St Kilda

A PEOPLE'S HISTORY

St Kilda

A PEOPLE'S HISTORY

Roger Hutchinson

BIRLINN

First published in 2014 by
Birlinn Limited
West Newington House
10 Newington Road
Edinburgh
EH9 1QS

www.birlinn.co.uk

ISBN: 978 1 78027 219 1

British Library Cataloguing-in-Publication Data
A catalogue record for this book is available from the
British Library

Typeset by Iolaire Typesetting, Newtonmore
Printed and bound by Gutenberg Press, Malta

To Caroline

Always take the turning

Contents

✖

List of Illustrations

Black-and-white plates

Early 19th-century sketches of the old, crowded clachan in Village Bay, before it was dismantled and replaced by the row of crofthouses on Main Street.

A Victorian imagination of Tigh an Stallair on Borerary.

'Being lowered on a homemade rope down the dizzying cliffs of Conachair required a superhuman quantity of courage.'

'Mid 19th-century St Kildan children, tow-haired and bright-eyed.'

Euphemia 'Effy' MacCrimmon: the last of the old St Kildan tradition-bearers, late in the 19th century.

Mother and child during St Kilda's short Indian summer.

A group of St Kildans in 1884, with temporary schoolmaster Kenneth Campbell.

Ann Ferguson, the media's 'Queen of St Kilda', on the eve of her intended marriage.

Ann's betrothed, Iain 'Ban' Gillies, before the show wedding was called off in 1890.

The widowed Ann Gillies awaits evacuation from Village Bay.

The celebrated 'St Kilda Parliament', posed in suitable dignity in 1885.

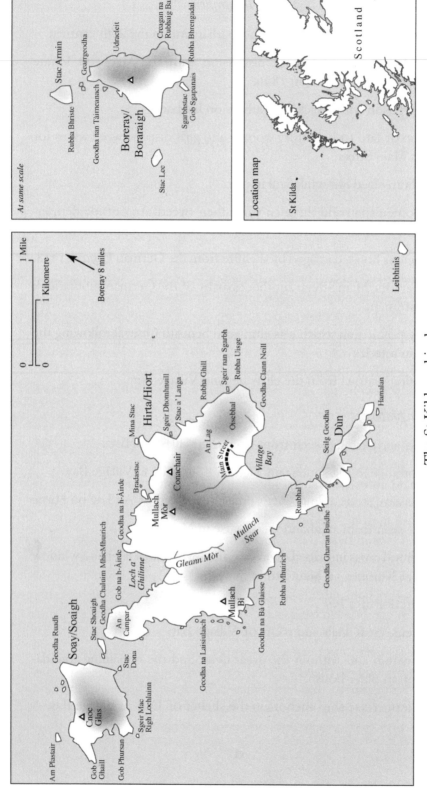

The St Kilda archipelago

At same scale

Rubha Bhriste
Stac Armin
Gearrgeodha
Udraicleit
Rubha Phursan
Geodha nan Tàirneanach
Creagan na Rubhaig Bana
Rubha Bhrengadal
Sgarbhstac
Gob Sgapanais
Boreray/
Boraraigh
Stac Lee

Location map

Scotland

St Kilda

0   1 Kilometre
0   1 Mile

Boreray 8 miles

Geodha Ruadh
Am Plastair
Soay/Soaigh
Stac Shcuigh
Geodha Chaluim MhicMhuirich
Gob Ghaill
Gob Phursan
Stac Dona
Cnoc Glas
Sgeir Mac Rìgh Lochlainn
An Campar
Gob na h-Àirde
Loch a' Ghàilinne
Geodha na h-Àirde
Bradastac
Mìna Stac
Sgeir Dhomhnuill
Stac a' Langa
Hirta/Hiort
Mullach Mòr
Conachair
Rubha Ghill
Sgeir nan Sgarbh
Rubha Uisge
Geodha na Laisiulaich
Gleann Mòr
Mullach Sgar
An Lag
Main Street
Oisebhal
Geodha Clann Neill
Village Bay
Mullach Bì
Geodha na Bà Glaisse
Rubha Mhuirich
Ruabhal
Seilg Geodha
Dùn
Geodha Ghàrran Buidhe
Hamalan
Leibhinis

Foreword

✳

'So much has already been written about St Kilda,' wrote Norman Heathcote in 1900 at the beginning of his book *St Kilda*, 'that I suppose I should apologise for adding yet another book on the subject, but I believe a good many people take an interest in the little island, the most remote corner of the British Isles, and … I venture to hope that my book may not be *de trop*.'

I know how he felt. The author of any new book about St Kilda is not standing on the shoulders of many giants. But he or she is perched perilously at the apex of an enormous human pyramid of predecessors. Since Heathcote wrote those lines more than a century ago several hundred books on aspects of the St Kilda islands have been published and republished. They have issued in such a flood that, in my occasional capacity as a book reviewer, I once threw up my hands and cried in print, 'Enough!'

Then I went there. It is difficult for a writer to spend any amount of time in St Kilda without being driven to write about the place. When that writer has spent an adult lifetime living in and writing about the north-west Highlands and Islands of Scotland, the urge is irresistible. All of the Hebridean islands are unique – all of the European islands are unique. St Kilda is simply the most unique of them all.

It is also, and has been for centuries, the most misinterpreted and misrepresented of island communities. For over 300 years, from the late seventeenth to the early twentieth century, St Kilda's apparent alienation from the rest of Europe tempted writers, even writers who understood both Gaelic and other Hebridean settlements and who should have known better, to impose upon it a popular idealisation.

The people who lived on Hirta moved, through no volition of their own, from being noble savages in the Age of Discovery to utopians and perfect communists and anarchists in the time of Marx and Bakunin, while simultaneously supposedly operating within an established Victorian hierarchy of a local male parliament and an insular constitutional monarchy.

The fallacy at the core of all such projections was that the inhabitants of those distant islands had somehow experienced a form of parallel evolution, uninfluenced in important social and political matters by the rest of Western civilisation. They were the reassuring antithesis of *Lord of the Flies*. They were an established gerontocracy abiding by ancient behavioural codes. They pulled off the unlikely but flattering trick of proving that, in at least one small set of circumstances, humanity was capable of perfecting the same philosophies and institutions which had evolved on the British and European mainland. The St Kildans were therefore both foreign and familiar.

St Kilda was unique not because its people were uninfected by outsiders – they were persistently infected, both literally and figuratively – but because their lives absorbed and adapted to powerful external influences while remaining, necessarily, more or less the same. It was an intriguingly different way of life but it was not mysterious. A means of surviving – and even thriving – on those unpromising outcrops of land which had almost certainly evolved in antiquity remained unchanged until the second half of the nineteenth century, and its remnants could be observed and identified in the twentieth century.

Since the departure of its last native residents in 1930, the ghost town of Main Street in Village Bay has been an empty space. Historical literature abhors a vacuum. That is the reason for the hundreds of volumes published in the last eighty years, which have clarified, muddied or left undisturbed the water in Village Bay.

Many if not most of those books have been excellent specialist studies. Few of the general histories of the islands, however, have managed to escape what the academic Fraser MacDonald describes as an 'erroneous narrative [which] ascribes an Edenic character to the St Kildans but implicitly blames them for having material aspirations'. That narrative was not, as MacDonald makes clear, restricted to St Kilda. It has been a common interpretation of the Highlands and Islands which merely found its most perfect subject in the most isolated and distant of the Hebrides – 'that mountain in the sea'.

St Kilda therefore became and remained the apogee of the sublime, the harsh, beautiful and innocent Highlands. That definition remains alive and active in the twenty-first century, as any Scottish tourism advertising campaign is likely to reveal. It has lost little of its power in four centuries of constant application.

There are numerous problems with sublime St Kilda, the most disturbing of which is that it denies St Kildans throughout history much agency in their own affairs. An unusually hardy, proud and articulate group of feudal vassals – 'the most knowingest people' in the words of a nineteenth-century labourer from the east coast of Scotland – have been reduced to cyphers.

This reduction has found its most outstandingly erroneous expression in accounts of the reasons for and handling of the evacuation in 1930. That was a momentous event in which the conduct of outside parties, most notably the British government through its Scottish Office, were models of sensitivity. But in the orthodox late twentieth-century interpretation, the St Kildans were buffeted into helplessness and then were led by their noses from the sublimity of Hirta to the mundanity of Argyllshire by politicians, civil servants, the medical profession and – most absurdly of all – their own Church. The false logic was straightforward. Having achieved a state of sublimity, nobody would voluntarily surrender it. They therefore must have been coerced.

Nobody benefits from such misrepresentation, least of all the St Kildans themselves. I hope that my presentation of an alternative version of their extraordinary history is not *de trop*.

I have learned about St Kilda from a great many people over the last four decades. There is a complete bibliography at the end of this book, but I must express particular gratitude to the authors Mary Harman and Michael Robson, both of whose forensically researched volumes have offered the comforting shoulder of hard and dependable fact. In St Kilda the hospitality and expertise of Susan Bain, Paul Sharman, Andrew Walsh, Kevin Grant and Dennis Fife did justice to the tradition of their surroundings. Angus Campbell, Christopher Gunn and the crew at Kilda Cruises got me there and back quickly and cheerfully. And for reasons that they will understand, thanks to Torcuil Crichton, Deborah Moffatt, Bill Lawson and John Murdo Morrison. I gratefully acknowledge the generous support of the Authors' Foundation and the K Blundell Trust in helping me to complete this book.

The publishers Birlinn – Hugh, Andrew, Jan, all of you – thanks again. My editor Helen Bleck once again rescued a manuscript from incoherence. Stan, never change.

ONE

Rachel's Unhappy Adventure in England

✣

ONE SUNDAY IN the spring of 1907 a government Fisheries Protection cruiser working out of Glasgow spotted a steam trawler netting in Village Bay, off the island of Hirta in the archipelago of St Kilda.

The trawler was from Fleetwood in Lancashire and was on a routine expedition to cast her nets on the North Atlantic Shelf 400 miles from home. On that Sunday she happened to be inside the official one-mile St Kildan limit which was designed to safeguard the marine assets of the islanders.

The cruiser bore down on the trawler and arrested her. When both vessels were anchored together in Village Bay some of the cruiser's officers went ashore. Instead of a grateful St Kildan welcome, they 'were met by a number of indignant natives, who questioned the right of the warship to arrest a friendly trawler'. The 'natives' were led by their young United Free Church of Scotland missionary Peter MacLachlan, who 'loudly complained of the heinous offence of arresting a steamer on the Sabbath'. ('The islanders,' observed the *Manchester Guardian*, 'evidently regarded this action as much worse than illegal fishing, which apparently had their blessing.')

MacLachlan then attempted to revoke the arrest of the Fleetwood vessel. He mustered a boatload of St Kildans who, in a gesture of solidarity and an attempt to stay the hand of the cruiser's captain, rowed out into the bay and boarded the trawler. It was to no avail. Peter MacLachlan and some other islanders were still on the arrested ship when it was put under tow by the Fisheries Protection cruiser and taken to Stornoway on the island of Lewis, where its captain was fined £90 and from where the St Kildans made their slow passage back home. 'The crew of the trawler, it is understood,' said the *Guardian*, 'had ingratiated themselves with the islanders by carrying their mails to and from the mainland and performing other friendly services.'

In the early decades of the twentieth century trawlermen from Fleetwood had a working relationship with the people of St Kilda. The Fleetwood trawler fleet was then the largest on the west coast of the United Kingdom. Since the 1890s its steam-powered boats (which were first introduced to the port by the Marr family of Dundee) had been sailing to the plentiful hake and dogfish grounds off the west of Ireland, off the Faroes, off Iceland, to Bear Island south of Spitzbergen and to the relatively homely north-west of Scotland, particularly the waters around Rockall and St Kilda.

The steam trawlermen spent weeks and often months at sea in brutal conditions. St Kilda was the most isolated human settlement in the British Isles. The islands lay 40 miles from the most westerly point of the Outer Hebrides and 100 miles from the Scottish mainland. On most days they were as invisible from any other part of Europe as a ship in mid-ocean. Their inhabitants led a subsistence lifestyle supported by an irregular commercial steamer service. Fishing boats were frequently the only vessels to approach St Kilda for months on end. A symbiotic connection developed. It started with trawlermen anchoring in Village Bay and putting ashore to pick up fresh water, enjoy tea and company and leave behind tobacco and other small luxuries. It grew into friendship and a form of inter-dependency. As they came to know the islanders and understand their needs, Fleetwood steam trawlers made a point of carrying sacks of meal and bottles of whisky as well as tobacco on their voyages north, and carrying news of the islanders' circumstances back to the British mainland. In return they were guaranteed a safe haven and a cheerful welcome in the hostile North Atlantic Ocean.

In 1906 this arrangement was officially recognised and formalised when the Fleetwood post office was given responsibility for delivering the mail to St Kilda in its local trawler fleet – a function which had previously lain with the post office at Aberdeen on the far eastern coast of Scotland.

In the summer of 1924 another steam trawler from Fleetwood in

Lancashire answered a radio signal for assistance from St Kilda. The ST *Philip Godby* put into Village Bay and picked up an elderly crofter and weaver named Finlay MacQueen who required medical treatment for a growth on his shoulder. When the trawler returned to Fleetwood it carried Finlay MacQueen in steerage. The 62-year-old widower spoke very little English, but a doctor with a smattering of Scottish Gaelic was found in Lancashire and an operation was carried out successfully. The morning after the operation Finlay MacQueen left Fleetwood on another trawler to return to St Kilda. He would, he told his interpreter, 'never leave St Kilda again'.

Four years after Finlay MacQueen's expedition for medical treatment from St Kilda to Fleetwood, three other islanders followed him on the same route. In April 1928 the fishing steamer *Loughrigg* carried to Lancashire a fifty-seven year-old unmarried St Kildan man called John MacDonald, a seventeen year-old girl named Rachel Ann Gillies, who had never previously left the island, and – at least in part as chaperone to Miss Gillies – Mrs MacLeod, the wife of the St Kilda missionary John MacLeod. None of the three had Finlay MacQueen's linguistic difficulties. Both John MacDonald and Rachel Gillies spoke English as well as Gaelic, and Mrs MacLeod was a native of Gloucestershire. (The English west country accent of the minister's wife must have contributed to the 'consternation' caused when she bustled into Fleetwood post office to pick up the St Kilda mail. 'They thought I was someone escaped,' laughed Mrs MacLeod, 'but I assured them I was quite tame.')

The arrival on the north-west coast of England of a teenaged girl from those fabled rocks caused even more of a stir. The captain of the *Loughrigg*, Reginald Carter, accommodated the three St Kildans at his Fleetwood home. They travelled from Carter's trawler to his house by taxi-cab, 'and the ride amazed Miss Gillies. Her drive through Fleetwood filled her with wonderment, though she was too excited to express herself'. This was, the newspapers pointed out, a girl who had never seen a horse, a cinema picture, a motor-car or a train. John MacDonald, who was in ill health and like Finlay MacQueen before him would require medical attention in Fleetwood, was less constrained. He told a reporter that most of the forty remaining St Kildans 'would leave the island if they had the opportunity of homes and work on the mainland'.

Within three months John MacDonald had returned to St Kilda. Rachel Gillies held out for slightly longer. She found a job in the town and appeared to settle in Lancashire. At the end of April an enterprising journalist took her to the cinema. The feature was an American silent movie starring Joan Crawford and titled *The Understanding Heart*. ('Monica Dale is a fire lookout in love with Forest Ranger Tony Garland', according to an online cinema datebase. 'Escaped killer Bob Mason hides out in Monica's observatory and falls in love with her. A fire encircles them and is put out by rain. Bob finally gives her up to Tony and is cleared of his earlier crime.')

When the film began to roll, reported the journalist, Rachel Gillies 'sat transfixed. Her facial expression was a study of wonder and fear. Gradually she settled down and rarely took her eyes off the screen … The film puzzled her as representing something different from what she imagined civilisation to be.' Rachel was obligingly grateful for the experience. 'We have heard about kinema pictures at St Kilda,' she said, 'but we never thought they were so wonderful. It is very wonderful. I never knew there were such things.'

In July Rachel Ann Gillies gave up her job and went back to St Kilda. 'She soon learned to dislike the hurried life of England, and after the first few weeks of excitement the novelty of things wore off and she longed for the solitary life at St Kilda, where the people during the winter are cut off from the outer world, save for the occasional visits of Fleetwood steam trawlers. She kept wanting to know how [her widowed] mother would be going to gather the peat for the winter'.

'When she left she discarded modern dress and went off in homely tweed, woven by her fellow-islanders. She returned to St Kilda with a feeling of pleasure at having finished with the hectic conditions of life on the mainland, and resolved never again to forsake the quiet of her home.' She was too polite to remark to the reporters that while until four months ago she may not have seen a moving picture, a motor-car or a train, they had never seen the sun set behind Mullach Mor, its last rays light up the black rocks of Dun and the evening draw down like a veil across Village Bay.

Two years later, in August 1930, Finlay MacQueen, Rachel Ann Gillies and John MacDonald would be among the last three dozen St Kildans who were evacuated from their island and offered new homes and jobs on the Scottish mainland. They sailed out of Village Bay on the Admiralty cruiser HMS *Harebell* with Rachel's forty-one year-old mother Ann, her eleven year-old younger sister Flora and another thirty of their relatives and neighbours.

It was not quite the first time in 4,000 years that the islands had been left uninhabited by humans. But it was the first time in 4,000 years that the islands had been considered uninhabitable. 'It was really quite sad,' Flora Gillies would recall, 'to see the chimneys and knowing we would never be back again.'

Four hundred miles away there was sympathy with Finlay MacQueen's reluctance to leave. It was reported that,

> The deep-sea fishermen of Fleetwood contemplate the evacuation of the small population of the lonely island of St Kilda, in the Outer Hebrides, with mingled feelings …
>
> In the gales that sweep across the west Scottish fishing areas almost continuously from December to March, St Kilda forms a harbour of refuge, and virtually every Fleetwood trawler has at some time or other run into Parson's Bay – a locality not indicated on any chart, but known to the deep-sea fishermen who so christened it because the house of the island's parson lay near the beach. The fishermen do not like to think that in the coming winter the island will be a scene of desolation and that the lights will no longer be a cheerful beacon to them during the winter storms.
>
> St Kilda without the natives is a disagreeable prospect in the eyes of every deep-sea fisherman.

As many of the older St Kildans would have known, they were not the first twentieth-century Hebridean Gaels to desert their native islands, and as some of them may have suspected, they would not be the last. Following the ravages of the nineteenth century, it was either the implicit or explicit policy of every twentieth-century British government to repopulate the north-west Highlands and Islands. They found the task more difficult to achieve than to pledge. The number of abandoned islands grew in every passing decade.

Between 1906 and 1912 the inhabitants of Pabbay and Mingulay, two islands at the foot of the Outer Hebridean chain 90 miles south-east of St Kilda, departed for lives in other places. At 2½ square miles, Mingulay is almost exactly the same size as Hirta, St Kilda's main island, and in 1881 it had supported 150 people, almost double the Hirtan population. By 1912 they had all left.

In 1920 the last few families deserted Eilean Mor in the Crowlin Islands between Skye and Applecross. In 1921 there were ninety-eight people living on Rona, an island off the north coast of Raasay which also lay between Skye and the Scottish mainland. By 1930 all but the Rona lighthouse keepers had departed. In the same decade the few people who had clung to the land on Ronay, an island off the east coast of North Uist which 100 years earlier had had a population of 180, gave up their unequal struggle.

In 1934 the twenty people of Sandray, another southern Hebridean islet, left for good. In 1943 Heisker – an island with curious historical links to St Kilda – was emptied. At regular intervals thereafter the fires were put out and the Gaelic bibles left open in empty homes on Soay, Scarp, Taransay, Boreray and Vallay.

They were all, like St Kilda, 'voluntary' evacuations, in the sense that a majority of the departing population considered life to be unsupportable without such twentieth-century services and amenities as electricity, access to hospitals, tapwater and telephones, and had either petitioned the authorities to be relocated or had simply put their furniture into skiffs and sailed away.

As well as electricity, the twentieth century brought motorised transport and a steadily improving network of roads to the mainland. The Hebrides were first settled and populated during the centuries when travel by water, particularly travel on the open sea, was hazardous but also faster, less arduous and therefore more popular than travel by land, especially in the mountainous Scottish Highlands. Long before and long after the Middle Ages, a clachan huddled at the end of a glen in Lochaber or Assynt was likely to be more remote and inaccessible than any insular community. The twentieth-century trawler fleets were St Kilda's last reminder of those happier days.

When it came to the moment of departure, St Kilda was typical of all the deserted islands in at least one obvious respect: the older folk regretted it most. Sorrow followed a comprehensible sliding scale. The children, such as Flora Gillies, were leaving only their infancies behind. The younger adults, such as Rachel Gillies, could insulate themselves against the rueful chill with the hope of a more comfortable and prosperous tomorrow. But for those of fifty years or more the past outweighed the future. They had neither the time nor the desire to recreate themselves. When they looked back over the ship's rail they saw, receding into the distance, everything that they had known, everything that they had loved and everything that they had been. 'May God forgive those,' said Finlay MacQueen, who was then sixty-eight years old, to a younger emigrant on HMS *Harebell*, 'that have taken us away from St Kilda.'

John MacDonald would have little time to mourn. The fifty-nine year-old moved to the Highland 'capital' of Inverness on the north-eastern coast, where he took a job as a labourer with the county council's roads department. John was accommodated in the Old Toll House at Culcabock on the main road east of the town, a picturesque but crumbling monument which he described as 'the worst place that my eye ever came across'. He died seven months after leaving St Kilda, in the Northern Infirmary, of acute pancreatitis on 18 April 1931. John MacDonald's death certificate was signed by a nephew who was living in Stornoway on the island of Lewis, two days' journey from Inverness.

A significant difference between the St Kildan evacuees and the emigrants from other Hebridean islands was that the St Kildans had no neighbouring settlement in which to relocate. The people of Mingulay could and did go to nearby Vatersay and Barra, where they already had friends and family. Many of the people of Rona shipped south to newly nationalised land on Raasay, land which they knew well partly because their grandparents had been cleared from it in the nineteenth century. The families from the Crowlins sailed across just two miles of sea to Applecross. The people of Scarp and Taransay transferred to the much larger parent islands of Harris and Lewis; the people of Heisker crossed over to Uist.

There were no such close and comforting neighbours to St Kilda. Some earlier emigrants had already moved to the Outer Hebrides, but when it came to an organised evacuation the authorities reasoned that almost any place in Scotland would be as suitable a destination as could be expected. If there was some Gaelic spoken in that place, so much the better. But the priority was to transfer the St Kildans into the twentieth century; to give them jobs and wages and access to trains and telephones and all the other benefits of modern civilisation.

The Forestry Commission, a government body which had been

established in 1919 to replenish British woodlands by planting trees chiefly in Scotland, shouldered the responsibility for employing and housing most of the islanders of working age. In 1930 the Forestry Commission operated almost exclusively on the mainland. It had recently acquired a large estate by Lochaline in the Gaelic-speaking district of Morvern on the west coast overlooking the Sound of Mull. Three-quarters of the evacuees, including Rachel Gillies's family, were resettled there. Much was made, then and later, of the apparent incongruity of moving people from a treeless island to live and work in a timber plantation. That was a condescending misinterpretation of the St Kildans. They were not aliens from the barren Planet Zog. Even those few of them who in 1930 had never previously left Hirta knew what a tree was, just as seventeen year-old Rachel Gillies knew about the cinema before watching *The Understanding Heart* on the big screen in Fleetwood. They had been educated; they read books. More importantly to the Forestry Commission, they knew how to cultivate plants in difficult conditions.

Fifty-four-year-old Neil Ferguson and his fifty-four year-old wife Ann were despatched to Tulliallan on the border of Perthshire and Fife in the south-east of Scotland. Its name derives from *tulach-aluinn*, meaning 'beautiful knoll', but twentieth-century Tulliallan was no longer a Gaelic-speaking area, and it was about as far from St Kilda as the Fergusons could travel without falling into the Firth of Forth. But the Forestry Commission had its main tree nursery in Tulliallan, where Neil could engage in relatively light work.

Their son and daughter-in-law, thirty-one year-old Neil Junior and his thirty-nine year-old wife Mary Ann, went to work and live at the Forestry Commission's more northerly Ardnaff plantation by Strome Ferry, close to the railhead and port at Kyle of Lochalsh in Wester Ross and 60 miles due north of the plantation at Lochaline by the Sound of Mull. Finlay MacQueen, who was Mary Ann Ferguson's father and whose English was still wanting, joined them at first in that Gaelic-speaking part of north-western Scotland.

One of Finlay's sons, John MacQueen, had joined the Royal Naval Reserve during the First World War and had since settled in Glasgow. In October 1930, two months after the evacuation, armed with a note which read 'Please see the bearer on the through train to Glasgow. He has no English', Finlay travelled south to visit John.

8

Inevitably, Finlay MacQueen was run to ground in Glasgow by journalists, who found the old man in an uncompromising mood. 'I wish
to God that I had never left [St Kilda],' he told them, 'in a voice which
trembled with feeling'. Four trains a day ran on the Kyle-to-Dingwall
line through the small and otherwise peaceful settlement at Strome
Ferry. 'A train runs within two yards of our new house,' said Finlay,
'and I am terrified.' He had been unable to get a smoke for a fortnight,
he asserted, because he 'dared not venture out to buy matches'.

'Finlay is to go back to the Kyle of Lochalsh,' concluded one report,
'but not to stay. He intends to collect his effects and go elsewhere.'

Finlay MacQueen did leave Wester Ross, but not for Lochaline, let
alone the Hebrides. He packed his effects and travelled to the anglophone south again, to join his near-contemporaries Neil and Ann
Ferguson in Tulliallan, where he lived in a farm building a long way
from the nearest railway line. He died there of heart failure ten years
later, in December 1941. He was seventy-nine years old.

On Sunday, 31 August 1930 the *Observer* newspaper soliloquised,

After a thousand years of human habitation, the winds and the seabirds have St Kilda to themselves. Economic circumstances have
brought about the migration, and while the islanders find a new, and,
as they hope, a fuller life by the Sound of Mull, nothing will remain
but the ruins of their homes and the wild sheep on Boreray to mark
the long settlement.

Sentimentalists in club smoke-rooms may be sorry for the change
and sigh for 'St Kilda no more', but the islanders will know better. The
retreat just conducted by the British Navy was a work of necessity and
mercy.

The islanders have not been self-supporting for some years.
Starvation faced them in the coming winter. They are not a helpless
people, but accident and emigration reduced the man-power below
the necessary minimum …

In a few days the steamer *Hebrides*, making her last call for the year,
may disembark a party of tourists to sentimentalise over the deserted
village. Hereafter the island will be left to itself and winter. Nor is it
likely that many people will go there again.

The proprietor, MacLeod of MacLeod, is against repopulation,
and the Department of Health is glad to be rid of a problem in

communications. Without the 'picturesque natives' the island will be of small interest to tourists and in a few years may be forgotten by all but trawlermen who shelter in its lee from the North Atlantic gales.

Some of the *Observer*'s correspondent's points were accurate and some were mistaken. Some were and remain debatable. But the newspaper's closing sentence could not have been more wrong.

TWO

Amazon Queens, Norsemen and Gaels

THEY WERE SHAPED by fire and ice. The four islands, their immense sea stacks and numerous smaller skerries and rocks which comprise the St Kilda archipelago are the remains of a volcanic crater which blew between fifty-five and sixty-five million years ago. The volcano was then part of a landmass which we now know as the Lewisian Complex in the Hebridean Terrane of the foreland of the prehistoric continent of Laurentia.

Two hundred million years ago in Laurentia, the north-west of Scotland was adjacent to the north-east of North America. They then drifted apart, and are still drifting apart, inch by inch over millennia, and the continent of Laurentia divided into America and Eurasia.

St Kilda would have been one of the tallest and most powerful volcanoes in the old Laurentian foreland. It erupted in roughly the same geological period as the mountains of Mourne in Ireland and the Cuillins of Skye. The results were strikingly similar: jagged, shattered ranges of igneous rock which look, as the travel writer H V Morton said of the Cuillin ridge, like 'Wagner's "Ride of the Valkyries" frozen in stone and hung up like a colossal screen against the sky'.

As the European and American regions of Laurentia separated, the Atlantic Ocean flowed into the void. Unlike the Cuillins and the mountains of Mourne, the peaks of St Kilda were stranded by the rising sea and left ultimately 40 or 50 miles west of the barrier islands of the Outer Hebrides. Then the ice came, and the far north of Scotland was once again linked by gelid water to the far north of America.

We may therefore summarise the prehistory of St Kilda as firstly a volcanic dome towering over a hilly primeval landscape, carpeted by ferns and inhabited by dinosaurs. The volcano then exploded, leaving behind black shards and splinters and crags and cliffs. Those dramatic remnants were later surrounded by salt water. The Earth's temperature fell, and St Kilda became a cathedral of rock covered in ice and snow, its glittering white steeples looming out of a frozen sea.

That Ice Age, from which Scotland is still emerging, began some fifty million years ago. It has regularly been interrupted by intervals of warmer weather, which are known as interglacials. There was an interglacial between 15,000 and 13,000 years ago. At that time our hominid ancestors had been foraging in the north of the continent of Eurasia, to which the British Isles were connected by a large land bridge, for hundreds of thousands of years. There is evidence of Palaeolithic settlement during a benign interglacial 800,000 years ago at Happisburgh on the Norfolk coast. According to Professor Chris Stringer FRS, those first Britons shared a grassy floodplain with 'a diverse range of animals ... such as primitive mammoths, rhino, horse, hyena and even sabre-toothed cats'.

Some of those pioneers took advantage of periods of warm weather to travel through the northern forests to the outer tips of Scotland. Flint artefacts discovered in South Lanarkshire and on the Hebridean island of Islay are residual evidence of that fact. Most other traces of their presence were scoured clean by the glaciers and meltwater of the last brief Ice Age. It descended some 12,900 years ago and once again covered with an ice sheet the whole of Scotland (with the north-easterly exceptions of the Orkney and Shetland islands, a few miles around John O' Groats and a few miles around Fraserburgh), the entire north of England and almost all of Wales and Ireland. The Hebrides were frozen and western waters from the Minch to the Irish Sea turned into pack ice.

That ice sheet began to retreat 11,500 years ago and has not yet returned. As it melted, vegetation and animals put down roots and took up residence in the high lands and the islands of northern Britain.

The outcrops which would become the British Isles were then connected like a hammerhead to the Eurasian continent. A 100-mile-wide extension of Belgium and the Netherlands reached westward to join Britain between Margate and The Wash. The prehistoric Stone Age settlement at Happisburgh, whose remains in modern times are on the English coast of the North Sea, was then an inland continental community, surrounded by freshwater courses, pools and marshes. For several thousand years, until the North Sea began to rise and cover that land bridge some 8,500 years ago, pedestrians were able to make their way to and from Rotterdam and East Anglia with relative ease. Even when 'Doggerland' was inundated, the few sea miles between the east of the new main island of Britain and the north-west of the Eurasian continent were navigable.

Post-Ice Age human colonisation began therefore in the south and east of Britain and travelled steadily north. There were Palaeolithic people in Lanarkshire 14,000 years ago and there were Mesolithic (the middle period of the Stone Age) settlements in the mild south-east of Scotland by 8500 BC. Over the next 4,000 years until around 4000 BC, when the hunter-gatherer Mesolithic Britons propagated the slightly more settled Neolithic Britons with their budding interest in agriculture, they hunted and gathered in the north-western islands of Rum, Colonsay, Skye, Islay, Jura and Oronsay and in such mainland littorals as Applecross. Those people were of course to be found in greater numbers elsewhere, but beside the Firths of Forth and Clyde their middens and arrowheads were ploughed over and buried beneath brick and concrete long before the nineteenth- and twentieth-century archaeologists arrived. In the sparsely populated Highlands and Islands their remnants were relatively undisturbed, if not preserved in peat bogs.

It is possible that Mesolithic hunter-gatherers set foot on St Kilda 6,000 years ago. Analysis of their Hebridean diet indicates the consumption of fish, shellfish, seals and seabirds. Birds, the surviving manifestation of the dinosaurs, were probably the first fauna to return to a post-Ice Age habitable St Kilda. There, in the absence of any serious predators – an absence which would last for thousands of years until being briefly disturbed by the arrival of homo sapiens – they thrived. Gannets, petrels, puffins and fulmars flocked to those distant cliffs, made homes upon the ledges and bred prolifically. The sea-going Stone Age men and women who found themselves looking westward from the Outer Hebrides are unlikely to have ignored so rich a source of protein. The first people to land at Village Bay on Hirta may have been a hunting party from North Uist or Lewis.

Mesolithic hunters left few footprints, and that proposition cannot be confirmed. Early in the twenty-first century our only certainty is that at some time after 3500 BC and before 1500 BC Neolithic people were living, for at least part of the year, on the main island of Hirta and the smaller island of Boreray in the archipelago of St Kilda.

They found a relatively hospitable island. Glacial retreat had carved two soft, substantial glens from either side of the main landmass of Hirta. In the east a bowl of fertile soil lay in the shelter of rolling hills. Loose rocks lay everywhere, but once they had been removed from the lowland machair and either deposited elsewhere or redeployed as building material, Hirta offered several acres of cultivable land. A few millennia later, in the eighteenth century AD, a land bridge would collapse and Dun would become a separate island. But in Neolithic times Dun was a promontory of Hirta. It was a crazy, jagged ridge emerging from the sea like an angry marine iguana in full profile. It formed one of the two strong arms of land that sheltered the small anchorage of Village Bay. The northerly arm was the rock-strewn mound of Oiseval, teetering over sheer cliffs and mysterious caves. The circular inlet of Village Bay is an almost perfect post-volcanic caldera.

Village Bay, with its natural harbour, good land and ample sources of fresh water, was an easy and obvious centre of settlement. Gleann Mor, the big western valley at the other side of a dip in the central hills, was more exposed to the prevailing Atlantic gales, less fertile and offered less suitable access to boats. But as the whole island was comprised of only 2½ square miles of land, and most of the rest of Hirta was barren hillside or peat bog, Gleann Mor was also settled by smaller and possibly more peripatetic groups of people. Although their cellular beehive dwellings were preserved and occupied as summer shielings during the annual transhumance until the twentieth century, it is unlikely that they were built to be used only seasonally. Their complex and durable construction suggests a permanent settlement in Gleann Mor during or before the Middle Ages.

One of those early dwellings was shrouded in myth and mystery by the later Gaels. They called it Taigh na Banaghaisgeich, the Amazon's House. Martin Martin in 1697 reported that,

This Amazon is famous in their traditions: her house or dairy of stone is yet extant; some of the inhabitants dwell in it all summer, though it be some hundred years old; the whole is built of stone, without any wood, lime, earth, or mortar to cement it, and is built in form of a circle pyramid-wise towards the top, having a vent in it, the fire being always in the centre of the floor; the stones are long and thin, which supplies the defect of wood; the body of this house contains not above nine persons sitting; there are three beds or low vaults that go off the side of the wall, a pillar betwixt each bed, which contains five men apiece; at the entry to one of these low vaults is a stone standing upon one end fix'd; upon this they say she ordinarily laid her helmet; there are two stones on the other side, upon which she is reported to have laid her sword: she is said to have been much addicted to hunting, and that in her time all the space betwixt this isle and that of Harries, was one continued tract of dry land.

Taigh na Banaghaisgeich, which in 1697 the St Kildans were using as a summer shieling while they pastured their cattle and sheep in Gleann Mor, may have been older than 100 years. It is medieval or earlier, and at the least offers an indication of the type of Stone Age dwellings in which the St Kildans lived until the Middle Ages. Those drystone sleeping chambered cells remained part of the architectural vernacular in the main settlement of Village Bay until the second half of the nineteenth century.

The Amazon's House did not date back quite to the time of the Hebridean Terrane of the continent of Laurentia, when St Kilda was connected by dry land to the island of Harris, although it is curious that such Jurassic phenomena should have been reflected in human folklore. A late nineteenth-century writer reflected, however unscientifically, that 'If there is any truth in my theory of the Warrior Queen, the first inhabitants of Hirta would have found their way there during the period succeeding the glacial epoch, while all this tract was still dry land, and the legend of how they got there would be handed down from one generation to another. Of course, the house that they now point out as the dwelling-place of their renowned Amazon may be of much later date than the lady herself, and the stories which Martin says were current in his time about her, but which he unfortunately does not record, may have been improvised or added to by the imaginative narrator, but I do not think that it is the sort of legend that would be invented in toto.'

The peat bogs offered a reliable source of fuel – in the form of slabs of black peat dug out of the earth and dried in the wind – on islands with no trees or other supplies of wood. Their presence could indicate, as the naturalist John Love suggests, that at some time before or shortly after the last Ice Age, in a warmer and calmer climate, St Kilda had been home to birch and hazel scrub. In 1758 Kenneth Macaulay reported that, 'In the turfpits dug there, a prodigious number of trees, almost entire, are frequently found, which must have been buried in these places, after having been killed or plucked away from their roots, by the vast quantities of earth which had been washed away from off the faces of the hills above.' Peat is no more than decayed vegetation, however, and at least some of the bogs on top of Mullach Mor, on the upper slopes of Gleann Mor and on Cambir may simply have been the seasonal deposits of dead turf which rotted and accumulated over centuries before humans arrived to excavate them with stone or iron tools.

Beyond Gleann Mor, a few hundred yards off the western tip of Hirta, sat the small, green grazing island of Soay, which at first was part of St Kildan common land but which later was reserved for the proprietor's stock. Six miles north-west of Village Bay was the group's third island of Boreray and its two prodigious stacks of Armin and Lee. The sea cliffs below the 1,400-foot summit of Conachair on Hirta are easily the highest in Britain (they are also the eleventh highest in Europe), and Stac an Armin and Stac Lee are, at 643 feet and 564 feet, respectively the highest and second-highest sea stacks in the British Isles. Stac an Armin is a fine arrow piercing the sky, and Stac Lee a vertiginous axehead of a rock. They are all but sheer from sea-level to summit, and gannets and other birds nest in their thousands on their diagonal thinly etched ledges. Before the arrival of humans and after their departure, in spring and early summer the upper slopes of both stacks have been made as white as an Alpine summit by the presence of thousands of young gannets and their guano. The island of Boreray had a high sloping pasture for sheep and even the possibility of some crop cultivation. But its main attraction was the seabird harvest from the Boreray cliffs and from Stacs an Armin and Lee, upon whose sheer rock faces bothies were somehow built by the bird-catching cragsmen of Hirta to offer shelter from the weather and even a temporary home, as if a window cleaner were to pitch a tent halfway up the Empire State Building.

That lethal, thrilling, skilful activity was and remained the central function and support of human settlement on the St Kilda islands. Whether in clambering up Stac Lee or being lowered on a home-made rope down the dizzying cliffs of Conachair, bird-catching required a superhuman quantity of courage, the skills, coordination and upper-body strength of an extreme rock climber and Olympic gymnast combined, and the indifference to heights of the Mohawk people who were employed to build Manhattan's skyscrapers. It was a valuable activity because for centuries a bottomless supply of seabird meat insulated the entire St Kildan community from the famine years which afflicted other, more agricultural Hebridean islands. It was also profoundly masculine. From the Stone Age to the twentieth century, seabird hunting in St Kilda offered its men the opportunity for physical assertion, displays of courage and strength and adrenalin rushes that others might find only in battle.

The Neolithic people left behind them stone hoes, knives, axes, grain grinders and shards of pottery. The pottery alone indicates that those prehistoric St Kildan settlers were from the Western Isles. It was Hebridean Ware, and in the words of the archaeologist Professor Ian Armit, Hebridean Ware pottery is a 'localised style, so far known only from the Western Isles of Scotland':

> Hebridean vessels are characteristically deep jars with multiple carinations; their upper parts are profusely decorated, generally with incised herringbone patterns … elaborately decorated pottery was to be a recurrent trait of Hebridean prehistory until almost the end of the Iron Age. The quantities of ceramics and the effort put into their decoration shows that pottery played an important role for the communities of the Hebridean Neolithic. In functional terms it provided containers for cooking and food storage. It also held offerings which were placed in the chambered tombs. It may also have played a role in feasting and ritual activities …

Shortly before or shortly after the birth of Christ a small souterrain was dug out and walled in Village Bay on Hirta. The word comes from the French *sous terrain*, under ground, and although the structures are found throughout Atlantic Iron Age Europe, the majority of good surviving specimens are in the early Celtic domains of Ireland and Scotland.

Souterrains were hallmark buildings of that culture. Hardly a single populated Hebridean island was without one. They were essentially underground passageways and chambers lined with slabs of stone or wood. They appear to have had no particular religious significance, nor were they used for burial. Souterrains were dwelling places, subterranean storage facilities or defensible hiding places, or all three.

The miniature example on Hirta later became known to locals as Tigh an t-Slithiche, House of the Fairies. Significantly, the souterrain Tigh an t-Slithiche was located a few yards from the medieval and modern settlements in Village Bay. The later inhabitants had known of its existence since the middle of the nineteenth century and probably earlier, without comprehending its historical importance. Until the middle of the twentieth century it was believed, as the newspaper reports of the evacuation in 1930 reiterated, that St Kilda had been populated for about 1,000 years. The presence of Tigh an t-Slithiche adds another 1,000 years to that figure, and possibly more. It certainly indicates a settled prehistoric community.

There are on Hirta, Soay, Boreray and even on the precarious top of Stac an Armin almost 1,400 ruined or intact cleitean. Those unique drystone sheds-cum-pantries define the landscape as certainly as bird-hunting defined the people. They are on the tops of mountains, the bottom of glens and the sides of cliffs. They sit in clusters, in rows and in isolation in surprising places, like the homesteads of some alien parallel civilisation. Village Bay is a shanty town of *cleitean* – they far outnumber the houses, old and new, even on the precious arable land – but nowhere in St Kilda is out of sight of a *cleit*.

Cleits are oval stone igloos which vary in size from that of a dog-kennel to a small cottage. The term, if not the construction, is common throughout the Scottish *Gàidhealtachd*. It can mean a quill or feather, which, probably coincidentally, describes some of what was stored in St Kilda. A cleit is also the Gaelic word for a natural rather than a man-made feature; it is a rocky outcrop on land or sea. At the foot of the cliffs of Conachair in Hirta there are reefs named Na Cleitean. The word derives from the Old Norse *klettr*, *klett* or *klet*, which simply means rocks (the Orkney surname Linklater is a conflation of *lyng* and *klettr*, meaning heather rocks). But only in St Kilda was the corruption of the Norse noun klettr into the Gaelic noun cleit adopted as the architectural description of a building made from stones, as well as still being applied in its more usual context as a feature of the landscape. That is unusual but not inexplicable. When the St Kildans first began to build their unique storage sheds they simply named them after the familiar geological phenomena which the *cleitean* best resembled – the large rocks which butted out of the sea and hillsides all around them.

As with almost all constructions on St Kilda the people made a virtue of the necessity of building without wood. Since no trees grew on their islands, if they needed it they were always almost entirely dependent on imported timber. Planks and logs were washed up as flotsam or saved from wrecked ships, but most of their wood came in the steward's galley from Harris, where it was also rare and therefore doubly valuable. Wood was a precious material in Village Bay and was used sparingly. Whatever their size, cleits have several main features in common. One is their sloping sides, which reach incrementally inwards until the roof can be spanned with rectangular slabs of rock. The slabs of rock are then amply covered with turf, which develops its own little self-sustaining eco-system on the top of each cleit and restricts the ingress of rain-water – not unlike the 'green' or 'living' roofs of late twentieth-century architecture. They have no windows and their other common feature is their single entrance at ground level, some so tiny that only a child could creep in, some half the height of a standard doorway.

Until the very end in 1930 they were used for cold storage, as ventilated larders for seabirds and mutton, as sheds for tools, nets and hay, and even for storing peat. (The last function was as unusual in north-western Scotland as the *cleitean* themselves. Everywhere else peats were, and are, cut outside, dried outside and stacked outside beside the dwelling place.) A visitor in the 1880s recorded that 'Formerly they were used by the people for drying birds ... In these houses the St Kildian crofter [now] dries his grass and grain. He has a habitual distrust of the weather, and never attempts to dry any of his crops in the open air.' Their deployment into modern times – cleits were still being built as well as used in the late nineteenth and early twentieth centuries – distracted outsiders from their actual antiquity. Later archaeology has suggested that some of them were in continuous use for at least 1,000 years.

Until the twenty-first century it was thought that all permanent human habitation had been restricted to Hirta, and that the islands of Soay and Boreray were occupied only during seasonal bird-hunts and sheep gathering. But in the summer of 2011 archaeologists working for the Royal Commission on the Ancient and Historical Monuments of Scotland and the National Trust for Scotland dug out an intact stone building with a corbelled roof among three settlement mounds from beneath the turf and soil on Boreray. This was the legendary construction known as Taigh an Stallair, or Staller's House. It was examined in the middle of the eighteenth century by Kenneth Macaulay. He wrote:

> At the distance of many ages back (the precise time cannot be ascertained) a bold, public-spirited, or self-interested person, whose name was Staller, or the man of the rocks, headed an insurrection, or rebelled against the governor or steward, and at the head of a party engaged in the same disloyal conspiracy (or rather struggle for liberty) possessed himself of Boreray, and maintained his port there for some time. Here he built a strange kind of habitation for himself and his accomplices. – The story is of an antient date, but is, by this extraordinary monument, in some degree authenticated.
>
> The house is eighteen foot high, and its top lies almost level with the earth, by which it is surrounded; below it is of a circular form, and all its parts are contrived so that a single stone covers the top. – If this stone is removed, the house has a very sufficient vent. – In the middle of the floor is a large hearth. Round the wall is a paved seat, on which sixteen persons may conveniently fit. Here are four beds roofed with strong flags or stone lintels, every one of which is capable enough to receive four men. To each of these beds is a separate entry; the distances between these different openings, resembling in some degree so many pillars.
>
> The rebel (or rather friend of liberty) who made this artificial cove, had undoubtedly sufficient reasons good enough to justify his taste of architecture; that he must have wanted timber to build in the common way is morally certain; it is equally so, that he must have been apprehensive the enemy would invade his little kingdom in the nighttime.

Taigh an Stallair entered St Kildan folklore in the following tale, told by the elderly Euphemia MacCrimmon to a visitor in 1862:

> The house is called Taigh an Stallair, after the name of him who built it. It was built on stone pillars, with hewn stones, which it was thought

were brought from the point of the Dun. It was round inside, with the ends of long narrow stones sticking through the walls round about, on which clothes might be hung. There were six croops or beds in the wall, one of them very large, called Rastalla; it would accommodate twenty men or more to sleep in. Next to that was another called Ralighe, which was large, but rather less than the first. Next to that were Beran and Shimidaran, lesser than Ralighe, and they would accommodate twelve men each to sleep in. Next to that was Leaba nan Con, or the Dog's bed, and next to that was Leaba an Tealich, or the Fireside bed. There was an entrance [passage] within the wall round about, by which they might go from one croop to another without coming into the central chamber. The house was not to be noticed outside, except a small hole on the top of it, to allow the smoke to get out and to let in some light. There was a doorway on one side (where they had to bend to get in and out) facing the sea, and a large hill of ashes a little way from the door, which would not allow the wind to come in. Bar Righ was the name of the door. The present inhabitants of St Kilda [in 1862], when in Boreray fowling, or hunting sheep to pull the wool of them, which is their custom instead of shearing them, used to live in the house until about twenty years ago, when the roof fell in. Some of the croops are partly to be seen yet.

The building and settlement mounds looked over a primitive field system and crop terraces. Whoever created them, whatever they were named, had lived there.

'This is an incredibly significant find,' said the RCAHMS surveyor Ian Parker, 'which could change our understanding of the history of St Kilda. This new discovery shows that a farming community actually lived on Boreray, perhaps as long ago as the prehistoric period.

'The agricultural remains and settlement mounds give us a tantalising glimpse into the lives of those early inhabitants. Farming what is probably one of the most remote – and inhospitable – islands in the North Atlantic would have been a hard and gruelling existence. And given the island's unfeasibly steep slopes, it's amazing that they even tried living there in the first place.' The unfeasibly steep slopes may have provided part of the reason. Boreray was an easily defensible island. The gradient of its cultivable land would not have deterred Hebrideans who were accustomed to ploughing on the sides of hills.

It is possible, although archaeologists now consider it unlikely, that there was also a megalithic stone circle on tiny Boreray. In 1764 Reverend Kenneth Macaulay reported there 'a Druidical place of worship, a large circle of huge stones fixed perpendicularly in the ground, at equal distances from one another, with one more remarkably regular in the centre, which is flat in the top'. A hundred years later a visitor to St Kilda said that 'there was a temple in Boreray built with hewn stones. Euphemia Macrimmon remembers seeing it. There is one stone yet in the ground where the temple stood, upon which there is writing: the inhabitants of St Kilda built cleitean or cells with the stones of the temple.'

Those were the people who built the oldest surviving crannog pile dwelling of Eilean Domnhuill in Loch Olabhat in North Uist around 3000 BC, and who therefore must have had a hand in inventing that architectural form. Crannogs, artificial inhabited islands, are almost unique to the lochs and rivers of Scotland and Ireland (one has been discovered in Wales), where they were iconic structures from prehistory to the early centuries AD.

They were the people who between 2900 BC and 2600 BC erected the magnificent standing stone complex at Callanish in the west of the island of Lewis. They were the people who 1,000 years later mummified and reconstructed their dead at Cladh Hallan in South Uist. As the stone hoes in the big glen on Hirta attest, they were early farmers. That was no overnight progression: for millennia they will have combined hunting and gathering with their increasing interest in and aptitude for crop cultivation and animal husbandry, and in St Kilda hunter-gatherer activity was still alive and viable in the twentieth century. But farming brought with it two major changes. It made nomadic tribes into settled communities, and it gave the people of those communities enough time and leisure to develop complicated beliefs and philosophies and build the monuments to honour their creeds.

The presence of hoes and pottery on Hirta 4,000 to 5,000 years ago indicates two things about those early St Kildan settlers. The hoes and the later souterrain suggest that they lived on the islands all year round. Their people may first have landed and camped there on summer fowling expeditions, but sooner or later a family or two chose to set up house, cultivate crops and winter on Hirta. To men and women who had sailed 30 or 40 miles from the Scottish mainland to the Western Isles, an extra 40 or 50 miles of travel by sea to St Kilda was not an insurmountable obstacle.

And the pottery, that Hebridean Ware, proves that they were part of the Western Islands' Neolithic sub-culture. They had not come from Ireland in the south, or from the established Stone Age civilisations on the Orkney or Shetland islands. They were not Scandinavian adventurers. They had not travelled even from the mainland of Scotland. They were Western Islanders, Hebrideans, bound by blood, language, lifestyle and culture to the people of Lewis, Harris, Skye, Barra and the Uists. That was and would remain the case until the year 1930.

Throughout its 4,000 to 5,000 years of almost permanent human habitation, St Kilda could be a difficult home. Infections and epidemics spread quickly through its small, tightly-knit population. The inhabitants were all but wiped out during recorded history, and the islands re-settled by people from the other Hebrides. It is inevitable that similar catastrophes struck the St Kildans during the 4,000 years before anybody made written reports of their condition. Following such years of famine or disease, St Kilda would have been repopulated by fresh settlers from the Western Isles. If there was ever such a thing as an original St Kildan gene, a strand of DNA unique to the aborigines of Hirta and Boreray, it was lost long ago. No twentieth-century St Kildan could claim a direct, unbroken ancestral line to the first Stone Age inhabitants of their particular archipelago. They were generic Hebrideans.

We do not know exactly what language was spoken by the earliest St Kildans. It is likely to have been an archaic Celtic dialect. By the last centuries BC the long millennia of Stone Age humanity were over, the industrial revolution of the Iron Age had begun, and it is probable that along with most of the rest of the population of Scotland, England and Wales the St Kildans were Brythonic Celts speaking an antique variant of what we now know as Welsh, Cornish or Breton. If so, they were a tiny, insular tribe of the people that the Romans called *Picti*.

That is a probability and not a certainty only because of St Kilda's extreme westerly position. Two thousand years ago the Scottish mainland and inner islands were overwhelmingly Pictish. But there were already small colonies of Goidelic Celts, Gaels who lived chiefly in Ireland and spoke a different Celtic vernacular, in Galloway, at the tip of the Mull of Kintyre and in Argyll. Those Gaelic-speaking Irish

Celts would also establish and maintain a strong relationship with the southernmost Western Isles, and would achieve hegemony in the Isle of Man. It is feasible that they had an early foothold in the westernmost Hebridean islands of St Kilda. Feasible, but unlikely. No such rumour or tradition exists in Ireland or Scotland, and St Kilda was more than 200 sea miles from the Gaelic people of the north of Ireland but less than half that distance from the Pictish strongholds of northern Scotland.

If we accept the likelihood that 2,000 years ago St Kilda was, like the rest of the northern Highlands and Hebrides, inhabited by Iron Age Picts speaking a regional form of what we now think of as Old Welsh, another intriguing supposition presents itself. Between roughly 1,600 and 1,100 years ago the Gaels whose forebears had crossed the North Channel from Ireland, and who sustained familial and tribal connections with Gaelic Ulster, moved out of the south-west of the country and conquered the whole of Caledonian Pictland. The land of the Picts was subsequently renamed after the Roman name for Irish raiders, *Scoti*.

Where Pictish tribes proved difficult to subdue and subsume, the Scottish conquest was achieved by military means. Skirmishes were fought in islands such as Skye before Pictish elders gave up their lands to Gaelic warlords. But mostly the process took the form of the gradual submission of one culture to another. The Irish Gaels wielded such powerful weapons as the convincing new religion of Christianity. Their language was a relative of Pictish, with many shared root words, and their culture was not entirely foreign. They had been peaceably present on the fringes of Pictland for centuries before they took over, and for a long time their expansion may have gone almost unnoticed.

However it was achieved, by the tenth century Scotland was a Celtic Christian nation named for the people with Irish roots who had imposed upon the country their language, religion, sports and customs. There was almost certainly no systematic attempt made by the triumphant *Scoti* to destroy the Pictish language. It was not necessary. Once Gaelic had become the dominant vernacular of authority, Picts voluntarily adopted the language over succeeding generations, and equally pragmatically forsook their grandparents' native tongue. In the slow, disparate and largely illiterate Middle Ages, spoken languages did not fade quickly away. We do not know when the last speakers of

Caledonian Pictish lived and died, although it has been suggested that it might still have been heard in remote pockets of northern Scotland as recently as the sixteenth century.

If Pictish clung to life anywhere, untouched by the inexorable advance of Scottish Gaelic, it would have been in such a place as St Kilda. Nothing exists to bolster this surmise. But we could do worse than imagine a group of Picts living their self-sufficient lives on the most remote islands in Britain who were slow to realise that a new political, religious, cultural and linguistic force was alive in the land far to their east.

It worked both ways: the ascendent Gaelic Scots had little reason to be interested in, let alone try to change, how the few dozen people of St Kilda lived and communicated. Pictish, that dialect of Brythonic/Brittonic Celtic which was once the lingua franca from Exeter to Eyemouth and from London to Llandudno, may have survived as a spoken language in St Kilda long after it had been lost from Edinburgh and Inverness. Pictish would have left the islands gradually, from necessity, as even the St Kildans' cousins and trading partners in the Western Isles ceased to speak or understand anything but the new Scottish dialect of Irish Gaelic. Before that evolution it is fair to assume that Dark Age St Kildans would have adhered to their Pictish language as faithfully as, more than a millennium later, their nineteenth- and twentieth-century successors adhered to its usurper, Gaelic.

Initially, they would have survived by landing with bone hooks some of the fish which, three millennia ago, teemed around the shores of St Kilda, and by catching birds. As they built their homes and storage cleits on Hirta, Soay and Boreray, their stone hoes were used to till the land and grow oats and barley. They introduced the small semi-feral Soay sheep, which survive still on St Kilda, and later the meatier Boreray sheep – a cross between the early Hebridean Blackface and the old Scottish Shortwool – were added to the stock. They would light their homes with fulmar oil lamps. They would heat them with central open cooking fires of peat.

Few of the routines or practices in that lifestyle were unique to St Kilda. It was how prehistoric peoples lived in all the Hebridean islands, from the tiny Shiants to the large mass of Lewis. Some St Kildan creatures evolved in isolation from the remainder of their species and became unique to the islands. Pairs of breeding wrens which somehow found their way to the archipelago became, far from the rest of their kind, categorical sub-species. An indigenous St Kildan house mouse evolved, which became extinct in the 1930s after the human evacuation left its habitat cold, damp and without food. The large, voracious native St Kildan field mouse still exists.

But the human population was never entirely isolated from the rest of its species. In common with so many of their Hebridean neighbours, they lived their unrecorded lives for several thousand years. In a seafaring age they were not disconnected from the outside world. On the contrary: St Kilda sat in the western shipping lane between Ireland, Wales and England, and Iceland, continental Scandinavia and the Arctic Sea.

One day – probably in the summer and probably in the eighth century – longships from Norway were pulled up onto the shore at Village Bay on Hirta. The few nervous St Kildans had probably sought refuge on the nearby defensible promontory named Dun. By example as much as by words, the crews of those and other, later longships informed the St Kildans that they were no longer part of Scotland. They, along with most of the rest of the west coast and the islands as far south as Man and Ireland itself, had been subsumed into the Norse Empire.

They were easy pickings. Scandinavian expeditions must have put into St Kilda for shelter and supplies for centuries. Neither Pictish nor Gaelic Scotland was a kingdom strong enough to defend its western mainland, let alone its distant islands. There was no shame in that. The throne of England could not preserve York from the Vikings, and the Irish High Kings lost Dublin. For 400 or 500 years, until 1266, St Kildans were at first effectively and later constitutionally subjects of the King of Norway.

Mysteries still surround those centuries of Norse dominance over western Scotland. They left behind their proper nouns. In the St Kildan island group more than half of the placenames come from Old Norse. The island names of Soay and Boreray are corruptions of the Norse names for Sheep Island and Fort Island.

A nomenclative tour of St Kilda yields a rich synthesis of language and culture. On Gob an Duin, the Point of Dun at the western tip of the promontory are the remains of the fortress – in Gaelic, the *dun* – which must once have been the defensive redoubt of the early

Gaels of Hirta. In the eighteenth century the remains of the 'old ruin-ous fort' were still visible, and a visitor decided that it had been built from rocks quarried in Hirta and carried along the promontory – 'The stones of which this strange fabric was constructed are large, nearly square, and must of consequence have been wrought out of a quarry; there being none of the same colour or substance to be found in the island [of Dun], above ground.' The word gob literally means a bird's beak or bill. It found its way from Gaelic into English as slang for a garrulous mouth – in Gaelic a gobair is a talkative person – but in this instance it indicates a modest nose, or beak, of land.

A few yards from Gob an Duin is another small point called Gob na Muice. *Muc* is Gaelic for a pig and *muice* is the noun's genitive form, so Gob na Muice can best be translated as the Pig's Snout. Offshore to the south of both of those points there sits an mallet-shaped rock named Hamalan, which probably derives from one of those Old Norse words which travelled far across land, sea and time: *hamarr*, or hammer.

To the east of those lies the highest peak on Dun, the towering slab of rock which greeted the inhabitants of Village Bay when they woke in the morning and which reflected the dying sun at night, is simply Bioda Mor, the Big Hilltop. In the sea to the south of Bioda Mor, hidden from view, sits Sgeir Cul an Rudha, the Skerry Behind the Point. This is a nicely literal combination of terms. *Sker* is Old Norse for a rock or skerry; *cul* is Gaelic for the backside of, or beyond, or forgotten, or absent, and *rudha* is Gaelic for a promontory.

On the Village Bay side of Dun, just below Bioda Mor, is the Norse/Gaelic Geo na Ruideig. Geo, or gully, came from the Old Norse *gja*, meaning cleft. There are numerous geos throughout the Hebrides. Geo na Ruideig is named after the Gaelic word for a kittiwake. Geo na Ruideig therefore amounts, in two ancient tongues, to the resonant Gully of the Kittiwake.

Across the narrow kyles from the promontory/island of Dun, its jagged black rock is replaced on Hirta by gentler, more roseate slopes. Ruaival rises over the south side of Village Bay. Although it trickled into Gaelic, where *ruaidh* came to mean a brownish red, this term is purely Norse, *rauda-fjall* in that language meaning simply Red Hill.

All around Ruaival lie placenames which echo, however enigmati-cally, the history and lore of St Kilda. At the foot of the hill is Geo na

Seanaig, Grandmother's Gully. On the eastern shore is Uamh Cailleach Bheag Ruabhail, the Small Lady of Ruaival's Cave. Uamh Cailleach Bheag Ruabhail is integrated in one of the most powerful of St Kildan legends. The story, as it was told many times in subtly different versions, told of two strangers, possibly from Lewis, named Dugan and Fearchar, who in the past (a St Kildan émigré would later specify 'the thirteenth or fourteenth century') landed in Village Bay with evil intent.

Having ingratiated themselves with the St Kildans and enjoyed their hospitality, one day Fearchar and Dugan climbed Oiseval and raised a false alarm of pirate ships approaching Hirta. They persuaded the St Kildans to seek sanctuary in the church. They then set the thatch alight, incinerated every man, woman and child, and began to discuss the division of the island's resources.

Unknown to Fearchar and Dugan, for the past few weeks an old lady had been tending cattle in Gleann Mor. She was on her way back home and from the high pass at Am Blaid she saw the dense, billowing smoke. Hurrying downhill, she then saw Fearchar and Dugan and deduced what had happened. She promptly hid in the cave which would be named after her, Uamh Cailleach Bheag Ruabhail. She sneaked out at night to take food from the cleits and water from the burns.

She survived. When the factor's galley arrived, Cailleach Bheag Ruabhail appeared and – to their surprise and horror – denounced Fearchar and Dugan. The factor ordered the two men to be bound and thrown onto his boat. What happened next is debatable. Fearchar at least was condemned to be marooned on Stac an Armin. He may have died there, or drowned after throwing himself in the sea from the stack and trying desperately to swim after the factor's vessel. Dugan was deposited on the more hospitable shores of Soay, where he built or adopted a small dwelling whose remains still stand and are still named Tigh Dugan.

If it is based on an actual incident this tale is the fable of an extermination of the St Kildans in the Middle Ages, possibly at the hands of pirates. It also implicitly suggests the island's subsequent repopulation from the other islands. The story is, however, reminiscent of at least two other fabled Hebridean atrocities. In the sixteenth century almost 400 people on the small island of Eigg were trapped in a cave by raiding MacLeods and asphyxiated by a fire built at the cave's mouth. A year later the MacDonalds of Uist retaliated by sailing to Waternish in the north of Skye and firing the church at Trumpan while it was full of MacLeods at worship. One family is rumoured to have escaped from the first massacre; one person from the second. It is at least possible that the seeds of the story of Dugan and Fearchar and Uamh Cailleach Bheag Ruabhail travelled to St Kilda with immigrants from Skye or elsewhere and was later, during the long winter nights around the peat fire in Village Bay, adapted to local circumstances and geography.

Further up the east coast of Ruaival, at the other side of the hill from Uamh Cailleach Bheag Ruabhail, is the inhospitable Laimhrig na Gall, the Stranger's or Foreigner's Anchorage, and Geo na Ba Glaise, a gully which was either thought to resemble a grey cow or, more likely, down which a grey cow fell. There is Gob Chathaill, Catherine's Point, and Geo an Eireannaich, the Irishman's Gully. A nineteenth-century visitor was told that one day in the distant past an unfortunate Irishman had been blown in a small boat from his own land to this distant shore. Marooned at the foot of the gully – which had presumably previously been an anonymous feature of the landscape – he was finally hauled to safety by St Kildans with ropes. He lived with them for about a year before catching another boat back home. North of Irishman's Gully, illuminating an otherwise lonely coastline, is Geo na Lashulaich, probably an abbreviation of Geo na Laise-Suileach, which means nothing less extraordinary than the Gully of the Flaming Eye and may describe a reflection of the bright afternoon sun. Nowhere is the contrast between placename nouns offered by the practical Norse and their adjectives affixed by the lyrical, fantastic Celts more luminous.

Curling protectively around Village Bay, the top of Ruaival leads to the ridges of Mullach Sgar, Mullach Geal and Mullach Mor, the Bare Summit, the White Summit and the Big Summit, and thence to the highest point of St Kilda, the 1,400-foot slope of Conachair.

Its name is singular and its origins are unclear. Throughout the year fierce gales blow down and around the side of Conachair into Village Bay and Gleann Mor, and it has been suggested that the Gaelic word for a tempest, *cona-ghaothach*, or that for a noisy uproar, *conghair*, has been corrupted into Conachair. But a visitor in 1885 reported that the locals thought Conachair to be named after 'some local hero' and consequently offered as explanation the Norse term for a king: *konungur* or *konungr*. In that interpretation Conachair was more likely the monarch of Hirta's hills than a homage to the King of Norway.

At its north Conachair descends in sheer cliffsides to the waves below. At its west it reaches towards the northern arm of Village Bay. It declines firstly into a fortuitous geographical feature known as An Lag bho'n Tuath, or The Hollow from the North. At around 250 feet above sea level, a short uphill walk from Village Bay, a sheltered grassy plain forms an oasis in the hills. Despite the fact that it frequently flooded (and occasionally overflowed into Village Bay), An Lag became a perfectly convenient holding area for hundreds of sheep gathered for shearing or slaughter.

To the east of An Lag bho'n Tuath, which was named entirely by Gaelic pastoralists, the 900 stony feet of Oiseval rise gradually and then collapse precipitously down to the Atlantic. Oiseval is the Eastern Hill, or in Old Norse *eystra-fjall*. The Vikings held the higher ground. At its inaccessible base is Sgeir nan Sgarbh and Geo nan Sgarbh, where, undisturbed in the morning sun, the cormorants fished for bream.

At between 700 and 800 feet, in a dip between Mullach Sgar and Mullach Geal, there is an opening known as Am Blaid, The Wide Mouth, which leads over the ridge into the head of Gleann Mhor, the Big Glen which in counterpoint to Village Bay rolls down to the western ocean. (Am Blaid is immediately beneath a knoll known as Cnoc a' Bheannaichta, the Hill of the Blessing, and it is tempting to conjecture that the blessing was issued by people who had reached the top of the ridge with a creel full of peat from Gleann Mor, and thanked God for the fact that after Cnoc a' Bheannaichta it was all downhill into Village Bay.)

South of Am Blaid, on the heights surrounding the top of the glen, is Claigeann an Tigh Faire. It is a knob of rock commanding views of the sea to the east, south and west and translates from Gaelic as Skull of the Watch House. Two strong rivulets flow down Gleann Mhor. Their Gaelic names are Abhainn Glinne Mhoir and Amhuinn Alltan – the River of Gleann Mhor and the River of (Smaller) Burns. They irrigate the land at the foot of the glen, where the fabled Amazon's House and its beehive equivalents are named in Gaelic according to their later, more practical application: Airigh Mhor, the Big Shieling where youngsters lodged while summering with the flocks and herds. Just by Airigh Mhor is another of St Kilda's many freshwater springs, Tobar nam Buadh, the Well of Excellence or Virtue. 'During the reign of Popery,' wrote an eighteenth-century Protestant, 'the St Kildians paid a kind of religious adoration to it [Tobar nam Buadh], from a very serious persuasion that the water had obtained some extraordinary benediction, and in consequence of that, had virtue enough to perform miraculous cures'.

On the rugged coast of Loch a' Glinne, Glen Bay, Norse kicks in once more. There are several geos running down those inhospitable rocks. Geo nan Ron and Geo Chruadahan indicate Seal Gully and Dangerous (literally Hardship) Gully. The flat flags of shoreline rock at Leacan an Eitheir – Slabs of the Boat – suggest the only place in Loch a' Glinne where it might be feasible to land a vessel.

Above the south side of the bay a neck of peat bog and high green meadowland reaches westward towards the nearby island of Soay. It is called Cambir, from the Norse, *kampr*, for a crest of land. Soay itself, which is 244 acres of decent grazing land, derives from the Old Norse *saudr*, meaning sheep, and *ey*, meaning island. It is surrounded by such rocks and small stacks as Am Plastair, which could simply mean a stone or could derive from *peallastair*, which in Gaelic means a rascally, cheeky fellow. If the latter, the name will be due to Am Plastair presenting a permanent hazard to anybody attempting to reach one of Soay's few decent landing places, Laimhrig Adinet.

Those are the home islands. Six or seven miles away to the north lie the hunting and adventure grounds of Boreray and the big stacks. Boreray is slightly larger but considerably less welcoming than Soay, which is reflected in its Old Norse name of Borg Ey – Fortress Island. Its two immense offshore stacks, Stac Lee and Stac an Armin, have dual nationality. Stac comes from the Norse *stakkr*. Armuinn is Gaelic for a hero or brave man, which is self-explanatory, and Lee probably comes from the Gaelic *li*, meaning either sea or grey or both. Stac an Armin is the stack which heroes climb; Stac Lee is grey and/or belongs to the heaving ocean.

On Boreray itself the two cultures fuse. The small high pasture of Sunadal probably comes from the Norse *sunnudalr*, the dale which catches the sun. It overlooks Udraclete, the Outer Cliff or *utarr klettr* in Norse, which is another example of the word for cleit being used in St Kilda in its original, natural context. There are also Cleitean Mac Phaidein on Boreray, which signify the man-made cleits built by a certain Gael called MacFadyen. And there is Gaelic in Creagan Fairspeag, the Crag of the Great Black-backed Gull.

Occasionally the traditions meet and mate in extraordinary style. A small rock sticks out of the sea just to the south of Soay. It is intriguingly named Sgeir Mac Righ Lochlainn. The name is almost purely Gaelic. But it means the Skerry of the Son of the King of Norway. Its origin in local legend offers an intriguing hint of Gaelic resistance to, or at least resentment of, Norse rule: 'A son of the king of Lochlan was wrecked on a rock a little west of St Kilda. He came ashore in a small boat, and while he was drinking out of a water-brook a little west of the present church, those who were then the inhabitants of St Kilda came on him and caught him by the back of the neck, and held his head down in the brook until he was drowned. The rock on which he was wrecked is called Sgeir Mac Righ Lochlain, or the Rock of the Son of the King of Lochlan, until this day.'

The Norse also left the forenames and the family names of people, which would survive throughout Scotland and in much of the rest of the world, including St Kilda, until modern times. Aulay, Ivor, Ragnall, Somhairle, Tormod and Torcuil all arrived on the longships. The surnames MacAskill, Macaulay, MacCorquodale, MacIver and MacLeod are Norse in origin. They left behind them in St Kilda a few coins, some pottery, carved Scandinavian stone, two brooches, a sword and a spearhead which was found in the souterrain.

But they did not leave their language. If, as some scholars have suggested, Old Norse did not surrender unconditionally to Gaelic in such Hebridean islands as Lewis until as late as the sixteenth century, the former left surprisingly few loanwords with the latter. The twentieth-century Norwegian linguist Magne Oftedal, who became an authority on the Gaelic dialects of Lewis, estimated that Scottish Gaelic's lexicon of over 7,500 words included only 182 from Old Norse. By contrast, the Church and international trade and diplomacy had planted almost 400 Latin derivations into Gaelic, and the proximity and rapid post-medieval expansion of English had later introduced almost 1,000. Oftedal's conclusions have been criticised as inadequate. Such common Gaelic words as *tarsgeir* and *sgarbh*, respectively a peat-cutting tool and a cormorant, come from the Norse *torfskeri* and *skarfr*. By relaxing his terms of admittance Thomas W Stewart has increased the number of Old Norse words in Scottish Gaelic to well over 200, and suggested an even greater influence on its alphabet and syntax.

But when the Norsemen arrived, Gaelic was already an old language and had no need to borrow such basic words as those for a house, a river, a fortress or the wind. They were and remained *tigh, abhainn, dun* and *gaoth* in the Scottish *Gàidhealtachd*. The Norse words hus, *fljot, kastali* and *vindr* were unnecessary there – although they were greedily absorbed by the infant English tongue in the south. Scottish Gaelic remained the default everyday language of St Kilda and most of the rest of the west despite four centuries of Scandinavian sovereignty.

The Norsemen were at first pagans – their kingdom did not officially convert to Christianity until the eleventh century – with no respect for the icons and valuables of the Celtic Church, but they did not attempt to eliminate Christian worship from their territories. From Stornoway to Dublin by way of St Kilda and the Isle of Man, the Norse conquerors assimilated themselves to their new subjects. Those escapees from the overcrowded fjords and hillsides of Atlantic Scandinavia called such places as St Kilda 'sudreys', or southern islands, and they seem frequently to have settled with more relief than arrogance in the temperate climate of their machair greensward.

The Gaelic-Norman kings of Scotland, Alexander II and Alexander III, who between them reigned from 1214 to 1286, attempted throughout the thirteenth century to regain the west of the country from its Norse authority, which had been nominal since the eighth century and legal since 1098, when King Edgar of the Scots signed away all of the western islands and some of the western mainland to King Magnus Barefoot. In 1262 Alexander III presented King Haakon Haakonsson at his new estate in Bergen with a formal claim to the Western Isles. Haakon rejected it. In the following year, 1263, having received credible intelligence that Alexander planned to invade his sudreys, Haakon set sail with a battle fleet to the west of Scotland. He passed through Shetland, Orkney and the Hebrides, reinforcing his squadron with local tributaries. His curious coalition of Norsemen, Shetlanders, Orkney chieftains and Hebridean warriors occupied the Firth of Clyde and reached the coast of Ayrshire at the end of September. On 2 October they fought an inconclusive land action at Largs against Alexander's Lowland Scottish cavalry and infantry. Haakon and his people retreated to their vessels, sailed to Orkney and planned a further incursion for 1264.

Unfortunately, the fifty-nine year-old King Haakon died in Kirkwall in December 1263. While Haakon was on his deathbed Alexander mounted punitive expeditions against Haakon's Norse-Gaelic allies and vassals in the west, many of whom did not require much convincing that the Norse Empire was on the wane and that their future lay elsewhere. Three years later, in 1266, Haakon's successor Magnus VI sent representatives to meet with Alexander's nobles at Perth on the east coast of Scotland. A treaty was signed there, in which Norway retained the Shetland and Orkney islands but ceded the Western Isles and the Isle of Man to the Scottish crown for a down payment of 4,000 merks and an annual rental, to be paid in perpetuity, of 100 merks. (The down payment was made in full but the rental defaulted during the fifteenth century, and was finally written off in 1468 when Shetland and Orkney also became part of Scotland. The Isle of Man, despite being a wholly Gaelic community, had been disposed as a semi-autonomous dependency to the English crown in 1399.)

St Kilda had a new monarch and was part of a new polity. It would be condescending to suggest that the islanders knew nothing of this momentous train of events. It would be wrong to suggest that it offered them much material change. During the last centuries of Norse ownership the Gaels of the Western Islands had established a confederation which became variously known as the Lordship or the Kingdom of the Isles.

While its people were still vassals of Norway, the Lordship of the Isles was a functionally autonomous Gaelic domain which, at its peak at the end of the eleventh century, ran from the Isle of Man in the south to the Butt of Lewis in the north, embraced every one of the hundred and thirty-six Hebridean islands, large and small, inhabited or not, and took in for good measure the mainland Mull of Kintyre.

The Lordship of the Isles was fractured after the Treaty of Perth, and by the subsequent three centuries of campaigning by the Scottish Crown to bring the former Norse-Gaelic regions into its legislation. A network of increasingly quarrelsome clanships remained to pick up the pieces. Early in the fourteenth century St Kilda fell within the territories of John MacDonald of Islay, who gifted 'insular de hert' to his son Reginald in 1346. At some point in the following 100 years the little islands fell, by treaty, by purchase, by default or by force, to the MacLeods of Harris. The MacLeods were of direct Norse lineage. Their founding father was a thirteenth-century Norse Gael named

Leod who was born in the Isle of Man and raised on the island of Skye, where he married into substantial properties.

Leod's sons Tormod and Torcuil inherited and expanded the family estate until it included Assynt on the mainland, most of northern Skye, the small island of Raasay and the larger Western Isles of Lewis and Harris. By the fourteenth century the MacLeods, the sons of Leod, had become and would remain the most numerous and powerful Scottish clan after the MacDonalds.

Naturally they were not consulted about the matter, but it made more practical sense for the St Kildans to be in the stewardship of a clan chief on the comparatively nearby island of Harris than of one based in distant Islay. For the next 500 years, the last 500 years of the islands' inhabitation, their residents would be citizens of Scotland, citizens of the United Kingdom and citizens of the grandest empire on earth. They would be unenfranchised subjects of Inverness County Council and members of the parliamentary constituencies of Inverness-shire and then of the Western Isles. But first and foremost, they would be tenants of the MacLeods of Harris and of Dunvegan.

THREE

The Saint Who Never Was

THE ST KILDANS FIRST entered recorded history – the recorded history that has survived for us – in 1202 AD. A pugnacious forty-one year-old Icelandic clergyman named Gudmundur Arason set sail that summer for Norway, where he was due to be consecrated as bishop of one of the two Icelandic seats. Strong winds blew Arason's ship off-course and south to the Hebrides. Arason's crewmen were apparently familiar with their surroundings (they were of course still within the Kingdom of Norway) and they ran for shelter 'to the islands that are called Hirtir'.

That simple, and by no means solitary, incident sheds two strong beams of light on medieval St Kilda. In common with many other islands in the European North Atlantic, Gudmundur Arason's Iceland had first been settled in the eighth century by eremitic monks from the Irish/Scottish Celtic Church. The *papar* (from 'pope' or 'father' – the name is recalled in the host of small Scottish offshore islets called Pappay, Pabbay, Papey, Papa and other variants) built cabins, cells, chapels and hives on the Faroe Islands, halfway between the Hebrides and Iceland, as early as the sixth century, and then progressed to Iceland itself. The Norse people who were to form the permanent population of those islands arrived in the Faroes at least two centuries after the Celtic monks, in around 800 AD, and in Iceland perhaps a century after the Gaels, later in the ninth century.

It is unclear whether the Celtic monks had departed from those northern fastnesses before the Norse arrived, whether they were driven out by the Scandinavians, or whether they co-existed relatively amicably until the Norse converted to Christianity at the beginning of the second millennium AD.

It is certain that the Celts were there. In the words of the *Landnámabók*, or *Book of Settlements*, which was contemporaneous with Gudmundur Arason, 'before Iceland was inhabited from Norway, there were there the men whom the Norwegians call papar; these were Christian men, and it is believed that they had come from the west beyond the sea, because Irish books, and bells, and croziers, were found behind them, and many other things besides, so that one might know that they were Westmen.'

It is equally certain that so active and knowledgeable a priest as Gudmundur Arason would have been aware of the missionaries who had preceded him 500 years earlier. Arason's metropolitan see and archbishopric may in the thirteenth century have been at Trondheim in Norway, but his Icelandic Christian heritage lay in the old sudreys, the Gaelic islands to the south.

When Gudmundur Arason beached his ship and jumped ashore at Village Bay on Hirta in July 1202, thanking God for his preservation, he was almost certainly conscious that he was treading in the footprints of the indomitable pioneers of northern Christianity.

Arason may even have been greeted by holy men. There were in Village Bay on Hirta at least three antique chapels, two of which were named after the early Christian missionary saints Columba and Brendan. Both of those sites stood on the south side of the bay, on the lower slopes of Ruaival. Directly below the latter chapel Geo Chile Brianan, St Brendan's Gully, leads down to the sea. According to the Reverend Kenneth Macaulay, who visited the island in 1758, St Brendan's had 'an altar within, and some monkish cells without it. These are almost entire and must of consequence be of later date, than the holy places dedicated to Christ and Columba.' Macaulay also noted that the names of land portions in Village Bay in the eighteenth century were neither Gaelic nor Norse, but 'of an English and Latin origin'. They included 'Multum agria, Multum taurus, Multum favere, or Multum fodere, Queen o Scot, Land dotteros, or the Doctor's ground, Lanphalin, or Paul's division.' Macaulay proposed that the Latin land divisions in particular suggested that in the past holy men had lived alongside a lay community on Hirta –

[S]everal Ecclesiastics, and some Laymen too, from a foreign land, must have visited this island in some distant periods.

These men must have been undoubtedly accounted able Statesmen, and profound Scholars, by the poor ignorant people of St Kilda. It is extremely probable that one or more of these men may have usurped a kind of Tribunitian power, or may have exercised it in a legal way, that is, with the full and unanimous consent of the community; and we have reason to believe, that this Lay-Tribune or Ecclesiastical Demagogue would have framed a body of Agrarian laws for the use of this little state: and though it is hard to determine whether these Legislators were Priests or Laics, though it is more likely they were of the former order, it is plain they had craft or vanity enough to give mysteriously learned names to every distinct portion of the ground, which their superior knowledge, or public character, gave them a right to divide and to distinguish with what appellations they pleased.

Kenneth Campbell, a Skyeman who taught at the St Kilda school in 1884 and 1885, said in 1886 that such remains inclined him to the belief 'that St Columba or at least some of his disciples established themselves on the island'. When Campbell asked the locals, who by the 1880s were all communicants of the Presbyterian Free Church of Scotland, who had been responsible for the old religious foundations, 'the inevitable answer is "Papanaich a ghraidh, droch dhaoine a ghraidh"' ('Papists my friend, wicked men my friend.')

If Macaulay and Campbell and other scholars and chroniclers are right, when Gudmundur Arason landed on St Kilda in 1202, those chapels and monks' cells were either in use or had been quite recently abandoned. They might have been the reason why Arason sought shelter on St Kilda rather than in any of the larger Hebrides to the east. If Arason did not find there fellow members of his own Church, he found the relics of the Celtic holy men who had first taken Christianity to his own land in the distant frozen north. In modern times, three stone slabs marked with crosses have been discovered where they were re-employed in the building fabric of a nineteenth-century house, as the cover of a drain and as a roof crossbeam in a nearby cleit. They are all within 100 yards of one another in the settlement at Village Bay, and they are all medieval or earlier. The two crosses which are now by a windowframe at Number 16 Main Street and in the roof of a cleit are similar. They are elegant incised symbols. Each is a simple, standard single-line crucifix inside the border of a larger cross. The crucifix which was turned into a drain cover has been subjected to more wear and weather but nonetheless seems to be older. The slab is broken but has the quarter-circular remains of a ring-head at both ends, which would place it in the tradition of the early Columban Dark Age Celtic Church.

One of the springs in Village Bay was traditionally known as Tobar a' Chleirich, or the holy well. Even on little Soay there are the remains of a 5-foot-square stone structure which is supposed to have been an altar. Taken together, those relics amount to convincing evidence of a settled Christian community in medieval St Kilda.

The second illumination provided by Gudmundur Arason's visit is that he referred to the place as 'Hirtir' and not as St Kilda. Until almost 400 years later, in the late sixteenth century, nobody used or had heard of the name St Kilda. There is not and never has been a Saint Kilda, let alone anywhere named after him or her. Its application to those islands was a freak of cartography.

In 1570 the Flemish map-engraver Abraham Ortelius, a friend and colleague of the great Gerardus Mercator, began to publish his *Theatrum Orbis Terrarum*, the 'Theatre of the Earth', the first modern atlas of the known world. The Theatrum came to include a *Scotiae tabula*, or specific map of Scotland. It contained substantial errors, particularly in the north and west of the country, but the 'Hebrides insule' were relatively well done. Just to the west of 'Barray minor', which we now know as Little Bernera on the Atlantic coast of Lewis, was depicted an oval island which Ortelius named 'S. Kylder'.

In 1551 a thirty-four year-old French soldier of fortune named Nicolas de Nicolay, Dauphinois Sieur d'Arfeuille et de Belair, was appointed *geographe du roi* by his king, Henri II. During the next thirty years Nicolay – whose military career had taken him to Germany, Denmark, England, Sweden, Italy, Spain, Greece and Turkey – produced with enthusiasm and increasing aptitude a series of maps of foreign countries and of the regions of France.

His last map, which was published in 1583, the year of his death, was of Scotland including the north of England and Ireland (in his own words, 'une Vraye et exacte description Hydrographique des costes maritimes d'Escosse et des Isles Orchades Hebrides avec partie d'Angleterre et d'Irlande servant a la navigation'). The map of the

Outer Hebrides is good. In the ocean directly to the west of the Uig district of Lewis there sits a single lump of land named by Nicolay 'Skilda'.

In 1592 the Dutch nautical cartographer Lucas Janszoon Waghenaer published a book for sea-going pilots titled *Thresoor der Zeevaert* ('Treasure of Navigation'). Waghenaer's *Thresoor der Zeevaert* included the first printed map of the three main islands and two big sea-stacks which were then in the archipelago (Dun was still connected by a fragile rock bridge to Hirta). But he gave them just one name. In the middle of the largest island of Hirta he wrote 'S. Kilda'.

Each of them drawing from an original confusion, and then from one another, Ortelius, Nicolay and Waghenaer – none of whom ever went near the Hebrides – made a complete break with precedent. Whenever the islands had been registered on a map or a manuscript in all of the previous centuries, they had been called by one rendition or another of the main island, Hirta. It became at different times Hert, Hyrte, Hirther, Irt, Zirta (in 1615, by its proprietor Sir Ruaridh MacLeod), Art, Hirtha, Uirt or Hirte, and one early sixteenth-century map had it as Torta. In Gaelic the name is Hiort, and it is either Norse or Gaelic in origin. Unlike Boreray, Soay and Dun, the exact meaning of Hirta is unclear. It may derive from the Gaelic *h-Iar-tir*, or the western land. It may be taken from the Old Norse for a stag, *hjortr*, referring to the silhouette of the island rather than to the presence there of any deer, or from *hirth* or *hirt*, which meant such a horned animal as a sheep, of which there were many in the archipelago of St Kilda. The Scottish historian and philosopher Hector Boece thought in 1527 that the island 'namit Hirtha' was so called after its sheep.

Among many other hazardous interpretations it has been suggested that Ortelius' and Nicolay's first deployment of S. Kylder and Skilda were misuses of the Old Icelandic term *skildir*, meaning shields. Boreray and Soay could at a stretch be said to shield Hirta from some of the elements, and Village Bay is a well-protected harbour, but it is difficult to understand why late sixteenth-century Flemish and French cartographers should suddenly adopt a mysterious word from the dialect of a thinly populated Arctic island of which they knew little. It is also possible that the islanders' own pronunciation of Hirta or Hirte or Hiort – they used a guttural 'h' and lisped the 'r' into more of an 'l' – misled visitors. A misinterpretation of Hirta as Kilda would not be the worst damage done to a Gaelic placename by a mapmaker who was unfamiliar with the language.

Ortelius, Nicolay and Waghenaer were making maps chiefly for the use of mariners, and were necessarily taking their information from those mariners and other travellers as well as from their fellow cartographers. By the sixteenth century St Kilda was best known to seafarers as a place of refuge, and especially as a source of that most valuable provision: fresh drinking water. Two centuries later another Hebridean remarked that 'The fountain water of St Kilda is beyond comparison the finest I ever tasted, and one will easily find inexhaustable quantities of it in every corner of that isle. In this respect the natives have a very considerable advantage over their neighbours in some parts of the Long-Island [the Outer Hebrides].'

There were numerous springs in Village Bay and Gleann Mor – and even in the stacks – and they were all given names, kept clean and clear and carefully surrounded by dry-stone frames. The Old Norse word for a freshwater well is *kelda*. As a result one of the most dependable natural water sources on the island, situated 300 yards from the shore, was given that simple name by the Norsemen. It was later described as 'near the heart of the village, and ... of universal use to the community. The water of it is sweet, light and clear like crystal'.

The Gaels of the island obviously retained it, and in their lexicography it became Tobar Childa. (It was an interesting tautology. As tobar is the Gaelic word for a well, the name meant Well Well in two languages, which indicates that the Gaels of the island either never came to understand basic Norse words or quickly forgot them.) From the Dark Ages to the present day, that freshwater source on Hirta was and is known as kelda or childa. It is possible that under interrogation by Abraham Ortelius a sailor told the cartographer of some lumps of inhabited land way out in the western ocean, which were of importance mainly because of a very sweet well which was called something that sounded like 'kylder'.

The initial 'S' could be explained in many ways or none. Abraham Ortelius was an Antwerp Protestant without a comprehensive knowledge of Catholic saints, and he may have presumed that the well had been named – as was common – after some venerated holy person named Kylder. Or he may have misheard his informant, or his inform-ant might have been mistaken. It could even have been an engraver's error. If an earlier sage could represent Hirta as Torta, almost anything was possible.

Ortelius, Nicolay and Waghenaer could also have been deliberately pointing in their own languages to a well which was named Kelda. The Flemish and Dutch for a freshwater outlet is 'springbron', and the French is 'source'. In Flemish, Dutch and French maps of that and later eras the terms were abbreviated to a simple 'S'. There is therefore the possibility that St Kilda started life as a reduction of 'Springbron Kylder' or 'Source Kilda'.

Whatever the origin, whatever the reasons, it stuck. Within decades, while the island's inhabitants, other Gaels and most Scots continued to refer to Hirta, map-makers were fixated on S. Kilda. In English and in Scots, 'S' was an abbreviation not of the words 'springbron' or 'source' but of the word 'saint'. A description of the Western Isles in the manuscripts of Sir Robert Sibbald, Geographer Royal to King Charles II after 1682, states that 'the Isle of Hirta ... is calld Saint Kildar Island ...'

The Skyeman Martin Martin, who visited the islands in 1697, wrote in a book which he chose to title *A Late Voyage to St Kilda* that 'This isle is by the inhabitants called Hirt, and likewise by all the Western Islanders; Buchanan calls it Hirta; Sir John Narbrough, and all seamen call it St Kilda; and in sea maps St Kilder, particularly in a Dutch sea map from Ireland to Zeland, published at Amsterdam by Peter Goas in the year, 1663 ...'

Buchanan was George Buchanan, a sixteenth-century Scottish historian and native Gaelic speaker from near Stirling, whose *History of Scotland* was published in 1583, a year after his death. Sir John Narbrough was a seventeenth-century English naval commander and commissioner. In blaming poor Peter Goas for using the term St Kilda in his map of 1663, Martin was understandably unaware of the works of Ortelius and Nicolay a century earlier.

In 1714, shortly after the parliamentary union of England, Wales and Scotland, a German or Dutch immigrant to London named Herman Moll drew up his definitive illustrated chart of 'The north part of Great Britain called Scotland: with considerable inprovements [sic] and many remarks not extant in any map.' Moll offered a group of 13 islets and stacks 55 miles off the west coast of North Uist. One of them was labelled 'Boreray I.' and to its south another, larger island with a 'Landing-Place' was named St Kilda. In the sea beside the archipelago Moll wrote 'The Inhabitants of the Isle St Kilda are about 200 in Number, the Solan geese are very numerous here, in so much that the people commonly keep yearly above 20,000 yong and old in their little Stone Houses, of which there are some hundreds, and there is Plenty of Cod, and Ling of a great size all round these Isles.'

St Kilda it had become and St Kilda it would remain.

Between 1202 and 1698 there were many short written accounts of and references to the islands, almost all of them composed by people who had never been there. Long before Sibbald and Buchanan, in around 1360, John of Fordun, a scholar from the Mearns in the east of Scotland, mentioned in his seminal *Chronicle of the Scottish Nation* an island named 'Hirth, the best stronghold of all the islands.' Near to Hirth, wrote Fordun, 'is an island twenty miles long, where wild sheep are said to exist, which can only be caught by hunters.' As Lewis and Uist, which are each roughly 20 miles long, are listed separately in Fordun's roll-call of medieval Scottish islands, and as neither Lewis nor Uist could reasonably be described as 'near to Hirth', he may have been referring to Boreray and its flock of semi-feral sheep. Boreray is less than a mile in length, but it was the fourteenth century and John of Fordun was writing at the opposite end of the country.

Hector Boece, a Dundee boy who befriended Erasmus at the University of Paris and in 1500 became the first principal of the University of Aberdeen, displayed in his 1527 *History of the Scottish People* an acute awareness of the extent of the old Gaelic Scottish islands. 'The last and outmaist Ile,' wrote Boece in translation from Latin to Scots, 'is namit Hirtha; quhare the elevatioun of the pole is LXIII greis. And, sen the elevatioun of the pole abone the Ile of Man is LVII greis, ilk gre extending to LXII milis and ane half in distance, as Ptolome and uthir astronomeris nowmeris, I conclude, that fra the Ile of Man, the first Ile of Albion, to Hirtha, the last Ile thairof, ar CCCLXXVII milis.' Boece's astronomical calculation was courageously wrong: the distance between the northernmost tip of the Isle of Man and Village Bay on Hirta is closer to 500 than 377 miles.

'This last Ile is namit Hirtha, quhilk, in Irsche, is callit ane scheip;' he continued, 'for in this Ile is gret nowmer of scheip, ilk ane gretar than ony gait buk, with hornis lang and thikkar than ony horne of ane bewgill, and hes lang talis hingand down to the erd.' A bewgill was an ox. Boece was not the last person to remark on the size of the horns and the length of the tails of St Kilda's sheep.

'This Ile is circulit on every side with roche craggis;' said Boece correctly, 'and na baitis may land at it bot allanerly at ane place, in quhilk is ane strait and narow entres. Sum time thair micht na pepill pas to this Ile but extreme dangeir of thair livis; and yit thair is na passage to it bot quhen the seis ar cawme but ony tempest.'

He concluded by affirming, in 1527, the St Kildans' Roman Catholic faith. 'In the moneth of Juny, ane preist cumis out of the Lewis in ane bait to this Ile, and ministeris the sacrament of baptisme to all the barnis that hes bene borne in the yeir afore. Als sone as this preist hes done his office, with certane messis, he ressavis the tindis of all thair commoditeis, and returnis hame the same gait he come.'

Twenty-two years later the superior of that Lewis priest who travelled annually to baptise infants and take masses on St Kilda made his own survey of the islands. Donald Monro was a Ross-shire man from the eastern Highlands who started his pastoral career as a Roman Catholic priest in Skye and Raasay. In around 1549 Donald Monro was made Archdeacon of the Isles. In order to advance his own and his Church's knowledge of the Hebrides, he promptly prepared *A Description of the Western Isles of Scotland*:

… Out in the mayne ocean seas, be three-score of myle of sea, layes ane ile callit Hirta, ane maine laiche ile, sa far as is manurit of it, aboundant in corne and gressing, namelie for sheipe, for ther are fairer and greiter sheip ther, and larger tailled, then ther is in any uther ile about.

The inhabitants thereof ar simple poor people, scarce learnit in aney religion, but M'Cloyd of Herray, his stewart, or he quhom he deputs in sic office, sailes anes in the zear ther at midsummer, with some chaplaine to baptize bairnes ther, and if they want a chaplaine, they baptize ther bairns themselfes.

The said stewart, as he himself tauld me, uses to take ane maske of malt ther with a masking fatt, and makes his malt, and ere the fatt be ready, the comons of the town, baith men, weemin, and bairns, puts their hands in the fatt, and findis it sweeit, and eets the greyns after the sweeitness thereof, quhilk they leave nather wirt or draffe unsuppit out ther, quharwith baith men, women, and bairns, were deid drunken, sua that they could not stand upon their feet.

The said stewart receives thir dewties in miell and reistit mutton, wyld foullis reistit, and selchis. This ile is maire nor ane mile lange, and narrest als meikle in braid, quhilk is not seine of aney shore, bot at the shoresyde of it lyes three grate hills, quhilk are ane pairt of Hirta, quhilk are seen affar off from the fore landis. In this fair ile is fair sheipe, falcon nests and wyld fouls biggand, but the streams of the sea are starke, and are verey eivil entring in aney of the saids iles. This ile of Hirta perteins of auld to M'Cloyd of Herray.

Donald Monro thereby confirmed – presumably from the testimony of the steward of MacLeod of Harris – that in the first half of the sixteenth century the community of Hirta was so economically healthy that it produced an export surplus, and that a Catholic priest sailed each year to St Kilda to perform certain sacraments. That would not happen for much longer. In 1560 the Scottish Parliament broke away from the Roman Catholic Church and established its own Reformed Confession of Faith. Donald Monro himself then joined the Protestant Church of Scotland and became a commissioner of its General Assembly in the Highlands, with responsibility for building new places of worship.

Not all of the remote Western Isles followed their Edinburgh Parliament's injunctions against the Papacy. With the encouragement of missionaries despatched from Ireland, the southern Outer Hebrides from Mingulay through Barra and South Uist to Benbecula retained the old faith. North of there, however, from North Uist up to Harris and Lewis, Presbyterian Protestantism took hold. As St Kilda was chiefly connected and answerable to Harris, its people followed suit. 'Simple' and 'scarce learned' as they might have been, they adapted to the transition.

As well as laughing with MacLeod's steward about the St Kildans' propensity for getting communally legless by eating mashed malted grain before it had fully fermented, Monro laid emphasis on the islands' abundance of cereal, dried mutton, seals and big wild birds. By the standards of sixteenth-century Scottish peasantry, St Kilda was not a hungry community. The St Kildan people – references from between 1615 and 1673 agree on about ten adult men and ten adult women, who at that time could have been expected to produce sufficient children to take the total population to over a hundred people – husbanded and caught a surplus of food. The fact that most of the surplus disappeared each summer as rental to MacLeod of Harris was no more or less than God's ordering of their estate. The population was fluid and may occasionally have been increased by emigrants from the MacLeod properties in Skye. A late-nineteenth-century factor of St Kilda and the rest of the MacLeod estates, John MacKenzie of Skye, was convinced that 'the progenitors of the St Kildans were undoubtedly transported from Skye by the Chief of MacLeod for various offences', and in evidence of this points out that 'whenever there is a row in that island [Skye] the restorers of peace will still threaten to send the disturbers to St Kilda. Further, that [Skye] mothers say to their children when they are troublesome, "If you don't be quiet, I'll send you to St Kilda."' If that was true, if St Kilda was used as a penal colony by MacLeod of MacLeod in Skye, Hirta would later stand beside Australia as irrefutable evidence that anti-social behaviour is not hereditary.

Their superfluity of produce did not go unnoticed elsewhere. In 1615 a neighbouring warlord, Coll MacDonald of Colonsay, raided St Kilda. By 1615 the old Lordship of the Isles was in dissolution. One hundred and twenty years earlier, in 1493, John Macdonald of Islay, the Earl of Ross, had finally ceded to the Stewart kings of Scotland and their parliament his claim to sovereignty over the Hebrides.

That epochal surrender did not mean that King James IV or his successors suddenly assumed complete control over the Western Islands, which remained beyond the jurisdiction of the state for centuries. It did mean that a fissile coalition of clans which had previously been united, at least nominally, by common cause, was sundered. There was never much love lost between the MacLeods and Clan Donald, the two largest entities of the Lordship of the Isles. After 1493 they saw less reason than ever to respect each other's property.

Alasdair Coll MacDonald, 'Colla Chiotaich', Ambidextrous Coll (his nickname was anglicised and slipped into history as Colkitto), was an archetypal rapscallion of his time. He was also a good example of the enduring trans-nationalism of Irish and Scottish Gaeldom. Coll was born in 1570 in County Antrim in the north of Ireland, and was moved as an infant to be raised in the small Scottish island of Colonsay. There he grew in power, reputation and pretension, and at the age of about 17 he gave away his inherited Antrim estate (whose castle had anyway been severely reduced by English cannons four decades earlier) and adopted Colonsay as his home.

A militant, unrepentant Catholic in newly Protestant Scotland as well as an assertive clan chieftain, Coll MacDonald's life was one long round of skirmish and feud. During a dispute in 1615 with the Earl of Argyll, who on behalf of the Scottish Privy Council was attempting to curb the Colonsay warlord, Coll made his way to St Kilda for respite and supplies. Sir Ruaraidh Mor MacLeod wrote bitterly from Skye to the Privy Council claiming that Coll and his men 'slew all the bestiall of the ylle, both cowes, and horses, and sheep, and took away all the spoolyee of the yle, onlie reserved the lyves of the enhabitants thereof.'

Ninety years later the grandchildren of those who had been on Hirta in 1615 gave a visitor a gentler version of events. They recognised that they had been invaded by a celebrity –

[T]here was one Coll M'Donald, alias Ketoch … a commander in chief of the Irish army, and was of the M'Donalds in Ireland, or of the family of Antrim, the M'Donalds' chief there; this Coll M'Donald alias Ketoch being defeat in battle, losing his right-hand, and his army which he had raised for the Popish interest rooted, was forced, with a few to flee for his life; and getting his foot in a vessel comes to land in St Kilda, whom when the inhabitants saw, they ran away from him and his men, into a cave in some remote corner of the island, where they thought they might be most safe from him, whom they thought to be an enemy come to destroy them; but he sending some few of his men after them, told them of his friendly designs, and he himself advancing gradually, enforces what his men had said, by telling them he had no hostile design against them, and that tho' he had, he was not in condition to effect it, since he wanted the right-hand (shewing them the stump;) so pulling out his mill, and giving them a snuff, with which, and some other significations of kindness, they came to be delivered of their former fears; so that he lived in safety and quietness with them for the space of three quarters of a year;

This Coll M'Donald at length examining them of their religion and principles, found that the priest was very ignorant, and had not taught the people the Lord's prayer, decalogue, and creed aright: so rebuking the priest, he corrected this, by causing them repeat these aright: He

likewise established them in their superstitious and idolatrous practices, being himself a begotted papist.

The poor people, judging the priest to be in the wrong, and looking
on him to be ignorant, resolved to depose him; for the doing whereof,
they referred it to the sentiments of this Coll M'Donald, whether they
should do it or not; but this Coll put them off such thoughts, by telling
them, he never saw a priest deposed in his country for ignorance; with
this and other such like reasonless reasons they were satisfied.

There are significant errors in both accounts. Coll MacDonald was not
one-handed in 1615, nor did he lose a hand at any time before he lost
his head in 1647. It is possible that the people of Hirta in 1705, some
of whom would have been children when Coll was still alive but none
of whom would have known him in St Kilda, had come to misinterpret
his Gaelic nickname as meaning not ambidextrous or left-handed, but
one-handed. Colla Chiotaich did, however, have a notorious fondness
for snuff. By the time of his death he had become a legendary figure
in the Scottish *Gàidhealtachd*. The supposed peacemaking action of
'pulling out his mill, and giving them a snuff' could be a reflection of
his fame, or it could as easily have been based on hard fact. Snuff was
a memorable luxury in St Kilda in the early seventeenth century. The
wit of his reported observation that 'he never saw a priest deposed in
his country for ignorance' certainly rings true.

He certainly did not stay on the islands for nine months, and nor
did he slaughter all the livestock in St Kilda. One of his sailors, who
claimed to have been travelling with Coll under duress, said later that
the Colonsay man had gone first to Uist, where he was given food and
offered two pilots to guide him to 'Art', 'far out in the ocean sea'. (Sir
Ruaraidh Mor MacLeod suggested to the Privy Council, with some
credibility, that the Macdonalds of Uist had deployed Coll as a merce-
nary to plunder the MacLeod realm of St Kilda and return with his ill-
gotten gains to Uist.) Once in Hirta, 'They took great store of barley,
and some thirty sheep for their provision ... There they remained
a month. From Art they sailed to another island called Burribaugh
[Boreray], which is six miles from Art ... there is no dwelling therein
... there Coll had a purpose to keep himself, for it is of such strength
[Boreray was so easily defensible] as not to be gained but by famine.
And from thence they returned back the same way they went thither.'

Forty years later in 1654 Sir Robert Moray also found it prudent to visit the Western Isles. Following an extraordinary career as a French soldier and spy in the employ of Cardinal Richelieu, Moray had joined the Royalist cause in the British Civil War. When Charles I was executed and Oliver Cromwell established the English Commonwealth in 1649, Sir Robert, a son of Perthshire, joined the Royalist resistance in Scotland. That was duly crushed by the New Model Army in 1653 and Robert Moray made himself scarce, firstly in the Outer Hebrides and then on the continent. He returned to Britain immediately after the restoration of Charles II to the throne in 1660.

In a paper which was published in 1678, five years after Moray's death, by the Royal Society of which he was a co-founder in 1660, the adventurer reiterated information about Hirta which had probably been given to him by the hereditary laird Macdonald of Clanranald in South Uist.

Moray reported that ten families lived on the island. He said that the women harrowed the land while the men climbed the high cliffs, using thick ropes plaited from strips of cured cow-hide, in search of seabirds. The Hirtans' only food, said Sir Robert (blithely disregarding his own line about women tilling the earth), was young fowls and eggs.

Moray described a method of rock-climbing which would be familiar to later mountaineers. The men worked in pairs. 'Each end of the rope is tied about each one of their middle, and he that is foremost goes till he comes to a safe standing, the other standing firm all that time to keep him up, in case his feet should have slipped: when the foremost is come to a safe standing; then the other goes, either below or above him, where his business is; and so they watch time about; seldom any of them being lost when this is observed.' If Sir Robert Moray is to be believed, that sophisticated practice was insufficiently observed. 'The men seldom grow old, and seldom was it ever known that any man died in his bed there, but was either drowned or broke his neck.' They died as Christians. Moray wrote that the fifteen- and sixteen-year-olds of Hirta were shipped to Harris to be baptised.

Another Royalist who was returned to eminence by the restoration of the monarchy, George Mackenzie, Earl of Cromartie and Viscount of Tarbat, offered in the early 1680s an account of Hirta which he received 'from intelligent Persons, dwelling in the same'. Robert Sibbald recorded Mackenzie as saying,

The island of Hirta, of all the isles about Scotland, lyeth furthest out into the sea, is very mountainous, and not accessible but by climbing.

It is incredible, what number of fowls frequent the rocks there, so far as one can see the sea is covered with them, and when they rise they darken the sky, they are so numerous. They are ordinarily catched this way: a man lies upon his back with a long pole in his hand, and knocketh them down, as they fly over him.

There be many sorts of these fowls; some of them of strange shapes, among which there is one they call the Gare fowl, which is bigger than any goose, and hath eggs as big almost as those of the Ostrich. Among the other commodities they export out of the island, this is none of the meanest. They take the fat of these fouls that frequent the island, and stuff the stomach of this fowl with it, which they preserve by hanging it near the chimney, where it is dryed with the smoke, and they sell it to their neighbours on the continent, as a remedy they use for aches and pains.

Their sheep upon that island of Hirta are far different from all others, having long legs, long horns, and, instead of wool, a blewish hair upon them, for the figure and description it seems to approach in resemblance to the *Ovis Chilensis*: Some natural historians make mention of the milk of those sheep, they make butter and a sort of cheese, which my Lord Register [that is, George Mackenzie himself] saith, pleaseth his taste better than Holland cheese.

They have no salt there, but what they make by burning of sea-tangle, which is very black. Their greatest trade is in feathers they sell: And the exercise they effect most, is climbing of steep rocks; he is the prettiest man who ventures upon the most inaccessible, though all they gain is the eggs of the fowls, and the honour to dye, as many of their Ancestors, by breaking of their necks; which Pliny observes of these people which he calls Hyperborei.

Ovis Chilensis was a reference to the hardy sheep which grazed at the other end of the earth in Patagonian Chile. Pliny's, or any other ancient's, Hyperborei were the mysterious people who dwelt far from the warm Mediterranean, beyond the north wind. The Gare fowl (a name which derives from the Gaelic *gearra-bhall*, and is echoed in the Icelandic *geirfugl*) was the Great Auk, a large, flightless seabird which became extinct in the middle of the nineteenth century, with implications for the reputation of the St Kildans. While it still bred on the islands, Great Auk stuffed with other bird fat was a valuable medicinal export from St Kilda – just as so refined a gentleman as Sir George Mackenzie, who tasted it elsewhere in Scotland, preferred St Kildan sheep's cheese to Edam or Gouda.

At the end of May 1697, the exhausted crew of a storm-tossed open galley which had set sail from Harris sixteen hours earlier, saw through the cloud and spray of the North Atlantic Ocean firstly the birds and then the island of Boreray. Having previously considered themselves lost, the boatmen gathered their residual strength, ate some of their remaining victuals, took down their mast and sail and rowed to anchor – while fortifying themselves with so much brandy that they had difficulty handling the cable – in the shelter of the high cliffs off the coast of Boreray.

The violent weather held them there for two nights and a day, throughout which time they were constantly showered with gannet excrement. On 1 June the sea calmed, and after some forty hours at sea the birlinn with its complement of fifty crew and passengers made its way south from Boreray to Village Bay in Hirta. As they approached the shore several men who were fishing from the rocks with limpet bait hailed their arrival, and then walked with uncanny balance and agility along the precipitous shoreline to receive the ship. It was fended off the rocks with poles while pairs of St Kildans walked into the sea and carried ashore on their shoulders the vessel's passengers, 'where we were received with all the demonstrations of joy and kindness they were able to express'.

So began the visit which would introduce the modern world to St Kilda, and the St Kildans to the modern world.

Martin Martin, Màrtainn MacGilleMhàrtainn, was the university-educated son of a factor and tenant farmer from the Trotternish peninsula in the north of the island of Skye. Having graduated Master of Arts from Edinburgh University in 1681 he travelled abroad and also became familiar with members of the Royal Society. (The Royal Society of London for Improving Natural Knowledge was founded in 1660 by twelve luminaries including Christopher Wren and Robert Boyle as well as Sir Robert Moray, and was given a royal charter by Charles II two years later.) Those gentlemen, apparently including Charles Montagu, first Earl of Halifax, Chancellor of the Exchequer, hobbyist poet and President of the Royal Society between 1695 and 1698, persuaded the Skyeman 'to survey the isles of Scotland more exactly than any other'.

Martin was naturally aware of St Kilda, and was doubly aware that previous accounts of the islands were no more than 'relations from second and third hands'. He resolved to become the first scholar to visit, study and make a written record of the archipelago. His opportunity came when Ruaridh Og, the 19th MacLeod of Harris and Dunvegan (who was also Martin's father's landlord and employer and whom Martin described as 'the kindest friend I had on earth') directed the reformed, Protestant Church of Scotland minister in Harris, Reverend John Campbell, to attend to the spiritual needs of the St Kildans. Martin was invited to accompany Campbell on the steward's annual visit to St Kilda, leaving Harris on 29 May 1697, and 'this occasion I cheerfully embrac'd'.

Martin Martin discovered what appeared, even to a Skyeman, to be a healthy and happy community of about 180 people, which ate extraordinary quantities of eggs. After he and Reverend Campbell had been carried ashore, tired, cold, wet, hungry, thirsty and covered in birdshit, they were taken to the small thatched clachan in Village Bay,

> ... where there was a lodging prepared for us, furnished with beds of straw, and according to the ancient custom of the place, the officer, who presides over them (in the steward's absence) summoned the inhabitants, who by concert agreed upon a daily maintenance for us, as bread, butter, cheese, mutton, fowls, eggs, also fire, &c. all which was to be given in at our lodging twice every day; this was done in the most regular manner, each family by turns paying their quota proportionally to their lands.
>
> I remember the allowance for each man per diem, beside a barley cake, was eighteen of the eggs laid by the fowl called by them lavy [guillemots], and a greater number of the lesser eggs, as they differed in proportion; the largest of these eggs is near in bigness to that of a goose, the rest of the eggs gradually of a lesser size.

Their dwellings, which Martin considered to indicate 'extream poverty', were nonetheless of standard Hebridean vernacular in the late seventeenth century:

… the houses are of a low form, having all the doors to the north-east, both on purpose to secure them from the shocks of the tempest of the south-west winds. The walls of their houses are rudely built of stone, the short couples joining at the ends of the roof, upon whose sides small ribs of wood are laid, these being covered with straw; the whole secured by ropes made of twisted heath, the extremity of which on each side is poised with stone to preserve the thatch from being blown away by the winds. This little village is seated in a valley surrounded with four mountains, which serve as so many ramparts of defence, and are amphitheatres, from whence a fair prospect of the ocean and isles is to be seen in a fair day.

The spit of rock which would later lose its narrow land bridge and become the separate island of Dun was, in 1697, still a peninsula of Hirta.

There is a little old ruinous fort on the south part of the south-east bay, called the Down. It is evident from what hath been already said, that this place may be reckoned among the strongest forts (whether natural or artificial) in the world; Nature has provided the place with store of ammunition for acting on the defensive; that is, a heap of loose stones in the top of the hill Oterveaul, directly above the landing-place; it is very easy to discharge vollies of this ammunition directly upon the place of landing, and that from a great height almost perpendicular; this I myself had occasion to demonstrate, having for my diversion put it in practice, to the great satisfaction of the inhabitants, to whom this defence never occurred hitherto.

Two years earlier a crew of Lowland Scottish seamen had put ashore on Hirta. The visitors had reportedly worked on the Sabbath, underpaid for cattle and attempted to rape women.

'They are resolved to make use of this for the future,' said Martin of his own strategy for the defence of St Kilda, 'to keep off the Lowlanders, against whom of late they have conceived prejudices. A few hands may be capable of resisting some hundreds, if the above-mentioned weapons be but made use of.'

Martin found 'about one hundred and eighty' people living on Hirta, the oldest of whom was a little over eighty years. They kept around

2,000 sheep on that island and on Soay and Boreray, as well as ninety head of cattle, eighteen horses and numerous cats and dogs. There were 'no sort of trees, no, not the least shrub grows here, nor ever a bee seen at any time', but the land below the hills was good. They grew bere barley and oats on 'subdivisions', or what would come to be called crofts, of soil fertilised by a mixture of peat-ash, straw, the bones and entrails of wildfowl and human urine. They were also 'plentifully furnished with variety of fishes, as cod, ling, mackarell, congars, braziers [bream], turbat, graylords [large coalfish], sythes; these last two are the same kind, only differing in bigness, some call them black mouths; they are large as any salmon, and somewhat longer; there are also laiths, podloes [small coalfish], herring, and many more ...' They were caught by primitive line and baited hook, 'for they have neither nets nor long lines'. The locals also reckoned seals to provide 'very good meat'.

Martin Martin, who we must constantly remind ourselves was another Gaelic-speaking Hebridean, albeit one with metropolitan pretensions, claimed to be highly impressed by the St Kildans. 'They are a sort of people so plain, and so little inclined to impose upon mankind,' he wrote, 'that perhaps no place in the world at this day, knows such instances of true primitive honour and simplicity, a people who abhor lying tricks and artifices, as they do the most poisonous plants, or devouring animals.' They spoke only Gaelic, and that of a 'purity' which Martin recognised as common to the Western Isles.

> The inhabitants of this isle are originally descended of those of the adjacent isles, Lewis, Harries, South and North Uist, Skiy: both sexes are naturally very grave, of a fair complection; such as are not fair are natives only for an age or two; but their off-spring proves fairer than themselves.
>
> There are several of them would be reckoned among beauties of the first rank, were they upon a level with others in their dress.

That dress, Martin was told, had in earlier centuries been fashioned from sheepskins,

> ... which has been wore by several of the inhabitants now living; the men at this day wear a short doublet reaching to their waste, about that a double plait of plad, both ends join'd together with the bone of

a fulmar; this plad reaches no further than their knees, and is above the haunches girt about with a belt of leather; they wear short caps of the same colour and shape with the capuchins, but shorter; and on Sundays they wear bonnets; some of late have got breeches, and they are wide and open at the knees; they wear cloth stocking and go without shoes in the summer-time; their leather is dress'd with the roots of tormentil.

The women wear upon their heads a linnen dress, strait before, and drawing to a small point behind below the shoulders, a foot and an half in length, and a lock of about sixty hairs hanging down each cheek, reaching to their breasts, the lower end tied with a knot; their plad, which is the upper garment, is fastened upon their breasts with a large round buckle of brass in form of a circle; the buckle anciently worn by the stewards' wives were of silver, but the present steward's wife makes no use of either this dress or buckle.

The women inhabiting this isle wear no shoes nor stockings in the summer-time; the only and ordinary shoes they wear, are made of the necks of solan geese, which they cut above the eyes, the crown of the head serves for the heel, the whole skin being cut close at the breast, which end being sowed, the foot enter into it, as into a piece of narrow stockin. This shoe doth not wear above five days, and if the down side be next the ground, then not above three or four days; but, however, there is plenty of them; some thousands being catch'd, or, as they term it, stolen every March.

Both sexes wear coarse flannel shirts, which they put off when they go to bed; they thicken their cloaths upon flakes, or mats of hay twisted and woven together in small ropes; they work hard at this employment, first making use of their hands, and at last of their feet; and when they are at this work, they commonly sing all the time, one of their number acting the part of a prime chantress, whom all the rest follow and obey.

They married 'very young', when the girls were thirteen or fourteen years old, having taken care to examine the lineage of each bride and groom to avoid the taint of incest. The island's bachelors routinely courted their sweethearts with gifts of the fattest plucked seabirds, 'and it is the greatest present they can make, considering the danger they run in acquiring it'.

During his visit in June 1693 Reverend John Campbell formally married fifteen St Kildan couples 'who immediately after marriage, join'd in a country dance, having only a bagpipe for their musics, which pleased them exceedingly'. It is likely that several of those partnerships had earlier been joined more or less informally, in the absence of a resident pastor, by MacLeod's ground officer,

> ... as when any two of them have agreed to take one another for man and wife, the officer who presides over them, summons all the inhabitants of both sexes to Christ's Chappel, where being assembled, he enquires publickly if there be any lawful impediment why these parties should not be joined in the bond of matrimony? And if there be no objection to the contrary, he then enquires of the parties if they are resolved to live together in weal and woe, etc. After their assent, he declares them married persons, and then desires them to ratify this their solemn promise in the presence of God and the people, in order to which the crucifix is tender'd to them, and both put their right hands upon it, as the ceremony by which they swear fidelity one to another during their lifetime.

They were good Christians, and (despite 'a brazen crucifix', which would shortly be removed) by 1697 confirmed Protestants, 'neither inclined to enthusiasm nor to popery. They swear not the common oaths that prevail in the world; when they refuse or deny to give what is asked of them, they do it with a strong asseveration,which they express emphatically enough in their language to this purpose, You are no more to have it, than that if God had forbid it; and thus they express the highest degree of passion. They do not so much as name the devil once in their lifetimes.'

As the roguish Lowland sailors had discovered, late seventeenth-century St Kildans were also convinced Sabbatarians. In 1686 a ship manned by French and Spanish seamen went down off Rockall, a tiny lump of uninhabitable granite which pokes out of the ocean 170 miles west of St Kilda. The sailors made their way by pinnace to Hirta, where they were given food and drink and shelter. They then began to prepare their pinnace to take them further east. Unfortunately, the Catholic Frenchmen and Spaniards began that work on a Sunday, 'at which the inhabitants were astonished, and being highly dissatisfied, plucked the hatchets and other instruments out of their hands, and did not restore them till Monday morning'. Martin tells us,

They leave off working after twelve of the clock on Saturday, as being an ancient custom delivered down to them from their ancestors, and go no more to it till Monday morning. They believe in God the Father, the Son, and Holy Ghost; and a state of future happiness and misery, and that all events, whether good or bad, are determined by God. They use a set form of prayer at the poising of their sails: they lie down, rise, and begin their labours in the name of God. They have a notion, that spirits are embodied; these they fancy to be locally in rocks, hills, and where-ever they list in an instant.

There are three chappels in this isle, each of them with one end towards the east, the other towards the west; the altar always placed at the east end; the first of these is called Christ Chappel, near the village; it is covered and thatched after the same manner with their houses; there is a brazen crucifix lies upon the altar, not exceeding a foot in length, the body is compleatly done, distended, and having a crown on, all in the crucified posture; they have it in great reverence, though they pay no kind of adoration or worship to it, nor do they either handle or see it, except upon the occasions of marriage, and swearing decisive oaths, which puts an end to all strife, and both these ceremonies are publickly performed.

The church-yard is about an hundred paces in circumference, and is fenced in with a little stone wall, within which they bury their dead; they take care to keep the church-yard perfectly clean, void of any kind of nastiness, and their cattel have no access to it. The inhabitants, young and old, come to the church-yard every Sunday morning, the Chappel not being capacious enough to receive them; here they devoutly say the Lord's prayer, Creed, and Ten Commandments.

They observe the festivals of Christmas, Easter, Good-Friday, St Columba's Day, and that of All Saints; upon this they have an anniversary cavalcade, the number of their horses not exceeding eighteen; these they mount by turns, having neither saddle nor bridle of any kind, except a rope, which manages the horse only on one side; they ride from the shoar to the house, and then after each man has performed his tour, the show is at an end.

They are very charitable to their poor, of whom there are not at present above three, and these carefully provided for, by this little commonwealth, each particular family contributing according to their ability for their necessities; their condition is enquired into weekly, or monthly, as their occasions serve; but more especially at the time of their festivals, they slay some sheep on purpose to be distributed among the poor, with bread proportionable ...

Their diet was simple and healthy:

Their ordinary food is barly and some oat-bread baked with water; they eat all the fowls, already described, being dried in their stone-houses, without any salt or spice to preserve them; and all their beef and mutton is eaten fresh, after the same manner they use the giben, or fat of their fowls ... They use this giben with their fish, and it is become the common vehicle that conveys all their food down their throats. They are undone for want of salt, of which as yet they are but little sensible; they use no set times for their meals, but are determined purely by their appetites.

They use only the ashes of sea-ware [potash from burnt seaweed] for salting their cheese, and the shortest (which grows in the rocks) is only used by them, that being reckoned the mildest.

Their drink is water, or whey, commonly: they brew ale but rarely, using the juice of nettle-roots, which they put in a dish with a little barley-meal dough; these sowens (i.e. flummery) being blended together, produce good yest, which puts their wort into a ferment, and makes good ale, so that when they drink plentifully of it, it disposes them to dance merrily.

They preserve the solan geese in their pyramids [cleits] for the space of a year, flitting them in the back, for they have no salt to keep them with. They have built above five hundred stone pyramids for their fowls, eggs, &c.

We made particular enquiry after the number of solon geese consumed by each family the year before we came here, and it amounted to twenty-two thousand six hundred in the whole island [that is, two-and-a-half gannets a week were eaten by each man, woman and child], which they said was less than they ordinarily did, a great many being lost by the badness of the season, and the great current into which they must be thrown when they take them, the rock being of such an extraordinary height that they cannot reach the boat.

Both men and women are well proportioned, nothing differing from those of the isles and continent. The present generation comes short of the last in strength and longevity. They shew'd us huge big stones carried by the fathers of some of the inhabitants now living; any of which is a burthen too heavy for any two of the present inhabitants to raise from the ground; and this change is all within the compass of forty years. But notwithstanding this, any one inhabiting St Kilda, is always reputed stronger than two of the inhabitants belonging to the Isle of Harries, or the adjacent isles. Those of St Kilda have generally but very thin beards, and those too do not appear till they arrive at the age of thirty, and in some not till after thirty-five; they have all but a few hairs upon the upper lip, and point of the chin.

Both sexes have a lisp, but more especially the women, neither of the two pronouncing the letters, d, g, or r ...

For recreation, the men played shinty, the Highland Scottish version of Irish hurling or camanachd:

They use for their diversion short clubs and balls of wood. The sand [on the shore of Village Bay] is a fair field for this sport and exercise, in which they take great pleasure and are very nimble at it; they play for some eggs, fowls, hooks, or tobacco; and so eager are they for victory, that they strip themselves to their shirts to obtain it; they use swimming and diving, and are very expert in both.

The women have their assemblies in the middle of the village, where they discourse of their affairs, but in the mean time employing their distaff, and spinning in order to make their blankets; they sing and jest for diversion, and in their way, understand poetry, and makes rhimes in their language.

There are some of both sexes who have a genius for poetry, and are great admirers of musick; the trump or Jewish harp is all the musical instrument they have, which disposes them to dance mightily.

Their sight is extraordinary good, and they can discern things at a great distance; they have very good memories, and are resolute in their undertakings, chaste and honest, and the men reputed jealous of their wives. They argue closely, and with less passion than other islanders, or those inhabiting the highlands on the continent.

They are reputed very cunning, and there is scarce any circumventing of them in traffick and bartering; the voice of one is the voice of all the rest, they being all of a piece, their common interest uniting them firmly together ...

Providence is very favourable to them in this, that they are not infested with several diseases which are so predominant in the other parts of the world; the distemper that most prevails here, is a spotted fever, and that too confin'd to one tribe, to whom this disease is, as it were, become hereditary; others are liable to fluxes, fevers, stitches, the spleen; for all which they have but very few remedies; to get away their stitches, they commonly lie upon a warm hearth, with the side affected downwards; this they look upon to be almost infallible for dispelling the humor, or wind, that torments them.

Martin then delivered a terrible hostage to fortune, declaring,

The smallpox hath not been heard of in this place for several ages, except in one instance, of two of the steward's retinue, who not having been well recovered of it, upon their arrival here, infected one man only.

The plants produced here, are lapathum vulgare, the common dock, scurvy-grass round, being large as the palm of the hand, mille-foil, bursa pastoris, silver-weed, or argentine, plantine, sage, chicken-weed; sorrel, long, or the common sorrel; all-hail, or siderites, the sea-pink, tormentil, the scurf upon the stones, which has a drying and healing quality, and is likewise used for dying. The inhabitants are ignorant of the virtues of these herbs; they never had a potion of physick given them in their lives, nor know any thing of phlebotomy; a physician could not expect his bread in this commonwealth.

They have generally good voices, and sound lungs; to this the solan goose egg supp'd raw doth not a little contribute; they are seldom troubled with a cough, except at the steward's landing; which is no less rare, than firmly believed by the inhabitants of the adjacent isles.

Martin recorded a phenomenon which would intrigue outsiders for a further three centuries. 'Those of St Kilda, upon the whole,' he wrote, 'gave me this following account, that they always contract a cough upon the steward's landing, and it proves a great deal more troublesome to them in the night-time, they then distilling a great deal of flegm; this indisposition; continues for some ten, twelve or fourteen days …'

This was cnatan nan gall, the 'boat-cough', or 'stranger sickness'. It was rarely if ever fatal, but it indisposed almost all of the St Kildans for up to a fortnight after a visitation from the outside world. Martin continued,

> I told them plainly, that I thought all this notion of infection was but a mere fancy, and that, at least, it could not always hold; at which they seemed offended, saying, that never any, before the minister and my self, was heard doubt of the truth of it; which is plainly demonstrated upon the landing of every boat; adding further, that every design was always for some end, but here there was no room for any, where nothing could be proposed; but for confirmation of the whole, they appealed to the case of infants at the breast, who were likewise very subject to this cough, but could not be capable of affecting it, and therefore, in their opinion, they were infected by such as lodged in their houses.
>
> There were scarce young or old in the isle whom I did not examine particularly upon this head, and all agreed in the confirmation of it. They add farther, that when any foreign goods are brought thither, then the cough is of longer duration than otherwise. They remark, that if the fever has been among those of the steward's retinue, though before their arrival there, some of the inhabitants are infected with it.
>
> If any of the inhabitants of St Kilda chance to live, though but a short space, in the isles of Harries, Skey, or any of the adjacent isles, they become meagre, and contract such a cough, that the giben must be had, or else they must return to their native soil. This giben is more sovereign for removing of coughs, being used by any other islanders, than those of St Kilda, because they love to have it frequently in their meat as well as drink, by which too frequent use of it, it loses its virtue; it was remarkable, that after this infected cough was over, we strangers, and the inhabitants of St Kilda, making up the number of about two hundred and fifty, though we had frequently assembled upon the occasion of divine service, yet neither young nor old amongst us all did so much as once cough more.

Martin Martin was not the last to be sceptical about *cnatan nan gall*, the stranger sickness. It seems to have disappeared by the beginning of the twentieth century, by which time St Kilda was receiving so many visitors that the 'boat cough', had it still taken hold, would have prostrated most of the island for most of the year. But until then it was commonplace, and until the very end St Kildans were susceptible to epidemics of influenza. According to the nineteenth-century minister Reverend Neil MacKenzie, three of the sixty-eight deaths which occurred on St Kilda between 1830 and 1846 were due to *cnatan nan gall*.

Many of the sceptics noted that the stranger sickness was in earlier days a reaction to the steward's annual visit. Samuel Johnson expressed that diagnosis by jibing that, 'The steward always comes to demand something from them, and so they fall a-coughing!'

But it was not always provoked by the steward. As late as 1860 a naval vessel called by with the friendliest of intentions, and following its departure '"the trouble" made its appearance – the entire population being more or less affected by it'. Shipwrecked sailors also had the same effect. A visitor in the 1870s analysed the condition. 'It usually begins with a cold sensation, pain and stiffness in the muscles of the jaw,' he wrote, 'aching in the head and bones, and great lassitude and depression – the ordinary symptoms of catarrh in an aggravated form – and is accompanied by a discharge from the nose, a rapid pulse, and a severe cough, which is particularly harassing during the night. The malady first attacks those persons who have come most closely into contact with the strangers, and then extends itself over the whole community.'

The sceptics assumed that the stranger sickness was at best psychosomatic: a habitual response to the stress of a possibly hostile and certainly avaricious boat's crew arriving in the bay. But so many sensible clergymen and islanders attested to it for so very long that it must have had a grounding in medical fact – in the St Kildans' lack of immunity to viruses which were commonplace everywhere else.

Cnatan nan gall attracted some sympathetic attention from nineteenth-century eminences. In a footnote to Chapter 19 of *The Voyage of the Beagle*, which was published in 1839, Charles Darwin lent it his credibility, writing,

Captain Beechey ... states that the inhabitants of Pitcairn Island are firmly convinced that after the arrival of every ship they suffer cutaneous and other disorders. Captain Beechey attributes this to the change of diet during the time of the visit.

Dr MacCulloch ... says: 'It is asserted, that on the arrival of a stranger (at St Kilda) all the inhabitants, in the common phraseology, catch a cold.' Dr MacCulloch considers the whole case, although often previously affirmed, as ludicrous. He adds, however, that 'the question was put by us to the inhabitants who unanimously agreed in the story'.

In Vancouver's Voyage, there is a somewhat similar statement with respect to Otaheite [Tahiti]. Dr Dieffenbach, in a note to his translation of the Journal, states that the same fact is universally believed by the inhabitants of the Chatham Islands, and in parts of New Zealand.

It is impossible that such a belief should have become universal in the northern hemisphere, at the Antipodes, and in the Pacific, without some good foundation. Humboldt (*Polit. Essay on King of New Spain*, vol. iv.) says, that the great epidemics of Panama and Callao are 'marked' by the arrival of ships from Chile, because the people from that temperate region, first experience the fatal effects of the torrid zones.

I may add, that I have heard it stated in Shropshire, that sheep, which have been imported from vessels, although themselves in a healthy condition, if placed in the same fold with others, frequently produce sickness in the flock.

Mr John E Morgan of the Manchester Royal College of Physicians, who visited Hirta briefly in 1860, noted the phenomenon at first hand and suggested 'that the usual isolation of the inhabitants – who are under exceptional conditions both as regards diet and occupation – when followed by sudden contact with strangers may exercise an infectious influence on the more susceptible of their number.'

Shortly afterwards another physician, Dr C R Macdonald of Beith in Ayrshire, wrote in the British Medical Journal:

When I visited St Kilda in June last year (1885), I noticed that almost every person on the island was suffering from a cough. This cough, I was told, they contracted from a party on board a steamer which was there a few days previously. I examined the chest of a few of them, and I could hear the moist rales of bronchial catarrh in one or two of the worst cases.

I asked the minister [Reverend John MacKay] if he could in any way account for this affection. He told me that he had no doubt as to its cause. The air in St Kilda, he said, was so pure, and as the natives were unaccustomed to inhale any impurities from their atmosphere, they were liable to be attacked in this way whenever people from other parts, where the air is more or less polluted, visited St Kilda.

Although works on germ-theories and micro-organisms have never figured in the St Kilda minister's library, yet I do not think that his theory of the cause of this disease is far from being correct. It is very probable that the atmosphere in St Kilda is free from a number of disease-causing organisms, which are rife in other parts, where the inhabitants are more or less inured to them. In this way it is possible that these agents of disease are innocuous unless a chill, damp, or other condition inimical to health predisposes the individual to their attack.

Not so in St Kilda. This inoculation of the inhabitants does not take place, consequently they suffer, as a rule, when they are exposed to their influence.

Darwin, Morgan, Macdonald and Reverend MacKay were right. In 2011 Peter Stride, an Australian physician and academic who has paid particular attention to the ailments of St Kilda, studied the stranger sickness and attributed it to 'limited genetic diversity' and 'low herd immunity'. 'St Kilda, as a "virgin soil" environment,' concluded Dr Stride, 'had a non-immune adult population, with increased morbidity and mortality from most infections.' The immune systems of St Kildans were unusually low even by Hebridean standards owing to their extreme isolation and possibly also their inevitable occasional consanguinity, or intermarriage.

Mostly Martin Martin discovered the St Kildans to be in robust good health, which was fortunate because they hunted birds. That pursuit may have been an early motivation of settlement in the islands, but it was never restricted to the inhabitants of Hirta and Boreray. All along the coastline of the British Isles, men hunted seabirds and harvested their eggs until the supply was exhausted or the species extinct, and either the cragsmen then found a safer and more rewarding occupation or the Wildlife and Countryside Act of 1981 outlawed the practice.

The first three terminators were slow to arrive in the Western Isles of Scotland, where a small population of crofters and fishermen exploited an apparently limitless number of seabirds until the twentieth century and beyond. The most celebrated survival of this Mesolithic, hunter-gatherer activity is the annual guga hunt from the north of the island of Lewis, which is uniquely exempted from the 1981 Act. Each autumn in the twenty-first century a select band of ten men from the Ness district sail 40 miles due north to the small, uninhabited outcrop of Sula Sgeir, where they live for two weeks in stone bothies and kill a maximum of 2,000 gannets. On the less precipitous slopes of that island the Ness men work almost exactly as had the St Kildans: in pairs, using poles and rope nooses to lasso young gannets from their nests before knocking them on the head and eventually returning with their catch to friends, relatives and customers in Lewis.

For the male St Kildans, bird-hunting was more of a proud and honourable year-round vocation than an annual adventure. It was literally how they defined themselves. Infant boys, newly able to walk, practised for their future occupation by clambering up the sides of their parents' homes. When the national census first reached St Kilda in 1851, all but one of the twenty-six adult men and teenaged boys on Hirta described their 'Rank, Profession or Occupation' to the enumerator as 'birdcatcher'. The exception was a seventy-five year-old who labelled himself 'retired birdcatcher'.

There was pride and honour because it was an extremely skilled and hazardous undertaking. Martin Martin described it:

> They furnish themselves with ropes, to carry them through the more inaccessible rocks; of these ropes there are only three in the whole island, each of them twenty-four fathoms [44 metres] in length; and they are either knit together and lengthened by tying the one to the other, or used separately as occasion requires; the chief thing upon which the strength of these ropes depends, is cows' hides salted, and cut out in one long piece, this they twist round the ordinary rope of hemp, which secures it from being cut by the rocks; they join some-times at the lower end two ropes, one of which they tie about the middle of one climber, and another about the middle of another, that these may assist one another in case of a fall; but the misfortune is, that sometimes the one happens to pull down the other, and so both

fall into the sea; but if they escape (as they do commonly of late) they get an incredible number of eggs and fowls.

The ropes belong to the commonwealth, and are not to be used without the general consent of all; the lots determine the time, place, and persons for using them, they get together in three days a much greater number of fowls and eggs than their boat is able to carry away, and therefore what is over and above they leave behind in their stone-pyramids: they catch their fowls with gins made of horse-hair, these are tied to the end of their fishing-rods, with which the fowlers creep through the rocks indiscernably, putting the noose over their heads about their necks, and so draw them instantly; they use likewise hair gins which they set upon plain rocks, both the ends fastened by a stone, and so catch forty or fifty a day with them.

The inhabitants, I must tell you, run no small danger in the quest of the fowls and eggs, insomuch that I fear it would be thought an hyperbole to relate the inaccessibleness, steepness, and height, of those formidable rocks which they venture to climb.

I my self have seen some of them climb up the corner of a rock with their backs to it, making use only of their heels and elbows, without any other assistance; and they have this way acquired a dexterity in climbing beyond any I ever yet saw; necessity has made them apply themselves to this, and custom has perfected them in it; so that it is become familiar to them almost from their cradles, the young boys of three years old being to climb the walls of their houses: their frequent discourses of climbing, together with the fatal end of several in the exercise of it, is the same to them, as that of fighting and killing is with soldiers, and so is become as familiar and less formidable to them, than otherwise certainly it would be.

I saw two young men, to whose share the lots fell in June last, for taking the nest of a hawk (which was in a high rock above the sea) bringing home the hawks in a few minutes, without any assistance at all.

Their dogs are likewise very dexterous in climbing and bringing out from their holes those fowls which build their nests far under-ground, such as the scraber, puffinet, &c., which they carry in their teeth to their masters, leting them fall upon the ground before them, though asleep.

Martin Martin's *A Late Voyage to St Kilda, the Remotest of all the Hebrides, or the Western isles of Scotland with a History of the Island, natural, moral, and topographical: wherein is an account of their customes, religion, fish, fowl, &c.* was published in London in 1698, the year after his visit, and dedicated to the Right Honourable Charles Montague.

Martin concluded of the islands that,

> The inhabitants of St Kilda, are much happier than the generality of mankind, as being almost the only people in the world who feel the sweetness of true liberty: what the condition of the people in the Golden Age is feign'd by the poets to be, that theirs really is, I mean, in innocency and simplicity, purity, mutual love and cordial friendship, free from solicitous cares, and anxious covetousness; from envy, deceit, and dissimulation; from ambition and pride, and the consequences that attend them.

> They are altogether ignorant of the vices of foreigners, and governed by the dictates of reason and Christianity, as it was first delivered to them by those heroick souls whose zeal moved them to undergo danger and trouble to plant religion here in one of the remotest corners of the world.

> There is this only wanting to make them the happiest people in this habitable globe, viz., that they themselves do not know how happy they are, and how much they are above the avarice and slavery of the rest of mankind. Their way of living makes them condemn gold and silver, as below the dignity of human nature; they live by the munificence of Heaven; and have no designs upon one another, but such as are purely suggested by justice and benevolence.

They were timely conclusions, and would have a profound effect upon St Kilda. In 1698 the idea of the good or noble savage was in its infancy. The term itself had first been coined by the playwright John Dryden twenty-six years earlier, in the lines:

> I am as free as nature first made man,
> Ere the base laws of servitude began,
> When wild in woods the noble savage ran.

But the concept had been fermenting for decades among the Western European intelligentsia. Initially a liberal reaction to the maltreatment by European colonists of indigenous 'barbarians' in America, Africa and Asia, it developed into a fully-fledged theory. The Age of Discovery was well underway. Human civilisations large and small were being 'discovered' by Europeans in faraway parts of the globe. The nature and lifestyles of those peoples, whether they were Caribs in the Antilles or Bandanese in the Spice Islands, even as they were being exploited, reduced or exterminated by Europeans, led many Western philosophers and poets to develop a romantic theory of noble savagery, of human beings in uncorrupted harmony with their environment and each other.

The theory limited itself at first to claiming that whatever their state of development, indigenous peoples from the Caribbean to the Ivory Coast shared the same humanity as their 'civilised' conquerors. It progressed to the suggestion that Iron or Stone Age tribespeople lived in a state of natural grace which was actually superior to the mendacious, acquisitive and warlike mentality of Europeans. This latter development found one of its purest voices in 1699, the year after the publication of Martin's *A Late Voyage to St Kilda*, when the French author François Fénelon published his novel *The Adventures of Telemachus*. Fénelon described a band of soldiers landing on a foreign shore, from whom 'a savage race' fled to the hills. When finally the soldiers met up with the leader of the savages they were told, 'We abandoned for you the pleasant sea-coast, so that we have nothing left but these almost inaccessible mountains: at least it is just that you leave us in peace and liberty.

'Go, and never forget that you owe your lives to our feeling of humanity. Never forget that it was from a people whom you call rude and savage that you received this lesson in gentleness and generosity.'

The 'Golden Age' referred to by Martin Martin in his assessment of St Kilda was a reference to an Arcadian epoch imagined in classical times to embody those virtues. An extremely loose translation of the Roman poet Ovid's epic 'Metamorphoses', which was originally written in the years AD 7 and 8, was made by Martin's contemporaries John Dryden, Alexander Pope, Joseph Addison and William Congreve. It included the lines:

> The Golden Age was first; when Man, yet new,
> No rule but uncorrupted Reason knew:
> And, with a native bent, did good pursue.
> Unforc'd by punishment, un-aw'd by fear.
> His words were simple, and his soul sincere;
> Needless was written law, where none opprest:
> The law of Man was written in his breast.

This was Martin's St Kilda and those were Martin's St Kildans: simple, sincere, gentle, generous and uncorrupted in their enviable isolation from the modern world. Even his story of the St Kildan influenza which was caught from visitors echoed the tales which were already reaching Britain of native Americans and indigenous Pacific islanders being exterminated by imported European diseases against which they had no immunity. The extraordinary cachet of St Kilda, of which Martin Martin was the midwife, was that instead of being on the other side of the earth it was to be found – complete with its noble savages – less than 150 miles from the mainland of Great Britain.

For all of that to be true, the seventeenth-century St Kildans would have lived in a hermetically sealed vacuum of peace, good health, harmony and stability. They plainly did not. As well as regularly hosting passing ships' crews from the rest of the British Isles, from Iceland and the Faroes and from the continent of Europe, the people of Hirta were visited at least once a year by their landlord's steward and by a priest or a minister. The traffic also went the other way. Martin himself wrote that the St Kildans occasionally 'chance to live … in the isles of Harries, Skey, or any of the adjacent isles'. He told a story about 'one of their number having travelled in the Isle of Sky, to the south part of it, thought this a prodigious journey; and seeing in the opposite continent the shire of Inverness, divided from Sky only by a narrow sea, enquired of the company, if that was the border of England.' Even if true, that is contradictory. If the St Kildan was so insular and unworldly, what was he or she doing over 100 miles away in the south of Skye? And having got there, a seventeenth-century Outer Hebridean can be forgiven for wondering where Scotland ended and England began.

St Kildans had gone and would go much further afield than England, let alone Skye. Strangely for a fellow Highlander, Martin either mistook or deliberately misrepresented the common integrity and essential self-regulation of a remote farming, fowling and fishing community for a mythological state of natural grace. Very far from being by 'none opprest', or free from 'the base laws of servitude', or in Martin's own words 'almost the only people in the world who feel the sweetness of true liberty', the St Kildans were feudal vassals of MacLeod of Harris, and above him of Martin's friend MacLeod of MacLeod in Dunvegan. They lived on their islands by MacLeod's permission and, until 1886, could be evicted at his whim. MacLeod's steward collected a large proportion of their annual produce, for which they laboured hard and frequently lost their lives, as rental payment. MacLeod's ground officer was their de facto ruler. MacLeod dictated to them even the finer details of their religious faith. None of those things was unusual in European peasant communities, but few other European peasant communities were acclaimed as actually living in 'what the condition of the people in the Golden Age is feign'd by the poets to be'.

Five years later, in 1703, Martin Martin published a sequel to *A Late Voyage to St Kilda*. It was a fuller 'Description of the Western Isles of Scotland, taking in Lewis, Harris, Skye, North and South Uist, Benbecula, Barra, Orkney, Shetland, Bute, Arran, Islay, Mull, Tiree and many smaller islands, including St Kilda'. It was prefaced by a first copy of the map of the Scottish coast by the Londoner Thomas Moll, which would later be expanded and published separately. Possibly because Martin had by then visited similar Outer Hebridean communities in Uist and Lewis there was no more talk of St Kildan noble savagery or Golden Ages in *A Description of the Western Isles of Scotland*. Martin Martin then studied to become a Doctor of Medicine at the University of Leiden in the Netherlands. He died in London in 1719 at about the age of sixty. His influence on the future of St Kilda would be enormous.

Most people would still find difficulty in getting there, but in the early eighteenth century literate Britain knew – or thought it knew – about St Kilda. The islanders would not reap the full harvest of their celebrity for a further 150 years. But they were literally and metaphorically on the map.

FOUR

False Prophets and Ministers

✹

T HE EIGHTEENTH CENTURY was a time of political and military upheaval in most of the rest of Scotland. It was a period of social and spiritual upheaval in St Kilda.

The islands entered the Georgian era with a new name (albeit one which the inhabitants abjured, continuing to refer to their homeland as Hiort, or Hirta), a new reputation and a settled way of life. While turmoil reigned on the other islands and on the mainland to their east, 200 St Kildans dined off oatcakes and barley bread, nettle and barley ale, sheeps' milk and cheese and more seabirds and fish than they could eat. They were never disconnected from major events in Scotland, but they always lived at a certain remove.

They lived in a huddle of round or oval thatched stone cottages, each warmed by a central open peat fire, in the middle of the arable land around the shore of Village Bay. They practised transhumance. In the spring they planted their crops in Village Bay, and sent their sheep and cattle over the hills and down to Gleann Mor. There the livestock would stay behind a long stone wall, broken only by gateways, which curved around the top of the glen from peak to peak and effectively enclosed the entire valley. Some people, mainly the young, would summer with the animals in Gleann Mor, sheltering and sleeping in the old cellular stone houses which were maintained as sheilings for that purpose, although even at the very foot of Gleann Mor they were never more than an hour's sprint from their homes in Village Bay. When the crops had been harvested the animals were led back over the hill to winter in Village Bay, or to be penned and shorn and slaughtered in several enclosures on the hillside outside the village bounds – most notably on An Lag, the large grassy plateau between Oiseval and Conachair just north of the village, which came to be dominated by large, high-walled sheep fanks.

They had one and sometimes two boats in which each man had a share and a seat, which was large enough to navigate their own inshore waters, but could safely go no further. The men did not use it for fishing. They were reluctant to eat much fish – and therefore to catch them – until late in the nineteenth century 'as they said it had no substance (oil) in it. They simply took the liver out of such as they caught, and either cured the body for exportation or threw it to their dogs.' To people raised on the ripe flesh of gannets and on mutton, seafood made a paltry meal.

Instead their boats were used to row from Hirta to the surrounding islands and stacks to collect eggs and catch birds before returning, filled to the gunwales with their prey, to Village Bay. Between one and two men or youths died each decade by falling from the cliffs and stacks. That occupational mortality rate remained more or less standard. They had more than enough sheep's wool to spin and weave their own clothes. In the Hebridean fashion, the women proved tweed together while chanting familiar songs. Until the twentieth century they plucked feathers from the dead seabirds and remitted them as rent to MacLeod's steward, after which they were sold to stuff the mattresses of the privileged elsewhere in Britain. The St Kildans slept on straw.

The publication of Martin Martin's *A Late Voyage to St Kilda* in 1698 alerted the Church of Scotland to the regrettable fact that there was no resident minister on St Kilda, and that as a consequence couples often married by jumping the broom in the presence of the ground officer. Infants went unbaptised and people were buried without sacrament. The Reformed Protestant Church was also uncomfortably aware that it had not succeeded in dislodging the Roman Catholic Church from several enclaves in the Highlands and Islands, including such Outer Hebridean islands as Barra, Eriskay, South Uist and Benbecula, which were close to St Kilda.

And then there was Martin's story of Roderick the Imposter. This was the bizarre account of a false prophet on Hirta who was able to take some advantage of the community's isolation at a time of religious uncertainty. Roderick was certainly delusional and may have been little worse than a local schizophrenic who was tolerated and humoured by most of his neighbours. He may also have been something of a rascal. But however seriously he was taken by other St Kildans (and we are told that even his own father warned him that he was heading for a sticky end) Roderick established a heretical ministry there which could not be tolerated by the established Church. Word of Roderick's activities had reached Harris in the 1690s and formed a large part of the reason for the visit to St Kilda in 1697 of Martin's companion, Reverend John Campbell.

When Martin met Roderick in Hirta in 1697 he found 'a comely, well-proportioned fellow, red-hair'd, and exceeding all the inhabitants of St Kilda in strength, climbing, &c'. At the age of eighteen, Roderick had broken the Sabbath by fishing from the rocks one Sunday. On his way home to Village Bay with his catch, Roderick said that he had met John the Baptist wearing a cloak and hat of Scottish Lowland fashion. John had 'immediately come from Heaven with good tidings to the inhabitants of that place, who had been for a long time kept in ignorance and error; that he had commission to instruct Roderick in the laws of Heaven for the edification of his neighbours'.

Those laws included a strict Friday fast, penances such as standing in cold water 'without regard to the season, whether frost or otherwise', and throwing feasts at which Roderick himself was the principle guest. He replaced the Lord's Prayer, the Creed and the Ten Commandments with his own versions, which included 'several unintelligible words ... of which he could not tell the meaning himself'. He invented what he called 'the Virgin Mary's hymn', which could only be taught to women in private, and which 'afforded him a fair opportunity of debauching the simple women'.

This last activity – 'his villainous design upon the women' – led to Roderick's downfall when he tried it on the ground officer's wife while the ground officer was in the next room. The ground officer burst in when 'this letcher began to caress his wife'. Shortly afterwards a boy from Harris who was visiting family in St Kilda eavesdropped on one of Roderick's night-time congregations. The steward was informed and Roderick was taken from St Kilda to the seat of MacLeod of MacLeod at Dunvegan Castle in Skye. MacLeod, 'being informed of this fellow's impostures, did forbid him from that time forward to preach any more on pain of death'. Roderick was then returned to St Kilda, with Reverend John Campbell and Martin Martin in his wake. 'The minister and congregation,' reported Martin, 'jointly prayed for repentance and pardon to this poor wretch ... We reproved the credulous people for complying implicitly with such follies and delusions as were delivered to them by the imposter; and all of them with one voice answered, that what they did was unaccountable; but seeing one of their own number and stamp in all respects, endued, as they fancied, with a powerful faculty of preaching so fluently and frequently, and pretending to converse with John the Baptist, they were induc'd to believe his mission from heaven ...'

The result was Reverend Alexander Buchan.

Alexander Buchan was a native of Halkirk in Caithness in the north-eastern Highlands. He had been a catechist and schoolteacher in Halkirk, on the Argyll-shire mainland, in the islands of Jura and Mull and in the Caithness town of Thurso before the commission of the General Assembly of the Church of Scotland decided in 1704 to send him to St Kilda to offer lay and scriptural education. Buchan would be the first Protestant pastor to live in Hirta, and probably the first Christian divine of any denomination to make his home there since those ghostly cross-carvers and chapel builders of the early Middle Ages. He was a Gaelic speaker – a 'master of the Irish tongue' as one of his daughters put it – as he had to be to work at that time in Jura, Mull and Argyllshire, let alone St Kilda.

It took Alexander Buchan almost a year to reach St Kilda from the Scottish mainland. Travelling with his wife Katherine and two young children, he was marooned by the weather at MacLeod's steward's house on the island of Pabbay, in the west of the Sound of Harris, throughout the winter of 1704–05. There he learned, to his dismay, that the St Kildans baked hardly any bread and ate a lot of eggs and seabirds. Even if MacLeod could arrange a supply of bread 'to my familie', the Buchans were unlikely be given butter, cheese or milk 'for they have litl of it to themselves'.

Buchan eventually arrived in Village Bay on 20 June 1705. A month later he wrote to the Moderator of the Church of Scotland. Some of his fears had been confirmed and he had discovered fresh grounds for unease. There was indeed no bread – a single farmer's family elsewhere, said Buchan, threw away more bread than was consumed by the twenty-five families on St Kilda. The locals could in fact give him nothing but fuel for his fire and 'wild fouls' to eat. He had managed to persuade just two boys to be educated, not least because word had got around that Alexander Buchan was not being paid (his remittance was nowhere in sight) and consequently the Hirtans did not expect him to stay with them for long.

Their observance of the Sabbath was limited. They certainly, as had been previously attested, stopped all work on Saturday. But the St Kildans did not believe that the same proscription applied to recreation, and 'men and women and children were sporting and gaming when I came here Sunday'.

On top of all that, they stank. 'They have the same wild smell that the wild fouls on which they live hath so that I must go between them and the wind.' Buchan would later tell a friend that he found it impossible to enter a cottage in Village Bay 'because of the smell of their rotten unsalted foules, and their guts, they mix with their ashes, una cum hominum urina [together with human urine], to make gooding or manure for their Land.' The locals were so particular about the latter custom that if they found themselves in need of relief in a neighbour's house, they would promptly excuse themselves and return home to piss on their own ashes.

It was the early eighteenth century. Everybody in Britain stank, and almost every dwelling room and enclosed public space reeked to high heaven. More than a century later another visitor noted that the habit of keeping middens indoors was commonplace even in the town of Stornoway in Lewis. Alexander Buchan had previously worked among other Highland cottagers in Jura, Mull and Argyll, and the streets of his native Halkirk and Thurso would have had their own distinctive odour. Buchan must initially have taken exception in Hirta to the unusual omnipresence of pungent gannet carcasses and peat ash mixed with urine, which would have dominated the everyday redolence of stale sweat and unwashed clothes to which he was accustomed. He will have become familiar with them.

Reasonably enough, the St Kildans persisted in their belief that whoever had sent Alexander Buchan and his family to Hirta should also support them. The St Kildans had not much use for cash, but MacLeod's steward could be prevailed upon to buy and deliver supplies. After two years, however (three if you counted, as he did, the year spent in transit), Buchan had not been paid a penny of his agreed salary. He was living in debt to the steward and on the goodwill of the islanders. His lack of means was a burden on his congregation and a cause of humiliation and frustration to himself. In August 1707 his wife Katherine, who was pregnant, left St Kilda to give birth in civilisation. She took the opportunity to petition old friends in the Kirk, with little success – her husband was forwarded a few merks to see him by – before returning to the islands with their third child in the following year.

Not until 1710, when the newly formed Society in Scotland for the Propagation of Christian Knowledge accepted his cause as their own, did Alexander Buchan begin to receive a regular income. Buchan forced his case by arriving in Edinburgh with the two young St Kildans, Finlay MacDonald and Murdo Campbell, 'whom I have been Intertaining and Learning since ... I first went to the Isle', and who had achieved some fluency in English. It was enough. St Kilda perfectly suited the SSPCK's remit to confirm Protestant 'religion and virtue' in parts of the Highlands and Islands where Roman Catholicism (which the Reformed Church also knew as 'idolatry') was still capable of asserting or reasserting itself. The Society sent Alexander Buchan back to St Kilda in 1710 with his two boys, with a guaranteed annual stipend of 300 merks, and with the authority 'to Erect and keep up a School in the Said Island and to teach the Inhabitants thereof to read Especially the holy Scriptures and other good and pious books, as also to teach writting Arithmetick and such like Degrees of Knowledge and to use Such means for Instructing the people in the Christian Reformed Protestant Religion as may be proper'.

Buchan would remain on St Kilda for the rest of his life. After 1710, when he was ordained as a full minister of the Church of Scotland, he quickly had built a basic manse and schoolroom close to the village. His ministry was not an immediate success. By 1717 Alexander and Katherine Buchan had six children of their own who comprised the majority of the school roll. (They produced a total of thirteen offspring, several of whom died in infancy or childhood.) Four young St Kildan scholars made the total up to ten. 'The people of Hirta,' Katherine Buchan told the SSPCK, 'are not forward to send their children to school.'

The people of Hirta had probably, by 1717, accepted that the Buchans were going to be around for a while. They seem not to have been convinced of their value. The school's books were all in English. Even the Bible itself had not yet been translated into Scottish Gaelic. The St Kildans must have doubted the purpose of education in a language which hardly any of them of could understand, let alone read.

To Buchan's frustration they had no ambitions for their children in the wider world. St Kildans could travel hundreds of miles to the east, beyond the other islands and far into the mainland of Scotland, and still be able to communicate in Gaelic. Throughout most of northern and western Scotland in the early eighteenth century, English speakers rather than Gaelic speakers were disadvantaged. In St Kilda itself the ability to scale a cliff, catch a wild bird, herd and shear sheep, spin wool, weave cloth and till the land were all vastly more profitable – not to say essential – accomplishments than the ability to read an English language book. They would send their children to school only if Buchan would then pay for their upkeep. As a result the new minister found himself with a houseful of orphans, all of them imbibing English along with their soup within the confines of Reverend Buchan's makeshift manse. His own children were sent away in their early teens to complete their education in Glasgow or Edinburgh. Before then they led a curiously divided life within the community: absorbing everyday Gaelic vernacular and Hirtan traditions from their contemporaries and playmates before returning to eat and sleep within the devout anglophone walls of their father's home.

Nor would Buchan's disciplinary procedures have endeared him to the locals. In order to improve the quality of Sabbath observance he would dip old sackcloths 'in the filthiest gutter in the toun' and then force miscreants to stand wearing the sackcloth, dripping sewage, in public view. On one occasion, Buchan reported to a superior, the ground officer's wife commanded two other women to kill a dog – presumably as a result of some canine trespass or assault – on the Lord's Day. Buchan fined the ground officer's wife (whose youngest son was in 1712 his only voluntary pupil) one merk for her part in breaking the Sabbath. The two less privileged women were dressed in filthy sackcloth and ordered to stand 'dreeping doun black gutter' until penance had been done.

In 1709 Alexander Buchan hit upon a way of raising some of the money which, in that year, he so desperately needed. He would take the bulk of Martin Martin's eleven year-old volume *A Late Voyage to St Kilda*, add to it some of his own observations and republish it at a cheaper price. Although its author was still alive, Martin's book was temporarily out of print, and in 1709 copyright laws were in their infancy. Buchan could get away with quoting, and attributing to Martin, almost the whole of *A Late Voyage to St Kilda*, so long as he appended sufficient original material to justify his own volume.

A Description of Saint Kilda was many years in the compiling and was not actually published until 1727, three years before Alexander Buchan's death on Hirta in 1730 of a 'high fever'. Its authorship was at first attributed to an anonymous 'Inhabitant'. Only when it was reprinted in 1741 by his daughter Jean was 'the Rev. Mr Alexander Buchan, late Minister there' credited as the book's creator.

Jean Buchan had several reasons to continue promoting and publishing *A Description of Saint Kilda*. In her preface to later editions Jean admitted that 'The Description of Saint Kilda, was first written by one Mr Martine ... [but] ... His book being dear, and out of date; the Rev. Mr Alexander Buchan, their late Minister, and my deceast father, thought fit to write the following Description, which he gathered partly by good information, and partly by his own observations; he having been their first settled Minister, and lived amongst them twenty-four years, till his death.'

Her father's ministry had, asserted his daughter, been a success. 'And he being master of the Irish tongue, and qualified with ministerial gifts suitable to his office, did labour amongst them during the foresaid time with great success in the work of the gospel, having found them most ignorant, and much given to idolatry. But by the blessing of God upon his labours, he brought them to the knowledge of the Christian Protestant religion, and had the Sacrament of the Lord's supper several times dispenced amongst them; and erected an eldership and Kirk-session, with other steps of reformation and order ...'

But Jean Buchan had not enjoyed good fortune since leaving St Kilda and the proceeds of her father's book would help her through difficult times. 'I the second daughter,' she wrote, 'was sent from St Kilda to the schools in Glasgow for my education, and was shipwreckt upon the Mull of Cantire [Kintyre] when I was about 15 years of age; yet I went to Glasgow for my education, where I continued for some time; from thence I went to Edinburgh where I had the misfortune to be beat by a horse on the street, and broke my jaw-bone, which has rendered me uncapable of earning my bread by the needle, to which I was brought up. I had also another misfortune to get my arm broke, and not being carefully sett, is mighty uneasy to me.'

Her father's book said that the population had increased slightly since the visit of Martin Martin, which could mean that in the early eighteenth century 200 people or more lived in the clachan by the shore in Village Bay. 'The inhabitants, whose number is about 27 families in Mr Martine's time, but now 30 or 33, live together in a little village, having all the signs of an extreme poverty; their houses of a low form, and very rudely built. It is surrounded with four mountains, which are as so many ramparts of defence, and amphitheatres, from whence a fair prospect of the ocean and isles are to be seen in a fair day. This village hath a rivulet, running closs by it.'

For all its author's superior experience, Alexander Buchan's *A Description of Saint Kilda* is little more than a series of lengthy footnotes to Martin Martin's *A Late Voyage to St Kilda*. Buchan added some tantalising, if possibly exaggerated, vignettes. 'One of [the St Kildans],' he wrote, 'as he was walking barefooted along the rocks, where he had fixed his gin, happened to put his great toe in a noose, and thereby stumbling, immediately fell down the rock, but hung by the toe, the gin being strong enough to hold him, and the stones that secured it on each end being heavy, the poor man continued hanging thus for the space of a night on a rock 20 fathoms high above the sea, until one of his neighbours, hearing him cry in the morning, came to his rescue, who drew him up by the feet, and so saved him.'

St Kildan men were noted for their large feet and strong toes. Those assets were unlikely to have been an evolutionary process. They were more probably an occupational development. St Kildans had exceptionally broad feet and pliable toes for the same reason that coalminers had immensely strong biceps and upper bodies: their lifelong vocation had developed those parts of their physique. It is nonetheless unlikely that the big toe even of a St Kildan was strong enough to support the weight of a man's body overnight. If the incident occurred – as it very likely did – the victim was more probably lassoed around his ankle. The Gaels were ever great storytellers.

When such falls (which Buchan asserted were 'frequenter now than formerly, by reason of their weakness, thro' coarse feeding, tho' formerly they were reckoned stronger than any of the other isles about') proved fatal, the widowed women 'make doleful songs ... which they call Lamentations. The chief topicks, or subject matter of these elegies, are their courage, their dexterity in climbing, and their great affection which they shewed to their wives and children.'

There are no statistics which prove that latterday St Kildans suffered greater mortality on the cliffs than had their forebears. In the middle of the nineteenth century, when birdcatching was still the predominant male activity and deaths on the island were first registered, it was recorded that four men had 'gone over the rocks' in the course of thirty-seven years. All of those deaths were lamented and some entered the island's folklore.

> On one occasion, the rope having given way, a young cragsman, the only support of a widowed mother, fell down a depth of several fathoms, lighting upon a grassy shelf, where unfortunately no assistance could be rendered.
>
> All that his friends could do was to approach as near as possible with a boat and comfort him by words at a distance. On the evening of the third day, parched with thirst, and starving with hunger, he became deranged, and was heard chanting a simple native song, till death sealed his lips.
>
> On another occasion, a father and son happened to descend by a single rope. When they were being drawn up, the son observed that a sharp rock had nearly cut through the rope, but he came to the conclusion that it was still capable of bearing the weight of one of them.
>
> On hearing this, the father urged his son to avail himself of it, as he was old and of comparatively little use in the world. The son burst into tears, and urged his father to ascend. With great reluctance he yielded, and reached the summit of the cliff in safety. On the son trying the rope after him, it gave way, as was expected, and the anxious father saw his son mangled by the projecting rocks, before he had reached the yawning gulf below.

Buchan repeated the details of the St Kildans' feudal bondage to the MacLeod of Harris. They were at the bottom of a societal pyramid which ran from MacLeod of MacLeod at the apex in Dunvegan Castle, to MacLeod of Harris, to MacLeod of Harris's steward and from the steward to the ground officer. The hereditary MacLeods rarely if ever visited their distant province. The steward of St Kilda, with whom Martin had travelled to St Kilda in 1697 and with whom Buchan had overwintered in 1704 to 1705 at his traditional home on the island of Pabbay, was 'some Cadet of his name [Macleod], whose fortune is low'. He crossed in great state to St Kilda each spring or summer, taking a large retinue which was accommodated, fed and watered by the St Kildans for weeks on end before the steward returned to Harris with as much 'Down [feathers], wool, butter, cheese, cows, horses, sheep, fowls, [fulmar] oil, and barley' as his galley could contain.

Beneath the steward was the ground officer, 'a deputy always on the place … and is one of the natives; he has free lands from the Steward, and is at present the richest man in the island, having about 20 Cows, if not more … and 2 or 300 sheep'. Nobody else on St Kilda had 'above 8 Cows, 2 or 3 Horses, and 80 Sheep' and most had fewer stock. The ground officer was also given two pecks (about 26 dry litres) of barley a year by each family in Hirta.

The ground officer was effectively MacLeod's steward's viceroy. His word was law on St Kilda, and he and his family were well rewarded. The ground officer was 'obliged to adjust [between islanders] the respective proportion of lands, grass, and rocks, and what else could be claimed by virtue of the last tack or lease, which is never longer than for three years … he is president over them in their debates, takes care that the lots be managed impartially, that none to whose share they may fall may have cause to repine, whether it be for the Steward's service, or the commonwealth's'. He punished any common assault with 'a fine, not exceeding the value of 2 shillings sterling, except there be blood drawn, and then it is 4s 6d'.

When there was no resident minister, as Martin described, the ground officer officiated at weddings which were later, if possible, sanctified by a visiting pastor. He did it according to the book and according to established ritual. The betrothed couple were taken to the old Christ's Chapel near their Village Bay settlement. There he 'enquires publickly, if there be any impediment why these parties should not be joined in the bond of matrimony? And if there be no objection to the contrary, he then enquires of the parties, if they are resolved to live together in well and woe, &c. After their assent, he taking out his durk naked, and thereupon causing them to swear it, declares them married persons; and then desires them to ratify this their solemn promise in the presence of God and the people, in order to which the crucifix is tendered to them, and both put their right-hands upon it, as the ceremony by which they swear fidelity one to another during their life-time'. As an unwelcome vestige of popery the crucifix was removed from St Kilda in the eighteenth century, but otherwise the ceremony seems to have remained constant for centuries.

In earlier years the ground officer had been 'chosen, or at least approved' by the St Kildans, 'but now the Stewards have the nomination of them absolutely'. There was nonetheless a vestige of local accountability. There were occasional disputes about the quantity of produce and livestock which the steward extracted as annual homage from the islands. One such argument over sheep in the seventeenth century resulted in some St Kildans attacking the steward's brother. In the event of differences, what Alexander Buchan described as 'a general council, in which the master of every family has a vote' appointed the ground officer as their envoy to present the St Kildans' case to MacLeod of Harris himself. Such envoys took the St Kildan ground officer to Harris or even to Dunvegan Castle in Skye, the seat of the supreme MacLeod of MacLeod, where 'he and the islanders look on M'Leod's family to be equivalent to that of an Imperial Court, and the King to be only superior to him'.

There was another downside to the position. On fowling or sheep gathering expeditions the ground officer 'as a point of his honour, must be the first that lands in the lesser isles and rocks; which point of honour exposes him to frequent dangers: For, when they come near the landing rock, he catches the first opportunity of the calmest wave, and having a rope tied about his middle, with the other end fastened to the boat in case of danger, jumps out upon the rock: If he lands safe, he fixes his feet in a secure place, and with his rope draws all the crew to him, except those whose turn it is, to look after the boat; but if in jumping he falls into the sea, as sometimes he does, then he is drawn in again by the rope ...'

The seventeenth and early eighteenth centuries were times of cultural and spiritual change in the islands, as the arrival of such Protestant ministers as John Campbell and Alexander Buchan chipped away at the old traditions, many of which were rooted in Catholicism or even in older ways. As we have seen, the St Kildans still thought 'that spirits are embodied; these they fancy to be locally in rocks, hills ...'

In earlier times when a death occurred – either by an accident on the cliffs or in a cot at home – 'they give a cry through the whole island, that all the people at work, whether in field or mountain, may thereupon come home'. They then abstained from work for a day, within which time the corpse was interred.

They esteem the grave, where the corps of the dead is to be interred, so sacred a bed, that they set a person at each end of it, that no dog, cat, or other brute creature, approach to, nor crose over the same. After prayers, a snuff box or two goes round the best respected; and the poor gets only a ped-full or two in their palms, especially if in haste to be away.

The women also have a superstitious custom, when they meet with any cross providence, that they go ordinarily to the grave stone of their husband, or nearest relation, and there weep and howl.

The weeping and howling at cruel fate, as well as the great cry around the island that one of their own had died, was dissuaded by Campbell and especially by Buchan as 'foolish and mimical' and 'unreformed'. Once the minister found himself closer than usual to the grave at a burial and 'he espied one of the tenants using some superstitious motions, which he took not heed to, untill he took up a spade, and lifted as much earth out of the grave, as would fill a child's hand or fist, and did spit a little in the grave, and threw in the little quantity of earth he had on the spade into the grave; all which he did the second or third time. All the reason he had from him or others was, that they are obliged to do it for antiquity or custom's sake.' But Buchan could not prevent them from observing the old habit of burying their dead only on an even-numbered day in the year.

'The reverend Mr Alexander Buchan their late minister,' wrote his daughter Jean, 'gives us to know, that he found them in as a bad a case as Mr Campbell, and as much addicted to superstition and idolatry, at his first coming among them; he having their idolatrous monuments to throw down, the razing whereof, and the getting them brought to a better temper of mind, cost him no small pains and trouble; as might be particularly instanced, but hereby it might swell this book to a greater length than is designed.'

A pastoral portrait swims slowly into focus. Between 180 and 200 people lived in Hirta in the seventeenth century and first two decades of the eighteenth century. In those early modern times they lived a not unusual rural life. They cultivated the good land in Village Bay. They overwintered their livestock there, and in the spring, when the ground was tilled and their crops were planted and sown, they took their hundreds of sheep and forty or fifty cattle – excepting each household's milking cow – up the hill and over the ridge at Am Blaid, led the animals through an entrance in the stone dyke which ran all the way around the top of Gleann Mor and down into the lush grass at the foot of the glen. In the middle of the eighteenth century a visitor noticed that in Gleann Mor and on neighbouring Cambir, 'The cattle of St Kilda feed most luxuriously during the summer season … and here they yield, it may be naturally expected, more than ordinary quantities of milk. I had occasion to know the quality of it. The cream it gives is so luscious, or rather so strong, that some of my people sickened upon drinking it.'

There the beasts summered and lambed and calved, watched over by young men and women who used as shieling dwellings the antique beehive houses which were fabled to have been in olden times the home of Amazons. Peat was cut from the sides of Gleann Mor and from Cambir, which was carried back over to Village Bay for household fuel. Their homes were lit with fulmar oil lamps – every fulmar 'yields near an English pint of this liquid substance, which drops out at the nostrils of the fowl while warm, and a considerable quantity of it is annually preserved in the isle'. As the birds laid few eggs the St Kildans rarely killed mature fulmars or collected their eggs, harvesting only the younger ones whose 'oil was clear like kerosene, but darker'.

In the autumn, when the Village Bay oats and barley were harvested 'before the beginning of September; and should it fall out otherwise, the whole crop will be almost destroyed by the equinoctial storms', the animals and their herders returned through Am Blaid. The sheep and cattle were pastured on An Lag and elsewhere around the township. They had around ten small Hebridean horses which were chiefly used as beasts of burden.

The men also kept sheep and hunted birds for meat and feathers on the two other islands and on some towering sea stacks. Their 25-foot open boat was therefore vitally important. Without it they could neither gather and butcher their flocks on Soay and Boreray nor harvest seabirds and their eggs from Stac an Armin. As it lay idle in the winter, the boat was 'filled up with stones and earth in a secure place, to prevent the greatest of all public calamities, that of its being swept away into the sea, or dashed against a rock by a violent gust of wind'. Fishing from the shores around Village Bay was as much a recreational as a necessary activity.

The boat occasionally came to grief. In 1712 it was lost on the west side of Boreray. Some of the crew climbed a sheer rock face to safety, and from there let down a rope to haul up their companions. On that or another occasion (the dates are uncertain, as Martin describes a similar incident early in the seventeenth century: it must have happened with relative frequency in those wild seas) when the boat was wrecked the men were stranded on Boreray between the middle of March and the end of May when the steward's galley arrived to rescue them. They were able to survive on mutton and birds and fish, but when they failed to return their women back on Hirta thought them drowned. So this time they lit on top of Boreray as many fires as there had been men in the boat. Their families saw and counted the fires, got the message and were suitably overjoyed.

It being seeding time, the women on Hirta then did all their absent men's work of foot-ploughing the land and casting grain, and for years thereafter the story was told in the island that that year saw the best harvest of corn in decades. It was probably in the same year, 1712, that 'two poor girls' were lost when 'for want of men' they went fowling on the cliffs of Hirta.

Various means of communication were developed between Boreray and the high north coast of Hirta. In the 1870s a visitor reported that.

> One day shortly after my arrival an old man happening to be up the hill at the back of the village descried what he imagined to be two marks cut on the turf on the top of Boreray. A party of men, it is necessary to explain, had gone to that island about a fortnight before to pluck the sheep which are kept there, for shears are as yet unknown in St Kilda. He came down in great distress, and communicated the intelligence to the rest of the people, who, to my surprise, were thrown into a state of consternation. The women seated themselves on the ground and chanted lamentations. On inquiring the reason, I was informed that a system of telegraphy had been long established in St Kilda, and that two marks cut in the turf in Boreray signified that one or more of the party were sick or dead, and that a boat was wanted immediately.

Further light was cast on this tale in 1896, when another visitor to Boreray,

… noticed three or four strips of ground, about two feet wide and twelve feet long, with the sod cut out and turned wrong-side up. The cuttings ran straight up and down the steep hill-side, and upon inquiry I discovered that they had been made by the members of a party which had recently been staying upon the island as a signal to their friends on St Kilda that the work which had occasioned their visit had been done, and they were ready to be taken off. If anybody should fall ill whilst sojourning on Borrera for more than a day this signal, or a fire lighted on the open hill-side, is used to warn the St Kildans at home that something is wrong and that the boat is wanted. During the time friends are absent from home on a prolonged wool-gathering, or bird-catching, expedition, daily watch is kept from the top of the hills behind St Kilda village for any signals which they may make for assistance.

In 1727, three years before Alexander Buchan's death on the island, a major catastrophe occurred. The smallpox pandemic of that year cannot have been the only occasion when the St Kildans were massively reduced by infection. Martin hinted as much when he wrote thirty years earlier that smallpox 'hath not been heard of in this place for several ages', implying that it had been heard of in former years. The 1727 outbreak is merely one of the few which were recorded – in 1721 Buchan had written from St Kilda to Edinburgh mentioning 'the great mortality' of 1720 which 'had Scattered the school', but we have few further details.

The details from 1727 are approximate but appalling. In the winter of that year more than eighty St Kildans died. By the following July around forty-two were still alive. Those sums do not agree with Martin's total of a hundred and eighty people thirty years earlier, nor with Alexander Buchan's daughter Jean, who claimed that during her father's ministry the population had risen from a hundred and eighty. It is likely that the 'the great mortality' of 1720 had already reduced the island, after the departure from Hirta of both Martin Martin and Jean Buchan.

According to Reverend Daniel Macaulay of Bracadale in Skye, who went in the early summer of 1728 to report on St Kilda for the SSPCK, seventy-seven of the eighty had died of smallpox and the other three 'of other Diseases'. The smallpox had apparently been imported from Harris. A St Kildan died there of the disease in 1726. The dead man's clothes were returned to Hirta, carrying the bacillus

with them. It spread quickly and ferociously. In the middle of the following century an eighty-three year-old St Kildan woman would tell
of the tragedy in these words: 'Donald Macdonald lived in St Kilda
till he was an old man. He then went to Harris, where he was seized
with the smallpox, and died there, about 133 years ago. The next year
his clothes were brought to St Kilda by one of his relations, when the
inhabitants were all seized with the disease, so that only four grownup
persons were left alive on the island; but they are the descendants of
this same Macdonald, who continue in the island yet.' Eleven males –
three men and eight boys – were harvesting seabirds on Stac an Armin
when Hirta was devastated. When no boat came out from Village Bay
to collect them they somehow survived over winter on that seabound
Matterhorn. The steward's birlinn relieved them in May and took them
at first to quarantine in Soay rather than to Hirta to mourn their dead.

But for that stroke of dubious good fortune, death's harvest would
have been even greater. As it was, between the summer of 1727 and
the summer of 1728 the island's population was slashed by two-
thirds. Daniel Macaulay reckoned that twenty-one households had
been reduced to just four. The residual inhabitants in summer 1728
amounted to nine men, ten women, fifteen boys and eight girls, many
of the children being orphans. (A century later another visitor would
be told that the total death toll had been ninety-four and that twenty-
five families had fallen to five. Bodycounts may not agree but the scale
of the disaster is beyond dispute.) The minister, Alexander Buchan,
was spared. Daniel Macaulay reported to the SSPCK that Buchan was
doing a decent job, despite his opinion that Buchan was not very bright
and most of his books were both out of date and damp.

The response of the MacLeods of Harris and of Dunvegan was
not dramatic. They sent over sufficient supplies to see the survivors
through what otherwise could have been a year of famine – crops
were unreaped and cattle left to run half wild during the epidemic. For
several years thereafter they exported annually a few new settlers, who
may or may not have been antagonists of MacLeod of MacLeod, and
they let St Kilda regenerate more or less at its own pace.

Much of this new blood came from Skye. There is no official record
of St Kildan surnames before the smallpox epidemic in 1727. We know
that fifteen or twenty years earlier Alexander Buchan had taught two
boys named MacDonald and Campbell. MacDonalds and Campbells

were two of the biggest clans and were to be found all across the Highlands and Islands. But in the seventeenth century neither of them was especially common in the northern Hebrides of Lewis and Harris. Campbells were firmly rooted in Argyllshire, and MacDonalds in the Uists, Skye and the southern Hebrides.

St Kildan placenames refer to a Murchison's Gully, a MacNeil's Gully and MacFadyen's Cleits. Later in the eighteenth century St Kilda had an unpopular steward named William MacNeil, who could for unknown reasons have loaned his name to a minor gully. If not, if those features all were named after pre-1727 residents, they suggested ancestries in western Inverness-shire, the Outer Hebridean island of Barra and the Inner Hebridean island of Mull. A St Kildan tradition had it that 'one Macquin, an Irish rover, was the first person who settled himself and a colony of his countrymen in their land'. (St Brianan's chapel on St Kilda suggests another possible antique connection to Barra. St Brianan was otherwise known as St Brendan, a much-travelled Irish missionary of the sixth century who was locally credited with introducing Christianity to that Hebridean island.)

When the census was first taken in St Kilda, more than a century after its post-smallpox repopulation, there were no Campbells, Murchisons, MacNeils or MacFadyens living there. There were MacDonalds, Gillieses, Fergusons, MacCrimmons, MacKinnons, Morrisons, MacQueens (Macquins) and one MacLeod.

With the possible exception of the Morrisons, a surname which smacks of Lewis or Harris, and of the Fergusons who claimed to spring from a boatman named Finlay Ferguson of the island of Berneray in the Sound of Harris (Finlay Ferguson took new settlers to St Kilda after 1727, fell in love with a girl on board his boat named MacDonald and stayed in Hirta), those names point to Skye.

In particular they point to the MacLeod estates in the north of Skye, where the names Gillies, MacQueen and MacCrimmon were common. Gillieses and MacQueens lived in Staffin and Kilmuir on either side of the Trotternish Ridge and until early in the nineteenth century the MacCrimmons were hereditary pipers to MacLeod of Dunvegan. Certain members of the 1851 population, such as at least some of the MacDonalds, were the descendants of smallpox survivors, but some if not most of them were certainly the grandchildren and great-grandchildren of eighteenth-century immigrants.

By the nineteenth century there was also a limited number of forenames in each gender on St Kilda. Catherine, Rachel, Ann and Mary were most common among women, who were differentiated in Gaelic tradition by a suffixed reference to their father or husband. So Mary Gillies, whose father was called Norman, became Mhairi a' Tormod, which distinguished her from Mary MacQueen, and indeed from another Mary Gillies whose father was not called Norman. The men, Finlay, Donald, Neil and John, were more often identified by physical characteristics such as their height, their complexions or the colour of their hair. Four different Johns could then become Iain Mor, Iain Beag, Iain Ban and Iain Dubh.

The slow introduction of new settlers after 1727 was not as neglectful as it might seem. The remaining nineteen adults and twenty-three children, augmented by newcomers from elsewhere, had their pick of the best land and fewer mouths to feed. Their stocks of sheep, horses and cattle, once redomesticated, would have been as high as before, leaving each of the households with a larger share. The island's cleits would have contained the dried fowls and mutton of the lost families, and perhaps some grain. Twenty or more men and boys would have been doubly cautious on fowling expeditions – if they were lost, so was the last of the community – but those who had survived on Stac an Armin clearly retained the old skills, and new arrivals from the other islands would not have been unfamiliar with the art of bird-catching.

St Kilda did regenerate, as it must have revived following earlier, undocumented disasters. But its population never completely recovered. If there were, as Martin Martin and Jean Buchan asserted, between 180 and 200 villagers on Hirta in the late seventeenth and early eighteenth centuries, their numbers never again reached that level. Even a century later, in the years leading up to the 1830s, when the populations of the rest of the Hebrides and western Highlands doubled and trebled and reached their highest levels in history, the population of St Kilda remained at around 100 people – almost half that of the early 1720s.

If St Kilda had not been so reduced by a fatal virus and if it had been allowed to follow the demographic pattern of its neighbouring islands, by the nineteenth century Hirta would have been home to well over 200 people. Thirty years after the epidemic Kenneth Macaulay would write that 'It is a fact indisputably true, that the inhabitants of St Kilda were much more numerous heretofore, than they are at present ...

'I shall only venture to affirm, that the island, if under proper regulations, might easily support three hundred souls. Martin, who visited it about the end of the last century, found an hundred and eighty persons there.

'The number is now dwindled down to eighty-eight: an extraordinary change this in less than two generations ...'

In such a place a community of 100 folk was measurably more vulnerable than one of 200 or 300 residents. The 'great mortality' of 1720 and the smallpox epidemic of 1727 sowed the seeds of the final population collapse exactly two centuries later.

In 1734, just seven years after the smallpox outbreak, one of Hirta's newest inhabitants was a most unfortunate woman from a most unusual place.

In 1730 Rachel Erskine, Lady Grange, separated from her husband James in acrimonious circumstances. She was fifty-one years old and had delivered him nine children. A 'wild beauty', Rachel was noted for her independent mind and fiery temper. Her portrait at the age of about thirty shows a proud and confident woman.

James Erskine, Lord Grange, was exactly the same age as his wife and by 1732 was a notable figure in Edinburgh society, having been Lord Justice Clerk since 1710 and briefly the Member of Parliament for Aberdeen Burghs in 1715. In the early 1730s Grange planned to revive his parliamentary career with the hope of eventually becoming Secretary of State for Scotland. In 1734 he became MP for Clackmannanshire. His portrait at the age of about seventy shows a Scottish grandee with a Roman nose and a weak right eye. He has no laughter lines and his left eye is not kind.

In the 1730s two hurdles obstructed Lord Grange's political career. One was the fact that in an age of Jacobite rebellions he was a younger son and brother of the famously Jacobite Erskines of Mar. James's oldest brother John, who succeeded to the family title in 1689, had helped to launch the Jacobite Rising of 1715 and led troops against the Hanoverian crown. Following the suppression of that insurrection the Mars' title was forfeited. John died in exile in Aix-la-Chapelle in 1732.

Jacobitism was still alive and kicking, as its greatest military manifestation would prove in 1745, and an ambitious man such as James

Erskine could not afford to labour under suspicion. Despite his family's recent history he publicly embraced both the Reformed Church of Scotland and the British Hanoverian line. Lord Grange tip-toed cautiously through the minefield of early eighteenth-century British politics and society.

His second problem was his wife. By the 1720s the marriage of James and Rachel Erskine had failed. James took a mistress in London and his infidelities were tearfully reported to his children by their mother in Edinburgh. In July 1730 she submitted to her husband a letter offering in return for £100 a year to 'retire and live by myself ... and shall not trouble you nor sett my Foot within your Doors ...'

Rachel also conceded the care of her children to her former husband. She had no choice in the matter: the law unambiguously favoured his claim to their offspring. Her behaviour became troubled and troubling. She caused embarrassing scenes in public places. Lord Grange worried that she might turn up one day in his courtroom and hector him. At some point in 1731 James Erskine was informed that his estranged wife had possession of letters which implicated him, and probably also such of his friends and acquaintances as Sir Alexander Macdonald of Sleat in Skye, Norman MacLeod of Dunvegan and Simon Fraser, Lord Lovat, in anti-government Jacobite conspiracies. We do not know if those letters existed or not. We do not know whether or not Rachel Erskine ever mentioned such plots, let alone threatened to expose them.

We do know that shortly before midnight on 22 January 1732 men burst into her bedroom, tied her hands and gagged her, put her into a sedan chair and carried their captive west. Slowly, over a period of months, Lady Grange was escorted by way of Stirling to the wild and inaccessible north-western coast of Scotland. In September 1732 she was put aboard a sloop on the shore of Loch Hourn, a deep fjord which cuts into the mainland opposite the island of Skye. She was by then in the hands of Highlanders and in the company of men whose language was incomprehensible to her. She was in the presence of just one speaker of English. His name was Alexander Macdonald and he was the tacksman, or tenant farmer, of Sir Alexander Macdonald of Sleat's Monach Islands, three miles off the west coast of North Uist in the Outer Hebrides. Rachel would live in that little archipelago for the next two years.

The Monach Islands, which were and are known locally as Heisker, are small, flat and sandy. They had a population of about 100 people when Rachel Erskine stayed there with Alexander Macdonald and his wife. At first she was not told where she was. When she discovered her whereabouts, from Alexander MacDonald, from his wife, or possibly through her own beginner's Gaelic from other islanders, Rachel tried unsuccessfully to get a minister from Uist to sail over and pray for her salvation. Then she made a failed attempt to escape. Then Alexander MacDonald went off to see his namesake, employer and feudal superior, Sir Alexander MacDonald, and said that he considered it a sin to keep Lady Grange imprisoned. Sir Alexander himself began to repent his own involvement in the kidnap (possibly because his tacksman's doubts threatened to make the affair more public than he would have preferred) but could see no way out of the situation. He soon found one. Sir Alexander persuaded his fellow Skye-based clan chief, MacLeod of MacLeod, to take the lady off his hands.

In June 1734 the steward of MacLeod of Harris sailed his galley from Pabbay to Heisker. He told Rachel Erskine that she was to be taken from there to the Orkney islands. It was a lie. He took her to St Kilda. When the steward's birlinn arrived in Village Bay in the early summer of 1734 it carried as supercargo a bedraggled and distressed fifty-five year-old Edinburgh gentlewoman. When the birlinn sailed back to Harris with the St Kildans' produce, it left her there. She would live for the next seven years in the steward's summer house beside the settlement in Village Bay.

Even by the unemancipated standards of the eighteenth century, this was an extraordinary chain of events. Because she threatened to hinder his career, a titled and well-connected Scottish politician and practitioner of law had his estranged wife, who was elderly by the measure of the time, abducted and confined in the most far-flung island in the kingdom – a dangerous place with a hostile climate, where almost nobody spoke English and from which there was no chance of escape. Although James Erskine was clearly involved in the plot, its chief mover seems to have been Simon Fraser, Lord Lovat, who certainly was a committed Jacobite and who was executed for treason in 1747. Lovat in his turn was able to coerce such other Highland clan chiefs as MacLeod of Dunvegan and MacDonald of Sleat. Their unmistakable intention was that Lady Grange should become demented and die alone and unremarked without anybody being obliged to commit the capital offence of killing her. That was, in the end, exactly what happened.

Rachel Erskine did not, however, die on St Kilda, although her years there were marked by misery and despair. Finlay MacDonald, one of the St Kildan boys who had been taught English by Alexander Buchan twenty-five years earlier, was by then a middle-aged man who had survived the smallpox epidemic and was still living on the island. Finlay MacDonald appears to have lived for a time in a tiny apartment of her small house in the position of manservant, companion or guard. His ward was impressed neither by St Kilda nor, initially, by Finlay.

'When I came into the Island,' she would write, 'I found it as I dreaded a very desolate barren miserable spot no body in it but the Natives of the place ... I am sure [MacLeod's steward] left me in a miserable Condition there being no Provisions left me but what the Island afforded and no body to assist me but an ill-natured Man who understood a little English and Explained to others what I wanted, he not only was surly but half witted he having one day taken out his Durk to kill me ...'

A century later one of Finlay MacDonald's grandchildren told a visitor that relations between Finlay and Lady Grange had improved. According to the family version he made her a seat of twisted straw, entertained her with legends of the Hebrides and as well as taking the opportunity to refresh his own command of English, Finlay helped Rachel Erskine to acquire some Gaelic. She was later given a serving girl named Florence MacLeod, who probably came from elsewhere in the Hebrides and seems to have spoken no English.

Shortly after Lady Grange was bundled onto Hirta there arrived from Skye a new minister named Roderick MacLennan. 'Had it not been for the care [MacLennan's wife] took of me I shou'd have died for Want,' wrote Rachel Erskine, 'for there was no provisions sent me but two Pecks [26 dry litres] of flower and such as the place can afford such as Milk, and a little Barley knocked [crushed], and that forced from them by threatening, the people being miserably poor and much oppressed: I have no body to serve me but a little highland Girl and the Minister or his Wife is obliged to explain to her [my requirements] ...'

Fifty years later, as a 'poor old woman' in the 1780s, the 'little Highland girl' Florence MacLeod seems to have met the Church missionary John

Buchanan. She told him that while she served Lady Grange on St Kilda, her mistress's 'whole time was devoted to weeping; and wrapping up letters round pieces of cork, bound up with yarn, and throwing them into the sea, to try if any favourable wave would waft them to some Christian, to inform some humane person where she resided, in expectation of carrying tidings to her friends in Edinburgh'.

Like Lady Grange, Reverend Roderick MacLennan did not have a happy time on Hirta, but unlike Lady Grange he was relatively free to leave. When he did depart, after five years in 1739, he took with him two letters from her which implored the outside world to heed her fate. The minister was instrumental in the composition of those letters, in the small but essential matter of giving Rachel a pen, ink and paper which she would not otherwise have been able to obtain, and in writing some of the content from her dictation. Reverend MacLennan went from Village Bay back to Skye. For whatever reason, Rachel Erskine's letters did not surface in Edinburgh until over a year later, at the end of 1740. Then they caused a stir.

One was addressed to her former husband and the other was an open account of her travails. It included the lines:

> I was in great misery in the Husker [Heisker], but I am ten times worse and worse here … You know I'm not guilty of any crime except that of loveing my husband too much. He knowes very well that he was my idol, and now God has made him a rode [rod] to scourgeth me; if friends cannot prevail with Lord Grange, then let me have the benefit of the law. It is impossible for me to write, or for you to imagine all the misserie and sorrow and hunger and cold and hardship of all kinds that I have suffered since I was stolen; if my paper allowed me I would give a particular account of the way, but I must be short and I have a bad pin [pen].

Copies were made of the letters and distributed around the tea- and coffee-houses of Edinburgh, to James Erskine's intense displeasure. Both of them were so articulate and well-reasoned that they scorned the slander that Rachel Erskine had lost her mind. As may have been intended, they fell into the hands of a distinguished elderly lawyer named Thomas Hope of Rankeillour. Hope was a sixty-three year-old baronet who was familiar with the Erskine family troubles. Ten years earlier he had agreed that Rachel Erskine should be separated from her husband. When she disappeared, Hope was assured that 'all care was taken of her'. When he received copies of her letters from St Kilda in December 1740, Sir Thomas Hope was horrified. 'I doubt not but she may be dead by this time,' he wrote to the Solicitor General for Scotland, 'but if she is alive, the hardest heart on earth would bleed to hear of her sufferings, and I think I can't in duty stand this call, but must follow out a course so as to restore her to a seeming liberty and a comfortable life.'

Lord Grange attempted to placate Sir Thomas with an extraordinary mixture of threat and reassurance, writing to him: 'I wish you had advised with these gentlemen (lawyers) sooner, for they would have advised you at least to write to me before that by your means (I know none else who would or could have done it) strange stories were spread over all the town of Edinburgh and made the talk of coffee-houses and tea-tables. I am willing to impute this to your want of consideration, for it's very injurious to me and my children, and the welfare of the person you say you have so much regard for could not have prompted a considerate man to take such a course.'

Undeterred, Hope commissioned a ship to sail to Hirta and rescue Lady Grange. When the *Arabella*, containing twenty armed men and the former minister's wife, Mrs Roderick MacLennan, to guide and interpret for them, arrived in Village Bay in March 1741, its captain was informed 'that she was removed from that place some time ago'.

She had in fact been removed just weeks or even days earlier. With her story unravelling before the Edinburgh public, Rachel Erskine had been whisked away to Harris and was a house prisoner of the MacLeods. She stayed there for seven months before being transported, possibly by way of Uist, to north Skye. There she died and was buried in May 1745, all but forgotten once again in a Scotland which was about to be rocked by tumultuous events.

There were around seventy islanders living in Hirta during the confinement there of Lady Grange. They were not unaccustomed to unusual visitations and they left no first-hand accounts of this strange interlude. Their descendants told stories of Rachel Erskine trying to bribe the St Kildans to help her escape; of her vain attempts to contact passing seagoing vessels which put into Village Bay for water. We have been told that 'She was kind to the peasantry, giving them from her own stores; and sometimes had the women to come and dance before her; but her temper and habits were not such as to gain their esteem.' We are told that she was often drunk, for which she could be forgiven. And we are told that when she was finally hurried off the island by MacLeod's men in 1741, she left behind twelve silver shillings for Finlay MacDonald.

As much as anything else, the Lady Grange affair illuminates the relationship of St Kilda and the other north-western Hebrides with the rest of Scotland as late as the eighteenth century. The kidnap occurred more than a century after the union of crowns and nearly three decades after the union of the parliaments of Scotland, England and Wales. It occurred in the lifetimes of such Enlightenment eminences as Adam Smith and David Hume. It was 250 years after the collapse of the Lordship of the Isles and almost 500 years after the incorporation of the Hebrides into the kingdom of Scotland. But places such as Heisker, St Kilda, Uist, Harris and even Skye were so remote and isolated from Edinburgh society that they might still have been part of Norway. It was perfectly feasible, given the right connections with those clan chiefs who held feudal power over the islands, for an unscrupulous abductor to conceal there a distinctive Edinburgh lady who was desperate to return home. In Skye and Harris as well as in St Kilda, Rachel Erskine found herself immured in a foreign country without a formal border.

In July 1745, two months after Rachel was interred at Trumpan in the Waternish peninsula of Skye, Prince Charles Edward Stuart landed on the island of Eriskay, announced his claim to the throne of Great Britain and the last and biggest of the Jacobite Risings was under way. Lord Lovat played an active part, which cost him his head two years later. James Erskine, who was living in London as the Member of Parliament for Stirling Burghs, kept his feelings to himself. Neither Macdonald of Sleat nor MacLeod of Dunvegan joined the '45 Rising, which in its turn meant that few people from the Hebrides were involved.

St Kildans might not have fought at Culloden in April 1746, but they felt its aftermath. Following his defeat Charles Edward Stuart went on the run. He made his way across the Highlands to the west coast and took a boat to the Outer Hebrides. The pursuing government forces reached the conclusion that he 'had set sail from the continent to St Kilda, being a place so remote that no suspicion would be readily entertained of his being there'.

Charles was actually wandering between Benbecula and Lewis in the Western Isles, in search of a ship to France. He would never be caught. But on 20 June 1746 three government sloops put into Village Bay and sent 100 armed men ashore to search the island of Hirta. 'The greater part of the poor inhabitants ran off to the clifts of their rocks to hide themselves, being frighted out of their wits ...' The few who remained expressed their convincing bafflement, and the troops and the ships departed. Charles Edward Stuart, who had travelled in the opposite direction, back to Skye and the Scottish mainland, eventually reached the safety of continental Europe.

The Risings were finished and the cause was done, but that was not the St Kildans' last connection with Jacobitism and the bewildering events of 1745 and 1746. In 1758 the Society in Scotland for the Propagation of Christian Knowledge demonstrated its renewed interest in the well-being of the islanders by despatching Reverend Kenneth Macaulay to research and deliver a report. The world got much more than a report from Macaulay.

Kenneth Macaulay came from an extraordinary family. He was born in Harris in about 1723, the son of a celebrated Church of Scotland minister named Aulay Macaulay. In 1746, when Kenneth was a young man, Reverend Aulay Macaulay was one of the few Highlanders who made a serious attempt on behalf of the British government to apprehend Prince Charles Edward Stuart during the Young Pretender's long break for freedom after the disaster at Culloden.

While soldiers were searching St Kilda, the prince had strayed from the Catholic Outer Hebrides into the Protestant islands and was hiding in the small island of Scalpay, off the east coast of Harris, when the elderly Reverend Aulay assembled a posse and ventured out to arrest him. The minister was dissuaded in Scalpay by a fellow islander, who professed his own personal distaste for the Jacobite cause but invoked the inviolable rules of Highland sanctuary and hospitality. Reverend Macaulay returned empty-handed to Harris and Charles Edward Stuart broke free for France. We do not know whether or not Aulay's son Kenneth, who was then in his early twenties and assisting his father's ministry in Harris, had been a member of the frustrated raiding party.

Aulay Macaulay had fourteen children. One of his other sons,

John Macaulay, became the father of the anti-slavery campaigner Zachary Macaulay. Zachary, who settled in London, was in his turn the father of Thomas Babington Macaulay, 1st Baron Macaulay, the famous nineteenth-century historian and politician. The newly ordained Reverend Kenneth Macaulay who visited St Kilda in 1758 was therefore one of a very long line of eminent Hebridean Macaulays. He was the son of a dedicated representative of the Reformed Church, the uncle of a prominent abolitionist, and the great-uncle of a reforming Whig parliamentarian who wrote *Lays of Ancient Rome*. It is not difficult to trace in Kenneth Macaulay's own work the enlightened, liberal, literary gene.

Six years after his voyage to Hirta, in 1764, Kenneth Macaulay adapted and published his SSPCK report as another book on the islands. The very publication of *The History of St Kilda* so soon after the appearance of Martin's and Buchan's volumes is evidence that the small archipelago and its inhabitants were already objects of great literary and public fascination in the middle of the eighteenth century. Macaulay acknowledged as much in his opening paragraph: 'The island of St Kilda may be ranked among the greatest curiosities of the British Empire. The situation of the place, the genius of its inhabitants, their manners and customs, the constitution of their little Commonwealth, that amazing dexterity with which they manage the most important branches of their business, that unexampled courage, with which they encounter dangers insurmountable to any other race of men, and that perhaps happy ignorance, which renders them absolute strangers to those extravagant desires and endless pursuits, which keep the great and active world in a constant agitation ...'

Like his predecessors, Kenneth Macaulay was not writing a guide-book. When Macaulay compared the main island of Hirta to 'the Teneriffe of Britain' he was making an extravagant topographical simile, not recommending St Kilda as a winter tourist resort. Then, as later, few of his readers would ever visit the islands. Then, as later, the combination of the proximity and the elementary inaccessibility of St Kilda was a cornerstone of its popular appeal.

Kenneth Macaulay was in his mid-thirties when he visited St Kilda in 1758. The History of St Kilda presents us with a man appealingly anxious to explore the past and present of an island group whose high peaks he would have gazed upon, out on the horizon due west of his home at Scarista in Harris, since he was a boy. He had seen boats come from the archipelago and boats leave for it; heard stories of the people and the place; glimpsed or even met St Kildans on their visits to Harris; wondered over the years what it really must be like.

At last he had the chance to find out. He embraced it wholeheartedly. Like others before him, he was impressed by the St Kildans' exceptional welcome to visitors. Macaulay sailed from Harris in a relatively small, six-oared boat which due to rough seas was unable to tie up at the usual rocky landing place in Village Bay. His crew had no option but to drop anchor and 'stand there for five hours more in a most distressful condition, drenched all over, shivering with cold, and under the dreadful apprehension of being swallowed up every moment'.

They were saved by the St Kildans, who 'flew down from the village to our assistance, men, women and children'. The locals directed the boatmen to weigh anchor and make for the nearby beach, a sandy strip below the cluster of houses which was only revealed for a few hours at low tide, where the visitors were treated to a particularly spectacular version of the time-honoured treatment of being carried ashore. It was described in grateful detail by Kenneth Macaulay:

[T]hey, with an amazing intrepidity flew into the water to meet us; a most desperate adventure, in which any other race of men would hardly think of engaging, were they to see their nearest relations in the same danger.

The disposition they made was this: After having divided and formed themselves into two lines, the two ablest men among them marched forward into the sea, each in the front of his own little corps.– Those next in strength and stature, seized these two leaders by the middle, and the rest, from one end of each row to the other, clung fast to those immediately before them, wading forward till those who were formost in the rank, and after them every one else in the order in which he stood, got hold of the boat.– Those who go from year to year to St Kilda, always take the precaution to wrap a strong rope round the stern of their boat, and tie another to the prow. As soon as the St Kildians have posted themselves round it, they immediately hand about the two ropes from one to another, till the women and children who stand upon the beach come at it, so as to have their share of the work.– This operation which is so very necessary, being soon over, a general signal is given, and every individual exerts himself with all his strength and spirit: The consequence is, the boat and every thing contained in it, are with surprising quickness and dexterity hauled on beyond the reach of the sea.

All the strength of this art was with the greatest alacrity tried upon this occasion, and with a success beyond any thing I could have expected.– Without giving time to any one of us to jump out into the water, the St Kildians hoisted up, almost in a moment our little vessel, ourselves, and all the luggage that belonged to us, to a dry part of the strand.

Once safely on dry land Kenneth Macaulay was relieved to discover himself in the company of,

> ... a very hospitable race of barbarians (if any one incline to call them so) ... those seafaring people, who have the misfortune to be shipwrecked about the Western Islands, or are reduced to extreme distress there, are treated with much greater humanity and Christian benevolence, than many of their fellow sufferers, whose harder fate drives them to the more barbarous shores of some other divisions of Scotland, and even of England. It is certain that these unhappy persons would meet with stronger marks of true politeness, or, what is infinitely more valuable, of real compassion and generosity at St Kilda, than in the more civilized places I now allude to.

He then set out to explore Hirta. He noted that apart from Village Bay and Glen Bay 'Its whole circumference is faced with an inaccessible barrier of rocks.' Village Bay was 'formed by two promontories, the first [Oiseval] running out to the north-east side of the island, and the other [Dun] to the south end: The former extends no great way, but the latter occupies a considerable tract of ground; and from its southern extremity describing a sort of curve, insinuates itself gradually into the land, till it comes to the north, where the bay terminates'.

Something momentous had occurred in the years before 1758. Kenneth Macaulay made the first mention of the land bridge between Dun and the lower slopes of Ruaival on Hirta having been swept away by the wind and the sea. When Macaulay arrived 'the Peninsula [Dun], which terminates the larger bay on the south side ... at high water is surrounded by the sea, and [is] in every respect an island'.

The narrow kyle between Dun and Hirta, which was first opened in the middle third of the eighteenth century, widened and deepened incrementally, even imperceptibly, in the following decades. In the twenty-first century Dun was still just about accessible on foot from Hirta, across slippery rocks at the lowest of spring and neap tides. St Kildans of the eighteenth, nineteenth and twentieth centuries could still reach Dun from Hirta at certain seasons without a boat. That may be why they were able to dig raised strips of *feannagan*, or lazy beds, on the steep green slopes of Dun nearest to Hirta. The people could reach the beds to plant and harvest their potatoes, but their animals could not get across the kyle to graze on the vegetable leaves.

Macaulay was powerfully impressed by the summit and cliffs of Conachair.

> The top of this enormous mass of matter commands a very extensive prospect. In a clear day, if the weather be settled, all the Long Island [the Outer Hebrides], that is to say, a tract of land and sea, more than 140 miles in length, may be seen from it.– But the most striking circumstance about this great and wonderful object, is the figure it makes on the north-side: there it hangs over the deep in a most frightful manner. A view of it from the sea fills a man with astonishment, and a look over it from above strikes him with horror.– Most of the crew were so terrified that they would not venture to gratify their curiosity in this respect, till the natives took hold of their heels as they lay flat to look over it; yet a St Kildian will stand or sit on the very brink of this stupenduous precipice, with the most careless indifference.

Macaulay described the old, traditional township on the Village Bay sward, which had been in place since at least the Middle Ages and would only be dismantled during the second half of the nineteenth century.

> Here the whole body of this little people live together, like the inhabitants of a town or city. All their houses are built in two rows, abundantly regular and facing one another, with a tolerable causeway in the middle, which they call the Street.
>
> These habitations are made and contrived in a very uncommon manner. Every one of them is flat in the roof, or nearly so, much like

the houses of some oriental nations.– That from any one of these the St Kildians have borrowed their manner of building, no man of sense will entertain a suspicion. They have been taught this lesson by their own reason, improved by experience.

The place in which their lot has fallen, is peculiarly subject to violent squalls and furious hurricanes: Were their houses raised higher than at present, they believe the first winter storm would bring them down about their ears.– For this reason the precaution they take in giving roofs much flatter than ordinary, to them, seems to be not altogether unnecessary.

The walls of these habitations are made of a rough gritty kind of stones, huddled up together in haste, without either lime or mortar, from eight to nine foot high.

In the heart of the walls are the beds, which are overlaid with flags, and large enough to contain three persons. In the side of every bed is an opening, by way of door, which is much too narrow and low to answer that purpose.

The beds were situated in wall cavities, he proposed, so that the St Kildans did not have to sleep on the steadily growing layer of peat-ash and urine compost which accumulated in the main room.

All their dwelling houses are divided into two apartments by partition walls. In the division next the door, which is much the largest, they have their cattle stalled during the whole winter season; the other serves for kitchen, hall and bed room.

Macaulay observed not only the island men's breathtaking feats upon the cliffs, stacks and crags, but also those of their dogs. The men captured gannets and their eggs; the dogs caught puffins:

During the summer season the women of Hirta are much employed in fowling: The principal game that falls to their share, is the small sprightly bird called the Puffin.

This fowl hatches under ground, and is easily traced out by means of the hole through which it makes its way; the hole it digs with its beak. The wife or daughter of a family makes a short excursion from home in a morning, attended by a dog, and catches what may be a sufficient provision for the whole family, at least for one day; every family in the island is furnished with one or more of those extraordinary dogs. They are a mixture of the tarrier, spaniel, and those that take the water: Of their own accord they sally out early enough and soon return, bringing five or six puffins at a time.

Sitting on the side of a hill with some of the people, I saw one of these little dogs stealing away from us: The men told me he would soon return with a considerable booty, accordingly he came back in half an hour and laid down his prey at his master's feet; being taught by experience and some friendly stroakings, that his owner had a just sense of the obligation, he went off the second time, and had much the same success.

Kenneth Macaulay was as impressed as were many other visitors of his time by the bounteous life of St Kildans, by their plentiful natural resources and apparent freedom from hunger and want:

The inhabitants of this the obscurest island in the world, have strong proofs of the equal dispensations of Providence.

The Lavie [guillemot] visits them most seasonably in the month of February, when their fresh mutton and bread are perhaps nearly exhausted, and continues to furnish plentiful repasts till the Solan Geese [gannets] appear in March. These supply their wants till they begin to lay. Then are these succeeded by the Puffins and a variety of eggs. When their appetites are cloyed by a frequent use of this food, the salubrious Tulmer [fulmar], and their favourite young Solan Goose [guga], crown their humble boards with grander entertainments, and hold out all autumn over: In winter they have generally a greater stock of bread, mutton and salted fowl, than they are able to consume: I shall speak elsewhere of the fish very liberally furnished by their seas.

Upon the whole, in spite of hard usage, and peculiar disadvantages, they feed more luxuriously, if that be a part of human felicity, than perhaps any small or great nation of Slaves, upon the face of the whole earth.

A key word here was 'slaves'. As we have seen, sixty years earlier Martin Martin had extolled the people of St Kilda as being 'above the avarice and slavery of the rest of mankind' and living 'by the munificence of Heaven'.

It was a caricature which nonetheless became almost definitive. Even after the theory of a Golden Age had been abandoned by most of the sensible world, the St Kildans found the image impossible to shake off, up to and after their evacuation in 1930. Even in the twenty-first century the islands are occasionally portrayed as Paradise Lost and their former inhabitants as fallen angels.

Kenneth Macaulay knew it to be largely nonsense. As a native of Harris, Macaulay understood that the residents of St Kilda were not a unique race, hermetically sealed from and untouched by the world beyond their shores. On the contrary: they were Hebridean fishermen, fowlers and crofters, connected by ancestry, intermarriage and repopulation to the rest of the Western Isles and the larger Scottish *Gàidhealtachd*.

Some of the most remarkable features of *The History of St Kilda* are Macaulay's repeated denunciations of MacLeod's dictatorship. They were doubtless enabled by the fact that when he wrote the book, Macaulay had left Harris and was ministering to congregations elsewhere in Scotland, beyond the reach of the petty chieftains of Clan MacLeod.

As a son of Harris as well as a minister of the Church of Scotland, Kenneth Macaulay had the experience and authority to assert that MacLeod's steward,

> …will always have it in his power to monopolise the whole trade of this island … excepting what is necessary to keep the people alive; or render them fit for the labouring …
>
> Nor is it an easy matter to redress this grievance. So peculiarly unhappy is the place in its situation, that the inhabitants must, I am afraid, to the end of time, be wholly at the mercy of some one person, who may swallow all the small commodities this island can afford, and rule the whole community with a rod of iron …
>
> While despotism reigns over that little community, industry will be effectually discouraged, and poverty must be the natural consequence of both, which by the by is no evil, as the necessaries of life are easily purchased by the St Kildians, and any thing else is hardly of any use to them … the people though unacquainted with the peculiar felicity of the British constitution, and never unaccustomed to the yoke of slavery, are not of the same low spirit with those servile Cappadocians, who refused the invaluable present of freedom, offered to them by the Romans.

The hard pressure of grievances they feel like other men, are ready enough to murmur in corners ...

From the account given of St Kilda under the preceding articles, it is evident, that the steward may, if he pleases, reign despotically over it; and will any man answer for a succession of absolute government. Humanity and religion are the only laws to controul him. From his sentence the helpless people neither dare nor can appeal to any other judge; such is the situation of their land, they cannot have recourse; nor is it in their power, were they men of spirit or letters, to transmit their complaints to the proprietor without the steward's privity: He may confine them within the isle during life, torture their persons if cruelly inclined, confiscate their goods, and do every act of violence, unless restrained by his own heart or understanding.

In the end, Kenneth Macaulay admired the St Kildans. In the best traditions of his family, he extolled their lack of worldly or military ambition, their freedom from 'all the vile arts of avarice, frauds, extortion and servility' which were requirements for advancement in the rest of Georgian Britain. They were not a race apart and they certainly were not noble savages; they were 'born philosophers' with 'sense enough to confine their ambition within the bounds prescribed by nature'. They were decent people, making the best of their life at the edge of Europe. Like Alexander Buchan before him, Macaulay was made keenly aware that, 'The smell of their houses, cloaths and breath, is very offensive to a stranger; he is uneasy when a St Kildian is near him, and for two or three days he breathes a thick loathsome air.' But unlike Buchan he was happy to record that in return, the St Kildans 'will tell you, that your company for some time is as offensive to them, as theirs can be to you; and that they find a difficulty in breathing a light sharp air when they are near you'.

There were three notable codas to this unusual book. In 1773, fifteen years after his visit to St Kilda and nine years after the publication of *The History of St Kilda*, Reverend Kenneth Macaulay was the Church of Scotland minister in Cawdor, which was then known as Calder, between Inverness and Nairn in the north-eastern Highlands. Unknown to Macaulay, in that year Dr Samuel Johnson and his amanuensis James Boswell were touring the Highlands armed with a copy of Macaulay's *History of St Kilda*, 'a book which Dr Johnson liked'.

Johnson and Boswell duly called in at Cawdor Manse, where Dr Johnson shortly broadcast his opinion that Kenneth Macaulay had not in fact written *The History of St Kilda*. Since his celebrated bitter feud with James MacPherson, the author and putative recorder of the Ossianic legends, Samuel Johnson had been hypersensitive to Highland imposters. As a High Church Tory, the Englishman was also automatically inclined to dislike Macaulay's Scottish Presbyterianism. Johnson probably tested Kenneth Macaulay's classical learning and found it inadequate for an author of the many Latin phrases and references in *The History of St Kilda*. A frosty evening ensued.

Samuel Johnson had been right about James MacPherson, but he was wrong about Kenneth Macaulay. A friendly minister in Skye with his own fixations on antiquity had assisted with the preparation of Macaulay's final manuscript, but the journey to St Kilda had been made by Kenneth Macaulay and *The History of St Kilda* had been written by Kenneth Macaulay.

The second coda came in the 1780s and 1790s. John Lane Buchanan, a native of Gaelic-speaking Perthshire and another friend of Kenneth Macaulay, toured the Western Islands as a Church of Scotland missionary between 1782 and 1790. In 1793 Buchanan published a book about his experiences. A reviewer in *The Gentleman's Magazine* correctly complained that Buchanan's chapter on St Kilda offered 'little new … Martin is more quoted than Macauley [sic]'. It is in fact doubtful whether John Lane Buchanan, who certainly travelled among most of the other islands, ever set foot on Hirta.

But Buchanan took up Kenneth Macaulay's criticisms of Hebridean clan chiefs and landowners and pursued them at blistering length. Most Hebrideans were, he repeated, merely slaves, and their proprietors ruthless slaveholders. MacLeod of Harris was deliberately keeping the population of St Kilda low, asserted Buchanan, in order to exploit the St Kildans more easily – 'their present master having forgot his former insignificance, has assumed all the turbulent pride of a purse-proud demagogue, to keep them under'. Musing on the condition of St Kildans stranded on the stacks or on Boreray when their single boat was wrecked, Buchanan pointed out that their relatives and neighbours left in Village Bay 'were deprived of a six-shilling Norway yawl to go in quest of them … How cruel and impolitic does the heritor of this isle behave to these brave men!' That criticism at least did not fall on deaf ears; within four years there were two boats at the disposal of the people of Hirta.

When his *Travels in the Western Hebrides* was published John Buchanan sent copies to William Wilberforce and the Duke of Clarence 'with letters entreating them to take up the cause of the oppressed Hebridians'. His choice of recipients could not have been more eccentric. The Duke of Clarence would in 1830 become King William IV. In 1792 he was no more than the recently titled third son of William III. Clarence was not known for his radical views, but he had visited the Outer Hebrides and later told the House of Lords – while arguing in favour of slavery – that the living standard among freemen in the Highlands and Islands of Scotland was worse than that among slaves in the West Indies. That statement undoubtedly earned him a copy in the post of John Buchanan's *Travels in the Western Hebrides*.

In 1792, when the book landed on his own doormat, William Wilberforce MP had recently undergone a religious conversion and joined the anti-slavery movement to which his name would be forever attached. Wilberforce was becoming accustomed to abuse, which was fortunate as during his House of Lords debate the Duke of Clarence – the son of the king – had also said 'the proponents of the abolition [of slavery] are either fanatics or hypocrites, and in one of those classes I rank Mr Wilberforce'.

There is no record of either man acknowledging receipt of John Buchanan's plea on behalf of the St Kildans and other 'oppressed Hebridians'. Buchanan had mistaken his targets. One of them considered that oppressed human beings were part of the natural order; the other had the eradication of a more vicious form of oppression in his sights.

The third coda was closer to time and home. In 1759, the year after Kenneth Macaulay visited St Kilda, he was told of another calamity there.

On the sixth of October that year, nineteen of their men put to sea, bound for the island of Boreray, ten of them landed there; the remaining nine intended to go back to Hirta: For three successive days the wind blew so furiously that there was no possibility of landing any where.

They sheltered themselves all that time under the lee side of one of the high rocks of St Kilda, being half starved with cold and hunger. On the fourth day of their distress they made for the bay, though without any prospect of safety; they steered for the sandy beach on which we landed; here three of the men were washed away, and the remaining six were driven by the force of a wave on the beach, the boat was broke to pieces.

The unhappy men left at Boreray were soon made sensible of the common calamity, and their own misery; their wives and surviving companions, made repeated signals in the main island. Finding there was no other timely resource, after the first violence of their anguish began to abate, they bethought themselves of securing some wild fowl for provisions; they lived on these and the flesh of the sheep that graze there all the year over. Before they quitted this prison, the skins of these sheep, and of the larger fowls tacked together with feathers, were all the clothing that some of them wore: What a grotesque figure they made in this distressful situation, one may easily imagine.

It was providential that Boreray was the place of their exile. The Staller's house or curious grotto, of which an account has been given already, afforded them a very comfortable habitation. Here they slept securely all night, and loitered away the whole winter season. They had taken the necessary precaution to dry some turf in the best way they could, and enough of that to last till the spring should be pretty far advanced.

On the return of the wild fowl, in the month of March, after having relieved their own necessities, they laid up in their storehouse a cargo of these, sufficient to load the steward's eight-oared boat. Their friends at home, willing to give them the satisfaction of knowing that their share of the arable ground was not neglected, turned up ten different small spots of ground on the northern face of the hill which stood over against them. In fine, the ten prisoners remained in this situation without sustaining any great loss, other than that of being much out of humour, till relieved in the month of June by the Steward.

There may have been a birth or two on St Kilda, and infants who survived the hazardous first weeks and months of life, between the summers of 1758 and 1759. There may also have been other deaths. If neither occurred, the population of eighty-eight – which was previously composed of thirty-eight men and boys and fifty women and girls – had been reduced by the loss of three active males. That was the first recorded indication of a gender imbalance which would, in future years, take a toll on the community in Hirta.

FIVE

The Whole Island Dancing

✹

B Y T H E E N D O F the eighteenth century there were two St Kildas. There was the St Kilda of public perception: a fabulous, new-found land which had first reached the attention of many of the citizens of the rest of Great Britain at about the same time that Captain James Cook was 'discovering' the Hawaiian islands. And there was the St Kilda in which fewer than 100 Gaelic-speaking Hebrideans lived and laboured. The two were not the same.

The St Kildans were different from most other British islanders in a couple of respects. They had developed an extraordinary sub-culture of working with stone. This was best exemplified by their thousand cleits. It was also expressed in a growing network of cyclopean dry-stone dykes and walls which would not have shamed Mycenean Greece, small enclosures and huge, complex sheepfolds, or fanks. It was a utilitarian rather than decorative or spiritual sub-culture – the enclosures protected vegetables; the dykes separated animals from crops; the fanks were needed to gather their flocks.

But while it was never purely decorative, it was not all strictly essential. Much of the building, such as of dykes, was necessarily com-munal, but there was a social dividend attached to the number of cleits owned by families, with the result that while they were not built willy-nilly, they certainly were built with status in mind. Having been built, the cleits must obviously be used, which helps to explain the mystery of why they contained the households' peats. Once cut and properly dried in the wind, slabs of peat are virtually impervious to rainwater. That is why all other Highlanders stack them outside. There was no shortage of drying wind on Hirta and no more rain than in other parts of the Highlands. Their peats could be, and probably sometimes were, stored outdoors. But for as long as there was a space in a cleit to fill, they seem to have been laboriously and unnecessarily taken in through the small doorway and then brought out again to feed the fire.

A hundred yards above the village, standing among cleits at the edge of the arable land, was an old small roundhouse known as Taigh Ruaraidh Mhoir. Apart from its great old age, Taigh Ruaraidh Mhoir was and is an unexceptional house, but it had legendary status because of the circumstances of its construction. One day in the distant past Ruairidh Mor, for reasons which are unclear but seem to have been connected to his youth and his supposed lack of strength and aptitude, had been denied a place in a boat going fowling on Boreray. In pique, and to establish his worth, Ruairidh Mor then built this roundhouse from gargantuan stones, single-handedly and in a single day. In other words, unable to prove himself in one classical St Kildan manner on the cliffs, Ruairidh Mor made his claim for proper respect and recognition in another esteemed St Kildan discipline, the craft of masonry. For that reason alone he and his small roundhouse entered the island's heroical canon.

While life even in bountiful Hirta, with its cleits full of meat and cheese, was hard work, the men and boys enjoyed a greater degree of spontaneity than did their fellow Gaels elsewhere. In almost all of the other Hebrides and in the Highlands, communities were tied to a strict annual round of planting, cutting peats, gathering, reaping, bringing peats home and a score of other subsistence activities. They often came to dread the summer months, when they were obliged to labour throughout eighteen hours of daylight, and look forward to the hostile but less physically arduous winter.

In Village Bay, where fowling was such a vital activity, the women lived a routine life, but between spring and autumn – and occasionally in the winter – the men often did not know whether or not they would go off in their boat until they woke to calm or windy weather in the morning. They were noted for their ability to forecast the climate, as well they might.

But on many days after dawn the men would gather with their clay pipes in the middle of the village to observe the sky and the waves and debate whether to go to sea or stay at home; whether to row to nearby

Soay or to distant Boreray and the big stacks; whether to catch birds and take eggs from their own cliffs on Hirta or to work on a stone dyke; whether to fish from the rocks or plough the earth; whether to cut peat or pluck sheep.

Those gatherings of men were the origin of what later became known, and photographed, as the St Kilda Parliament. It was a legislative body of a kind, but its judgments were limited and short-term. It simply agreed what work was best suited to that day (or if Boreray and the stacks were on the schedule, the next few days), according to the weather, the forecast, the season and the community's needs.

That intriguing lifestyle was exhaustively described to the rest of Britain by Martin Martin and his eighteenth-century successors. The result was not only the label of noble savagery; it was also that a more accurate impression was made of an insular community which, while the rest of the country was on the cusp of enormous social and economic change, had altered hardly at all since the Dark Ages. However close it might have been to the developing world, St Kilda was apparently as distant from the agricultural and industrial revolutions as any inhabited South Sea atoll. The St Kildans were as ignorant of the Rotherham plough as they were of the English language. They were living museum exhibits. It remains a minor miracle that they were not, as were some Australian aborigines, Pacific islanders and Native Americans, kidnapped and displayed at the court of King George III. Instead, they attracted tourists. As soon as they were able, the more affluent of their fellow Britons went to observe them in their native habitat.

If a tourist is somebody who travels to foreign lands purely for pleasure and for the satisfaction of curiosity, the first recorded non-Gaelic-speaking tourists to sail from the south to St Kilda as a result of reading Martin and Macaulay were the Honourable Berkeley Paget and his tutor, the widely travelled naturalist and mineralogist Edward Daniel Clarke. They arrived there in 1797, when Paget – the sixth son of the Earl of Uxbridge and a future Member of Parliament and Lord of the Treasury – was seventeen years old, and Clarke – a future professor at Cambridge University – was twenty-eight.

In the words of Clarke's biographer William Otter, the teenaged Paget 'had finished his education at school, and had been admitted at Oxford: and, it having been thought advisable that the summer before his residence in College should be spent in travel, Mr Clarke was desired to undertake the tour of Scotland with him ...' Before they set off Edward Daniel Clarke wrote to his fellow naturalist Thomas Pennant, who had travelled around the Highlands and the Inner Hebrides in 1769 and 1772 and had published two books on the region. Pennant suggested that Clarke and Paget should explore the Outer Hebrides, which had 'escaped his own notice'. They travelled by land to Greenock, where Lord Uxbridge had ensured that a revenue cutter was placed at their disposal, and they set sail for the Western Isles.

In the early morning of 30 July 1797 Clarke was urged hastily from a bed in the Outer Hebridean island of Barra with the news that the wind was set fair for St Kilda. None of the revenue cutter's crew had ever been near those islands, so MacNeil of Barra and two of his men piloted them out of the sound and set the cutter on its course before the three Barraich turned back for home. Within an hour the lookout in the cutter's topmost crow's nest made sight of Hirta and Boreray, and in the early afternoon, with a mist descending, the islands were visible from the fo'c'sle. When they found themselves close to 'the immense rocks of the island, rising above our topmast' both crew and passengers were impressed and disturbed. With some difficulty Clarke persuaded the cutter's captain to order out a long boat with six oarsmen and Mr Ritchy, the first mate, to attempt to land himself and Berkeley Paget. Within the heaving bay 'Mr Ritchy shot a fulmar, the first we had seen, which fell into the sea, and created a partial calm all around him, by the quantity of oil he ejected from his mouth ...

'The magnificence of the stupendous cliffs about the island [Hirta] astonished every one. Mountains of rock lay one within the other, as if defending each other with a vast artificial wall.' They could see the 'smoking settlement' in Village Bay, and 'the natives in great confusion, some running towards the hills, others on the tops of their huts ...' When Clarke, Ritchy and the sailors waved in a friendly fashion the Hirtans ran to the shore and hauled them onto dry land.

They shook hands and Clarke handed out tobacco and snuff, and 'one of them, a good-looking young man, address[ed] me in broken English. He was pale, almost breathless with apprehension, asking repeatedly, "Whence come ye? What brought ye to our island?"'

Clarke replied that they were friendly English and Scottish

gentlemen, 'coming without any hostile intention merely to see their island'. At that their host relaxed.

'Oh, God bless you,' said the young man. 'Come! Come along! Will you eat? Will you drink? You shall have what you will of our island.'

Some older men asked him in Gaelic to inquire how their visitors knew of St Kilda. Clarke replied that they had read about the place in books.

'Books!' said the young man. 'What books? We have no books; is our island told in books?'

Clarke said that Martin Martin and Kenneth Macaulay had written about St Kilda.

'Oh, Macaulay! We know him very well – he came to see us,' said the young man, presumably after consulting with his elders, as Kenneth Macaulay had visited St Kilda forty years earlier. This young man would accompany Clarke throughout the whole of his visit. The biologist learned that his guide had been married for a little over a week, the steward's ship having departed with its booty only eight days before and 'they postpone their marriages until the arrival of the steward'. Clarke should have been there for the wedding, said the young man … 'you would have seen the whole island dancing, and the whole island drunk'.

'And what do you find to get drunk with here?'

'Whiskey! The steward always brings whiskey, and, when he comes, we dance and sing merrily.'

'And don't you dance through the rest of the year?'

'Not so much; when the steward comes, we dance all night, and make a fine noise altogether.'

That information led Edward Daniel Clarke to formulate a theory about *cnatan nan gall*, the St Kildan influenza that invariably arrived with the steward's boat. It was, he decided, little more than a prolonged hangover.

They walked from the shore towards the village and Clarke asked how his new friend had learned English. 'Our minister taught me,' he was told. 'Here he comes.'

The current pastor was Lachlan MacLeod, a man in his late thirties who was the son and grandson of former catechists on Hirta and who was probably the first and last St Kildan Protestant minister to have been born in Village Bay. The probability is increased by the fact that

– unusually in a representative of the Church of Scotland at that or any other time – Lachlan MacLeod shared his congregation's belief in the old Gaelic phenomenon of second sight. MacLeod was relatively uneducated – John Lane Buchanan described him as being illiterate. But he clearly knew the parish and its circumstances, he had a grounding in the gospel, and he was bilingual and therefore able to communicate both with the islanders and with the SSPCK in Edinburgh. In 1789 the SSPCK had accepted his hereditary appointment and agreed to pay his salary with almost audible sighs of relief and resignation. St Kilda was dirty work, but somebody had to do it.

Clarke noted that Lachlan MacLeod 'was only distinguished from the other natives by wearing a hat, instead of a bonnet, or cap of wool'. MacLeod explained that the St Kildans had initially feared that the visitors might be French or Spanish privateers. The steward had warned them of such raiders, he said, as a devious ploy to prevent his valuable tenants from venturing too far afield, 'but he need not fear this, for they are too much attached to the island to leave it'.

There followed some uncomfortable incidents. The women loudly objected to Lachlan MacLeod giving Clarke and Paget a tour of the interior of their homes. One of the landing party, possibly the trigger-happy first mate Ritchy, fired his gun at a gannet which was hovering over the clachan – 'a universal scream broke forth from all the women; the men all surrounded their minister; and a general alarm once more prevailed, which was not easily dispelled'.

They adjourned to the minister's house, 'which differed from the rest only in having two chairs, and a couple of bedsteads, and a bare earth floor, instead of a covering of peat-ashes and heath'. There Clarke and Paget were introduced to Lachlan MacLeod's wife, mother and three small children. They decided that everybody but Clarke would return to the revenue cutter, leaving him alone on Hirta for as long as the weather permitted.

The moment Paget, Ritchy and the six oarsmen had rowed away with Ritchy's gun, everything changed. '[T]he natives gathered round me in a crowd,' recorded Clarke in his journal, 'seeming highly delighted, that I remained among them alone, and with no other object but curiosity. I was now admitted freely into all their huts, and having distributed the remainder of my stock of tobacco, received a general welcome from them all …'

Edward Daniel Clarke was consequently able to make a detailed study of domestic life in Village Bay as the eighteenth century turned into the nineteenth, just 130 years before the evacuation.

There were, he assessed, 'about one hundred persons' living in twenty-two family groups, 'each family upon an average consisting of five or six persons'. The village itself was a higgledy-piggledy organic construction. 'I saw none of the causeways mentioned as forming what they term a street, between their huts. The huts are built without the least attention to regularity, not fronting each other, but standing in all directions. The passages between them were almost knee-deep in mud when we were there …'

The houses themselves were oblong, consisting of 3- or 4-foot high dry-stone walls and a roof thatch of straw tied down with rope made from marram grass. Inside they were full of peat smoke, which the St Kildans welcomed 'as it adds to the warmth of the hut, and long custom has rendered so unpleasant an atmosphere habitual, if not requisite'. Unlike the blackhouses in the other Hebrides, there was no central chimney hole in the roof. Ventilation was achieved through 'two small holes in the sides of their huts, opposite to each other, about seven inches in diameter, one of which is open and the other closed, as the wind happens to blow.' He discovered peat ash mixed with water on every floor, 'all of which is trodden together and pre-served for manure', but made no mention of any admixture of urine. Indeed, he suggested that the 'strong smell' of the ubiquitous fulmar oil was responsible for the impression given to strangers that the St Kildan people reeked.

Clarke crawled with a lamp into one of the sleeping cavities attached to the main room. It was 'a vault like an oven, arched with stone, and defended strongly from the inclemencies of the weather … in this, I was informed, four persons slept. There is not sufficient space in them for a tall man to sit upright'. Forty-four years later an early Victorian minister would tell another visitor that as the sleeping cavities were not big enough to accommodate every member of a large family, 'a peculiar and by no means praiseworthy practice prevailed, of the young people of different families being assembled in the evening, and all passing the night together in a separate building, adjoining but not identical with their parents' dwelling'. The same clergyman asserted that the pile of ash manure on the cottage floor grew so high by the end of winter that people could not stand upright and had to dive 'like rats or rabbits' over the pile of ordure and into the aperture of their sleeping chambers.

They ate two meals a day; their principal repast being at noon when they enjoyed a fulmar and laver (an edible seaweed) broth cooked in a pot over the central peat fire. And they seemed to be doing very well on it. 'I did not see a single instance of a St Kildian with bad teeth, and many of them had the most pearly whiteness, as even as possible. Their faces are somewhat pale, owing to continual residence in smoke, but their skins are fair and pure, and free from cutaneous eruption … They are generally short and stout made; I saw no tall persons on the island.'

He walked 'through the little cultivated patches of oats, barley and potatoes' to the foot of Ruaival, where the remains of St Brianan's, or St Brendan's, chapel could still be seen. It was 'a circular pile of stones, very little larger than one of their common huts. Among these they pointed out a broad stone, on which the saint used to read mass to their ancestors'. But the late eighteenth-century Protestant St Kildans 'had no tradition extant' of the saint or of his chapel.

Following an exhibition of rock climbing down the cliffs of Conachair – something which the St Kildans would quickly adopt as a proven tourist attraction – Clarke decided to spend the night in Village Bay. 'We now all adjourned to the little hut of the minister. The whole village was convened, and having stowed them as well as we could, the women on the floor round the wall, and the men standing behind, and those who could not get in, placed on the outside; some of the oldest and most respectable of the inhabitants, assisted by the minister as interpreter, thus opened the history of their grievances.'

Edward Clarke did not list those grievances in full. But he had read Macaulay, and he referred in his journal to the exploitation by MacLeod and his steward of what was a comparatively prosperous and productive little island. Their home-grown peat-ash manure, for instance, was 'not, as has been supposed, to cultivate lands for their own use; but to feed the rapacious avarice of distant taxmen, who have nothing more to do with the island, than to visit it once or twice a year to plunder the inhabitants of every thing they possess'.

The inhabitants could not eat as many seabirds' eggs as they would prefer, because MacLeod's steward had taken to demanding from them a huge quantity of feathers which he could then sell to the upholstery market on the mainland. Feathers came from live grown birds, and live grown birds came from undisturbed eggs. While he was in the hills above the village Clarke found it 'a melancholy spectacle to behold plenty of cows and sheep ... not one of which the natives are suffered to enjoy; although their island offers them pasture, and they are burdened with the care of them'.

That was not all strictly true. The Hirtans used some of their own crops, and therefore benefited from the manure which had fertilised it. It is doubtful that they suffered from an insufficiency of eggs, although they had traditionally eaten so many of them that a reduction in the ration could have been keenly felt. Some of the sheep and cattle on the hill were their own: the steward did not claim every beast.

But he claimed enough. Buchanan reported that the steward removed fifty bolls of barley and potatoes each year in the 1790s. Fifty bolls was the rough equivalent of 2,500 dry gallons, which was a lot of grain and root vegetables. They had also to relinquish, in the form of butter and cheese, all the milk produced in the five summer months between May Day and Michaelmas.

On top of that their new proprietor, Captain Alexander MacLeod of Harris, was eager to cash in on the growing national demand for feather beds. He built a stone featherstore beneath Oiseval at the north side of Village Bay and between 1793 and 1840 the St Kildan feather export trade grew from 20 to 240 stones a year. The trade went into slow decline as the Victorians developed cheaper and more convenient forms of upholstery, and by the end of the nineteenth century they were sold only on contract to the British Army for soldiers' pillows – 'Before being used they are thoroughly fumigated, but in about three years the smell returns to them so strongly that Tommy Atkins refuses to rest his sleeping head on them until they have been again roasted.'

But while the going was good, feathers weighing what feathers weigh, 240 stones of them represented an incalculably huge amount of labour. In 1847 the London retail price of feathers for bedding was between 1 shilling and 3 shillings a pound, dependent on quality. If St Kildan feathers were middle-of-the-range, during that decade the islanders sent off £350-worth of feathers each year. But the people of Village Bay, who risked their lives catching the birds, who then plucked, gathered and stored them, saw not a penny from the business.

They handed over every feather as part of an annual rental which was arbitrarily assessed and which effectively amounted to everything that they caught, grew, raised and produced over and above their basic diet. They ate seabirds and slept on straw, heather, dirt or stone.

The late eighteenth century and early nineteenth century were famously a time of clan dissolution. Hereditary chieftains, who were increasingly educated at southern public schools and universities, discovered the free market. That significant connection between Highland landholding and the new economics was nowhere better illustrated than in the 1760s when the young Sir James Macdonald of Sleat on Skye, High Chief of Clan Donald (and by that time a neighbour and colleague rather than bitter enemy of MacLeod of MacLeod in Dunvegan), who had been educated at Eton and Oxford, enjoyed a European Grand Tour in the company of his hired tutor, Adam Smith.

Often reluctantly, for despite the practical teachings of the Enlightenment their sentimental familial attachments were centuries old, if they could not make money from their estates they sold them to people who could, and then disappeared with the cash to Edinburgh, London or Australia. In many parts of the Highlands and Islands their day of reckoning was delayed by the kelp industry. The giant kelp sea plant grows lavishly around the northern shores of Scotland. Harvested and burned, its ashes produce a multi-functional substance named alginate. Among a dizzying array of other goods, alginate can be used in the manufacture of gunpowder. During the wars with revolutionary France between 1793 and 1815, and with the United States of America between 1812 and 1815, there was a high demand for home-grown alginate in Great Britain. That demand was fed by Highland landowners who put their tenants to work on the coastline and grew rich on the profits. Partly as a result of the alginate boom the population of the north-west Highlands and Islands reached its historical apex at the end of the first third of the nineteenth century. As the Pax Britannica dawned, however, and cheaper alginate became available from overseas, the people who had recently been so valuable to their overlords became quickly redundant. Huge numbers of them were subsequently removed from their ancestral homelands to make room for sheep ranches. The clan chiefs who had claimed ownership of those homelands were usually unwilling or incompetent to operate in the early nineteenth century cut-throat free market, and those who had not already abandoned their people and property quickly did so.

The alginate bubble did not affect the 100 people of St Kilda. Their shoreline was too precipitous to allow much harvesting of seaweed. The small quantity that they did gather was, as we have seen, burned and its salty ashes used as a food preservative. Even if they had produced surplus quantities of alginate it could not profitably have been transported for sale. And their islands were already sheep ranches, which required a year-round population of humans to sustain. They had always delivered a comfortable profit to their steward and laird. Their exploitation had been, and continued to be, of a feudal rather than industrial nature.

They noticed the advent of the new era chiefly through a revolving door of new proprietors and their agents. Hundreds of years of undisputed heritable suzerainty by the MacLeods of Harris and their superiors in Dunvegan was broken by a succession of men who could afford to buy St Kilda, and who hoped perhaps to recoup their investment. Alexander MacLeod was the first of these. A deep-sea captain from the island of Berneray in the Sound of Harris, Alexander returned home from the East Indies trade in his middle age as a prosperous man. In 1779 he bought Harris and its associated islands for £15,000. That was no mean sum and Captain Alexander MacLeod promptly invested in improvements across the estate. Elsewhere that chiefly meant encouraging fishing. In St Kilda it meant the feather trade, the featherstore and a slipway. In 1790 Captain Alexander died and his son Alexander Hume MacLeod, who was still amassing money in the Far East, inherited.

In 1804 Alexander Hume MacLeod sold the islands of St Kilda and Pabbay for £1,350 to Lieutenant-Colonel Donald MacLeod. The Lieutenant-Colonel was an exceptionally interesting proprietor. Although he too had made his fame and fortune in the Indian subcontinent, where he was a long-serving and distinguished officer in the East Indian Army, he had actually been born on St Kilda as the son of a missionary. He returned from active service to an Argyllshire estate and to his newly acquired Hebridean properties. One of Donald MacLeod's first actions was to dismiss the unpopular St Kildan steward William MacNeil from Rodel in Harris. MacNeil, who had by 1804 operated for many years more or less independently on behalf of a succession of absent employers, had long stood accused of being responsible for making the most excessive demands of the islanders, and of profiteering from the trade in feathers. The dismissal of MacNeil was in itself sufficient to establish Lieutenant-Colonel Donald MacLeod as a relatively popular proprietor of St Kilda.

Donald MacLeod died in 1813 and the islands of his birth were inherited by his twenty-one year-old son John MacPherson MacLeod. Young John was yet another Hebridean engaged in amassing a fortune from the East India Company. He also added the more promising Glendale estate in Skye to his portfolio. John MacPherson MacLeod first visited St Kilda as a twelve year-old in 1804, the year his father bought the islands, but did not return there until 1840, two years after his retirement from the East. He would nonetheless preside over an era of great change on Hirta until 1871, when he sold it back to the 25th MacLeod of MacLeod in Dunvegan for £3,000. After almost a century of merry-go-round in the marketplace, St Kilda was returned to its hereditary owners. The islands would remain in their hands until the last natives departed fifty-nine years later.

John MacPherson MacLeod was an absentee proprietor of two years' standing in 1815, when John MacCulloch's ship dropped anchor in Village Bay. John MacCulloch was born on Guernsey in the Channel Islands. His father's family came from Galloway, and after attending Edinburgh University he pursued an interest in geology which showed such promise that in 1811 he was commissioned by the Geological Society of London to study the stone and mineral history of Scotland.

He did much more than that. MacCulloch later embarked on a long tour of the Western Islands and not only reported on their geology but also delivered two highly opinionated books on their 'agriculture, scenery and antiquities'. His second volume of *A Description of the Western Islands of Scotland* included a report of his visit to St Kilda.

He and his escort of Argyll Highlanders were greeted by the whole population assembled on the beach and the minister's wife – the minister himself was not at home – calling out 'Friends or enemies?'.

It was not an unreasonable request. Piratical as well as peaceful vessels had anchored in Village Bay for centuries, and would continue to do so. As late as the year 1840 a brig with its crew 'armed to the teeth' skirted Hirta for ten days. When contact was made it was discovered that no English or Gaelic was spoken on board. Her captain was 'of swarthy complexion and foreign aspect'. He was not hostile – on the contrary, he treated the St Kildans to 'sundry foreign wines', which convinced them that the ship was merely a Spanish smuggler doing business on the north-west coast. But from the Middle Ages to the early twentieth century, they would not always be so lucky.

Most crucially in 1815 the people of Hirta had not yet been informed of the Battle of Waterloo, which had ended the Napoleonic Wars earlier that year, or of the Treaty of Ghent in December 1814 which brought a close to the contemporaneous British/American War. The latter was of greater concern to the St Kildans for two reasons. American privateers had run riot in the North Atlantic Ocean and 'their remote and defenceless island was subject to depredation from the ships of that enemy'. And the American war had forced up the price of tobacco, which delivered a serious blow to the average male St Kildan.

Having absorbed the comforting news that both conflicts had been resolved, the St Kildans proceeded to offer John MacCulloch and his party their usual unstinting welcome. MacCulloch noted that the church inside the graveyard outside the old clachan had fallen into such disrepair – it seemed to have all but disappeared – that the recently built featherstore had been adopted for religious services. The deserted church was the 'Christ Chappel, near the village' which had been noticed by Martin in 1697, 'covered and thatched after the same manner with their houses' inside the 'church-yard [which] is about an hundred paces in circumference, and is fenced in with a little stone wall, within which they bury their dead'. The old churchyard would continue to be used as a burial ground but would never again contain their place of worship. The 'debris' of Christ Chapel, which was also known as St Mary's, was still observable in the middle of the nineteenth century. But the new manse and church which was built twelve years after MacCulloch's visit, in 1827, was situated at the foot of Oiseval, around the north side of the bay 150 yards from the settlement. Those buildings, which would do active service for another century, were erected according to specifications presented by the civil engineer Robert Stevenson. (Stevenson was a grandfather of the writer Robert Louis Stevenson, a designer of lighthouses and, more pertinently, a member of the Society in Scotland for the Propagation of Christian Knowledge.)

MacCulloch also observed that in the temporary absence of her husband, Lachlan MacLeod, the minister's wife, Marion, was 'regent' of the island, which confirmed that since the more or less permanent establishment of a pastor in St Kilda the old position of a lay, native ground officer had been abandoned. The minister, or his wife, now spoke for the people.

He counted in that year of 1815 a total of a hundred and three people in twenty families, all living still in the 'little crowded cluster' of medieval houses in the clachan on the shore. He noted with surprise that 'each house has a door with a wooden lock and key, a luxury quite unknown in other parts of the Highlands'. He noted that the tradition of cultivating manure within the dwellings had ceased. The men, thought MacCulloch, were 'well looking and better dressed than their neighbours [in the other Outer Hebrides]'. The children were handsome, but the women 'like the generality of that sex in this country, are harsh in feature, and impressed with the marks of age in very early life'.

Since the sacking of William MacNeil, the steward's annual visit to collect homage and live large off the locals had also been suspended. The benevolent patronage firstly of Donald MacLeod and then of his son John MacPherson MacLeod had instead continued to provide the islanders with two boats, one of which was capable of sailing to the Western Isles, most usually to the familiar harbour at Obbe in Harris. This the St Kildans did 'once or twice in the year … to dispose of that part of their wool, feathers, and cheese, which is not required for payment of rent; purchasing with them such commodities as are wanted for the uses of their limited establishments'. The rent itself was £40 a year, which by 1815 MacCulloch thought to be all paid in feathers. At the same time as it yearned for more feather bedding the sophisticated outside world was losing its appetite for dried seafowl. The St Kildans must still have sold or given some of their immense haul of guga to their fellow Western Islanders, but they were left with increasing quantities to consume in their own cottages.

Their common arable land around the village was planted with what John MacCulloch judged to be the best barley in the Hebrides, with some of the worst oats and with fewer potatoes than were eaten elsewhere. He noted that the soil was excellent, especially in Gleann Mor, but the prevailing westerly wind which tore up that great, open valley limited its use to pasture for 'sheep and black cattle, very few horses being used: a few goats also wander about, kept chiefly for the purpose of milking'.

John MacCulloch thought the hundreds of astonishing cleits to be 'works of human art'. Those 'hemispherical or semi-ellipsoidal domes … appear to a stranger as inexplicable, as their numbers excite his surprise … It is in these that the peat, the hay, the corn, and even the winter stock of birds are lodged … these buildings speak much in praise of the industry and ingenuity of the natives …'

In terms of the old customs and superstitions, MacCulloch wrote with approval that they were dying as quickly in St Kilda as elsewhere in the Scottish *Gàidhealtachd*. Music seemed to have disappeared – he saw neither 'a bagpipe nor a violin in the island'. He thought, wrongly, that all Hebrideans including St Kildans had ceased to credit the claim to second sight. Apparently unaware of the smallpox epidemics of a century earlier (MacCulloch admitted to being ignorant of any reason why the population should have almost halved since the visit of Martin Martin) and the islands' subsequent repopulation from the other Hebrides, he wrote 'there appears no difference between the present inhabitants of St Kilda and those of the neighbouring islands. At the time that Martin wrote, the manners of the islands in general were far different from what they are at present. Had these people remained stationary while the others were advancing, there would indeed have been now an essential difference; but … they have sailed down the stream with their neighbours, the anchor alone remaining to indicate where they once lay.'

To a man like John MacCulloch, who had witnessed conditions in the rest of the West Highlands and Islands at that time, the 100 St Kildans were so fortunate, so favoured by the abundancies of their archipelago that it was little wonder that few of them wished to leave. 'The pampered native of St Kilda may with reason refuse to change his situation; finding his amusement where his chief occupation lies, in the pursuit of the sea fowl, that constitute at the same time his game, his luxury, and a considerable part of his wealth.'

MacCulloch's conclusions indicated the degree to which Martin Martin's assertions of a century earlier had taken root even in hard-headed men of the world. 'Free from the reputed evils of law, physic, politics, and taxes;' wrote MacCulloch in 1819, 'living under a patriarchal government, among a social circle of his relations; in a mild climate, without knowledge of a higher state of things; if he thinks not his island an Utopia, the pursuit of happiness is indeed a dream.'

There stood St Kilda in the second decade of the nineteenth century. Well fed and poorly housed. Both connected to and ignorant of the outside world. Still hunting birds, still practising transhumance, still building cleits, still grinding grain in querns, still the object of extraordinary speculation and fantasy. Still stable.

Change – unprecedented change – was about to occur.

SIX

From Thatch to Zinc

✻

S IR THOMAS DYKE ACLAND'S yacht was not the first aristocratic pleasure craft to drop anchor in Village Bay. But it left the
most substantial legacy.

Acland first visited St Kilda in 1812. He was twenty-five years old,
had been married for four years to Lydia Hoare and was about to
take an effectively hereditary seat in the House of Commons as the
Conservative member for Devonshire.

Thomas, Lydia and their infant son Thomas put ashore. Thomas
Senior made sketches of the hills and the huddle of houses and
declared himself to be 'shocked' by the islanders' poverty, before the
couple issued a promise to revisit the island and then returned to their
yacht. Acland's comments suggest an ignorance of the rest of north-
western Scotland, where early in the nineteenth century he would have
found poverty and living conditions to be as bad as or worse than in
Village Bay. But he did return.

Twenty-two years later, in 1834, Sir Thomas and Lady Lydia's new
ocean-going schooner put into Village Bay on her maiden voyage. The
vessel was named *The Lady of St Kilda*. It is unclear whether 'the lady'
was intended to be Lydia, the unfortunate Rachel Erskine or merely
the boat herself. Her name did however suggest a lifelong interest in
the islands from a man who apparently visited St Kilda only twice in
his long life. During a parliamentary career which spanned five decades
Acland did not once mention St Kilda in the House of Commons.

He nonetheless unwittingly sent its name to the other end of the
earth. In 1840 Acland sold *The Lady of St Kilda* and her new owner

sailed her to Australia. She docked in a quiet bay outside Melbourne and stayed there for so long that the immediate foreshore became associated with the schooner and was named St Kilda. To complicate matters further, one of the earliest thoroughfares in St Kilda was named Acland Street after the boat's first owner. And twenty years later a Melbourne property developer transferred the name St Kilda to a suburb of Dunedin in New Zealand. Some St Kildans did later emigrate to the Antipodes, but they transplanted not a single one of the archipelago's names. The St Kildas in Australia and New Zealand all derive, however indirectly, from Sir Thomas Acland's boat.

Back in 1834 Sir Thomas and Lady Lydia once again set foot on Hirta. They found the village quite unchanged, and this time Sir Thomas felt obliged to do something. The minister of the day, Reverend Neil MacKenzie, recorded that 'Sir Thomas and his lady, willing to confer a more lasting favour on the inhabitants of this island, or rather his benevolent mind being excited by their miserable homes, left me with 20 sovereigns, to help them build new houses ...'

The catch was that the new houses must be built 'within two years' or Reverend MacKenzie was to spend the 20 sovereigns on another useful purpose.

It was done. With the consent of John MacPherson MacLeod, who donated another £20, and his tacksman tenant, Donald MacDonald of North Uist, and with the active encouragement of Reverend Neil MacKenzie, the settlement in Village Bay was entirely rearranged. The traditional, semi-communal runrig land system was abandoned and each family was given a rectangular lot, or croft, which ran from the shore to the foot of Conachair. In 1836, two years after that first allocation, the Hirtans themselves redistributed their arable land into twenty new, more acceptable and consequently permanent crofts. A gargantuan stone dyke was built along the foothills from Oiseval to the burn called Abhainn Mhor, enclosing the cultivable land of Village Bay in a loud modern echo of the old wall at the head of Gleann Mor. As an incidence of this rearrangement the tacksman Donald MacDonald insisted that all the horses should be removed from St Kilda as they were 'destructive' to the new enclosed grazings.

A row of twenty-one sturdy new thatched blackhouses was erected – by men who were expert at building with stone – in the middle of the crofts, on the landward side of the old settlement, forming a graceful arc around Village Bay which echoed both the shoreline and the hollow of the hills. (It was during this process of rebuilding and relocation that the souterrain was properly uncovered, according to a local woman who was in her fifties at the time: 'When they were making a level space for the foundations, they discovered a house in the hillock, which was built of stone inside, and had holes in the wall ... which seems to have been the fairy's residence. There was another house of the same kind discovered a little afterwards above the burial-ground, and it is there yet; they found ashes and half-burnt brands in it.')

The donated money was spent chiefly on imported glass and wood for windows and roofbeams. In 1837 the Society in Scotland for the Propagation of Christian Knowledge gave Reverend MacKenzie £5, with which he bought in from Glasgow tables, chairs, bedsteads, kitchen dressers, stools and crockery.

The old clachan was not immediately emptied or dismantled. Most families moved into the new cottages but one or two old people remained for a short time in the houses which had provided shelter in Hirta for longer than anyone knew. But by the summer of 1841 nobody was left in the clachan in Village Bay, and just one roofless home was still standing on what was then allotted croftland. It fell apart, was ploughed over and planted upon, and was like all its former neighbours reduced to the faint outlines of its ancient walls. Sir Thomas Acland's 20 sovereigns were shared equally between the heads of each new household.

In August 1841 James Wilson witnessed the transformation. Wilson was a Paisley-born zoologist and Fellow of the Royal Society of Edinburgh. He spent much of 1841 navigating the coast of Scotland in the company of Sir Thomas Dick Lauder, the Secretary to the Board of the British White Herring Fishery. Like John MacCulloch before him, Wilson had a primary task to carry out – in his case to study the natural history of the herring – but also like MacCulloch, having washed up in so celebrated a place as St Kilda he found himself with much more to write about.

Wilson and Lauder were greeted by Reverend Neil MacKenzie, who showed them the new manse and church – a 'very respectable-looking slated house, of two storeys, with a little porch, and a longer and larger, but not much higher building (also slated) behind it and separated only by a narrow back court'. Inside the church they discovered the school. 'Near the pulpit there was a piece of railing, with a yard or two of desk-work … This portion seemed to be used as a writing school, and a copy-book which caught our eye had the words ST KILDA in large hand, repeated over and over again, very legibly upon its ample page. The good Minister is teacher and writing-master (literally prime minister), as well as priest …'

The men then walked up a footpath to the new crofting village. The houses were built looking at each other, with their gable ends facing the sea, sideways on to a rough main pathway 'sufficient for at least two people to walk abreast'. The cottages, 'or at least the front ones, form a pretty regular line, though some are placed farther back or behind the others, so, as in these parts, to make the line double … [They] have the appearance of being detached from each other, though sometimes two small dwellings join together … The door-way is very low, and the great thickness of these double walls produces a space as you enter, which may be called a passage. There are generally two rooms together, each apartment being covered by a separate roof, although there are smaller single tenements for widow women and old maids.' They were all thatched, with the bottom edge of thatch tucked inside the outer walls to stop the wind from taking purchase and lifting off the roof.

The goats of earlier years had been destroyed because they were prone to leap about the cliffs and disturb nesting birds. But 'more than enough of yelping curs were seen about the cottage doors,' wrote Wilson, 'lank long-limbed creatures of the terrier kind, with what seemed a dash of the shepherd's dog, and exhibiting something of a jackal aspect, though the tail was long. They are probably useful in cleaning garbage from around the houses …'

Wilson and Lauder visited a widow and her daughter in one house. Earlier that morning the older woman had been hunting puffins with her dog on the hill. She had already eaten some of the birds for break-fast and was boiling more for dinner – 'We saw their little fat bodies turning round and round in the pot …' There was a peat fire on the floor of each home, 'the smoke finding its devious way as it best can from the floor to a hole in the roof'. The two Lowlanders thought the furnishings 'scanty', but 'each house has one or more bedsteads, with a small supply of blankets, a little dresser, a seat or two with wooden legs, and a few kitchen articles; and almost every dwelling has also a small four-paned window ...' Wilson confirmed that manure was no longer cultivated indoors. Ashes were deposited in nearby cleits and other garbage was thrown into collective outdoor middens.

As well as the crofts, which were chiefly given over to barley, Wilson noted within the enclosure of Village Bay several small walled gardens containing cabbages and potatoes, and a little mustard in the vicinity of the manse, but noted that the salt spray distributed by the constant wind hindered the growth of almost all other vegetables.

While he was on Hirta a party of nineteen men and youths returned from a ten-day hunting trip to Boreray, Stac an Armin and Stac Lee. 'The large boat was half filled with huge bundles of feathers, and besides these there were a great number of smaller bundles of dark red rather repulsive-looking fleshy things, which we found to consist of the hind legs and backs of birds, chiefly young solans.' The boat also contained bags made from the stomachs of gannets which were filled with fulmar oil.

Although the St Kildan men 'were what we Southrons would call undersized, many of them were stout and active, and several of them handsome featured, with bright eyes, and an expression of great intelligence'. The 'noble countenance' of one man in particular reminded James Wilson of the famous actor John Kemble. He stood in the boat 'and with broad chest and brawny arms heaved on shore huge bundle after bundle of damp and weighty feathers, following each flight with keen observant eye ...'

Wilson was not the last visitor to see an idealised socialism in a small Hebridean community, and to wish for its adoption elsewhere:

Old age and sickness are of no disadvantage to the individual beyond the physical sufferings which they might entail, for his house, grazings, and fuel privileges belong to him as a member of the community, and the feathers are collected by the able-bodied, who also distribute a due proportion of the general stock of solan goose flesh, fulmars, and other delicacies, to the feeble and inefficient. Of course your widow woman and others who have no husbands to work for the general benefit, are expected when in health to do what they can to contribute in some small measure to their own support, by snaring puffins and other poultry at their convenience; but no one who is really unable to work need fear want, as he is sure of his share from the general stock. What a blessed change would it be for the poor of other places … if a similar system were pursued!

'From each according to his ability, to each according to his needs,' wrote Karl Marx in 1875, by which time James Wilson had been dead for two decades. In the meantime, Wilson's Hirtan Utopia continued to be compromised by external exploitation. As we have seen, the benevolent absentee owner John MacPherson MacLeod sub-let his island to the tacksman Donald MacDonald. Wilson was told that MacLeod 'obtains a very small rent from the tacksman, but that the latter gains a large proportional benefit from the people – in other words that any sacrifice which the owner inclines to make never reaches the natives, but is intercepted by the tenant, all of course in the fair way of business'.

That 'fair way of business' could be analysed. MacDonald took an annual rental of 240 stones of feathers from St Kilda. He valued the feathers at source at 5 shillings per stone, which gave him an in-kind notional income of £60 a year from the island. MacDonald then sold the feathers for 15 shillings per stone, which trebled his take to £180 a year. 'It would certainly be better,' wrote James Wilson, 'for these poor people to have no tacksman.'

Before very long, for better or worse, Wilson's best wishes came true. In 1842 Donald MacDonald of North Uist gave up the rented tack of St Kilda and John MacPherson MacLeod appointed the factor of his estate in north Skye, a man named Norman MacRaild, to handle directly his business in the islands. MacRaild was the son of a tenant farmer on the west side of Harris. A Gaelic speaker because of his Hebridean boyhood, his sympathies would nonetheless lie more with his own tacksman class than with the Skye and St Kildan crofters under his control.

Wilson and Lauder were treated to a spectacular example of cragsmanship. They took Reverend MacKenzie aboard their cutter for a cruise around the archipelago. The poor man fell upon the ship's victuals (curry soup and pancakes washed down with malt whisky) 'with an undisguised and almost youthful relish'. The minister then sent a note ashore to his wife, asking her to direct some of his congregation to Conachair cliffs while the Princess Royal sailed round Oiseval to the north of Hirta. The St Kildans who rowed over and collected the note asked some Gaelic-speaking members of the ship's crew whether they proposed to take Reverend MacKenzie to America. If so, they added cheerfully, given a bit of notice they also would come along.

The visitors reached the seaward foot of Conachair cliffs. They could see 1,400 feet above them men 'perched like jackdaws' on the summit. Reverend MacKenzie then stood on deck and waved his hat, and the acrobatic display began.

Suddenly we could hear in the air above us a faint huzzaing sound, and at the same instant three or four men, from different parts of the cliff, threw themselves into the air, and darted some distance downwards, just as spiders drop from the top of a wall. They then swung and capered along the face of the precipice, bounding off at intervals by striking their feet against it, and springing from side to side with as much fearless ease and agility as if they were so many school-boys exercising in a swing a few feet over a soft and balmy clover field.

Now they were probably not less than seven hundred feet above the sea, and the cliff was not only perfectly perpendicular in its upper portion, but as it descended it curved back as it were, forming a huge rugged hollow portion, eaten into by the angry lashing of the almost ceaseless waves. In this manner, shouting and dancing, they descended a long way towards us, though still suspended at a vast height in air ...

A great mass of the central portion of the precipice was smoother than the wall of a well-built house ... It was on this the smoother portion of the perpendicular mountain that one or two of the crags-men chiefly displayed their extraordinary powers, because, as there was nothing to interrupt either the rapid descent of the rope, or its lateral movement, or their own outward bounds, we could see them sometimes swinging to and fro after the manner of a pendulum, or dancing in the air with a convulsive motion of the legs and arms ... or tripping a more light fantastic toe by means of a rapid and vigorous action of the feet ...

But on either side, the precipice though equally steep was more rugged, and there we could perceive that the cragsmen, having each a rope securely looped beneath his arms, rested occasionally upon his toes, or even crawled with a spider-like motion along projecting ledges, and ever and anon we could see them waving a small white fluttering object, which we might have taken for a pocket-handkerchief, had we not been told it was a feathery fulmar. They twisted their necks, and then looped their heads into a little noose or bight of the rope above them, and by the time the men were drawn again to the top of the rock, each carried up a good bundle of birds along with him ...

How one man (for such is the case), himself standing with the points of his toes upon the very verge of a precipice, many hundreds of feet deep, can with such secure and unerring strength sustain the entire weight of another man bounding from point to point below him with irregular and frequent springs, is what a stranger cannot understand, and could scarcely credit without the 'ocular proof'.

Wilson learned that two ropes were used by each pair of men.

The rope which the upper man holds in his hands is fastened round the body and beneath the arms of him who descends, while another rope is pressed by the foot of the upper man, and is held in the hand of the lower ... it is said that scarcely more than one or two accidents have happened within the memory of the present generation ...

After thus showing off for a sufficient length of time, the rope dancers were hauled to the top, and made their way upwards almost as rapidly as they had descended. We could then also perceive more clearly the uses of the two ropes, for while the man above drew up one of them, hand over hand as sailors say ... the man below aided his own ascent by hauling also hand over hand upon the other, which was held by the tenacious foot of his assistant on the higher regions.

When James Wilson anchored in Village Bay in August 1841, nobody fled for the hills. He was not asked whether he was a friend or foe. Instead, as Wilson and Thomas Dick Lauder were rowed ashore, a few men watched them from the crofts and then approached the sea, showed them where to land, helped to hoist their lighter onto dry land and engaged in easy conversation with the cutter's Gaelic-speaking crew. The St Kildans were becoming accustomed to visitors. Fifty years after the arrival of the first aristocratic sightseers their age of tourism was underway.

It may have started properly seven years earlier, when the

ss *Glenalbyn* arrived in Village Bay in July 1834 with fifty or sixty well-heeled passengers from Lowland Scotland, England and continental Europe. The *Glenalbyn* did cause the St Kildans to run from their houses 'like a flock of bees ... to the steepest crags'. But that was because her captain, who had put into the bay at midnight, absurdly chose to announce his presence by firing two cannons at 4.00 a.m. When the people returned and met those early tourists on the shore their welcome was as hospitable as ever. The visitors gave tobacco to the men, sweets to the children and 'cotton handkerchiefs of gay patterns' to the women, and took away with them in return souvenirs such as brooches, cheese and even St Kildan dogs. When, upon his return to the mainland, a passenger published an account of his visit to Hirta in the *Scottish Guardian* magazine in Glasgow, it was headlined 'European Savages'.

That same visitor told Robert Carruthers of the *Inverness Courier* about the *Glenalbyn*'s trip. Carruthers reported that 'the party took leave of that simple-minded and warm-hearted little community, with feelings of deep interest and commiseration ... Yet they could not altogether suppress their fears, that if a visit to St Kilda should become a common occurrence in parties of pleasure, it might unfortunately happen, that the vices of civilised life would be imparted to them sooner than its virtues and its blessings.'

A St Kildan boy called Norman Gillies and a St Kildan girl named Ann MacQueen were nine and four years old respectively when the *Glenalbyn*'s passengers dispensed sweetmeats to the barefoot children of the clachan in Village Bay.

Seven years later, when James Wilson and Sir Thomas Dick Lauder landed in August 1841, Norman and Ann were sixteen and eleven years old. They were by then living in the new blackhouses at the head of the row of crofts. Norman Gillies lived with his father and mother, Finlay and Ann, and his younger siblings Betsy, Rebecca and Donald. Ann MacQueen lived three houses away with her father and mother, Finlay and Kirsty, her brothers Calum and John and her sister Rebecca.

Their schooling at the desks in the new church had been perfunctory. It certainly did not give them English; along with all of their neighbours and contemporaries they would remain monoglot Gaelic speakers. By 1841 the sixteen year-old Norman had all but grown into St Kildan manhood. He was possibly one of the nineteen men and youths whom Wilson observed returning from a fowling expedition to Boreray and the stacks. If not, that would very shortly become his lot.

At the age of eleven, Ann also was not far from adulthood. Her friend Norman's mother had given birth to him at the age of seventeen. Ann would have helped her own mother to look after the younger children. She would have gone hunting for puffins. She would have helped to cultivate the potatoes in the lazybeds on Dun. She would have collected peats and carried them back to the family's cleits.

They were not without friends of their own age. There were over two dozen children between the ages of five and sixteen in Village Bay in 1841, including the minister's offspring. They were the youngsters of whom John MacCulloch wrote 'as there is no want of food here as a cause ... the children of both sexes might even be considered handsome'.

They were also lucky to be alive. Infant, or neonatal, mortality – which is to say, the deaths of babies within roughly a month of their birth, not counting the stillborn – was viciously high in St Kilda. Between 1830 and 1839 the neonatal mortality rate in Village Bay was a terrible 57 per cent. In the next five decades it only once dropped below 50 per cent, reaching its apex in the 1860s when 69 per cent, more than two-thirds of all babies born to the small community, died within days of drawing their first breath.

That was appalling even by the standards of Victorian Britain's industrial slums, and it was therefore appalling to other Victorians. The highest average recorded level of neonatal deaths reached in England and Wales was 15 per cent in the late nineteenth century. In the 1870s, when only 50 per cent of children born in Hirta were still alive two weeks after their birth, in the Lowland Scottish industrial town of Kilmarnock 85 per cent of infants survived that period.

Even in the other Hebridean islands, where neonatal mortality was also higher than the mainland average but where there were often resident nurses or doctors, the figures were nowhere as depressing as in St Kilda. In Skye in the 1870s a third of all babies surrendered to infant mortality – twice as many as in Kilmarnock but half as many as in St Kilda. A mid-Victorian doctor contrasted 'the vital statistics of St Kilda with those of the Faroe Islands, in which the habits of life are, in many respects, very similar to those of the St Kildans.

From the conclusions ... it appears that notwithstanding their nauseous food and the open sewers in the immediate neighbourhood of their huts, the Danish islanders are the longest-lived community with which we are acquainted – their annual rate of mortality being only 12.5 in every thousand persons.

In St Kilda, on the other hand, the death-rate, during the ten years ending 1840, amounted to very nearly 61 in every thousand, or nearly twice as high as that of the most unhealthy of the manufacturing districts in England.

If the abnormal infantile mortality could only be checked, there seems to be no reason why the death-rate of St Kilda should not ultimately approximate to that of Faroe.

It was not a new phenomenon. In the middle of the eighteenth century Reverend Kenneth Macaulay, who as we have seen was a native of the Outer Hebridean island of Harris, was surprised to note that 'The St Kilda infants are peculiarly subject to an extraordinary kind of sickness; on the fourth, fifth or sixth night after their birth, many of them give up suckling; on the seventh day their gums are so clenched together that it is impossible to get anything down their throats; soon after this symptom appears, they are seized with convulsive fits, and after struggling against excessive torments, till their little strength is exhausted die generally on the eighth day. I have seen two of them expire after such agonies.' The fact that another Hebridean was persuaded to dwell at such length on St Kildan neonatal mortality suggests that even in the eighteenth century its frequency, its characteristics or both were highly unusual.

This apparently unique 'eight-day sickness', which claimed over half of the island's offspring and clearly restricted the growth, or revival, of its population, attracted the attention of different authorities. A Manchester physician named John Morgan visited St Kilda in 1860 and reported that 'At the time of birth, there was no appreciable physical inferiority on the part of those infants who were so prematurely and suddenly selected as a prey. They were all proper bairns, and so continued till about the fifth or sixth day. The mother's eye might then not infrequently observe on the part of her child a strange indisposition to take the breast.' That failure to take the breast was recognised as an invariably fatal sign. Between 30 and 70 hours later the infant was dead.

Five years later, in 1865, the deputy commissioner for lunacy in

Scotland, Arthur Mitchell, having discovered nothing untoward about the mental health of St Kilda's citizens, turned his forensic attention to the eight-day sickness. He wrote:

> Out of 125 children the offspring of the 14 married couples residing on the island in 1860, no less than 84 died within the first fourteen days of life, or, in other words, 67.2 per cent ...
>
> The pestilential lanes of our great cities present no picture so dark as this. It is doubtful if it is anywhere surpassed, unless in some of the foundling hospitals of the Continent ... One woman in St Kilda, at the age of thirty, has given birth to 8 children, of whom 2 live; while two others have borne 14 each, or 28 in all, of whom 24 are in their graves ...
>
> I made most carefull enquiry as to the mode of dressing the umbilical cord but I did not find anything so exceptional in this matter as to lead me to suppose that it was in any way connected with the disease.

He was wrong, but he was not alone in his fallacy.

In the 1870s the politician and journalist John Sands wrote that 'Doctors differ as to the cause: some say that it arises from the mothers living on sea-fowl; others to weakening of the blood from long continued intermarriage; some that an operation necessary at birth is not properly performed; others that the infant is smothered with peat-smoke; whilst some aver that the child is killed by improper feeding; and I am now inclined to believe that the last is the true reason. Comparatively few of the children born on the rock survive for more than a few days; they are seized with convulsions and lockjaw, and soon become exhausted.'

Lockjaw or 'trismus' were early terms for what would soon be known as the first signs of tetanus infection. By the early 1890s the tetanus toxin had been isolated and an antitoxin, or prophylaxis for immunisation, was developed. Trained nurses were by then resident on the island and between them they administered the prophylaxis, cleaned up midwifery practices with particular attention to the umbilical cord, and the number of infant mortalities on the island plummeted. (It remained common elsewhere. In the twenty-first century tetanus caused by infection of the unhealed umbilical stump is responsible for 14 per cent of neonatal deaths in developing countries.)

In the last thirty years of human settlement in St Kilda, between 1900 and 1930, just three children died within twenty-eight days of their birth. In the previous century there had been well over 200 such neonatal fatalities in a community which rarely numbered more than 100 people. The schoolteacher George Murray reflected in 1886: 'On looking through the churchyard, I felt sad at the sight of so many infant graves. One man, not yet fifty years old, I should say, pointed to the place to me where he buried nine children. He is left with four of a family. Another buried no less than a dozen infants and is left with two now grown up.'

The cause of all that suffering, of all that heartache and of irreparable damage to an increasingly fragile society, considered the Australian authority Peter Stride in 2008, was probably 'the knife used to sever the umbilical cord':

> The sterility of the instrument used to cut the cord is now recognised by many authorities worldwide as the most important factor in the prevention of neonatal tetanus. Many cultures throughout the world have for generations sterilised blades by passage through a flame before severing the cord to prevent infection. Any knife used for other purposes on St Kilda would inevitably have been contaminated with tetanus spores. Alternative possibilities are the unclean 'swaddling' clothing used in the first week of life, and the cord ligature ... We do not know what ligature was used for the cord stump. The St Kildans used horsehair to make ropes. If this was also used for ligating the cord, it could have been responsible for causing neonatal tetanus.

Peter Stride was undoubtedly accurate. It is also likely that tetanus was rife in the earth of Village Bay, where it survived as free-living, anaerobic soil bacteria. Cleaning the knife was a way of ensuring that tetanus was not transmitted to mother and baby, but it would not eradicate the bacteria.

At a time when infection was thought to be carried in the air and transmitted environmentally, nobody thought to look at the midwife's knife, let alone at the soil on their floors. The horror of the result was not only that most babies died, but also that their parents did not expect them to live. They rarely christened a child or made it clothes until they were sure that it might survive for long enough to suckle.

'The little creature is wrapped up in cloths of coarse home-made flannel,' wrote one journalist, 'and compelled to prove, so to speak, its right to wear the clothing of a decent Christian baby before a single stitch is sewed.'

They took some strength from their faith. With a belief that would be cruelly misinterpreted as indifference by visitors from outside, the St Kildans told themselves that if the Lord required their infants at His side, His will was paramount. 'If it's God's will that babies should die,' one St Kildan man was recorded as saying, 'nothing you can do will save them.'

The disastrous effect on the population of the island can be assessed. The psychological effect was incalculable. Remote islanders who had rarely been given reason to feel confident of their future were obliged to watch, month after unrelenting month, their human succession literally dying before their eyes.

Those who survived 'usually turn out healthy and vigorous'. There are sketches of the mid nineteenth-century St Kildan children, tow-haired and bright-eyed, clothed in miniature versions of their parents' long skirts and ganseys, draped around each other with easy familiarity.

Their young lives were occasionally fired with drama. In the early 1830s, some shipwrecked English sailors whose ship had gone down off Rockall were marooned in their flitboat at the foot of uninhabited Gleann Mor. After a couple of days a herdsboy discovered them and raised the alarm. The eighteen Englishmen, as incomprehensible to the St Kildans as any Spaniard, were taken to Village Bay where 'it was discovered that one of the poor fellows had broken his leg, and was in great pain. He was carried, as gently as possible, to the nearest hut and lowered into one of the odious wall-beds. The poor sailor afterwards told the minister that he thought the savages were lowering him into a well! Fortunately, Mr McKenzie was able to set the broken limb, having previously had a good deal of experience in surgical cases, connected with accidents in fowling expeditions.'

Many years later Ann MacQueen's oldest brother Calum would relate his memories of growing up in St Kilda. Calum MacQueen had been born in 1828. He was two years older than Ann and three years younger than Norman Gillies. He recalled that while he was one of four surviving children, four others had died in infancy. All of Calum and Ann's ancestors were descendants of the post-1727 immigrations.

His paternal great-grandfather Finlay MacQueen 'was not a native of the island. I think he came from Uist but I am not sure.' His maternal great-grandfather was the Berneray boatman Finlay Ferguson who a century earlier had fallen in love with a young woman called MacDonald while transporting immigrants to Village Bay, married her and settled in Hirta.

When Calum was born 'the houses were grouped together but when I was eight or ten [in fact when he was six or eight years old] surveyors cut the place up in lots and lots were cast and each man had to go to his own lot and new houses were put up … each man cultivated eight or 10 acres.'

Calum MacQueen remembered the excellent quality of St Kildan cheese. He remembered the tradition of each family killing a sheep for New Year's Day. He remembered spending more than five years being schooled in the 1830s, firstly by a teacher and then by the minister, in Gaelic and English, but 'we had no introductory books and didn't make much progress'. He remembered so much snow in the winter that 'I have seen drifts 40 feet deep', and so much shelter from the heights around the sun-trap of Village Bay 'that in summer it was very hot'. In those summer months almost everyone went barefoot 'except on Sundays or when visitors were about'.

Most of his young life, and the lives of his sister Ann and his neighbour Norman, was spent outdoors.

> It was very hard to tell exactly how many sheep etc we had as all were mixed together – each had his own earmark and the factor had to take the word of each man. It was thus easy for the crofters to cheat but I never knew of this being done … In the shearing the wool was not cut off but pulled. It usually lifted off like a blanket. The people paid £5 per annum for the grass on Boreray about eight miles away. Previous to my time vessels used to come and steal the sheep. The people at that time were very suspicious of strange vessels and used to retire and hide in inaccessible spots.

The potato blight struck in the late 1840s, when Norman and Ann and Calum were teenagers. Elsewhere in the Highlands and Islands, where potatoes were a staple of the diet, that epidemic caused famine and widespread emigration. In lucky St Kilda before the blight 'we had more potatoes than we could use and used to feed them to the cows'. After the blight the cattle were fed a more routine diet, but the people did not go hungry. There were still enough potatoes in the lazybeds for their personal consumption.

Calum MacQueen also told a story about Reverend Neil MacKenzie calling on an old woman to ask why she had missed a Church service. The minister was told that she had stayed at home to keep the crows from pecking holes in her thatch.

'Why did you not ask God to keep them away?' he said.

'But I knew he would not,' she said.

'How is that?'

'Because before I asked him and he would not.'

Such excuses would not always be acceptable – or become the subject of fond anecdotes – in St Kilda. As the teenagers Calum and Ann MacQueen and Norman Gillies were fully aware, early in the 1840s a powerful religious revival swept Village Bay. The Church of Scotland minister Neil MacKenzie observed it with some mystification, reporting to the Society in Scotland for the Propagation of Christian Knowledge that he was unable properly to preach as 'the whole congregation became so agitated that they could not contain themselves, some cried with vehement energy, some fainted, others sobbed, and the children participated in the distress of their parents'.

The young Calum MacQueen observed that at the height of the revival 'the people did very little work for two years'. 'Very little work' in St Kilda was a relative concept: there were church meetings in the evening of every weekday other than Saturday and Monday, and services occupied almost all of Sunday, but 'during the week the men were usually away in boats at one or another of the islands around, looking after sheep or occasionally fishing.'

As much as anything else, that revival indicated St Kilda's increased connections with the rest of northern Scotland, for the same revival was afoot in almost every Protestant parish in the Highlands and Islands. It had enormous repercussions. It meant that following the Disruption of 1843, when 474 of 1,200 Church of Scotland ministers left on grounds of congregational democracy and spiritual independence to create the Free Church of Scotland, most of the Protestant Highlands and Islands left with them.

The majority of the people of little St Kilda also came out for the inspirational, evangelical Free Church. In 1844 Reverend Neil MacKenzie departed for an established Church of Scotland parish on the mainland. The proprietor, John MacPherson MacLeod, who was also an established Church man, was therefore left with a problem. In the Church of Scotland tradition it was his right and responsibility to appoint a new minister. But the Free Church of Scotland repudiated that dictum and insisted that each congregation should be permitted to 'call' a minister of its own choosing. John MacPherson MacLeod could hardly impose a minister who most of them would repudiate upon the people of St Kilda. But the Free Church, which was their preference, had no access to the church and manse and glebe and other associated Kirk properties on Hirta.

John MacPherson MacLeod's factor Norman MacRaild attempted to bully the St Kildans back into the established Church with threats of eviction, but his employer told MacRaild to desist. Established Church of Scotland schoolteachers and missionaries who were sent to replace MacKenzie were effectively boycotted and quickly went home again. At first the Free Church islanders worshipped in one of the larger houses. 'We were there for nearly six months,' said Calum MacQueen, 'and all the people except fifteen or sixteen came there. Among those [still] going to the church were nine who got benefit from the minister's glebe ...'

For nine years after MacKenzie's departure, St Kilda was without a resident minister or catechist. When Norman Gillies and Ann MacQueen were married on Tuesday, 10 July 1849, the service was conducted, not in the church but probably in a family home on Main Street, by Reverend Angus MacGillivray, a Free Church of Scotland minister who had journeyed from his charge in the village of Dairsie in faraway Fife. MacGillivray – a native Gaelic speaker who had been born at Farr in Sutherland – was visiting St Kilda as part of a Free Church delegation which also held communion in Village Bay.

Norman was twenty-four and Ann was eighteen years old. Following their wedding in 1849 they moved into a thatched stone cottage adjacent to that of Norman's parents in the middle of the village. Their first child to survive the curse of neonatal fatality, a girl whom they christened Christian, would not be born until six years later, in 1855.

In the spring of 1851 Norman and Ann Gillies and their neighbours in Village Bay encountered the factor Norman MacRaild in unusual circumstances. In belated acknowledgement of St Kilda's position as part of the United Kingdom, MacRaild was deputed to enumerate its inhabitants in the national census. The full census had been conducted every ten years since 1801 in England and Wales, since 1821 in Ireland and since 1841 in Scotland. St Kilda's absence from the national register was a small anomaly. It was explicable on the grounds that steamships did not begin to visit the Outer Hebrides until the 1840s, and the journey by sail was too arduous and risky to be justified by such a small population. But it was also an implicit acknowledgement of the mystique of St Kilda as a place apart, a civilisation lost in the mists of the northern ocean a short day's sail from Atlantis.

MacRaild had an easy job. He walked the familiar length of Main Street, calling in at thirty-one adjacent cottages. He counted and recorded on his printed forms a total of 110 people, all but one of whom had been born on St Kilda. The exception was thirty-five year-old Betsy MacDonald from Lochinver in Sutherland, who had arrived as Elizabeth Scott in Hirta some twenty years earlier to keep house for Reverend Neil MacKenzie, and had shortly afterwards married the St Kildan Calum MacDonald. Betsy had some conversational English, which made her for many years a point of contact between visitors and her neighbours. She was also a stark embodiment of St Kilda's disproportionate incidence of infant mortality. By the time she was forty-two years old, Betsy MacDonald had been pregnant fourteen times. Betsy was the mother most often mentioned in case studies of neonatal mortality in Village Bay. Five of her children were stillborn, seven died 'in eight or nine days', and only two survived.

The oldest inhabitant recorded in the 1851 census was the seventy-nine year-old widow ('former birdcatcher's wife') Marion MacCrimmon, who was in receipt of alms and lived alone in a small cottage appended to the larger MacCrimmon family home towards the southern end of the row. The youngest was the three-month-old daughter of another MacCrimmon family which lived in the middle of the street. The manse was still unoccupied; there was no resident minister and therefore no minister's family; there was also no school-teacher. Not a single child was registered as a 'scholar'.

Almost every man and teenaged boy on the island registered his 'Rank, Profession, or Occupation' as 'birdcatcher' and 'farmer' – or in the case of the single male over seventy years old, Roderick Gillies, as 'formerly farmer and birdcatcher'. Most of their spouses were listed as 'farmer and birdcatcher's wife'. Young girls were usually 'employed at home'; young boys were sheep and cattle herders until the age of fifteen, when they became 'employed in the general service of the island – farming and birdcatching'.

Norman Gillies, who was then twenty-six years old, identified himself as the farmer of three acres of land as well as being, of course, a birdcatcher. His three acres were the croft of his father-in-law Finlay MacQueen, which was for the moment shared by the two men. Within eighteen months, Norman and Ann would have the croft to themselves. The short-term benefits of that inheritance were obvious and welcome. The reasons for the inheritance were deeply disturbing.

SEVEN

The First Exodus

✳

I T TOOK A FURTHER eighty years to prove fatal, but the mortal blow was landed on the Gaelic population of St Kilda in 1852, just twelve months after the island's first census enumeration. In that year thirty-six islanders – a full third of the population – left for Australia. The remainder, hunted and harried as they were by extreme levels of neonatal mortality, would never properly recover.

The emigrants' reasons were manifold. In the first half of the nineteenth century, thousands of other Highlanders and Hebrideans set sail for the Antipodes, most of them unwillingly but some in the voluntary search for a new and better life. St Kildans were not immune to those powerful social currents. Their call to the crew of James Wilson's ship in 1841 – that if Reverend MacKenzie was being transported to America, they would join him – was only half in jest. Other Highland communities had transplanted themselves, complete with their minister, in the New World and later in Australasia.

Victorian attitudes towards the St Kildans, of which they were aware, were mixed. While some, such as the increasing number of tourists, regarded them as a precious survival from a more innocent age, others, particularly in Scotland, saw them as an anachronistic embarrassment. 'We think the cause of humanity would be served,' said the *Glasgow Herald* in 1852, 'if [emigration] were continued until all the inhabitants were removed from this barren rock.'

The confessional schism of the previous decade also played a large part in encouraging the 1852 emigration. Calum MacQueen remembered the factor's unsavoury tactics. Norman MacRaild had arrived in

St Kilda after the Disruption of 1843, and 'He was vexed at the state of matters. He threatened to evict any who refused to go [back to the established Church of Scotland].'

It was broadly understood in Village Bay that MacRaild had 'overstepped his powers' and that the proprietor John MacPherson MacLeod would tolerate no evictions. But the threats caused unease. Elsewhere in the west Highlands and Islands adherents of the new Free Church were persecuted by factors and landlords who did not share their revived faith. Calum MacQueen recalled a family man in his thirties called Finlay Gillies, who had been one of the first to join the Free Church in St Kilda, as being especially concerned. 'He reckoned the people had made a mistake in coming out [for the Free Church]. "If it were not for that we would have been on our land from eternity to eternity," [said Finlay Gillies] ... Some folk had told him we were all to be put off the land and sent away.'

The struggle between the established and Free Churches for the souls of the people of Hirta would last for ten years. It was not resolved until 1853, when a Free Church catechist, a fifty-nine year-old Argyllshire man named Duncan Kennedy, was permitted by John MacPherson MacLeod to serve St Kilda and make use of the church, manse and glebe in Village Bay. Until then this deeply religious community was deprived of its central figure: a resident minister. As the minister was almost invariably educated, literate and English-speaking, during that decade, as the 1851 census indicated, a generation of St Kildan children also grew up without any schooling. The new Free Church catechist was therefore warmly welcomed. But by the time Duncan Kennedy moved into the manse at the northern side of Village Bay, a third of the previous year's population was in Australia – or had died in passage.

They included Ann Gillies's family. Her brother Calum MacQueen, who was then twenty-five years old and unmarried, left with their father, mother, younger brother and two younger sisters. Their travelling companions included seven other married couples and their children and older relatives.

The thirty-six emigrants left St Kilda in the late summer of 1852. They sailed first to Harris and then to Skye, where they waited for a steamer to Glasgow. In Glasgow they were sought out by their concerned proprietor, John MacPherson MacLeod, who travelled with them to Liverpool, all the time urging them to return to St Kilda. MacLeod offered to charter a steamer to take them home, and then to 'give them all they needed for two years'.

The St Kildans refused. They had already cut the umbilical cord. 'We told him,' said Calum MacQueen, 'probably the rest of the inhabitants would come away shortly.'

Doubly alarmed, MacLeod 'asked what he had better do to retain them'.

He was told that 'the people were not pleased' with continuing established Church interference while they themselves 'belonged to the Free Church. We suggested that the manse and church be given to the people'.

John MacPherson MacLeod said that he would see what he could do about that, and relinquished any hope of sending his thirty-six dissenters back to St Kilda. He even paid the fare to Australia of those who were hard-pressed.

They sailed from Liverpool in October 1852 aboard the barque *Priscilla*. Their voyage to the other end of the Earth took over three months, and it was a nightmare. An outbreak of measles killed eighty of the *Priscilla*'s passengers, including no fewer than sixteen of the thirty-six St Kildans. Calum and Ann's nineteen year-old sister Rachel died. An entire MacCrimmon family, husband and wife Donald and Ann and their children Donald, Marion, Margaret and Christina, all succumbed. Another family of MacQueens lost both parents and its two youngest children, leaving four others between the ages of eleven and eighteen orphaned upon their arrival in Melbourne's Port Phillip Bay in January 1853.

They were herded into a quarantine station, where further infections spread in the middle of the Australian summer and more people died. When the survivors were finally allowed ashore, weak and traumatised, the Australian authorities were dismayed to discover that they spoke little or no English. 'We could turn you out tomorrow if we liked,' said one official to Calum MacQueen. The irony was not lost on the man who was attempting to escape from feudal St Kilda. 'Thus,' he reflected, 'the tables were turned.'

They found work – any work, splitting logs, making bricks – and saved money, and built weatherboard cabins, and learned English, and bought land, and eventually were absorbed into colonial Australian society. Many months later news of their catastrophic voyage arrived back in St Kilda, where as a result of their relatives' departure Neil and Ann Gillies had the three-acre croft to themselves. There would be no further mass emigrations, but the damage was done. Unlike the aftermath of the smallpox epidemic 130 years earlier, St Kilda would not be repopulated from elsewhere following the 1852 depopulation. Times had changed. In the middle of the nineteenth century it was the view of both landowners and government that Hebridean islands were overpopulated. Most public opinion and most policymakers agreed that the kindest solution to the 'Highland problem' was to educate Scottish Gaels out of their old ways and their old language and offer them entry to modern society. If forced removal from their lonely glens and archipelagos was unpalatable, then controlled decline should be accommodated. Actually increasing the population of any Highland parish, let alone one so distant and worrisome as St Kilda, was beyond consideration.

The seventy or eighty remaining St Kildans absorbed the news of their tragic losses on faraway oceans and returned to their lives. The peats were cut, the animals summered over in Gleann Mor, the crops were sown and harvested and the remaining men and youths scaled the cliffs and stacks for seabirds, feathers, eggs and oil.

In 1855, as we have seen, Ann Gillies gave birth to Christian, her first surviving child. The baby girl was followed a year later by young Finlay. Norman and Ann finally had a family of their own to raise. The Free Church catechist Duncan Kennedy had re-established a school on Hirta in which he taught some adults as well as children. In 1856 it was reported to have thirty-five attendees of all ages, 'of whom twelve were able to read English at different levels though they had only very limited reading resources, letters of the alphabet and old reports being used for want of more suitable school books ... fourteen of them were "very fair" writers.' By the time of the 1861 census ten St Kildan children between the ages of four and thirteen years were recorded as full-time 'scholars'. The ten included young Christian and Finlay Gillies.

In 1860 another infant girl survived to Ann and Norman Gillies. They christened her, uniquely to St Kilda or anywhere else, Mary Jemima Otter Gillies.

Mrs Jemima Otter was the wife of Captain Henry Otter. Henry

Charles Otter was a career Royal Navy seaman from Derbyshire who spent much of the middle of the nineteenth century, in his own middle age, surveying the waters off the west coast of Scotland, latterly as captain of the paddle steamer HMS *Porcupine*. That was how he became familiar with, and concerned about, St Kilda.

In the course of his official duties Captain Otter would note that the best place to anchor was in the middle of Village Bay,

> ... with the narrow sound of the Dune open in ten or eleven fathoms, with a sandy bottom and good holding-ground. Great care must be taken to keep the anchor clear, as, except in southerly winds, terrible squalls veer all round the compass, and frequently, in northerly winds, a vessel will be lying with her head out. It is scarcely necessary to warn the careful seaman to leave this exposed position the moment the wind comes to the south ... it is high water, full and change, at 5h. 30m. The ebb sets S.W. by W., and the flood in the opposite direction; near the islands, and especially at Point of Dune, it runs at the rate of three miles an hour.

Such excellent surveys were not, of course, sufficient to win Captain Otter the honour of having a St Kildan child named for his wife. He also visited frequently on unofficial business. On one occasion Norman MacRaild's boat was wrecked in Village Bay during the factor's annual visit from Skye, and Captain Otter's *Porcupine* was despatched to rescue MacRaild and his crew who had been 'imprisoned to all appearance for the winter'. Another time Otter took 16 hundredweight of fish from the St Kildans, sold them for £16 and handed all the proceeds over to the islanders. He was 'one of the best of men', a teetotaller and a Christian who 'labours to disseminate religious principles and feelings among his crew, and, morning and evening, all hands are piped to prayer'. He happily conveyed Free Church missionaries and ministers to conduct communion in Hirta.

Otter became deeply concerned by the absence of a good jetty in Village Bay, and by the consequent aggravation of St Kilda's isolation. Following consultation with the proprietor John MacPherson MacLeod he engaged a mason from Nairn on the eastern mainland to build a landing place 'at the north edge of the nearly vertical rock below the manse. The large boulders when blasted were cleared away to some distance, and a small breast-work erected; but, in the course of two years, the drawback of the winter swells rolled back the stones and destroyed it. It appears that the Captain intended to have cleared away the rock, and then to have made a cutting of about 40 or 50 yards into the bank to the right of the minister's house, with the view of letting the sea run in at high water.'

Becoming, in the words of Michael Robson, 'for a few years … a link between material and spiritual branches' and the people of St Kilda, Henry Otter addressed many aspects of island life. One of them was, inevitably, the gross pandemic of the 'eight-day sickness', or neonatal mortality. It had been suggested that this might be aggravated by decades of intermarriage within the confined community. When the Scottish Lunacy Commissioner Dr Arthur Mitchell examined the troubling subject of 'consanguineous marriages' in St Kilda, Mitchell consulted Otter, who helped him to his conclusions that, 'In the case of not one of the fourteen married couples then in the island [in the early 1860s] was the relationship between husband and wife that of full cousins or cousins-german. Not less, however, than five of the fourteen couples were second cousins.' Of those five couples fifty-four children had been born, of whom thirty-seven died in early infancy, leaving seventeen alive. 'Of the seventeen survivors it is distinctly stated that not one is either insane, imbecile, idiotic, blind, deaf, cripple, deformed, or in any way defective in body or mind.' As Admiral Otter remarks, 'It is certainly strange that though they marry so much amongst themselves, there is only one – a spinster – who is weak in intellect.'

In July 1860 Captain Otter took the *Porcupine* into Village Bay with a small Free Church delegation and some representatives of the Highland and Agricultural Society of Scotland, including the president of the HASS, the Duke of Atholl, who satisfied a personal ambition to spend a night on a St Kildan cottage floor.

Otter had convinced himself that,

As to the mortality of the children, I believe the cause can be traced to the oily nature of their food, consisting chiefly of sea-birds, which build in incredible quantities on the different islands forming the group. The fulmar, which is found in no other place in the United Kingdom, is a peculiarly oleaginous bird, containing in its stomach a considerable amount of clear pinkish oil ... Though they have cows, potatoes, and meal, this is their chief article of food, and thus the system becomes so impregnated with fatty matter that it gives a peculiar odour to their persons, and the touch of their skin is like velvet. The startling mortality of the children before the ninth or tenth day (which has not been over-rated), is caused by the strength of the mother's milk while nursing ...

He was therefore delighted in that summer of 1860 to have the opportunity of a test-case. Henry Otter discovered upon landing that Ann Gillies was pregnant and nearing the end of her term. He also discovered that after eleven years of marriage Ann and Norman had only two surviving children. The Captain set to work: 'the mother was kept on cocoa, meat, and biscuit, and the child throve well.'

Having enjoyed an unusually comfortable late pregnancy, Ann Gillies herself clearly credited the good sailor with saving the young life of Mary Jemima Otter Gillies. She and her husband and their neighbours must also have allowed themselves to suspect that Henry Otter had discovered the cure for the holocaust of their newborn. They would realise within three years, in the worst of circumstances, that he had not.

In 1861 the census enumeration was carried out by the resident catechist Duncan Kennedy, who had been appointed registrar to the district of St Kilda in 1856. His successors in the manse would continue to hold that extra responsibility. The 1861 census recorded the grim effect on Hirta's population of the emigration to Australia nine years earlier and of continuing neonatal mortality. The number of inhabitants had fallen from a hundred and ten to seventy-eight people. Equally disturbingly, the average age in Village Bay had risen from twenty-five to thirty-one years.

It is difficult to estimate the minimum number of active men and women required to sustain a viable community on St Kilda. In 1861 there were still twenty-eight men and boys between the ages of fourteen and fifty-six who recorded their occupations as cragsmen, fowlers or cottars. The lexicographical change from 1851's 'farmer' to 1861's 'cottar' may have been due to the precision of Duncan Kennedy. Cottar was a more accurate term for the St Kildans, denoting as it did a peasant tenant smallholder with – at least in the Scottish Highlands and

Islands – no security of tenure. But the word negated the intimation of independence which was implicit in the term 'farmer'. In common with most other Hebrideans, until the middle of the nineteenth century St Kildans had regarded what they did with the land as farming. The introduction of uncertainty about both their function and their security was a recent phenomenon.

More crucially, the grown men still saw themselves as cragsmen first and foremost. Boys were mere fowlers until they won their spurs at the end of a rope, usually in their late teens. Climbing the stacks, belaying down the cliffs was a proud vocation in St Kilda even as it died out elsewhere in the British Isles. 'On conversing with them upon their intrepidity in scaling and exploring the stupendous cliffs in search of sea-fowl,' said John MacDiarmid in 1876, 'I could perceive that there exists among the men a great desire to excel as successful cragsmen. He is looked upon as the greatest hero who succeeds in capturing the largest number of birds at a time; and a young man was pointed out to me who, in a single night last year, bagged six hundred.' It was a vocation which narrowly escaped being outlawed in the 1860s.

The Sea Birds' Preservation Act of 1869 was a harbinger of things to come. It was the United Kingdom's first bird conservation legislation. The campaign which led to the Bill which led to the Act was a typical product of cross-party Victorian liberalism. Although almost nobody on the mainland of the British Isles any longer depended on seabirds for their livelihood, plenty of people still shot them for sport. Ornithologists and others had only recently been made aware of the extinction of the Great Auk, the 'garefowl' described by earlier writers. One of those birds, which turned out to be the last in the British Isles and one of the last in the world, had coincidentally been killed on Stac an Armin in the 1840s by a small party of men from Hirta who, when confronted later with the enormity of their deed, implausibly claimed to have mistaken the large flightless bird, which their ancestors had known as the Garefowl and had hunted for centuries, for a witch.

The worries of naturalists about further extinctions were exacerbated by both the wanton destruction caused by seaside daytrippers with shotguns, and in some eyes the equally wanton fondness of women for wearing the feathers of wild birds in their hats. An Association for the Protection of Sea-Birds was formed, and in 1869 the Sea Birds' Preservation Bill was moved in the House of Commons by Sir Christopher Sykes, a Conservative MP from East Yorkshire who had become concerned about shooting parties diminishing the seagull population around Bridlington and Flamborough Head. (During twenty-four years in the House of Commons Sykes made just six speeches. As most of them were in relation to his Sea Birds' Preservation Bill he became known as the 'Gull's Friend'.)

Sykes's Bill offered protection to a large number of sea birds and their eggs during the breeding season, including those avians upon which St Kilda's economy depended – fulmar, puffins and the northern gannet. Had Sir Christopher Sykes succeeded in protecting fulmar, puffins and gannets from human predation within the whole of the British Isles, the descendants of the killers of the last Great Auk would quickly have followed it into oblivion.

His Sea Birds' Preservation Bill went smoothly through the House of Commons. During its hearing in the House of Lords the Duke of Northumberland popped up to point out that 'The adult bird is not an article of food except at St Kilda; and this being far removed from the mainland I am willing to exempt [those islands] from the operation of the Bill.'

The Duke of Richmond opposed the St Kilda exemption on the grounds, odd for a legislator, that the St Kildans would ignore any legal prohibition – 'as policemen are certainly unknown in that neighbourhood, the Bill would probably not, in any case, make much alteration in the habits of the people; but if there are to be any exceptions, there are probably several other places that had an equal title to be exempted'. The Duke of Argyll then rode to the rescue, asserting that 'there is a reason for treating St Kilda exceptionally. I doubt whether there is any other case where the people practically live on sea birds'.

The amendment exempting St Kildans from the Sea Birds' Preservation Act was duly agreed. In one of the strangest manifestations of British parliamentary democracy, a conclave of unelected dukes had defended the interests of the cragsmen and fowlers of Village Bay.

St Kilda's rapidly declining population brought the best out of its proprietor. By 1861 John MacPherson MacLeod had returned from the East Indies to the United Kingdom and had received a knighthood. His response to the emigrations and to their effect was commendable. Having ensured that the Free Church of Scotland was allowed to use the church, manse and glebe, he set about once again improving the housing in Village Bay.

MacLeod was as concerned as anybody else by infant mortality. That blight, which reached its peak in the 1860s, had prevented the island's population from increasing throughout the previous 100 years, and following the exodus to Australia it restricted any revival of the Village Bay community. The sheer number of neonatal fatalities had also a depressing effect on St Kildans. Men, and women in particular, did not expect their babies to survive. They were scarred by loss and calloused by tragedy. How could they be expected to invest faith in the future of their islands when they buried so many tiny manifestations of that future with such numbing regularity?

In the 1850s and 1860s John MacPherson MacLeod had no more idea than anybody else of what was causing the deaths. But the concept of hygiene was developing throughout the British Isles, and he was awkwardly aware that in many respects the row of stone croft cottages erected in the early 1830s was little better than the medieval clachan which had preceded it. To people such as St Kilda's increasing number of visitors from the south who had not seen the old clachan, and who were also often ignorant of the blackhouse building vernacular in the other Hebrides, the homes on Main Street looked like rural slums. They wondered aloud what manner of proprietor would maintain his tenants in such appalling conditions. The influential Captain Henry Otter admitted in 1860 that 'while the people are very cleanly in person and manners', their houses 'are worse than any I have seen in the Highlands ... the soot lies two or three inches deep on the rafters and everything [indoors] is impregnated with it, rendering it nearly impossible to discern any object in the dwelling'.

In 1860 John MacPherson MacLeod commissioned a new row of sixteen modern cottages to be built. They would stand between and before the thirty year-old stone thatched houses along a pedestrian thoroughfare which would become known as Main Street. It was both a statement of good intent and an extraordinary achievement. MacLeod was doubtless, as Michael Robson suggests, shamed into the development by such comments as those of Henry Otter and by the various funds and donations established by outside bodies to subsidise the St Kildans and assist them in such matters as building a good landing place and breakwater – a responsibility which would ordinarily have fallen upon the proprietor. He was also probably still disturbed by guilt about the 1852 migration. Those motives can only qualify, not reduce his accomplishment.

He imported masons from Skye to direct the building work. Between 1861 and 1862 they constructed the sixteen neat, spacious, rectangular cottages from blocks of worked stone (including one bearing that 'papist' cross from the remnants of a neighbouring chapel). The walls were mortared and rendered. They had a fireplace and a chimney in each gable, so that no more soot would coat the interiors. They had two main rooms, each with a glass paned window on either side of the central door, 'nine panes of glass in each ... good, well-fitting door, with lock. The interior of each house is divided into two apartments by a wooden partition, and in some a bed-closet is opposite the entrance-door.'

Every window commanded one of the most powerful views in Europe: of Dun and Oiseval and the expanse of Village Bay. They were roofed with sheets of zinc nailed onto wooden planks. Channels routed downhill from the wells and burns and covered with slabs of stone (one of which was inscribed with another medieval cross) ran between each house, allowing drinking and washing water to be scooped out upstream, and waste and sewage to be deposited downstream as the small canals ran on to irrigate the crofts. They were all immediately occupied, although for many years after 1862 a few individuals and families continued to occupy the neighbouring blackhouses. Some young couples used them as starter homes. Until her death in 1914 at the age of eighty-one years the unmarried Rachel MacCrimmon continued to live with her cats 'in an ancient straw-thatched hut' at the north end of Main Street. Rachel was an exception. Most of the blackhouses were maintained as byres and turned over to cattle.

To an outsider, St Kilda suddenly boasted the most up-to-date model crofting village in the west Highlands and Islands. Three decades after they were erected an Englishman noted:

> All the houses in St Kilda ... are substantial one-storey stone structures with zinc roofs securely fastened down by iron bands. They contain two rooms, each of which is lighted by a small four-pane window. Although they have fair-sized chimneys, some of which are even surmounted by earthenware pots, they are generally full of smoke for

ABOVE. Early 19th-century sketches of the old, crowded clachan in Village Bay, before it was dismantled and replaced by the row of crofthouses on Main Street.

LEFT. It is known that humans lived on Boreray, perhaps for lengthy periods of time. This is a Victorian imagination of Tigh an Stallair on the small island, as it might have been in domestic harmony, with Stac Lee looming like a shark in the background.

'Being lowered on a homemade rope down the dizzying cliffs of Conachair required a superhuman quantity of courage.'

'Mid 19th-century St Kildan children, tow-haired and bright-eyed' – but lucky to be alive.

Euphemia 'Effy' MacCrimmon: the last of the old St Kildan tradition-bearers, late in the 19th century.

Mother and child during St Kilda's short Indian summer. (National Trust for Scotland)

A group of St Kildans in 1884. The temporary schoolmaster Kenneth Campbell is on the extreme left of the party wearing a bowler hat.

Ann Ferguson, the media's 'Queen of St Kilda', on the eve of her intended marriage before a boatload of tourists.

Ann's betrothed, Iain 'Ban' Gillies, 'a very religious man from his youth up', before the show wedding was called off in 1890.

RIGHT. Forty years after the famous non-wedding, the widowed Ann Gillies awaits evacuation from Village Bay.

BELOW. The celebrated 'St Kilda Parliament', posed in suitable dignity with their notable dogs by Norman MacLeod for the professional agency of George Washington Wilson in 1885. (National Trust for Scotland)

A more relaxed, and more representational, photograph of the 'parliament' (and a new generation of St Kildan dogs) early in the 20th century. (National Trust for Scotland)

Finlay MacQueen (right) in intense discussion with the MacLeod Estate factor, John MacKenzie, in 1896. (National Trust for Scotland)

Neil Ferguson with a sack of feathers on his back – upholstery was for almost a century part of the St Kildan export economy. (National Trust for Scotland)

Tweed became another essential product. Here a group of late 19th-century women and girls display the wares for sale on Main Street. (National Trust for Scotland)

A medium-sized *cleit* while still in use. Note the small doorway, crude lock and absence of windows. (National Trust for Scotland)

ABOVE. The women span and the men wove their tweed. This is an outside demonstration of what most usually would have been an indoor activity. (National Trust for Scotland)

LEFT. The factor's house damaged by shellfire from the German *U-90* in 1918. The enemy vessel failed to hit its target: the radio masts.

BELOW. Number One Main Street: another casualty of the German submarine's bombardment.

The 25-pound gun which was emplaced beneath Oiseval following the attack, and which was never fired in anger.

To the end the old traditions were maintained by young and old: collecting seafowl from the cliffs beyond Village Bay. (National Trust for Scotland)

Boreray and Stac Lee seen from Conachair cliffs on Hirta.
(All colour photographs by Caroline MacKechnie)

The entrance to the souterrain Tigh an t-Slithiche in Village Bay.

The massive stone animal enclosures in the basin of An Lag on Hirta, between Conachair and Oiseval, and a short walk from the village.

'Every window commanded one of the most powerful views in Europe.' Dun as seen from an abandoned house in Main Street.

A medieval cross inscribed on a rock, deployed much later as a window frame at Number 16 Main Street.

Building without wood. The interior architecture of a cleit showing the sloping walls reaching up to stone crossbeams.

The cleits, croft walls and roofs of Village Bay, enclosed by a Cyclopean stone dyke running around the foothills of Conachair. The opening in the dyke was to allow for the entry and exit of grazing animals.

Old and even older: cleits within and without the great dyke, and the remaining foundations of an older house. The Soay sheep in picture were originally confined to that island as the proprietor's stock, but since the evacuation have run wild in Hirta.

Two hundred years of St Kilda tourism. A modern cruise ship anchors in the shelter of Dun in Village Bay.

some reason or other, which is, I think, to be sought in the peculiar conformation of the hills around them. They are far ahead in point of comfort and conveniences of nearly all the crofters' dwellings I have been into in Harris, Uist, and other Hebridean Isles. As the stranger walks along the path in front of the houses, he is struck by three things – the strong smell of fulmar oil, the plenitude of birds' wings and feathers on the midden heaps, and the numbers of birds' eggs that adorn nearly every window.

To an insider the houses were not so perfect. They were of course quite unusual to a conservative, traditional people. But they were also genuinely more difficult to heat than the small, huddled, thatched blackhouses with their filled layers of drystone double walling. They were draughty. The doors and windowframes leaked. The roofs of sheets of zinc were particularly ill-considered. They let in water and let out heat. They were not waterproof, soundproof or energy-efficient. Ten years after their construction the minister John MacKay told a visitor that 'it rained inside whenever it rained outside, the plates not being made to overlap sufficiently to produce perfect security'. The zinc sheeting was by every practical measure hugely inferior to a thatch (the zinc was replaced several decades later by tarred felt).

But the people adapted. If this was progress, if this was the industrial age, they would not be found wanting in ambition to join the rest of Britain. All but one or two of the old folk moved their few belongings into the new row, got on again with their lives and waited stoically for the future. In the short-term, that future was violently mixed.

Following the visit of its representatives in 1860, in 1861 the Highland and Agricultural Society of Scotland sent to St Kilda 'a fine large boat, fully equipped, and which cost about £60 ... with the view of encouraging the inhabitants to extend their fishing operations'. The boat was named the *Dargavel*.

In April 1863 the *Dargavel* left Village Bay in favourable weather, bound for Harris on a trading expedition with seven men and boys and one woman aboard. The *Dargavel* was carrying 'cloth, salt-fish, and other native produce to the value of upwards of £80, as well as some money in notes, which the owners wished to exchange for gold'. Neither the boat nor her crew and passengers were ever seen again.

Towards night the wind changed to the south, blowing very hard, and it was supposed that the little craft must have gone out of its course, several miles to the north of the Sound of Harris. Nothing more was known regarding the lamentable occurrence, except the loss of the boat and all its occupants, as was supposed to be clearly indicated by certain articles of clothing cast ashore at Maelsta [Mealista], on the west coast of Lewis. The sad intelligence was conveyed to the islanders by three London smacks, about a month after the disappearance of the boat; and it is unnecessary to add that the sorrow produced among the surviving friends by the announcement was of no ordinary kind.

The lost woman was the forty-nine year-old Betsy MacDonald, the former servant to Reverend Neil MacKenzie, the girl from Sutherland who had been for decades the island's only resident incomer and, in the absence of a minister or catechist, its only competent English speaker. Betsy left behind her husband Calum and her only two children to have survived neonatal tetanus, who were then in their early twenties. She had apparently taken the opportunity of the *Dargavel*'s voyage to visit her family on the mainland. In a curious and possibly scurrilous coda to this tragedy, it was gossiped to a visitor thirteen years later that Betsy MacDonald was on the *Dargavel* that day because she had been 'unfaithful, and deserted her husband'. That same husband, Calum MacDonald, apparently 'does not credit this report [of the drownings] but believes that the occupants of the boat were picked up by a passing vessel and conveyed to a foreign country'.

Of the other deceased, 'Three of the seven men were married, and besides their widows, left seven children. The other four were skilful fowlers, in the prime of life, and were survived by mothers, sisters, and other dependent relatives.'

It was a terrible toll; as tragic and as ominous in its own way as the emigrations to Australia. One of the most capable and respected women on the island had died. The active male population was reduced by a further seven bodies. Fatherless children and widows had been left ashore. Young, unmarried men who could have been expected to grow up and raise families in Village Bay would no longer do so.

And it carried a stark lesson. For more than a century different individuals and organisations had been suggesting that the future of human life on Hirta lay in the fishing industry. Such proposals had never been greeted with enthusiasm in Village Bay. The men of Hirta were more than capable sailors – certain seafaring skills were necessary, if only to navigate regularly between Village Bay and Boreray and the stacks. But they did not regard and had never regarded themselves as deep-sea fishermen. Their skills, their supreme specialities, were on the cliffs and the stacks as cragsmen and fowlers. They fished incidentally, from the rocks or from the side of a boat on a fowling expedition, but never as a vocation. Those preferences may have been inherited from earlier centuries, when vessels were more fragile and too often overwhelmed by the wild North Atlantic Ocean. They might have become rooted in some proud machismo which maintained that fishing could not compare to extreme rock climbing as a true man's occupation. They certainly resulted in the fine irony of the males of the most sea-girt community in the British Isles becoming landsmen rather than sailors. The disaster of 1863 confirmed one thing at least to a St Kildan: whatever the relative rewards, deep-sea sailing was a more dangerous pursuit even than swinging down the highest cliffs in Britain on a hand-held rope.

On 9 May 1863, at about the same time that news arrived in Village Bay of the loss of the *Dargavel*, Ann Gillies gave birth to a baby boy. Ann and Norman did not tempt fate by christening the infant. He died, like so·many others, after just seven days of life. The catechist and registrar Duncan Kennedy wrote on the death certificate that the cause of death was 'unknown ... no Medical Attendant'.

Nineteen days later, on 4 June, Ann Gillies herself also died. This time Duncan Kennedy was confident enough to attribute her cause of death to tetanus, although he made no reference to the undoubted fact that Ann had been carried away by the same infection which destroyed her baby. She was thirty-three years old. The thirty-nine year-old Norman was left widowed with the care of their three young children, Christian, Finlay and Mary Jemima Otter Gillies. He was by then helped by the fact that each of the three children was old enough to spend at least some of their time as a scholar under Mr Kennedy, and of course the neighbours on all sides of their new house on Main Street cared for the motherless Gillies children as they cared for their own.

Four years later, in 1867, Norman married again, this time to twenty-seven year-old Mary Ferguson. Over the next fifteen years

Norman and Mary Gillies produced three surviving children. The last one, young Ewen, was born when Norman was fifty-six and Mary was forty-two years old.

It was frequently asserted that those nineteenth-century children grew up in a St Kilda which had abandoned its ancient Celtic folklore and musical traditions. In the late seventeenth century Martin Martin had referred to their love of dancing, of the pipes and jew's harp. In the late eighteenth century John Lane Buchanan commented (albeit probably from a second-hand source) that, 'Their songs are wonderfully descriptive, and discover great strength of fancy.'

But in 1815 John MacCulloch was disappointed to note that 'All the world has heard of St Kilda music and St Kilda poetry, just as all the world has heard of the musical and poetical genius of the Highlanders ... We were prepared to bring away some valuable relics; the staves were already ruled, the dragoman [interpreter] appointed; but alas! there was neither fiddle nor Jew's harp in the island, and it was not remembered when there had been either ... St Kilda has been celebrated for its music. That reputation, if it was ever well founded, exists no longer ...'

MacCulloch was a passing visitor with more than an edge of cynicism about Highland culture, and the St Kildans of any era could not be expected to drop everything and conjure up a tune or a song for the satisfaction of anybody who stepped ashore for a few hours. Other, later travellers observed such phenomena as 'an old man sitting on the low wall opposite his cottage, sewing clothes or making gins, and humming an oran Hirtaich or St Kildan song', or noted the nineteenth-century composition of a lilt whose words 'describe the performances of a skilful cragsman, and other exciting incidents'. A visitor in 1838 'was much affected by the tremulous but musical voice of an old woman – Margaret M'Leod by name – seated on a stone by the side of her cottage, and busily plying the spindle, as she sang an elegiac song or "lament", composed by a sorrowing mother in memory of a favourite son, who met his death on the cliffs of Soa.'

The legends of the place did survive. In 1860 another Royal Navy survey officer operating on the north-west coast took an interest in St Kilda. Captain Frederick Thomas landed at Village Bay, took a number of photographs and made the acquaintance of the missionary Duncan Kennedy. Thomas later posted to Kennedy 'a string of questions ...

on points of antiquarian interest'. Duncan Kennedy duly passed those on to his niece, who assisted him at the school and other duties, and in April 1862 Miss Anne Kennedy wrote from St Kilda to Frederick Thomas (the notes and parentheses are those of Captain Thomas):

Dear Sir,

I have endeavoured to collect some of the traditions of St Kilda according to your request. I do not find any one in St Kilda who can tell me more about Banaghaisgeach (the Amazon's House in Glen Mhor) or Gobha Chuain; they have heard of the Banaghaisgeach, but not of the Gobha Chuain. But I have got some other stories – though, may be, they are of no importance – from Euphemia Macrimmon, the oldest woman in St Kilda.

The (first) Macdonald who came to St Kilda was with his brother on the shore (of Uist?), gathering seaweed; he struck his brother on the head, and he thought he had killed him. He fled to St Kilda and had a family there.

He had a son named Donald. Donald and another man, named John Macqueen, were going up to Oiseval, the most eastern hill, to hunt sheep. As they were passing a little green hillock they heard churning in the hill. John Macqueen cried, 'Ho! wife, give me a drink.' A woman in a green robe came out and offered him a drink (of milk); but although he had asked for it, he would not take it. She then offered it to Donald, and he said he would take it with God's blessing, and drank it off. They then went to their hunting, when John Macqueen fell over a precipice and was killed; and it was thought he met his fate for having refused the drink.

Donald Macdonald lived in St Kilda till he was an old man. He then went to Harris, where he was seized with the smallpox, and died there, about 133 years ago. The next year his clothes were brought to St Kilda by one of his relations, when the inhabitants were all seized with the disease, so that only four grown up persons were left alive on the island; but they are the descendants of this same Macdonald, who continue in the island yet.

The houses were then (133 years ago) built in two rows with a causeway between them, which they called the Street. The houses were very different from what they are now; they had not beds, but holes in the heart of the wall, as in Tigh na Banaghaisgeach. There were two apartments, as at present, – one for themselves, the other for the cattle. In their own end they spread the ashes on the floor, then a coat of peat dust, then another of ashes, and so on, until the time for sowing barley, by which time the floor was raised to a great height. It was counted a good manure for barley and potatoes, and is still made, not in their dwellings, but in a little house beside their dwellings. About thirty years ago their houses were altered and set as they are now. When they were making a level space for the foundations, they discovered a house in the hillock, which was built of stone inside, and had holes [beds] in the wall, as in Airidh na Banaghaisgeach, or croops as they call them, which seems to have been the fairy's residence. There was another house of the same kind discovered a little afterwards above the burial-ground, and it is there yet; they found ashes and half-burnt brands in it ...

There is no other name known in St Kilda for the Dun, but the Castle of Dun; neither is it known who built it.

But there were two brothers, one named Colla Ciotach, the other Gilespeig Og or Young Archibald; each of them had a boat, and both were racing to St Kilda, for he who got there first was to be the proprietor. When they neared St Kilda, Coll saw that his brother would arrive there first; so Coll cut off his hand and threw it on the east point, which the boats pass as they come into the harbour, and he cried to his brother, 'This [the hand] is before you;' and the point is called Gob Cholla, or Coil's Point, to this day; and there is also a well not far from the point, called also Tobar Cholla, or Coll's Well.

Coll and his brother used to war with each other. Coll resided in the Dun, and Archibald in a large house, built underground in Boreray. The house is called Tigh a Stalair ...

It is not known in St Kilda whether Tigh a Stalair was built when the Dun was built.

There was a temple in Boreray built with hewn stones. Euphemia Macrimmon remembers seeing it. There is one stone yet in the ground where the temple stood, upon which there is writing; the inhabitants of St Kilda built *cleitean* or cells with the stones of the temple. Euphemia Macrimmon has seen stones in Tigh a Stalair on which there was writing. There was also an altar in Boreray, and another on the top of Soay ...

Anne Kennedy

Some of those tales, such as that of the fatal temptress on Oiseval, were still being told to their children by St Kildan parents in the twentieth century. Frederick Thomas annotated Anne Kennedy's fieldwork with comments that suggested the intricate meshing of St Kildan folklore with the stories and legends of the rest of the Scottish *Gàidhealtachd*. Of 'the first Macdonald', he wrote,

> This tradition may refer to Archibald (Gillespie) Dhu, who murdered his two (legitimate) brothers about 1506 ... he afterwards joined a band of pirates; and it is quite possible that he harboured in St Kilda and had children there ... This, however, does not square with the tradition that the clothes of the son of the 'first Macdonald' caused the outbreak of small-pox in St Kilda, which happened in 1730 [actually 1727]; nor with the account by Macaulay (pp. 263, 266, 'Hist. of St Kilda'), that the Macdonalds of St Kilda claimed kinship with Clanranald of South Uist; for Gillespie Dhu was of the clan Huisten of Slate [Sleat in southern Skye]. Of the two clans formerly in St Kilda, the Mac Ille Mhoirre (Mac Ghille Mhuire = son of the servant of Mary) is plainly Morrison, from Lewis; but I can make no sense out of Mac Ille Rhiabich, which appears to mean the son of the servant of the Grizzly (man). Perhaps this can be explained in South Uist.

Of Effie Macrimmon's death-dealing milkwoman, he commented:

> The adventure related is one of a large class. On the mainland, at Achadh-na-ghirt, or the field of the standing corn, I am told by one of my correspondents, that two men were ploughing; one of them said to the other that he wished his thirst was upon the dairymaid that he heard churning the milk in the rock. A few minutes after a woman came out with a cog of milk. The first man to whom she offered it refused to take it, on which he fell down dead. The other took it; the woman then said to him (in Gaelic, of course) 'May it be as nourishing to you as your mother's milk.'

In 1865 the highest contemporary authority on such matters appeared in St Kilda. Alexander Carmichael was born in the Argyllshire island of Lismore in 1832. He worked for all of his life as an Exciseman in the Highlands and Islands, 'from Arran to Caithness, from Perth to

St Kilda'. While on his professional journeys, by boat and packhorse and on foot, lodging, travelling and meeting with all the people of the north and west of Scotland, in the 1850s he began to collect their hymns, stories, songs, curses and incantations. He was struck time and again by the probable antiquity of what he heard from the mouths of his contemporary Gaels: 'It is the product of far-away thinking, come down on the long stream of time. Who the thinkers and whence the stream, who can tell? Some of the hymns may have been composed within the cloistered cells of Derry and Iona, and some of the incantations among the cromlechs of Stonehenge and the standing-stones of Callarnis. These poems were composed by the learned, but they have not come down through the learned, but through the unlearned – not through the lettered few, but through the unlettered many – through the crofters and cottars, the herdsmen and shepherds, of the Highlands and Islands.'

Carmichael was naturally fascinated by St Kilda, although he did not make the common error of supposing it to be the last redoubt of insular Gaelic culture. He was familiar with such islands as South Uist and Eriskay, whose much larger populations in the nineteenth century were the object of far less popular attention than the people of Hirta, and where Gaelic music, song and story thrived.

He had nonetheless gathered intriguing second-hand tales before visiting Village Bay. One was told to him by Captain Henry Otter's Gaelic-speaking pilot, John MacDonald. MacDonald, who was described by Carmichael as a 'kindly humorist' whose stories might not always be taken literally, said that he had once had the following exchange with two attractive young St Kildan woman:

'O ghradhanan an domhain agus an t-saoghail, carson a Righ na gile 's na greine! nach 'eal sibh a posadh is sibh cho briagh?'

['Oh! Ye loves of the domain and of the universe, why, King of the moon and of the sun! are ye not marrying and ye so beautiful?']

'A ghaol nan daona, ciamar a phosas sinne? Nach do chaochail a bheanghluin!'

['Oh! Thou love of men, how can we marry? Has not the knee-wife [midwife] died!']

From another source Carmichael discovered 'a joyous song' which the people of St Kilda used to sing on the arrival of their birds:

Bui'cheas dha 'n Ti thaine na Gugachan
Thaine 's na h-Eoin-Mhora cuideriu
Cailin dugh ciaru bo 's a chro!
Bo dhonn! Bo dhonn! Bo dhonn bheadarrach!
Bo dhonn a ruin a bhlitheadh am baine dhuit
Ho ro! Mo gheallag! Ni gu rodagach!
Cailin dugh ciaru bo 'e a chro –
N a h-eoin air tighinn! Cluinneam an ceol!

['Thanks to the Being, the Gannets have come,
Yes! and the Great Auks along with them.
Dark haired girl! – A cow in the fold!
Brown cow! Brown cow! Brown cow, beloved ho!
Brown cow! My love! The milker of milk to thee!
Ho ro! My fair skinned girl – a cow in the fold,
And the birds have come! – Glad sight, I see!']

In May 1865 Alexander Carmichael set sail in the very early morning from Lochmaddy in North Uist and caught his first sight of St Kilda six hours later:

Islands look magnificent rising up out of the water in the mist. Slight breeze on the starboard side. Arrived at St Kilda about 12 noon. Fine open bay. Bold rocks and remarkably grand. Landed in first boat. Was at manse. Poorly furnished but good house. Cameron the missionary oldish and common looking. St Kildans good looking s[t]out fellows with pale complexions. Woman good looking and ruddy complexions. Women high shoulders and crouched figures and bad ankles and feet. Beautiful white teeth. Pronunciation peculiar and lisping. People seem to be spoiled not polite ... Kissed a St Kilda lassie. A little beauty with dark brown eyes and fresh complexion about ten or eleven years. Kissed her so as to have to say that I kissed a St Kilda lassie. Saw men going on rocks. Fearful sights. The deep blue fathomless ocean roaring many hundred feet beneath them. Took out the fulmars and some eggs. Birds vomiting oil – painful sights.

Norman and the late Ann Gillies's oldest daughter Christian was the only girl aged 'ten or eleven years' on St Kilda in 1865. She may therefore have been the object of the folklorist's attentions. He was, however, more interested in an elderly female.

Euphemia, or Effie, MacCrimmon had reached the approximate age of eighty-six in 1865. An immediate first or second generation descendant of the Skye MacCrimmons who had arrived after the devastation of the 1727/1728 smallpox epidemic, Euphemia had absorbed a great deal of St Kildan lore which was occasionally confused – by her and by others – with the symbiotic tales and songs of the other Hebrides.

In Carmichael's words she,

> ... had many old songs, stories, and traditions of the island. I would have got more of these had there been peace and quiet to take them down, but this was not to be had among a crowd of naval officers and seamen and St Kilda men, women and children, and, even noisier than these, St Kilda dogs, mad with excitement and all barking at once. The aged reciter was much censured for her recital of these stories and poems, and the writer for causing the old woman to stir the recesses of her memory for this lore; for the people of St Kilda have discarded songs and music, dancing, folklore, and the stories of the foolish past.

Before he was advised by the minister to stop bothering the old woman Carmichael took from her three songs and one glorious poetic dialogue which she said had been composed by her parents during their courtship in the middle of the eighteenth century:

> Esan:
> *Is tu mo smùidein, is tu mo smeòirein,*
> *Is mo chruit chiùil sa mhadainn bhòidhich!*
> Ise:
> *M'eudail thusa, mo lur 's mo shealgair,*
> *Thug thu 'n dé dhomh 'n sùl 's an gearrbhall.*
> ['He:
> Thou art my turtle-dove, thou art my mavis,
> Thou art my melodious harp in the sweet morning
> She:
> Thou are my treasure, my lovely one, my huntsman,
> Yesterday thou gavest me the gannet and the auk.']

The minister who dissuaded Alexander Carmichael from paying further attention to the songs and tales of Effie MacCrimmon was Reverend John MacKay, Duncan Kennedy having left St Kilda two years earlier. MacKay was a fully ordained Free Church pastor. He had been born in the town of Inverness but came from a fishing family in the west coast Gaelic-speaking township of Lochcarron. A forty-eight year-old bachelor in 1865, he settled at first in the manse with his sister Margaret.

In the following decade MacKay was accused of examining a visitor's gift to the islanders of 'some perfectly unobjectionable Gaelic song-books', and announcing 'that as they were "neither psalms nor spiritual hymns", they could not be accepted'. If that was the case, Reverend MacKay, who had formerly been a schoolteacher, did not apply the same restrictions to his own library. Another visitor who stayed overnight with him in the Village Bay manse reported that 'The minister has several volumes, among which were the following: Smith's Moral Sentiments, Butler's Fifteen Sermons, Harvey's Meditations, Works of John Owen, D.D., Select Works of Dr Chalmers, Baxter's Call, Sir John Herschell's Astronomy.' Yet another man reported,

> I found the reverend gentleman seated in what appeared to be at once bed-room and study. He was engaged filling a short clay pipe, quite black enough to gratify the taste of a Lanarkshire collier. The minister wore his chimney-pot hat during the interview. I never saw one of a similar pattern before; possibly the style may have been fashionable in our grandfathers' days. I was waved in a kindly but cavalier way to one of the two chairs in the room, the rest of the furniture consisting of a rough plain table, two coarse chests resembling joiner's tool boxes, a Gaelic Bible, three or four books of theology, including Smith's *Moral Sentiments*, Harvey's *Meditations among the Tombs*, and Baxter's *Call to the Unconverted*, a candlestick, and a penny bottle of Perth ink. A fire of turf was simmering in a small broken grate.

Anne Kennedy's correspondent Captain Frederick Thomas would write of 'the belief that all secular music is vicious; and both in St Kilda and the Long Island, one of the ruling canons is that "it is easier for a camel to pass through the eye of a needle, than for a piper, etc."'

Those critics were foreign to the Protestant Highlands and Islands, largely ignorant of the precepts and appeal of the Free Church of Scotland, and usually deaf to the powerful Gaelic psalmody which had latterly been embraced by the St Kildans.

John MacDiarmid of the Highland and Agricultural Society attended one of Mr MacKay's three Sunday services and,

> ... counted 66 of the natives present – 21 men, 35 women, and 10 children [out of a population of 75 souls]. At the close of the service the men all sat down and allowed the women to depart first. All were decently and rather cleanly clad.
>
> The men wore jackets and vests of their own making, mostly of blue colour, woollen shirts, a few had linen collars, and the remainder cravats around their necks, the prevailing head-dress being a broad blue bonnet. The women's dresses were mostly all home-made, of finely spun wool, dyed a kind of blue and brown mixture, and looked not unlike common wincey.
>
> Every female wore a tartan plaid or large shawl over her head and shoulders, fastened in front by an antiquated-looking brooch, and upwards of twenty of these plaids were of the Rob Roy pattern, all got from the mainland. Several of the women wore the common white muslin cap or mutch, and only one single solitary bonnet, of a rather romantic shape, could there be descried, adorning the head of by no means the fairest-looking female present.
>
> All the men, and a few of the women, wore shoes; the rest of the women had stockings on, or went barefooted. They seemed very earnest and attentive to the discourse, and now and then heaved a long deep sigh, as if by way of response.

But when it came to their psalmody, a unique form of Gaelic worship which would take a further century and more to be appreciated outside the Presbyterian congregations of the Scottish *Gàidhealtachd*, 'The singing baffles description. Everybody sang at the top of his voice, and to his own tune, there being no attempt at harmony.'

There is no doubt that Protestant missionaries, catechists and ministers were nervous of the old traditions, many of which recalled the Celtic Catholic Church that had been renounced in most of Scotland since the sixteenth century. There is also no doubt that Reverend John MacKay was a devoted Free Church man. He would not tolerate an inattentive service. 'The minister is one who commands attention,' said another visitor, 'every eye fastened on him throughout the discourse; and if any one happens to drop asleep, he or she is immediately aroused by a stinging remonstrance from the pulpit! Such, for instance, as saying in Gaelic: "Arouse your wife, Lachlin – she won't sleep much in Tophet, I think, eh?" which causes Lachlin to poke his elbow in his wife's side immediately.'

But neither he nor any of his colleagues merit the published obloquies of 'a religious zealot who may have done more than any single individual to destroy the St Kildan way of life' and of establishing 'a vibrantly harsh rule over his parishioners'. An outsider who actually met and lodged briefly with MacKay when the minister was almost sixty years old described him as,

... not only an earnest and honest man, but a kind-hearted one withal, whom those of any or of no persuasion would respect.

There, posted like a sentinel on a rocky bank close to the sea, his whole aim is to keep the devil out of the island. Absorbed in this duty, he forgets the loneliness of his situation, and is deaf to the roaring of the waves that rage before his sentry-box during the long winter, and blind to the desolate aspect of the hills that tower steeply around, their lofty tops enveloped in drifting fogs. He is contented with plain fare and drinks none, is attentive to the infirm, and shares, in a stealthy way, what luxuries he has with them ...

Who so anxious as he when the boats happened to be caught in a storm? Methinks I see him now, wandering restlessly on the shore, watching the waves outside the bay lashed into foam by the strong north wind, until the boats came round the rocky point ...

Although a bachelor, he is seldom to be seen without a rosy-cheeked urchin – a lamb of his flock – hanging on to his breeches-pocket and following him like a dog. Personally I am indebted to him for numberless acts of friendship, – kindness continued from first to last. He pressed me to live in his house, and when, preferring freedom and the bagpipes, I declined his invitation, he did his utmost to render me comfortable in my own quarters. Take him for all in all, the Free Kirk has few soldiers she has more reason to feel proud of.

That is not a description of a tyrant.

If 'way of life' meant an abundance of popular music, the evidence suggests that was in decline in St Kilda many decades before John MacKay landed in Village Bay. If it meant such fond peculiarities as adhering to the old Julian calendar's feast days, the Free Church did not interfere. Until the end St Kildans celebrated the 'old' New Year on 12th January, often to the disconcertion of visitors.

Moreover, the Free Church was established as a democracy. In contrast to the established Church of Scotland which it supplanted in most of the Protestant Highlands and which often did exercise 'a vibrantly harsh rule' over its people, neither the views nor the ministers of the Free Church could be imposed on an unwilling congregation. John MacKay could not have followed the example of his established Church predecessor Alexander Buchan and discipline women by making them wear sackcloth soaked in sewage, not least because Buchan was the landowner's proxy and MacKay was not. Being neither appointed nor paid nor housed by the landowner, a Free Church minister was accountable only to his congregation and was free to support that congregation in lay as well as spiritual matters, even in opposition to the landlord. If Reverend MacKay and his message had not been popular on Hirta, he would not have drawn the entire able adult population to his services. The idea of three Church services each Sunday might have been unconscionable to southern liberals, but it would remain commonplace in the Hebrides for another 150 years and was precisely in tune with the requirements of the revivalists in St Kilda and elsewhere in the early 1840s.

Unlike many of its critics, the Free Church embraced the Gaelic language, which was as important a St Kildan tradition as any. Rather than attempt to educate its congregations out of Gaelic and into English, the Free Church of Scotland made a point of categorising west Highland and Hebridean ministries as 'Gaelic essential' – which was to say that it would not put forward a non-Gaelic speaking pastor to such places. It was also careful to introduce schools, conducted in the medium of Gaelic where necessary, and medical attention to places which had previously known neither. The Free Church of Scotland was popular for a reason. It had earned its popularity.

So when, many years later, an elderly Reverend John MacKay was interrogated by a government commission about the conditions of life in St Kilda, he was able honestly to say, 'I think they are better off today than they were when I came to the island.' He was able also to criticise the proprietor for taking in rent 'the whole, everything he can get; he will take the whole produce of the island'. He was able to suggest that 'they are very much needing a doctor at times'.

He was happy to confirm that the schoolchildren were 'perfectly' literate in Gaelic. But the only songs they committed to memory were the psalms. And the St Kildans had, 'No poets or poetry of their own … Well, perhaps they may have, but I don't hear.'

The census of 1871 showed the combined effects of the loss of the *Dargavel* and of a terrible decade for infant mortality. It also coincided with the end of the fifty-eight year-long proprietorship of Sir John MacPherson MacLeod, who in the same year sold the St Kilda archipelago for £3,000 to Norman MacLeod of Dunvegan, the 25th MacLeod of MacLeod. Norman MacLeod had no more money than his predecessors but he was determined to re-establish the family's status. Regaining St Kilda was part of that process, which was only partly subsidised by letting out Dunvegan Castle, making a good marriage to the only daughter of a Northamptonshire baron and embarking on a civil service career in London.

In the short term MacLeod retained the services as factor of Norman MacRaild, who was however dismissed in 1873 and replaced by the MacLeod estate factor from Skye, John MacKenzie, who was assisted and later succeeded by his own son John. (The younger MacKenzie had an embarrassing introduction to St Kilda. Unaware that over the decades the islanders had lost the inclination and ability to swim, on his first summer visit he went for a naked dip in the bay. 'So unusual was the sight that the entire population rushed down to the beach to watch him. This led to an extremely awkward situation, for the women squatted themselves down beside his clothes. He swam round and round for a while in the hope that their curiosity would ere long be satisfied, and that they would then return to their household duties. Not a bit of it. The sight of a man performing the part of a fish was far too entertaining a business to be regarded with indifference, and they sat on enchanted until he swam close in and told them to go away.')

Five years after the reassertion of MacLeod sovereignty a visitor discovered the islanders to be pleased with their new owner, and not least with the replacement of MacRaild by John MacKenzie Snr. 'None of the men keep an account of the quantity of produce they give to the factor, and the amount of goods they take in return,' he reported.

They have great confidence in Mr M'Kenzie, who, they say, is just and generous, and easy to deal with, and always anxious to attend to their wants in bringing from the mainland whatever they may order or stand most in need of. I have heard it stated that between £70 and £80 is the annual revenue derived by MacLeod from the island, for which he paid £3000 about five years ago. They are never pressed for arrears; and, so far as could be made out, they are contented with their lot, and consider that they are very fairly dealt with.

They are very much attached to their island home, and there is no inclination to emigrate. Of their landlord, MacLeod, they speak in the very best terms, and consider themselves very fortunate in being under his guardianship; and not one single word or expression did I hear uttered implying want of confidence or distrust in his dealings with them. As one old woman put it in Gaelic, 'It would be a black day for us the day we severed ourselves from MacLeod's interest.'

MacLeod of Dunvegan and the MacKenzies took over an unpromising island. By 1871 the population of St Kilda had fallen yet again, to just seventy people including the minister John MacKay and his sister Margaret. Along with the twenty-two year-old Isabella MacDonald, who had married into St Kilda from a Glasgow Highland family, they were by then the only residents of Village Bay who had not been born there. Margaret MacKay would die of a chronic respiratory complaint three years later at the age of forty-four. Isabella MacDonald would follow her into the small graveyard above Main Street in 1878 at the age of just thirty.

The average age on the island, which had been twenty-five in 1851 and thirty-one in 1861, had risen in 1871 to thirty-six. There were just seven children under the age of ten years and almost 30 per cent of the population was over the age of fifty years. The number of men who registered themselves as active 'cragsmen' had fallen to ten. Equally ominously, there were twenty-five unmarried females on Hirta and just ten unmarried males.

This dramatic collapse in population attracted national attention. In August 1871 the *Manchester Guardian* newspaper reported:

It is not often that we hear anything from or of the little island of St Kilda, or the few families which spend their lives on a spot some three miles long and two miles broad. Nor is it wonderful that, even if anybody cared for news from this lonely isle, there should seldom be any; for we are told that there is 'regular communication' between St Kilda and Stornoway only once a year, and that a reply to a letter sent to the island is deemed to be received by return of post if it comes at the end of a year.

But the census has revealed the fact that the population of St Kilda is diminishing, having decreased from about 100 to 71 [sic]; and besides it appears that among the 43 females and 28 males who make up the number of 71 there is but one child, 'and it is dying'. It seems that during the last eight years not one of the children born on or brought early to the island has survived.

This extraordinary mortality has been ascribed to the unspeakable filthiness of the islanders, who are said to dwell in huts which they turn into dungheaps. But their habits can hardly be filthier now than they were when their children did not perish with such certainty; and Mr J M MacLeod, who was until very lately the landlord of the island, declares that 'the inhabitants are well fed, well clothed, and for a Hebridean peasantry particularly well housed'. He declares too that the practice of collecting manure in their huts, though it may once have prevailed, has long ceased, and that they are as cleanly as the other inhabitants of the Hebrides.

Moreover, Mr McKay, the resident minister of St Kilda, states ... that the children die of a strange kind of paralysis. 'About ten days after birth the jaws begin to relax, the lower one soon sinking quite powerless, and through inability to suck the baby wastes away in a few more days.'

It was not strictly true that 'during the last eight years not one of the children born on or brought early to the island has survived'. There were in St Kilda in 1871 one three year-old, two five year-olds, one seven year-old and two eight year-olds, all of whom had been born in Village Bay or on Harris, where anxious St Kildan mothers often travelled to give birth in the hope of avoiding death by lockjaw. Nor was it true to say that in earlier days 'their children did not perish with such certainty'. As we have seen, Kenneth Macaulay recorded the phenomenon in graphic terms in 1758. The fatalities only became glaringly obvious in the nineteenth century, when increasingly accurate records of births and deaths were kept, even on Hirta.

As well as a dearth of infants, there were also a few displaced children. One of those was the eight year-old Finlay MacQueen, who was staying with his father and grandparents on Main Street. Finlay had been born on 18 November 1862. His mother was nineteen year-old Ann MacDonald and his acknowledged father was the twenty-two year-old cragsman Donald MacQueen. As the two were unmarried and still living with their own parents, the catechist Duncan Kennedy registered little Finlay as 'illegitimate'.

Even after the birth of their son, Donald and Ann did not marry each other. Ann MacDonald never married. Following his sister's death Ann was taken on by Reverend John MacKay as the minister's housekeeper in the manse. When MacKay left in 1889, the forty-six year-old spinster Ann MacDonald also departed St Kilda to live out her years with a nephew on Skye.

Donald MacQueen, Finlay's father, did marry. At the age of thirty in 1868, when Finlay was six years old, he wed twenty-three year-old Mary Gillies. In 1871 Mary died at the age of twenty-six. Two years later, in 1873, Donald was remarried to the sixteen year-old Marion MacDonald, who in the course of a long partnership would bear him five surviving children.

According to the law and custom of the day, the father had automatic claim to and responsibility for the son. So in the 1860s and early 1870s Finlay was brought up in the MacQueen family household on Main Street with two consecutive stepmothers, while his natural mother stayed 100 yards away in the manse.

As young Marion MacQueen began to produce her own children, and as Donald's father and mother were elderly but still alive, it quickly became a crowded cottage. A typically Hebridean solution then presented itself. Ann MacDonald's parents, John and Betsy, were in their late sixties and living alone since Ann had moved into the manse and her older brother Donald had left home to start his own family elsewhere in the village. In his mid-teens Finlay MacQueen was therefore transferred from the home of his paternal grandparents up the street to the house of his maternal grandparents, whose croft he could work with a view to inheriting. He would clearly also have regular contact with his natural mother in her parents' cottage, while his natural father lived a few doors down the street.

In the Gillies household on Main Street in 1871, forty-six year-old Norman was still one of the island's active cragsmen. His new wife Mary worked their 3-acre croft with the help of her stepchildren, sixteen year-old Christian and fourteen year-old Finlay. Twelve-year-old Mary Jemima Otter was one of the scholars at Reverend MacKay's Free Church School, absorbing psalms and a literacy in Gaelic.

One Sunday five years later Finlay MacQueen and the Gillies family experienced 'the most remarkable event … that had happened in St Kilda for many years'. The Lowland writer John Sands was then living among them, and he reported that on 17 February 1876,

> The people had just gone to church when, happening to look out at my door, I was startled to observe a boat in the bay.
>
> I had been nearly seven months on the island, and had never seen any ship or strange boat near it all that time. Robinson Crusoe scarcely felt more surprised when he saw the foot-print on the sand, than I did on beholding this apparition. I ran to the shore, where there was a heavy sea rolling, and shouted to the people in the boat; but my voice was drowned by the roar of the waves.
>
> A woman who had followed me gave notice to the congregation, and all poured out of the church. The St Kildans ran round the rocks to a spot where there seemed to be less surf, and waved on the boat to follow. I went with the others. When we arrived at the place indicated, the islanders threw ropes from the low cliffs to the men in the boat; but the latter declined to be drawn up, the captain bawling 'Mooch better dere', pointing to the shore before the village, and putting about the boat. All ran back; but before we got to the shore the strange boat had run through the surf. Instantly all the men in her leaped into the sea and swam to the land, where they were grasped by the St Kildans. In a few minutes their boat was knocked to pieces on the rocks.
>
> The strangers were invited into the minister's house and dry clothes given them. They proved to be the captain and eight of the crew of the Austrian ship *Peti Dabrovacki*, 880 tons, which had left Glasgow for New York five days before. The vessel had encountered bad weather; her ballast had shifted, and she lay on her beam-ends about eight

miles west of St Kilda. Seven men had remained in her, and no doubt perished. The ship was not to be seen next day.

When the survivors had got their clothes shifted, they were distributed amongst the sixteen families that compose the community, the minister keeping the captain, and every two families taking charge of one man, and providing him with a bed and board and clean clothes.

I myself saw one man (Tormad Gillies) take a new jacket out of the box in which it had been carefully packed, and give it to the mate to wear during his stay, the young man having no coat but an oilskin.

Tormod is the Gaelic equivalent of Norman. Sands's 'Tormad Gillies' was Norman Gillies, the husband of Mary and father of Christian, Finlay and Mary Jemima Otter. Norman, at the age of fifty years, thought little of offering both his home and his best clothes to a young, weary and cold sailor of a distant nation with whom he could exchange not a sentence of conversation.

The oatmeal being done, the islanders took the grain they had kept for seed and ground it to feed the shipwrecked men. The hospitable conduct of the St Kildans was all the more commendable when one considers that their guests were all foreigners. But long before the five weeks had elapsed during which the Austrians lived on the island, they had by their good behaviour removed the prejudice that had prevailed against them at first. They were polite and obliging to the women, and went from house to house to assist in grinding the grain.

When John MacDiarmid landed on Hirta on a Saturday evening in 1877 Norman and Mary's first surviving child, a five year-old daughter named Ann – touchingly, after Norman's first, deceased wife – was also at school. The population had increased to seventy-five people, all of whom lived in the zinc-roofed houses on Main Street except for the minister, who lived in the manse, and the spinster Rachel MacCrimmon and an 'eccentric old bachelor' named Rory Gillies, each of whom still occupied a surviving thatched blackhouse on the row.

John MacDiarmid was the clerk to the Highland and Agricultural Society of Scotland. He travelled to St Kilda with provisions to the value of £179, some of which were bought from a donation from the Austrian government in thanks for the islanders' care for the shipwrecked sailors and some of which came from the HASS's own St Kildan fund. The provisions were oat and bere seed, turnip seed, potatoes, oatmeal, flour, sugar, horsehair for making ropes, leather for making shoes, 30 pounds of tea, a very large parcel of sweeties and two cases of brandy, sherry and port 'for medicinal use'. Reverend John MacKay was also given potatoes, tea and sugar and a separate supply of oat seed for his glebe. The care package contained no tobacco, to the disappointment of the St Kildan men and especially of Reverend MacKay – 'among the first questions put by the minister was, if I had brought any tobacco, and when I had unfortunately to answer in the negative, I perceived he felt far from happy'.

Otherwise MacDiarmid and his goods received a wholehearted welcome: 'A few words spoken in the vernacular conveyed and spread the welcome intelligence that the supplies had come, upon which there arose a great shout, or rather wail, of gladness and thankfulness, the very dogs, of which there would be about a dozen, joining in the refrain, and, combined with the hollow murmuring sound of the Atlantic waves, made a weird din that sounded strange in our ears, and the memory of which will not soon be effaced.'

St Kildan dogs achieved a character and renown of their own. Fifteen years later a visitor would report,

> They are a mongrel breed of collie, used for bird-catching as well as following sheep. Every crofter has two or three, and the total number on the island is about forty. They run in packs like wolves, and are almost as savage and troublesome. Their loud barking as they congregate on the shore to give you welcome is very impressive when you first set your foot on St Kilda. The people are proud of their army of dogs, and it is their common boast when speaking of any offensive person that if he dares to plant a foot on their rock-bound shore the dogs will quickly 'do' for him.

According to yet another visitor,

> They have a wonderful intuition as to when a boat is going out or coming in, and even as to when a steamer is expected. No matter what time of day or night, a chorus of barks is a sure indication that something is happening or going to happen by the landing-place. As

long as a boat is at work on the fishing grounds they pay no attention, but the moment her nose is pointed towards the shore, down they all rush, barking and snapping and rolling over one another in their excitement. Occasionally one of them gets caught by a fish-hook, which sobers the individual affected for a time, but they seem pretty well accustomed to such a mishap and soon begin barking again.

There was a hiccup in John MacDiarmid's arrival.

The weather being fine, and knowing how unsafe and uncertain the anchorage was, we proposed to land the goods at once, and asked the natives to give us assistance with their boats … the old men shook their heads and gathered around their minister in solemn conclave; the minister thrust his hands deep into his trouser pockets, and cast his eyes upon the ground in pensive meditation; eager, anxious women and amazed children stood with bated breath awaiting the result of the deliberation.

An answer was given, that as it was now drawing near the Sunday, and as the people must be prepared for the devotions of the morrow, they could not think of encroaching on the Sabbath by working at the landing of the goods. This ultimatum was like the laws of the Medes and Persians, for no entreaty, expostulation, or persuasive language on our part, though uttered in the hardest Gaelic, would make them alter their decision; and as for reasoning with them upon its being a work of necessity, such a conception seemed to have no place in their creed.

They told us that rather than land the goods on Sunday they would prefer sending to Harris for them, should we be compelled by stress of weather to betake ourselves there before Monday. The captain endeavoured to land a few bags with the *Flirt's* boats, but was completely baffled on account of the surf. The boats were not strong enough to withstand the force with which they would be pitched on to the rocks. The attempt had to be abandoned; and as nothing more could now be done, on the minister's recommendation we resigned ourselves to Providence, and waited patiently for Monday's dawn, trusting the weather might be propitious.

Monday did dawn fine; the provisions were unloaded and MacDiarmid was given the opportunity to observe and survey life in Village Bay for a couple of days in the middle of the 1870s.

Although they had had a bad harvest the previous year and had as a result to go for a while without the porridge which comprised their standard breakfast and supper (they dined at midday on potatoes and fowl, mutton or fish),

> Judging from outward appearance, I cannot believe the St Kildians suffered much from want of food.
>
> They are, on the whole, full-faced, fresh-looking, and some of them well-coloured and quite rosy. Several of the women are, in my opinion, more than ordinarily stout. No doubt they might be wanting in farinaceous food, and had to take more than was good for them of cured meat ... It may be mentioned that at this moment there are twenty carcasses of good cured mutton lying in the storehouse in two barrels for the proprietor. These were killed for him from his own flock in the island of Soa. There can be no doubt, had the St Kildians been in great want they would have used this mutton, and been made quite welcome to it by MacLeod. Of course, since the arrival of the sea-fowl in March, they have had plenty of eggs.

MacDiarmid found,

> ... living on the island at present 22 grown-up men, including the minister, and 39 women; 5 boys and 4 girls under 14 and over 5 years of age; and 4 boys and 1 girl under 5 years of age – in all, 75 souls ... There are about a dozen marriageable women, while there are only two unmarried men. This it must be admitted, is out of all proportion, and it would be well if some means were adopted whereby the young women could be transferred to the mainland for domestic or farm service. They would no doubt make good out-door workers or farm servants, and might be much benefited by the change, acquire cleanlier and less slovenly habits, which they would carry back with them if ever they returned.
>
> It must tell on the prosperity of the island such a large majority being females: they have to be supported, and though able and willing workers, still are unfitted for the arduous and dangerous pursuit from which the St Kildian derives his principal support. The majority of the men are old, and comparatively few young lads are ready to take their places.

Staff-Surgeon Scott of HMS *Flirt*, the Royal Naval vessel which had delivered John MacDiarmid and his provisions to Village Bay, went ashore, examined a number of extremely willing inhabitants and later handed over his medical notes to MacDiarmid:

> The inhabitants are all of moderate stature (the men from 5 ft. 5 in. to 5 ft. 7½ in.), look healthy and well-fed; but closer inspection shows the muscular development to be of rather a flabby character.
>
> The ailment par excellence is rheumatism, as might be expected from the exposed nature of their island home. This disease is common to both sexes, and in a number is attended with pain in the cardiac region, with irregular heart's action. Dyspepsia is also common; and it is noticeable that the teeth were in general short and square, as if they had been filed down. There were several cases of ear disease, and there is a tendency to scrofula. One boy had disease of the bones of the leg.
>
> Their staple food consists of oatmeal porridge and the flesh of the sea-fowl. Colds and coughs are common enough, but no case of phthisis presented itself. We saw only two cases of skin-disease (one of herpes and one of sycosis menti), and these were trifling, for nature seemed to have endowed them with very clean, smooth epidermic coverings.
>
> There is said to be great fatality among children when from 7 to 14 days old, but why was not easy to make out. We were told that the women sometimes proceeded to the mainland of Harris to be confined there and have medical attendance: whether such a journey in a small open boat is at all beneficial for a woman in an interesting situation, is at least open to doubt. The children whom we saw were all healthy-looking. The medicines which would be of most use are those for cough and rheumatism; and for the latter, strong liniments would be the most appreciated.

John MacDiarmid was impressed by their curiosity:

> They all have a pretty fair idea of numbers and dates in Gaelic, and know the value of the current coins; but it cannot be said that there exists among them any great desire for money, and on offering some to the children they did not clutch at it, as children elsewhere invariably

do, which may be accounted for by there being no shop where the ha'pence might be converted into something more enjoyable.

There are two watches and one clock on the island. The people are fond of asking the time, and upon showing them a watch they could tell the time at once. They are anxious, and desire very much to be educated in English and arithmetic, and many earnestly beseeched that a schoolmaster might be sent to them. It is my opinion they would learn English very soon – the grown-up people as well as the young. They are very sharp and quick at picking up English names and words, and their keen, bright eyes bespeak an intellect easily susceptible of impression …

Judging from the well-built walls surrounding their patches of land, the men must be rather good masons. They have axes and hammers, and in one house there was a large box of joiner's tools. They are rather scarce of nails, which are always of use to them in the case of accidents to their boats. They had excellent candles, made from the tallow of the sheep; and suspended in the church were two chandeliers, each having three of these magnificent luminaries.

As an agriculturalist, John MacDiarmid was concerned to note the effects of a certain overuse of the land and the moor:

The soil is a fine black loam resting on granite, and by continued careful manuring and cleaning, looks quite like a garden.

Yet with all this fine fertile appearance, the return it gives is miserable; and this can only be accounted for, I presume, from the land never being allowed any rest under grass. The only crops grown are potatoes and oats, with a little bere. Within the remembrance of some of the older men, the returns were double, or nearly treble, of what they now are. Questioned several of the men upon this point, and got exactly similar answers. From a barrel of potatoes (about 2 cwt.), scarcely 3 barrels will be lifted. They require to sow the oats very thick—at the rate of from 10 to 12 bushels to the acre, and the return is never above two and a-half times the quantity of seed sown; formerly it used to be five or six times.

I was shown a sample of the oats grown, but they were very small and thin, and thick in the husk. If possible, they avoid sowing home-grown seed, as it never gives a good return. Flails are the instruments used for separating the grain from the straw. The ground is all turned over with the spade, of which they have a number in very good order. The Cas Chrom (spade-plough), so common in the Western Isles as an implement of tillage, was once in use, but has long ago given place to the spade, and not one is now employed. The land is harrowed with a sort of strong, roughly-made wooden hand-rake. They have iron grapes for spreading their manure.

The dungpits are situated generally a few yards in front of the house, in the end of the patch of land, sunk a few feet in the ground – rather convenient for being conveyed to the land, which is done by wooden creels or baskets. Saw no wheelbarrows; but there were one or two handbarrows. They have sufficient manure for their land. Sometimes they gather a little seaware for manure, but there being no beach, it is not to be got in any great quantity.

He found,

1 bull, 21 cows, and 27 young cattle on the island, all in wonderfully good condition – much better, in fact, than in many places on the mainland in this trying season. The bull, brindled in colour, is of the West Highland breed, about eight or nine years old, and by no means a bad animal. He was brought from Skye about five or six years ago, and has left a mark of improvement on the young stock. The cows are of a degenerate Highland breed, light and hardy-looking, and mostly all black in colour. The young cattle are red-and-black in colour; healthy-looking, and among them are a few well-shaped and well-coated animals ...

It was impossible to ascertain the number of sheep on the island, for none of the men questioned seemed to have any accurate idea of how many there might be, or if they had, perhaps they imagined it was the best policy to keep it dark; however, from what was to be seen in perambulating the hills, the number may be put down at over 400. There may be many more, but I do not think the number is less than that. Each family, it is said, should have between 20 and 40 sheep; but, on inquiry, it was found that some families had scarcely any at all, while others again had a good many more than the regulation number ...

The sheep are very wild; and though it was just after the lambing season, appeared in very good condition, and able to climb the steepest parts of the rocks. The yeld sheep are plucked about the beginning of June, and the ewes about the middle of summer. They sell neither sheep nor wool. From 2 to 5 sheep are killed by each family for the winter's supply, and the wool is made into blanketing and tweed, which they sell. They keep about 12 tups ...

The proprietor has between 200 and 300 sheep on the island of Soa, and between 20 and 30 of the native St Kilda breed on the island of the Dun. The latter I only saw at a distance, and they appeared of a light-brown colour. All the tups were on the Dun island, and there was not an opportunity of seeing them. The sheep are said to be very fat in autumn when killed, which may well be believed from the nature of the pasture; and the St Kilda mutton that was presented to us for dinner would favourably compare in flavour and quality with the best fed blackfaced. What is not used of the tallow for candles they sell to the factor.

They had no butter on the island, and make but very little of that article of diet. Saw no vessel of the shape of a churn, and omitted to ascertain their process of butter-making. Cheese is more made, as it sells better, and in order, they say, to give it a better flavour, they milk the ewes, and mix their milk with that of the cows.

There are a number of dogs on the island – in fact, too many for the number of sheep, unless they use them for some other purpose, such perhaps as catching the birds. They are collies of a kind – certainly not pure bred – and did not by any means look as if they had suffered from abstinence. In almost every house there was to be seen a cat, from which it is to be inferred that mice exist also. There are only two hens on the island. Within the recollection of several of the older men, a lot of ponies were kept and reared, some of the crofters having as many as four and five.

More ominously, he also noted the possibility of an exhaustion of the peat bogs, 'of which nothing worth mentioning was to be seen on the whole island'. Such a shortage would, as MacDiarmid said, have had dire consequences for 'the future fitness of St Kilda as an abode for man'. Other inhabited small Hebridean islands, such as Vatersay and Eriskay, had little or no peat, but they were within easy reach of the larger islands of Barra and South Uist and could either cut peat there or import fuel. No such solution was available to St Kilda. If isolated, treeless Hirta did run out of peat, human life there would very quickly have become unsustainable.

John MacDiarmid said that as a result of the apparent shortage of peat, 'A very large extent of their pasture has already been bared by the turf having been used for fuel. Slow as the process appears to be, yet with the lapse of time it will as surely work out the dire effect, and render St Kilda quite uninhabitable either for man or beast. In asking a woman who was piling dried grassy turf upon the decaying embers of what was recently a similar pile, if she did not feel sorry at reducing to ashes the best support of their cattle and sheep, she replied, "Yes; but we must have our food cooked."' He noted 'scores, it might safely be said hundreds, of acres bared of what was once the finest pasture. In some parts where a little soil was left to cover the rock after the first cutting, a second coating or skin is forming — a poor apology for the original sward.'

MacDiarmid was both right and wrong. The peat bogs on the tops around Gleann Mor and on the Cambir in particular were not and never would be exhausted. The St Kildans had taken to burning dried slabs of turf, especially in the warmer months, from the pastures around Village Bay and even over in Gleann Mor, because they presented a comparatively quick and easy alternative to cutting, drying and carrying home a full year's supply of peat from the other side of Hirta. It was a further consequence of the drastically reduced number of young and active people, especially of males who traditionally cut peat from the bogs. Twenty years later another visitor with experience of the Hebrides noticed the St Kildan preference for turf over peat. He recorded,

At present they are in the habit of burning turf – a very wasteful process. It burns away very quickly, and the fire is produced at the expense of the pastures. Some of the grass in St Kilda affords as good pasturage for sheep as is to be found anywhere in Scotland; but in all parts of the island one comes across bare patches, sometimes large strips from which the turf has been systematically taken, sometimes merely holes from which just one sod has been removed.

There is no excuse for this, as there is plenty of excellent peat. The reasons they give for burning turf instead of peat are, that it is less trouble to dig, lighter to carry, and that they cannot dry the peats in their damp climate. As it is mostly found on the tops of the hills at a considerable distance from the village, this sounds a fairly plausible excuse; but as a matter of fact the heavier peat would burn proportionately longer than the lighter turf, and it would not really be necessary to transport any greater weight. As to the drying, all I can say is that if peats can be dried in Skye they can be dried in St Kilda. The carrying is done for the most part by the women, and a fairly obvious improvement would be the importation of a few ponies or donkeys.

If continued indefinitely the practice of stripping, drying and burning turf would certainly have had a calamitous effect on the ecology of the island. But for reasons other than conservation, it would not be continued indefinitely.

John MacDiarmid also noticed the prevalence of weaving in St Kilda in the mid-1870s:

The men are mostly all tailors, shoemakers, and weavers; in every house there is a loom. Some of the men, attracted by the pattern of our Ulster coat, began to handle and examine it closely, when suddenly one of them, with a beaming countenance, which plainly indicated that the intricate deftness of the textile fabric had dawned upon him, exclaimed– *'Dheanadh sin fhéin sud!'* (we could manufacture that ourselves).

As before mentioned, they make all their own clothing, and sell a good deal of blanketing and tweeds. The St Kilda tweeds are a good deal sought after for suits. A number of their sheep are blackish-brown, and when their wool is properly mixed with the white, it gives the cloth a slight brownish tinge, which is the only colouring it receives. In mostly every house there was to be seen a spinning-wheel, and a large pot, in which they dye their yarn. Strange to say, it is the men who make the women's dresses. The women are very expert at knitting.

St Kildans had, of necessity, been manufacturing almost all of their clothing since the dawn of settlement. With an abundance of wool and leather grazing on the hills, obtaining the raw materials presented no problems. Primitive distaffs and spindles had been in use for hundreds of years and there were certainly homemade looms on Hirta early in the eighteenth century.

In the second half of the nineteenth century the amount of tweed and blanketing woven in St Kilda soared. That was partly because it was encouraged by MacLeod of Dunvegan and his factor John MacKenzie as a means of paying rent in kind. But the growth of the industry predated the MacLeod purchase in 1871. In 1851 six young women described themselves as 'weaveress (of wool)', one man in his thirties admitted to the same occupation as well as birdcatching, and sixty year-old Ann MacQueen told the census enumerator that before qualifying for the receipt of alms she also had been a weaveress.

Highlanders and Hebrideans had been making hand-woven twill for centuries. The home export industry that would become known as Harris Tweed ('tweed' being an accidental misnomer which stuck) was developed in the 1840s by the widowed chatelaine of North Harris Estate, the Countess of Dunmore, Lady Catherine Herbert. Catherine Herbert noted the quality of the fabric being produced in Harris and promoted it as ideal outdoor wear to the gentry, at the very time when that gentry was displaying an interest in Highland hunting estates. Harris Tweed, whether it was made on Harris, Lewis or any of the other islands, quickly became a fashionable textile. It was all but inevitable that St Kildans, with their antique connections to Harris, should be among the first to adopt the trade.

In 1861, 1871 and 1881 the censuses were conducted by the Free Churchmen Duncan Kennedy and John MacKay, and they made no mention of female occupations other than 'wife' or 'servant'. Only in the early twentieth century were the majority of adult St Kildans of both genders officially recorded as 'handspinners', 'homeloom weavers' and finally as occupied in the 'tweed industry'.

The operation of looms became a male occupation as its profitability grew. It is likely that in 1851, when most cloth was still produced on a small scale for domestic use, it was recorded in the census as a traditional female pursuit. Once tweed weaving became a wintertime cottage industry and a cash export the men took it over and the women's contribution was limited chiefly to spinning the yarn from sheep's wool. By the middle of the 1870s this division of labour by gender was established. A visitor who over-wintered on Hirta between 1876 and 1877 recorded that, 'In October, when the nights were getting long, spinning-wheels began to be busy in every house, making the thread which the men afterwards wove into cloth ... The men about [10 December] began to weave the thread which the women had spun. Both sexes worked from dawn of day until an hour or two after midnight. Their industry astonished me.'

Ten years later another visitor noted of the St Kildan male:

> His loom is in operation for only about two months of the year, when the nights are at their longest and out-door work is suspended. The loom is set up in one of the two apartments into which every house is divided, generally the kitchen. It is a primitive-looking machine, every portion of it home-made, and displaying much ingenuity and dexterity. The most heterogeneous and unpromising materials have been utilised. A little bit of timber thrown up on the shore has been scooped with a pocket-knife into a shuttle; for a spindle there is the quill of a goose, and a bobbin has been shaped out of the stalk of a common weed – the dockan!
>
> For two months the sound of the shuttle is heard in nearly every house. The work is carried on with astonishing zeal, the men often sleeping in their clothes and sometimes for but a few hours each night. The dawn of day finds them at the loom, which they do not leave till an hour or two past midnight. It is the same every winter.

Commercial weaving in Village Bay also served the tourist industry. The St Kildans were among the very first Highlanders to milk the cash cow of tourism. A combination of independent spirit, pride and their tradition of hospitality to strangers made most Scottish Gaels notably slow to exploit the spending power of visitors, who well into the twentieth century would frequently not be charged even for full board in a Highland or Hebridean cottage.

There were exceptions. When in 1818 the poet John Keats tramped across Mull and made the short crossing to the holy island of Iona, urchins on the shore tried to sell him ochre-coloured pebbles. The children had presumably honed their souvenir-hawking skills on earlier visitors, for Iona was already a celebrated place.

So too, for different reasons, was St Kilda. Iona was known as a cradle of Christianity and a burial ground of kings. St Kilda was known, thanks largely to Martin Martin and his successors and imitators, as the home of a semi-mythological tribe of people unpolluted by western civilisation. Iona was relatively easy to reach, being further south and closer to the Scottish mainland. St Kilda remained accessible only to wealthy people with ocean-going yachts until the arrival of steamships in the north-west of Scotland in and after the 1830s.

One of the earliest such tourists, the writer Lachlan Maclean who arrived in Village Bay on the steam yacht *Vulcan* in 1838, set the tone for most who were to follow. 'If St Kilda is not the Eutopia so long sought, where will it be found?' wrote Maclean, echoing Martin Martin's Golden Age of 140 years earlier.

> Where is the land which has neither arms, money, care, physic, politics, nor taxes? That land is St Kilda. No taxgatherer's bill threatens on a church door – the game-laws reach not the gannets. Safe in its own whirlwinds, and cradled in its own tempests, it heeds not the storms which shake the foundations of Europe – and acknowledging the dominion of M'Leod, cares not who sways the British sceptre.
>
> Well may the pampered native of happy Hirt refuse to change his situation – his slumbers are late – his labours are light – his occupation his amusement. Government he has not – law he feels not – physic he wants not – politics he heeds not – money he sees not – of war he hears not. His state is his city, his city is his social circle – he has the liberty of his thoughts, his actions, and his kingdom and all the world are his equals. His climate is mild, and his island green, and the stranger who might corrupt him shuns its shores. If happiness is not a dweller in St Kilda, where shall it be sought?

Following such absurd encomiums the trade grew slowly through the middle decades of the nineteenth century. Chartered and private vessels arrived with increasing frequency. By the early 1870s, remarked one visitor,

> Among recent visitors to St Kilda, I may mention Mr Bouverie Primrose, secretary to the Board for Manufactures, etc.; Mr Walker of Bowland, Chairman of the Board of Supervision; the Rev. Eric J. Findlater of Lochearnhead, on three different occasions; Captain Macdonald of the Fishery cruiser *Vigilant*; the Commissioners of Northern Lighthouses in the *Pharos*; Sir William and Lady Baillie of Polkemmet, with the late Mr Baird of Cambusdoon, in August 1874; Sir Patrick-Keith Murray in his yacht *Crusader*, in July 1875; Dr

Murchison of Harris, on two occasions, during the same year; Lord and Lady Macdonald, in the yacht *Lady of the Isles*, accompanied by Miss Macleod of Macleod, the Rev Archibald M'Neill, minister of Sleat, and Mr Macdonald, Tormore, on the fifteenth of June 1877 …

In 1877 the ss *Dunara Castle* began regular weekly summer excursions from Glasgow and Greenock which called at many of the other islands before culminating its grand tour in Village Bay. The ships anchored in the shelter of Dun and their passengers were rowed ashore to view the noble savages in their stunning natural estate. They brought with them gifts of whisky, tobacco and sweetmeats for the children, and they took away homemade brooches, gulls' eggs and lengths of tweed.

To many people St Kildan tourism was from the very beginning a contrary exercise. Visitors sailed there to witness '[one of] the greatest curiosities of the moral world' – a supposedly primitive communal society in a state of grace. But their very presence, for however short a time, was bound to infect that unspoiled community with the materialist virus of the outside world. That was why Lachlan Maclean had written in 1838, having failed to heed his own advice, 'the stranger who might corrupt [the St Kildan] shuns its shores'.

Before very long other intelligent men and women were returning from an afternoon spent on Main Street bemoaning the corruption of St Kildan life by a surplus of tourists. 'The children looked very healthy,' one such visitor entered in his journal, 'but I am sorry to say that there is in them a habit of trying to get a sort of backsheesh out of everyone and never leaving you alone.' The same diarist also visited an eighty year-old woman in her cottage and, having established that she could speak no English other than 'No farder, no mudder, no brudder, no sister', gave her a handful of copper coins and then fled hurriedly back into the light and air of Main Street.

'One cannot be long on the island,' wrote a Lowland journalist in the 1880s, 'without discovering the great moral injury that tourists and sentimentalists and yachtsmen, with pocketfuls of money, are working upon a kindly and simple people. They are making the St Kildian a fibreless creature, totally dissimilar to all that, with so much justifiable pride, we associate with the Scottish character. The best gift that can now be made to the St Kildian is to teach him to help himself.'

St Kildan men usually rowed out to boats anchored in the bay, from curiosity and a desire to offer help as much as any other reason. Those missions were often interpreted by the crew and passengers of steamships as begging errands, and the men were tossed food, drink and coins. Such exchanges developed their own momentum. One of the saddest stories in the later history of St Kilda is of a small party of men rowing out to a Uist fishing boat in Village Bay and the *Uibhistich*, assuming that they had come to ask for whisky, drenching them with the ship's hose.

They were no more mendicants than they had ever been noble savages. That view of the St Kildans reflected more on the visitors' fantastic misapprehensions than it did on the people of Hirta. People who supposed that those innocents knew nothing of such coarse activities as trade were vaguely disillusioned to discover that the St Kildans were acute and accomplished tradespeople. They had been bartering for their livelihood for centuries with ruthless factors and tacksmen. A handful of Victorian bourgeois from Edinburgh or London were easy meat. If those bourgeois chose to give St Kildan children lollipops, their parents were unlikely to object. If they chose to offer the men whisky and tobacco, that also would be received with civil gratitude. If they wished to buy objects such as seabirds' eggs and tweed which had cost the St Kildans time, skill and labour, then the St Kildans on their part were willing to sell. Their goods already had a market value: their proprietor himself took feathers and tweed from them in lieu of cash for rent. If their acuity disillusioned the purchaser, that was no business of the St Kildans.

They had not chosen to be a *tabula rasa* upon which any Victorian could chalk his or her idealised image, but that was their fate. In 1906 the radical activist W C Hart moved the people of Hirta up the contemporary political ladder. In *Confessions of an Anarchist* he wrote,

It is interesting to know that the British Empire includes at least two successful but unconscious Anarchist communities. The one is at the island of St Kilda, in the remote Hebrides, where government and police are conspicuous only by their absence; the other is at Tristan d'Acunha … The inhabitants practically enjoy the possessions in common, and there is no strong drink on the island, and no crime. It was, at one time proposed to give them laws and a regular Government, but this was found unnecessary, for the above reasons, and they remain under the moral rule of the oldest inhabitant ... The inhabitants are spoken of as highly religious, and this must be the explanation of their success.

A few years earlier a journalist had reported, with tongue only slightly in cheek,

Before you have long set foot on St Kilda you discover that there is a species of socialism firmly rooted among the people. Very likely you have brought with you some presents for the islanders, and, if you have consulted their well-known tastes, these are sure to include tobacco and confections. You are at once asked bluntly for both – the men begging the one luxury, and the women the other. To discover the socialistic principle you have only to toss a roll of tobacco – an ounce will serve the purpose as well – to the first man that accosts you. True to the apostolic theory of 'all things common' this latter-day Ananias will share his spoil, to the last leaf, with every smoker on the island ...

In some of their vocations ... some of these poor people are socialists out and out. Take, for instance, bird-catching. Let me explain how the socialistic principle is carried into practice in this – the principal industry on the island.

Every year before the nesting season begins the islanders divide the rocks where the fulmar breeds into sixteen portions, and these are allocated by lot, one falling to each of the sixteen crofts on the island. The fulmar is, of course, the principal bird of St Kilda, and the one with which the island is identified. It is the business of each crofter to look after the portion of the rocks which he has been allotted. Assisted by his family, he acts as a kind of policeman, being particularly careful that the birds are in no way molested. His special aversion is a fowling-piece, which cannot be tolerated near the nesting-ground for one moment. The sheep, too, have to be kept from disturbing the birds.

When August comes round the young fulmar is killed, and though each crofter is specially entrusted with his own particular bit of rock, getting whatever assistance he requires from the others, the total produce is shared equally among the happy sixteen. The feathers are the most valuable part of the bird, and these are scrupulously divided. Less value is put upon the carcasses, because they are so plentiful and are not marketable ... These are preserved for use during the winter, and salted fulmar is a delicacy which you may have served up to you along with your porridge even at the manse.

In fishing, too, the St Kildians are socialists. As a rule, two boats of six men each go out to the fishing, and here again the produce is divided among the lucky sixteen.

Part noble savage, part beggar, part pioneering socialist or anarchist community, this little Hebridean family clung tenaciously to life. In 1875 a freelance writer from Ormiston in East Lothian made his first visit to the islands. John Sands was fascinated by the customs and archaeology of Scotland's islands. Having spent June and almost all of July in Village Bay, Sands returned a year later and was marooned there for a further eight months. He learned some Gaelic, and the forty-nine year-old bachelor may also have been attracted to at least one young woman on Hirta. Sands also, however unwittingly, did more for the St Kildan tourist industry than any visitor since Martin Martin.

Sands would begin the first recorded full excavation of Tigh an t-Slithiche, the souterrain above Main Street. 'The most extraordinary relic of antiquity in the village is a subterranean house,' he wrote.

I had heard of it on my first visit; and on the 13th July 1876 determined to have it opened and examined.

A crop of potatoes grew on the top, and the owner at first refused to allow this to be disturbed. But by dint of raillery, persuasion, and a promise to pay the damage, he at length acceded to my request. This underground dwelling was discovered about thirty-two years ago by a man who was digging the ground above it, and was generally called the House of the Fairies. The aperture on the top was filled up again, and it had never been opened since. But after a little search the hole was found and an entrance made. Two or three men volunteered to clear out the stones and soil that had accumulated on the floor to a depth of several feet, and worked with a will.

The house was found to be twenty-five feet long by three feet eight inches wide, and about four feet in height. The walls consisted of three or four ranges of stones, a roof of slabs resting on the sides. This house runs due north and south, and curiously enough there is a drain under the floor. Amongst the debris on the floor I found numerous stone axes, knives, and fragments of a lamp, as well as pieces of rude pottery. As there was no tradition concerning this house, and as it is assigned to the fairies, it may be very old; but I am inclined to think that the stone period extended to a very recent date in St Kilda. I have some satisfaction in believing that I am the discoverer of stone implements in St Kilda …

In 1896 an English naturalist also explored the souterrain, which had by then been adopted as a personal curiosity by the Skye factor John MacKenzie. The naturalist reported:

The dwelling is something in the form of a huge drain, some thirty or forty feet in length, four feet in height, and three in width, with a passage of somewhat similar capacity, but only about nine or ten feet in length, running at right angles to it on the left-hand side, and about halfway from the entrance. This is, I believe, supposed to have formed the bedchamber of the people who inhabited the rude house, the entrance to which commands an excellent view of Village Bay. This last fact was, no doubt, of great importance, in order that the people might have early knowledge of the approach of enemies. Neither had the owners of this underground mansion been unmindful of the benefits of some sort of sanitary arrangement, for we found a drain beneath the floor, made, no doubt, to carry off the slops from their crude earthenware bowls. We also came across a lot of limpet shells and bones of sheep and birds of various kinds.

John Sands was also responsible for two of the more enduring modern St Kildan legends. He claimed to have invented the St Kilda mailboat – a small unmanned floating device which, cast onto the ebbing tide, could supposedly connect Village Bay with the Outer Hebrides or further afield in times of sickness, shortage or bad weather. During his enforced winter in Village Bay 'I made a miniature ship and put a letter in the hold, in the hope that she might reach the mainland. I was anxious that my friends should know that I was alive.'

On many occasions afterwards the St Kildans despatched messages at times of grain shortages or other hardship in different forms of small mailboats. There is no record of them having done so before the visit of John Sands. His claim to patent may stand up. Before the

1870s no native St Kildan could have despatched a message in a bottle because no native St Kildan could write his or her own name, let alone inscribe a request for help in English. The exception was the minister or missionary, who may not have considered it his function to pen such a letter. In earlier years the St Kildans were not in the habit of asking for assistance from abroad. Their grain was more carefully sown, harvested and stored. Shortages were rare and when they occurred they were stoically borne. Sickness was also a personal, family matter for which outside help had never been requested – and when such outside help later presented itself, it would often be resented. It is feasible if not proven that the St Kilda mailboat was invented by John Sands in the last quarter of the nineteenth century.

They were not entirely dependable. Some reached Scandinavia, from where they were sometimes despatched to the Foreign Office in London, whose personnel dutifully returned them to St Kilda. Others disappeared, and a few were washed up on the western shores of Lewis or Uist. Twenty years after Sands another visitor tested the efficacy of the mailboat, writing:

> As I had expressed a desire to hear from the St Kildans during the winter by means of one of their miniature mailboats, they dispatched one containing three letters for me at eleven o'clock on the morning of March 24th, during the prevalence of a north-westerly wind. On the 31st of the same month it was picked up by a shepherd in a little bay at Vallay, North Uist, and its contents forwarded to me by post. The letters had been placed in a small tin canister, and despite the fact that they had become soaked with sea water, they still retained a delightful aroma of peat smoke when they reached my hands, reminding me forcibly of my stay on the island.

Their mythology was established and in later years St Kilda mailboat replicas would become valuable tourist souvenirs.

As Sands was there when the Austrian seamen were stranded, one day,

> … the captain and sailors called on me and felt interested in seeing a canoe I had hewn out of a log. They helped me to rig her and to put the ballast right; but we had to wait until the wind was favourable. We

put two bottles in her hold containing letters, which we hoped would find their way to the mainland and be posted.

This canoe carried a small sail, and was despatched on the 5th of February, the wind being in the north-west, and continuing so for some days. I thought she would reach Uist; but the Gulf Stream was stronger than I calculated on, and she went to Poolewe in Ross-shire, where she was found lying on a sandbank on the 27th by a Mr John MacKenzie, who posted the letters.

Five days previous to the date when we launched the canoe, we sent off a life-buoy belonging to the lost ship. I suggested that a bottle containing a letter should be lashed to it and a small sail put up. This was done; but no one had much hope that this circular vessel would be of service. She was sent off on the 30th January, and strange to relate, drifted to Birsay in Orkney, and was forwarded to Lloyd's agent in Stromness on the 8th February, having performed the passage in nine days.

John Sands also introduced the modern legend of the St Kilda Parliament, that occasional, ancient convocation which would be interpreted as a daily gathering of tribal elders and pictured on many a tourist's postcard.

The men of St Kilda are in the habit of congregating in front of one of the houses almost every morning for the discussion of business.

I called this assembly the Parliament, and, with a laugh, they adopted the name. When the subject is exciting, the members talk with loud voices and all at one time; but when the question is once settled, they work together in perfect harmony. Shall we go to catch solan-geese, or ling, or mend the boat to-day? are examples of the subjects that occupy the House. Sometimes disputes are settled by drawing lots.

A system of mutual insurance has existed from time immemorial. A large number of sheep are annually lost by falling over the cliffs, and the owners are indemnified by the other members of the community, whose contributions are in proportion to the number of sheep they possess, and the consequent risk. As the calculations are all performed mentally, I think this shews no small arithmetical power.

Parliament, besides being necessary to the conduct of business, has, I think, a salutary effect on the minds of the people, and helps to keep them cheerful in spite of their isolated position and excessive religious exercises. Man is a gregarious animal, and there are no people more so than the St Kildans. In work every one follows his neighbour. If one puts a new thatch on his barn, a man is to be seen on the top of every barn in the village. If the voice of praise is heard at the door of one house, all, you may be sure, are engaged in worship; and so on.

As he makes clear, both Sands and the St Kildan men only jokingly described their meetings as 'parliaments'. Such gatherings were commonplace in every crofting community. They were rarely much different from the Village Bay morning debate described in 1876:

To sit on a boulder of rock in the strangers' gallery of a parliament, where all its members stand and speak at once in an unknown tongue, is a curious experience, which I have had the pleasure of indulging in. The St Kildans meet every morning – either in front of one of their cottages or on the rocks below the storehouse – and discuss how they shall go about the business of the day. One or two of the debates, at which I was present, became so animated and the din so prodigious that I thought the matter must inevitably end in blows and bloodshed; but I was greatly mistaken, for after awhile some satisfactory understanding was arrived at, and they all went forth harmoniously to share the toil and danger of the day.

The parliament's directives were flexible.

One day [in 1878] they were talking of going to Boreray on the morrow, but the factor wanted to get a little business done first, and, not to interfere with their plans, agreed to be ready for them at 5 a.m. The first man turned up at 10.30, and it was past six in the evening before they got off in the boat.

Every morning they spend a long time discussing what the plan of campaign for the day is to be, and seldom start doing anything before ten o'clock. Sometimes they will take a whole day making up their minds to go fishing on the next, but when once started they are most industrious, and do not seem to mind hard work.

The parliamentary tag usefully confirmed to others their misapprehension that St Kilda was a small, independent polity which had developed in isolation many of the grand institutions of the Western world. Later St Kildan men, anxious always to please their visitors, duly posed for parliamentary photographs outside a house in the middle of Main Street at any time of day. They then returned to the cliffs, to the gathering of animals, to mending boats or even to set sail for Boreray. A young St Kildan man who was allowed to join the parliament at seventeen years of age in 1919 wrote later that it met for serious business only occasionally. 'As certain conditions on the Island did not change that much, as far as certain work that had to be attended to at certain times of the year and this was a must, take for example peat cutting took approximately ten days – no parliament during that time. The yearly expedition of the Islanders to Boreray to shear sheep, that's another ten days or so. The parliament did not meet during harvest time, which took at least a fortnight, and I could go on and mention the months that the Islanders fished for ling and also cod, no parliament.'

By the early twentieth century and probably earlier 'the real purpose of the St Kilda Parliament was to see that all the islanders got their equal share of the cliff where the fulmar nested'. It also decided who was to be paid £1.00 a year for looking after the bull; it arranged the building of new cleits for widows; it apportioned grazing space on Dun and it decided from whose flock a visiting minister would be given a sheep when the clergyman arrived to conduct communions, weddings and baptisms.

Thanks to the reduced population in the 1870s, Sands discovered the women of Hirta to be unusually active in uncomfortable or dangerous outdoor pursuits. He accompanied a party of young women on a puffin-catching expedition to Boreray. The group must have included Norman and Mary Gillies's daughters Christian and Mary Jemima Otter, who were twenty-one and seventeen years old at the time, were no longer scholars and were among the dozen unmarried young women on the island in 1876. Sands reported,

Being acquainted with their habits, the women take dogs with them, which are taught to alarm the puffins and to catch them as they flutter out of their holes. The girls also place hair-ropes on the ground, held down at the ends by stones. Nooses of horse-hair are affixed to the rope, into which the birds (which frequent this island in incredible numbers) push their feet. In this way some of the girls catch as many as four or five hundred puffins in a day.

The young women remain about three weeks on the island, all alone by themselves. They work until they drop asleep. Every one takes her Gaelic Bible with her, for all can read with ease. They sleep in the clothes they wear during the day. On my second visit to this island, I took a glance at the houses in which these bird-catchers reside. They are three in number, and are covered outside with earth and turf, and look like grassy hillocks. One of them is fifteen feet long by six feet wide. It is six and a half feet high at the hearth, which is close to the door. A semicircular stone seat runs round the hearth. The rest of the floor is raised a foot higher, and is used as a bed. The door is about two and a half feet high, and has to be entered on hands and knees. These houses are built on the same plan as the *claetan*, but are covered outside with earth and turf for the sake of warmth.

It was not an easy lot. On one occasion in Sands' time the girls on Boreray all fell ill with what may have been the influenza to which St Kildans were ever susceptible – 'the weather had been bad, and these unprotected females had never changed their clothes, but slept in the garments that they wore during the day; and although accustomed to severe exercise in the open air, had sat exposed to the cold, plucking feathers from morning till night'.

They sent some puffins back to Village Bay to be plucked but stayed on Boreray to catch more.

They suffered great hardships, and only get the pittance of six shillings a St Kilda stone (twenty-four pounds) for the feathers, which are of excellent quality. At that time the few people left in the village were also busy plucking feathers; and the smell of roasted puffins – 'a very ancient and fish-like smell' – came from every door. These birds also furnish a feast for all the dogs and hooded crows that haunt the village. I ate a puffin by way of experiment, and found it tasted like a kippered herring, with a flavour of the dog-fish. Custom would no doubt make it more palatable.

On the 3rd of August a boat went to Boreray and brought back a cargo of puffins and gougan or young solan-geese. On the sixth two boats went again to that island, and brought back the twelve young women who had been catching puffins, together with the feathers.

Some of the women caught as many as six hundred puffins a day. I calculate that eighty-nine thousand six hundred puffins must have been killed by both sexes. The fingers of the girls had become so sore from plucking the feathers that they were obliged to use their teeth in drawing the tail and pinions!

Those were, needless to say, the same young women whose occupations were either unrecorded or were registered in the censuses of the time as 'servant'. In 1886 a schoolteacher on the island found himself hanging off Conachair cliffs from two ropes which were supported on the clifftop by 'three girls & [a] lad'. Another male visitor in the 1870s paid tribute to 'the manner in which [the St Kildan women and girls] carry heavy loads of turf from every corner of the island; the powerful aid which they render in dragging boats on their arrival over the rocks; their milking, cheesemaking, and herding in all states of the weather; their washing, spinning, and occasionally dyeing of wool; their alertness in knitting stockings while tending the flocks or when engaged in conversation; their snaring of puffins and plucking the feathers; their help in tilling the land; and their grinding the corn in hand-mills, after it has been thrashed with a flail, and scorched in a pot or basket containing hot stones'.

The querns referred to as 'hand-mills' were still in common use in the Hebrides, including St Kilda, in the late nineteenth century. They consisted of,

two circular stones of granite, from 15 to 18 inches in diameter, and about 4 inches thick, laid flat upon each other. In the centre of the lower stone, which has a hollow of some 5 inches in depth, there is an iron pivot on which the upper stone, which is flat, is turned by means of a wooden handle. The grain is dropped into a round hole in the centre of the upper stone, finds its way between the two stones as the upper one is kept revolving, and is supposed to be sufficiently ground when it comes out at the edge between the stones. [Earlier in the nineteenth century] the practice in St Kilda was to place the quern on a sheep-skin, in the centre of the floor, while two women, in accordance with the language of Scripture, sat cross-legged on each side – one feeding the mill with grain, while the other turned the handle with great rapidity.

Whether or not he fell for one or more of those girls, their appearance certainly appealed to John Sands. Once, while he was watching the men scale down Conachair cliffs for fulmars, two young women arrived, 'step[ped] with their bare feet to the very verge of the precipice and peer[ed] below.

'One of them, who has a light graceful figure, looks very picturesque as she stands poised on that stupendous cliff. She has a Turkey-red handkerchief on her head, and wears a coarse blue gown of a quaint shape, girdled at the waist, and only reaching to her knees. Her limbs are muscular and browned with the sun.'

Sands went also to neighbouring Soay, where he saw the proprietor's unique breed of sheep – 'They are of a fawn colour, and are very wild. They run like deer; and are only caught to be plucked.' He experienced the tricky business of getting off and then back onto a boat on Soay's rocky shores:

Two young men sat on the top of the cliff, each holding a rope, by the help of which the others slid into the boat.

Then came my turn. A line was fastened around my waist, and a hair-rope put into my hand. I was peremptorily requested to take off my shoes; and as I descended, I pushed my toes into any crevice or cranny that offered, until the rock became so smooth that I could find no hold for my feet. Then I was obliged to be passive, and allowed myself to be lowered like a sack until I reached a small limpet-covered shelf on which the waves rose about knee-deep. 'Jump! Jump!' shout the crew; and when the boat mounts on the wave, I leap, and fall in a heap amongst the fulmars – all right.

The air was quite calm, but the sea continued to rise, and the boat was in imminent danger of being dashed to pieces against the wall. At one time she became altogether unmanageable, and was forced by the sea into a place where the rocks were under her bottom, and caused several hard bumps. The water too began to pour over the gunnel, and I thought that every wave would send us to the bottom. It being impossible to get the two men on board at that spot, the boat was rowed along to a cliff farther south. The waves were quite as wild there; but a double line having been passed around a projecting stone, and the ends held firmly in the boat, the two men slid down and pulled the rope after them. A few strokes of the oars carried us out of danger.

In the excursion I experienced no little exhaustion. A morsel of cheese and a bit of oat-cake was all I had tasted during the day, as I had hurried off without breakfast. It was dark when we reached the village.

In October 1876 he watched as 'all the inhabitants went down the cliffs to pluck grass for their cattle. I saw the women lying on the narrow sloping ledges on the face of the rocks. A false step, and they would have fallen into the sea, hundreds of feet below, or been mangled on the projecting crags'. John Sands attended the harvest thanksgiving service conducted by Reverend MacKay on 7 November, and the celebration of the Old New Year on 12 January. He spent evenings in the homes of the St Kildans, listening to their folk tales and improving his Gaelic by attempting to translate the old horror story of Bluebeard into their language – 'the women sometimes improving my grammar, and helping me out of any difficulty'.

At 7.00 a.m. on 22 February 1877 'as I was lying in bed and thinking of getting up to make my breakfast, I was startled by hearing the sound of a steam-whistle. I lay back again muttering: "It was the wind;" when hark! the whistle is repeated.'

I leaped up, ran to the door, and saw, sure enough, a steamer in the bay! Huddling on my clothes, I rushed barefoot up the village, rattling at every door, and shouting 'Steamer – strangers!' In a few minutes all the people were astir and hurrying to the shore. I had just time to throw the articles that lay handy into my trunk and to get on board the steamer's boat, which I saw belonged to Her Majesty.

Then I discovered that I had left my purse and other property in the house; but the surf was too great to allow me to land again. I got on board the steamer, which I found to be the [Royal Navy's paddle-powered gunship] *Jackal.* 'How did you know we were here?' I inquired of one of the officers who stood on the quarter-deck. 'From the letter you wrote and put into the bottle lashed to the life-buoy.'

I ran to the side of the ship muttering to myself: 'There is a Providence that shapes our ends, rough-hew them as we will;' and bawled to the St Kildans in the boat along-side: 'It was the life-buoy [the mail boat] brought this steamer here, you incredulous people;' for they had smiled, although good-humouredly, at my efforts to send a letter home. A small supply of biscuits and oat-meal was given to them; and waving an adieu to my good St Kildan friends, we were speedily receding from the island.

On 2 July 1877, four months after John Sands's departure, the *Dunara Castle* arrived in Village Bay with her first charter cargo of tourists. Those tourists included the unmistakable figure of George Seton, a fifty-five year-old civil servant from Perth who stood 6 feet 5 inches tall in his stockinged feet. Seton's travelling companions were a mixture of the Scottish minor landowning (the major landowners travelled on their own yachts) and professional classes.

'Our party numbered about forty,' he recorded, 'and, besides three ladies, included the following gentlemen: Captain Macdonald of Waternish; Major James Colquhoun, Arroquhar, and a younger brother; Dr George Keith and son, Edinburgh; Mr Bulkeley, procurator-fiscal, Lochmaddy; Captain Macdonald of the Vigilant; Dr Messer, Helensburgh; Rev. John Macrae, minister of North Uist; Dr Mackenzie, Old Calabar [a town in the British colonial possession of Nigeria]; and Mr Thomas Ormerod, Brighouse. Miss Macleod of Macleod accompanied us on our return.'

Miss MacLeod was Emily MacLeod, the sister of the proprietor, Norman MacLeod of MacLeod. While her brother worked in London Emily remained at the family seat on Skye, from where she sallied forth to attend to the family's most distant dependencies. She was much admired for her charity by both her acquaintances and her tenantry. When Emily MacLeod left Village Bay, where she had lodged for over two weeks in the factor's house at the north end of Main Street, George Seton noted that 'The scene at her departure was not a little touching. While she was affectionately kissed by the women, the men "lifted up" their voices. I was, however, fully prepared for this display of attachment, having heard so much of the benevolent lady's acts of kindness at Dunvegan, where a woman, to whom I happened to speak of Miss Macleod's absence from Skye being a cause of regret in that quarter, warmly informed me that she was "an angel in human form!"'

The *Dunara Castle*'s maiden excursion created the template for almost all future charters to St Kilda. The tourists left An t-Obbe, which would later be renamed Leverburgh, in the south of Harris at about 3.00 a.m.

… we soon emerged from the Hebridean archipelago into the wide Atlantic; and between four and five, the islet of Borrera and its adjacent stacks began to disclose their picturesque outlines. Masses of white clouds were resting on the summits of St Kilda as we approached its rocky shores from the north-east side.

We dropped anchor at half-past eight, in smooth water, within a gunshot of the shore, and the impression produced by the surrounding scenery was heightened by the stillness that prevailed. After breakfasting on board the *Dunara*, the passengers began to land in detachments about half-past nine. Heavy rain fell during breakfast; but the weather speedily improved, and the sun shone forth most auspiciously. Some of the party landed in one of the boats of the islanders which came out to the steamer, while others went in the gig belonging to the *Dunara*. We received a warm and hearty welcome from the inhabitants, who had all assembled on the beach when the steamer entered the bay.

They were put ashore for four hours in Village Bay. If the weather was decent, four hours offered the younger and fitter members of the group the chance to climb Conachair, or even to stride over into Gleann Mor. Everybody had an opportunity to mingle with the natives on Main Street.

The visitors were offered an exhibition of cragsmanship reminiscent of that displayed to James Wilson and Sir Thomas Dick Lauder in 1841. As before, it was orchestrated by the resident clergyman.

The minister having made suitable arrangements with some of the most experienced fowlers in the island, we ascended to the summit of the [Conachair] cliff, which commands a magnificent view of Borrera and the adjacent stacks – a pretty stiff pull of fully half an hour – and from the verge of the precipice looked down a sheer descent of some 800 feet upon the heaving rollers of the Atlantic.

Furnished with the requisite ropes and other appliances, four or five of the cragsmen approached the edge of the cliff. One of the most agile of the party – a vigorous, bright-eyed islander of about thirty years of age – taking one rope in his hand, in order to steady his movements, and having another firmly secured round his waist, was gradually lowered down the perpendicular face of the precipice by two of his comrades.

Uttering a shrill Gaelic cry, he descended barefooted, skipping and singing as he went, and occasionally standing out nearly at a right angle from the beetling cliff! Arrived at the narrow rocky ledges where the fulmar and puffin sit in supposed security, a long stick, resembling a fishing-rod, with a noose at the extremity, was let down to him from above, which he cautiously extended, making the noose fall rapidly over the head of the bird, the fluttering victim being immediately captured.

Several fulmars and puffins were thus secured for different members of our party, one of the former – of which an accurate representation is given – being now in my possession. It is difficult, by means of verbal narration, to convey anything like an adequate idea of the sensation produced by the wonderful performance which I have endeavoured to describe ...

To any one who has witnessed the daring procedure of the St Kilda cragsman, the most startling feats of a Blondin or a Leotard appear utterly insignificant; and if the most venturesome member of the Alpine Club had been of our party, I feel satisfied that he would have been compelled to 'hide his diminished head'! [Charles Blondin was a French tightrope walker and acrobat who in 1861 had performed to public acclaim at the Royal Botanic Gardens in Edinburgh; Jules Leotard was a Gallic trapeze artist who gave his name to the garment.]

Some sensitive people are quite unable to contemplate the fowler's miraculous movements; and even in the case of the most callous spectator, the blood inclines to run cold, and for once in his life he discovers that he is possessed of a nervous system.

The St Kildan men were paid 'a few pounds' for this display. An earlier visitor, T S Muir, had complained in the 1860s about 'the bargaining that he had to go through before three or four of the islanders could be prevailed upon to accept a good day's wages for an hour's exhibition of their mode of descending the cliffs. "They had once got as many pounds as we were offering shillings for doing the same thing for a Lady Somebody, and what was there to hinder us from giving a like sum?"'

Muir concluded that 'in later times, money having become to some extent the medium of traffic, a thirst for it is now as keen in lonely St Kilda as it is in quarters where its acquisition is matter of hourly concern'. The Hirtans had certainly grasped the economics of the tourist trade. As early as 1860 they expected to be paid before they would pose for a photograph. The *Dunara Castle*'s passengers in 1877 'were presented with specimens of eggs and sea-birds; and the payments made for stockings, and other small articles knitted by the women, were very slightly in excess of an ordinary hosier's charge'.

At 2.00 p.m. those tourist re-embarked with their souvenirs on the *Dunara Castle* and took a trip around the islands and the stacks before returning to Harris.

It had been an extraordinary experience. 'It is not easy to convey anything like a correct or adequate conception of the magnificent and fantastic outlines presented by the rugged promontories and beetling headlands of St Kilda and the adjacent islets', wrote George Seton.

The vast variety of form and colour which delighted the party on board the *Dunara Castle* on the afternoon of the 2d of July will not soon be forgotten. Being in water of forty fathoms, we were able to keep very close to the shore; but the rate at which we steamed round the island – although probably not exceeding nine knots an hour – was not sufficiently slow to enable the most rapid observer fully to realise the grandeur of the remarkable scene.

I almost feel disposed to summarise my impressions by quoting part of an American author's description of Inspiration Point in the Yosemite Valley. 'In all my life,' he says, 'let it lead me where it may, I think I shall see nothing else so grand, so awful, so sublime, so beautiful ... It was only yesterday evening; – I cannot write of it yet. How long I sat there on the rocks I never shall know. I brought the picture away with me. I have only to shut my eyes, and I see it as I saw it in that hour of hours!'

... For two or three hours after we steamed away from Borrera in the direction of the Sound of Harris, the bold outlines of St Kilda and its satellites continued more or less in sight; and the last glimpse of the wonderful group was eagerly regarded by every member of our enchanted party.

In the following year of 1878 an extremely distinguished personage was among the tourists who visited St Kilda.

Nothing can be more picturesque than the approach to St Kilda … by degrees, we came upon the little green valley opening down upon the shore in which the people of St Kilda live. There were the few acres that are cultivated in the island, and there is the row of cottages, eighteen in number, in which the inhabitants live. There is also the chapel which has been built for their use, and there also lives their pastor, who has been now twelve years among them.

We went ashore in the ship's boats, and the inhabitants came out to meet us with gracious smiles. With them was their minister, and with them also was Miss MacLeod, the sister of MacLeod, the proprietor of the island … The first care was to land certain stores, – tea, sugar, and such like, – which Mr Burns had brought as a present to the people. It is the necessity of their position that such aid should be essential almost to their existence.

It is about forty-five miles from the nearest of the large inhabited islands, – forty-five miles, that is, from humanity; but St Kilda is in itself so small that there is no ready mode for traversing that distance. There is no communication by steamer, except such a chance coming as that of ours. The whole wealth of the small community cannot command more than a small rowing-boat or two. When we landed, the men were in sore distress for a few fathoms of rope, which they obtained from the liberality of Mr Burns.

The island is about two-and-a-half miles long, and about seven in circumference; the highest land is about 1,200 feet high … it contains about thirty acres of cultivated land, lying just in front of the cottages, on which potatoes and oats are grown … There is, too, a considerable amount of pasture-land among the rocks and hills, on which are maintained about 50 cattle and 400 sheep; but with them there is much difficulty. The winter here is very cold, and in winter the stock is necessarily left to shift for themselves … Then we walked up among the cottages, buying woollen stockings and sea-birds' eggs, such being the commodities they had for sale. Some coarse cloth we found there also, made on the island from the wool grown there, of which some among us bought sufficient for a coat, waistcoat, or petticoat, as the case may be.

In their want of other fuel, the inhabitants skin the turf from their pastures and burn it. Gradually, thus, the grass is going, for it is burned much quicker than it is produced. In this way the food for the sheep and cattle will quickly disappear.

They (the cottages) are soundly built of stone, and each contains two well-sized rooms; but it may, I think, be taken for granted that this is due to private munificence and not to the personal efforts of the inhabitants. There are still to be seen the wretched hovels in which the people dwelt before the stone cottages were erected, fifteen years ago.

The pastor, whose life here is certainly not to be envied, and who acts as schoolmaster as well as minister, receives £80 per annum from the Scotch Free Church ... There is but one person in the island but himself, a married woman, who can speak a word of English. No books can reach him; hardly a newspaper.

There are between seventy and eighty inhabitants on the island, of whom, among the adults, the female outnumber the male by nearly two to one. This, of course, comes from the fact that the young men can leave the harshness of such a life much more easily than the young women. I was told that at the present moment there were two marriageable young men at St Kilda, and twelve marriageable, but unmarried, females ...

Each man is his own shoemaker and tailor. They dye their own wool. Whatever furniture they use they make generally for themselves. They make their own candles. But perhaps the chief employment of the men is the catching of sea birds; the feathers of which they sell, and on the flesh of which they in a great part live. The bird which they eat is the fulmar ... Sometimes they have bread. Sometimes they make a stew with oatmeal and fulmar, – not delicious I should think to any but a St Kildarite; – sometimes they luxuriate with corned mutton. Sometimes they have porridge.

Those words were written by the novelist Anthony Trollope. In 1878 Trollope was sixty-three years old and at the height of his fame. The St Kildan islands were firmly on the social map.

EIGHT

Speaking Truth to Power

✸

W HEN REVEREND JOHN MACKAY took the census in 1881 the population had stabilised. There were seventy-seven people living in Village Bay.

The average age had risen yet again, from thirty-six ten years earlier to thirty-eight in 1881. One of the reasons was the unusual longevity of late nineteenth-century St Kildans. At a time when the United Kingdom's average life expectancy at birth was forty years, and the average life expectancy at forty years was seventy years, there were seven St Kildans – or 10 per cent of the native population – over the age of seventy and another twelve in their sixties.

Encouragingly, the number of children under ten years old had doubled to fourteen in 1881. But the result was still a highly unbalanced demographic. There were just sixteen people – including only five men – in their twenties and thirties in St Kilda – fewer than the number who were over sixty years old. Ten of the women of marriageable age were unmarried and there were only two bachelors over the age of eighteen. Overall St Kildan women outnumbered St Kildan men by forty-four to thirty-three.

Reverend John MacKay made two pioneering entries in the 1881 St Kildan census. It was the first survey which counted the number of Gaelic speakers in Scotland. The number of Gaelic speakers in Ireland (which was then part of the United Kingdom) had been enumerated since 1861 and Highland lobbyists pressed hard to gain similar treatment for the Scottish *Gàidhealtachd*.

Early in 1881 the Home Secretary Sir William Harcourt agreed.

But the census forms had already been printed without any reference to Scottish Gaelic. The enumerators were therefore instructed to ask Scots if they were 'habitual' users of the language, and if so to note the fact beside the individual's entry.

In Hirta the question was plainly ridiculous. Rather than detail each person's fluency in his or her native language, Reverend MacKay scrawled across the first page of the census return the words: 'All of the inhabitants of St Kilda speak Gaelic habitually.'

The second introduction to the census was more significant. In 1879 Miss Emily MacLeod, the proprietor's sister who made so many visits to St Kilda, employed a nurse and teacher to take up residence in the island. Ann MacKinlay was a widow from Bracadale in north Skye who had practised for many years as a nurse in Edinburgh. By 1881 she was sixty-seven years old, lodging in the two-storey factor's house at the north end of Main Street, and not in the best of health. But she was a native Gaelic speaker and, more crucially, the first trained nurse to work on Hirta. Her impact, and that of her successors, was most evident in reducing infant mortality.

The causes of the 'eight-day sickness' which carried off almost 70 per cent of St Kildan babies in the 1860s were not fully understood either by Miss Emily MacLeod or by Ann MacKinlay. Both women did however understand basic hygiene. Nurse Mackinlay had 'no hesitation in attributing the disease to improper food and treatment'. The everyday knives greased with fulmar oil and carrying other detritus which had traditionally been used to cut the umbilical cord in Village Bay, and which conveyed a fatal tetanus infection to newborn babies and, in many cases, to their mothers, were at least partly sterilised in hot water or over an open flame. Swaddling clothes were boiled and the infants' early days passed in a cleaner environment.

The results were not immediately dramatic. Throughout the 1870s and the 1880s, on Ann MacKinlay's watch, half of St Kildan children died before they were a month old. Even when Mrs MacKinlay delivered the infants the parents were frequently unwilling to forego old neonatal practices, with the same old tragic results and with consequential bad feeling between Ann MacKinlay and some St Kildans. There is little doubt that St Kildans were cynical about modern medicine. In 1896 a doctor arrived in Village Bay to inoculate the children against smallpox, 'but so small was the faith of the natives in Jenner's great discovery, that he was obliged to take his departure without having operated upon a single child'.

Basic personal and domestic cleanliness was however embraced. By 1898 a visitor who had expected the widely advertised bad breath, stinking clothes and disgusting homes of St Kilda was surprised to find that 'they were remarkably clean. I fancy that a little Keating's powder [an insecticide] would add to the comfort of any one sleeping in a native house, and they are not very particular as to where they throw the refuse parts of birds and fishes, but, to outward appearance, they are clean enough in their persons. Fishiness is not looked upon as a reason for refraining from the handshake, but if they have been handling tar or other unpleasant materials, they apologise for not being able to conform to the ordinary St Kildan mode of greeting.'

Nurse MacKinlay's 50 per cent survival rate was an improvement on 30 per cent, and the improvement continued over the following forty years. Many people who were born in late-nineteenth-century St Kilda lived to see the twentieth century chiefly because of the medical regime which was introduced by Ann MacKinlay.

Down on Main Street, in 1881 Finlay MacQueen was eighteen years old and still living with his elderly maternal grandparents. Finlay's mother, Ann MacDonald, was lodging as well as housekeeping at the Manse following the death of Reverend MacKay's sister. Reverend John MacKay had also taken into his house the nine year-old son of Isabella MacDonald after her death and her husband's remarriage.

Finlay MacQueen was one of just two young St Kildan men who still identified themselves as cragsmen. Further down the street at Number 13 the fifty-seven year-old Norman Gillies, in common with almost every other adult of either gender on the island, now described himself as a crofter.

There were political as well as occupational reasons for that change of vocation, and they indicate the connections between St Kilda and the rest of the west Highlands and Islands. The St Kildans had been working their allocated crofts since the abolition of communal runrig land in the 1830s, but they had always since preferred to describe themselves as birdcatchers or cragsmen. (In truth, as one writer observed, where 'every man follows five or six distinct callings' his vocation was difficult to pin down: 'He is at once crofter, cragsman, fisherman, weaver, tailor, and cobbler.')

Crofts at that time were insecure assets. Landlords and their agents were legally able to evict crofters for no reason at a moment's notice, or to rack-rent them, or simply to sell off a parcel of croftland to an aspiring farmer.

All of those things had occurred, even under the most apparently benign of landowners, elsewhere in the Highlands and Islands during the nineteenth century. In the 1870s and 1880s crofters on the Highland mainland and on the larger Hebridean islands such as Skye and Lewis began to campaign – and in some cases physically fight – for security of tenure and fair rents. By 1881 the political tide was turning in the crofters' favour. It began to look as though their battle might be won. In the event of such a happy outcome the people of St Kilda did not wish to be left behind. When Reverend John MacKay asked them for their occupations during the 1881 census enumeration, although all the able-bodied males still caught birds and scaled crags, almost to a man they replied that they were crofters. They might have liked the absentee MacLeod of MacLeod and they certainly appreciated the efforts of his sister Miss Emily, but the 1881 census indicates that they placed their long-term trust in a reform of the law rather than in the paternalism of Dunvegan Castle.

In 1883 William Gladstone's Liberal Government was persuaded by widespread unrest in the north and west of Scotland to establish a Royal Commission of Inquiry into the Condition of Crofters and Cottars in the Highlands and Islands. It was headed by Francis, tenth Lord Napier, and immediately became known as the Napier Commission. As well as Francis Napier the commission included the Conservative landowners Sir Kenneth MacKenzie of Gairloch and Sir Donald Cameron of Lochiel, the radical Member of Parliament for Inverness Burghs Charles Fraser Mackintosh, a Skyeman named Alexander Nicolson who was currently Sheriff of Kirkcudbright, and Professor Donald MacKinnon, the holder of the Chair of Celtic at Edinburgh University. Napier and his five colleagues then toured the region by yacht.

Typically, the St Kildans knew nothing of Napier's impending visit. They tended to be aware of broader events in the outside world without being up to date on the minutiae. Two years later a visitor learned that the men of Hirta knew that they had, for the first time, been enfranchised by the Representation of the People Act of 1884, and they knew that a general election campaign was being held in 1885.

They did not know much about the Crofters' Candidates who would, following the franchise extension, sweep the Highlands and Islands in that election, but they were aware of 'the Crofter Question'. A visitor in 1885 was instantly assailed by a barrage of questions such as 'How is the Crofter Question getting on?', 'What are the landlords doing?', 'Have their heads been chopped off yet?'. They did not know how they would be expected to vote – they hoped 'that when the polling day came they would be taken away in a boat to record their votes'. They were not. Many St Kildan adult men were nominally enfranchised by the 1867 Reform Act, even more of them in 1884, and all men over the age of twenty-one years and several women over the age of thirty should have been given suffrage after 1919. During those periods they were citizens firstly of the Inverness-shire parliamentary seat and after its creation in 1918 of the Western Isles constituency. They were never once given the opportunity to register their preference in a General Election. Voting forms and polling booths never arrived in Village Bay. Postal voting, which at certain times of year might have suited St Kilda, was not permitted to civilians in the United Kingdom until eighteen years after the last civilian had left the islands.

So it was to the great surprise of the St Kildans that Napier and his commissioners appeared in St Kilda on the evening of Friday, 1 June 1883, announced that they wished to hear of any grievances and then held their hearing about conditions on the island throughout the following Saturday. Almost all of the island attended but only three of them spoke.

The St Kildans nominated to present their case were the sixty-seven year-old Reverend John MacKay, the thirty-seven year-old Donald MacDonald and the thirty-five year-old Angus Gillies. Neither MacDonald nor Gillies could speak English and only two members of the commission – Nicolson and MacKinnon – were Gaelic speakers, so their questions and answers were filtered through a translator. They were intelligent, articulate and dignified. They displayed a marked lack of deference, which was at least in part due to the Free Church education which had taught them that all people were equal in the eyes of the Lord, and that a crofter in Village Bay owed nothing to the likes of Francis, 10th Lord Napier and 1st Baron Ettrick. Most valuably, they delivered a vivid portrait of the island as seen through the eyes of its inhabitants in the early 1880s.

Reverend John MacKay introduced himself to Lord Napier as having been on St Kilda 'eighteen years in the month of October'. He then raised the subject of the island's persistent isolation from mainland services. MacLeod of MacLeod, he said, sent two boats a year, in June and September. The tourist steamers *Dunara Castle* and the *Hebridean* each appeared on two or three occasions in June, July and August carrying mail. So St Kilda could have as many as six or seven postal deliveries in the summer months, but between September and the following June they were 'eight months without communications'.

'There is no stated visit on the part of a Government vessel?' asked Napier.
'No,' said Reverend MacKay.
'There is no communication here with the coastguard?'
'No.'
'No branch of the public service?'
'No.'

In raising this matter of long winter isolation, MacKay was representing a real and insistent grievance. That grievance would be represented in the House of Commons ten years later by their Inverness-shire Member of Parliament Donald MacGregor. MacGregor collected a petition from the St Kildans and presented it to the Admiralty, saying: 'I beg to ask the Secretary to the Admiralty if he has received a Petition from the natives of St Kilda, in the outer Hebrides, where they live isolated for nine months of the year from all communication with the rest of the world, craving for an occasional visit of the gunboats cruising in northern waters during the autumn, winter, and spring months; and whether it will be possible to comply with this request?'

MacGregor was told that 'the request is receiving immediate and careful consideration'. In 1905 yet another petition from St Kilda 'for improved communication with the mainland' was laid before Parliament. It also was ignored.

Asked in 1883 if during his eighteen years there had been 'any material change in the condition of the people', Reverend MacKay said: 'Well, I think there is some change for the better as to their moral character.'

'Their general character has improved?' said Lord Napier.

'Yes.'

'Are there any spirituous liquors sold in the island?'

'No.'

'Is there any private drinking in their houses?' Napier persisted. 'Have they got any whisky or spirituous liquors in their houses?'

'Well, they buy a bottle or two, and when they are out on the hill and catch a cold, they take a glass of whisky after coming home, but that is all they use.'

'When the steamers come here do they do any mischief by the sale of liquors or in any other way?'

'I don't think it,' said John MacKay. 'Some of these passengers are very loose in their character, and some of them are drunk when they come ashore, but the people avoid them as far as they can … They [the visitors] are very annoying when they remain here over the Sabbath … They go about the hills, and go seeing through the windows and striking the dogs and one thing and another.'

'What school is there here?'

'There is a school taught by a woman, Miss McKinlay … It is supported by the [Free Church] Ladies' Association in Edinburgh and by Miss McLeod.'

'Do the children attend regularly?'

'Yes, pretty fair. Sometimes their parents want them to go after some cattle, and they are sometimes absent in that way.'

'Have they more general knowledge of English than when you came, or is there no change in that respect?'

'Well, there is a little, not much.'

Charles Fraser-Mackintosh asked John MacKay if the St Kildans were 'as comfortable in their ways and means as they used to be'.

'Well,' said Reverend MacKay, 'I think they are better off today than they were when I came to the island … When the [tourist] steamers come here, they leave a good deal of money among the people; and again there is another thing, that McLeod gives a larger price for the kealt [home-woven cloth – the word was the origin of 'kilt']. It once sold for 2s and 2s 4d and now they get 3s … He will take the whole, everything he can get; he will take the whole produce of the island.'

'When the steamers come here, are they able to make purchases of fresh provisions? Are you able to sell any butter or fowls or eggs?'

'No, neither butter nor eggs. We have no hens on the island.'

'Then steamers can get nothing in the way of food here?'

'No, unless they buy a sheep; they generally buy a sheep here.'

Cameron of Lochiel was curious about the St Kildans' nuptial arrangements. Having been told that there had been no marriages on Hirta in the last year, he asked, 'What is the average – one or two?'

'That is the utmost – two,' said Reverend MacKay.

'Do any of the people ever marry with those who come from the mainland?'

'No, they never marry with any from the mainland; they marry among themselves.'

'Do they ever get the chance of marrying from the mainland?'

'I never heard it.'

'Do you think they would if they got the chance?'

'I think they would.'

'Do you know of any offer of marriage that was ever made by young men of the mainland to any of the girls here?'

'Well, I cannot call to mind. They are not very fond of strangers.'

John MacKay then informed the hearing that while the St Kildans were more interested in receiving supplies than letters or the newspapers by ship, they were 'very fond' of papers and corresponded frequently with people on the mainland.

'What do they live on chiefly?' asked Cameron of Lochiel.

'They eat fresh potatoes, fulmars and puffins.'

'Do they kill their beasts and eat beef?'

'Yes.'

'And mutton?'

'Yes.'

Sir Kenneth MacKenzie then wondered 'How many births are there on average in the year?'

'One or two. There were two last year.'

'Do the children live?'

'I am sorry to say they don't live very well. When they come to the age of seven or eight days they generally die.'

'Do you know if there are more deaths in the island than births?' asked Sir Kenneth.

'No, there are not more deaths than births … [the population] is increasing a little.'

'Do you feel the want of a doctor very much?'

'Well, they are very much needing a doctor at times.'

'Who attends the women in childbirth?' asked Lord Napier.

'Miss MacKinlay up here, the nurse … She was sent here by Miss McLeod, and she attends the women here.'

'Do the women frequently die in childbirth? Has there been any case of that sort?'

'Yes, last February a young woman died here in childbirth. She was only married a year and a quarter.'

'Are there any medicines kept in the island?'

'There is medicine kept in the island, but it will be sometimes very short.'

The Skyeman Alexander Nicolson wondered if the high infant mortality rate could be owing to 'the want of proper care or feeding of the infants at that early age'.

'I don't think it is from the want of any proper care at all,' said Reverend MacKay, 'but after seven or eight days they always – especially some of them who die – are struck with lock-jaw.'

'Do they give them anything but the mother's milk?'

'Nothing.'

'There was an old peculiarity of the inhabitants, that they took a cold when any strangers came to the island?'

'Well, they are very subject to that still. They always catch a cold when there is a cold in the vessel or among the passengers who land here. It begins with one, and goes through the whole village.'

'Have you noticed it yourself?'

'Yes, I have.'

'Following immediately after the visit of a ship?'

'Yes.'

'Have you been infected by it yourself?'

'Yes.'

'Then you think it was infectious?'

'It was, very. There were some fishermen here from Uist a few years ago, and they had a very severe cold. There was not a man or woman on the island I think but took it, and I was very ill myself.'

'Ordinarily they are not subject to colds?'

'No, they are not. They are very healthy that way.'

'Are there ever cases of consumption?'

'No, there is not a case of consumption, so far as I know, on the island: they take so much food, and these fulmars and birds they eat are so full of sap and oil.'

'What are the prevalent diseases? Are they subject to rheumatism?'

'Some of them are very bad with rheumatism.'

'Are they subject to any skin diseases?'

'They have nothing of that kind at all. Of course, they sometimes have [the skin of] their feet and legs broken out.'

'I suppose they are all very well clothed?'

'Very well.'

'I suppose there is not a ragged person to be seen in the island?'

'Not a ragged man or woman, if she or he pleases to clothe themselves.'

'Or child?'

'Or child. There is plenty of cloth on the island.'

'Are there any of them on the parochial roll of Harris?'

'None.'

'But I suppose there are some old women who cannot support themselves without help?'

'There are two women. There is one of them who is confined to bed for more than two years. She cannot do anything. She is very ill with rheumatism, and cannot move a limb.'

'How is she supported?'

'By her husband.'

'In the case of old persons of that sort being unable to do anything for themselves, or without near relatives, who takes charge of them?'

'Well there are none of them in the island who have not relations.'

'And their relations look after them?'

'Yes.'

'Are any of the inhabitants of the island engaged in work out of the island?'

'No.'

'They are never in the habit of going to work out of the island?'

'No.'

'Or to fish?'

'Yes, they fish in the island.'

'But not out of it?'

'No.'

'They never go to the east coast?'

'No.'

'How many boats have they in the island for their own use?'

'They have four or five boats.'

'Sufficient for their own use round the coasts of the island?'

'Yes.'

'Are any of them big enough for going to the mainland with?'

'Well, we sent for a boat last summer to Mr Fletcher Norton Menzies [the current secretary of the Highland Agricultural Society and consequently trustee of the St Kilda Fund], Edinburgh. They have some money there lodged in his hands, and they wrote him to send them a boat; and after sending the boat, they complained that the boat was too small for going to Harris. You will see the boat down on the beach. The boat is a very steady one, but they say she is rather too small for going to the mainland, and they left that boat and took the boat [a benefactor] sent them some years ago, about 1867.'

'Is it the case that nobody in the island can speak English except yourself and Miss McKinlay?'

'Well, they cannot speak very well, but they are coming on very well.'

'I suppose they are getting a little more knowledge of English?'

'Yes.'

'Is there ever any case of illegitimate birth here?' interrupted Lord Napier.

'There is.'

'Is it very rare?'

'Very rare, but I must say there is such a case.'

'How many have there been since you came to the island?' asked Alexander Nicolson.

'Two.'

'In these cases did the father marry the woman?'

'No, both of them were very young. There was a girl about twenty-four years of age, and a young lad. He was promising to marry her.'

'Was he a native of the island?'

'Yes, but she died in giving birth to the child. There was another case of a younger man who committed fornication.'

'How do you account for the very small increase of the population? Is it from the deaths among the children being very large?'

'Yes.'

Professor Mackinnon wondered if 'Miss McKinlay keeps a school quite regularly since she came to the place?'

'Yes.'

'Do you keep up your own class yet?'

'Yes, I teach them here every Sabbath evening – those whom she teaches.'

'Before she came you taught them yourself?'

'Yes.'

'Are they all able to read?'

'Yes, they are.'

'They can read Gaelic, every one of them?'

'Perfectly well, and commit portions of Scripture to memory.'

'Is there anything else they commit to memory besides portions of Scripture?'

'Nothing.'

'Nothing in the way of songs?'

'Nothing. Nothing whatever.'

'I suppose Miss M'Kinlay teaches them to read English?'

'Yes.'

'Do you think they are able to understand much of what they read?'

'Well, they understand very little.'

'I suppose the whole of the island is in their own hands? They have the whole island among them?'

'Yes.'

'Do they all pay the same amount of rent?'

'No.'

'What is the biggest rent?'

'I cannot say.'

'There is no great big man among them that has taken possession of the crofts of others?'

'No, they pay according to their grazings.'

'Is everybody allowed to put on as much as he likes?'

'I think he is.'

'I heard when I was coming here that there was an emigration from this place. How long ago is that?'

'A great many years ago. It will be well on for thirty years ago since they went to Australia.'

'Who had the property at that time?'

'Sir John MacLeod.'

'Can you tell how many families went away at that time?'

'Seven families, I think.'

'It was to Australia they went?'

'Yes.'

'Did they go away of their own accord, of their own free will?'

'It was poverty that made them emigrate.'

'Did the proprietor or factor compel them to go away in any way?'

'I think Norman [MacRaild], the factor, had a hand in it.'

'Did he make them go?' asked Lord Napier.

'He encouraged them to go, because some of them were poor, and he was giving them meal in order to get quit of them. He got some papers from Government for them to sign, and when some of them saw their friends going away, more came afterwards and signed it.'

'Did the proprietor pay their passage?' asked Professor MacKinnon.

'The proprietor did not know of it, and when he heard that they had gone, he was encouraging them to return, and said that he would do them every justice he possibly could; but as they had gone so far, they did not wish to return back, and he said he himself would send a ship for them if they would come back. This was Sir John McLeod.'

Charles Fraser-Mackintosh wondered if the commissioners' yacht was 'the first strange vessel that has come here this year?'

'Yes.'

'Of course you have received no newspapers this year?'

'Yes, the factor's ship was here on the 3rd of May. McLeod of McLeod sent a ship here. I wrote to him in July last, telling him the state of the island, and telling him he would require to send a ship in April with supplies for the people as the crop looked so bad.'

'Did you get any newspaper then?'

'Yes.'

'Did you see anything about this Commission?'

'Yes, I did; I read about this Commission, and about Glendale.' [At the end of 1882 and early in 1883 there had been serious land rebellions on the late Sir John MacPherson MacLeod's estate in Glendale on Skye, where – to the undoubted interest of the St Kildans – the unpopular Norman MacRaild had been factor.]

'But you did not know we were coming here?'

'No, I did not expect you here at all.'

Lord Napier concluded the examination of Reverend MacKay by asking, 'Is there any case of great longevity in man or woman in the place?'

'Well, some of them are very old.'

'How old is the oldest?'

'A woman is the oldest person on the island. She will be about eighty – Mrs Rory Gillies.' [Catherine Gillies was, in 1883, 81 years old.]

'You don't know any extraordinary case of a person being one hundred years of age?'

'No.'

The thirty-seven year-old crofter and fisherman Donald MacDonald then took the stage, and, through the medium of his native Gaelic, immediately clarified the matter of annual rent.

'We pay separately for the ground that is worked around here [the crofts],' said Donald MacDonald, 'and separately for the hill.'

'Then what do you pay?' asked Sir Kenneth MacKenzie.

'£2 for the arable ground.'

'And for the hill?'

'About £3.'

'Do the tenants all pay the same thing for the hill?'

'No.'

'Why does one pay more than another?'

'According to the proportion of the hill that they had when the laird [MacLeod of MacLeod] came into possession.'

'Then their hill is not in common?'

'Under the former proprietor [Sir John MacPherson MacLeod],' said Donald MacDonald, 'each man paid for the actual stock that he had; but since then the proprietor makes them pay according to the stock they had at that time, whatever it is now.'

'But their stock is all on the same hill; there are no marches on the hill?'

'No.'

'Do you pay this in money, or do you pay it in produce?'

'We pay it with all the produce which the island gives.'

'What is the produce of the island?'

'We pay it with feathers, and oil, and cloth, and also with cattle.'

'At what price does the proprietor take the feathers and oil?'

'5s. a stone for the grey feathers, and 6s. a stone for the black feathers – puffin feathers – which are finer.'

'What does he pay for the oil?'

'One shilling a pint.'

'What oil is it?'

'Fulmar oil.'

'What does he pay for the cloth?'

'Three shillings a Scotch ell.'

'What does he pay for the cattle?'

'The price varies.'

'How do they agree about the price?'

'The factor fixes the price.'

'Are you bound to give your cattle at the factor's price?'

'Sometimes when we are complaining, he adds 1s. or 2s. to the price.'

At that point a St Kildan in the gallery could be heard to say: 'We never got such good prices before as under the present factor.'

'We get £2. 10s.,' continued Donald MacDonald, 'and we have got £3 for a stirk from him. Though the former factor was as he was, we must admit he gave us better prices latterly.'

'Are you in arrears of rent, or are the arrears fully paid in St Kilda?'

'Yes, there are some in arrears.'

'Are they much pressed for payment of these arrears?'

'The factor does not press people at all.'

'A man behind [in the gallery] said, that though some were in debt some were the other way. What is the meaning of that?'

'As in many places, some people are well off and some are ill off.'

'Have any of them an account against the laird – money due to them?'

'Yes, that is so. The laird owes some of us money.'

'In what way does the laird pay them back?'

'Anybody that wishes it from him gets it from him in money.'

'Do you generally make meal enough to keep yourselves through the year?'

'The island would not keep us in meal any time.'

'What quantity of meal do you get from the mainland most years?'

'Some families get from eight to twelve bolls in the year.' [A boll was the equivalent of about 140 lbs.]

'And that is paid for in the produce of the island in the same way as the rent?'

'According to the families. Some don't get more than five or six bolls. Our accounts are made up at the same time for the rent and for the meal.

'You get all your meal and all your supplies from the proprietor?'

'Yes, except a few bolls we got by steamer last summer.'

'Is there any sale for your produce to the steamer?'

'We have sold a little cloth to them.'

'Were you getting good prices?'

'A little better.'

'You don't sell any cows to the steamer?'

'I have seen one cow sold to the steamer.'

'Did they get a good price for it?'

'A better price.'

Cameron of Lochiel then asked, 'Would you like to have a pier?'

'Certainly we would be the better of a pier.'

'How would you be the better of a pier if you got it?'

'If you saw some of the days when we have to land here you would understand then what need we have of it.'

'Is it for purposes of fishing you would be the better of a pier, or for the steamers when they come with supplies?'

'We would rather have it for ourselves – for purposes of fishing.'

'How many of the men fish on the island?'

'Two boats go out to fish now. We are fallen off in able-bodied men.'

'What time of the year do they fish?'

'Whenever we get the chance.'

'I suppose there are a great many days in the year when they cannot fish at all?'

'There are very many days when we cannot go to the fishing, and other days we have other work to attend to at home, and cannot go to fish.'

'Are you ever kept out at sea by the weather getting bad, and your being unable to land here after being once out?'

'Yes, we have sometimes been obliged to try and seek shelter in a creek opposite us on the other side of the island when we could not land here.'

'Does that happen often?'

'Not often.'

'Have any boats ever been lost?'

'There have been no drownings that I remember, but we have lost a boat at Boreray.'

'What fish do you catch?'

'Ling and some cod.'

'At what time of the year do you catch the sea birds?'

'We catch the birds [fulmars] to get the oil at the beginning of summer.'

'How do you catch them?'

'We catch the young ones with our hands before they are able to fly away off their nests.'

'Do you catch any birds at this time [June], or in the spring of the year?'

'We catch the old birds in spring, and at this time of the year with the rod and snare.'

'On the nest?'

'Yes.'

'You put the snare over the nest?'

'We descend the rocks on a rope, and place the snare over the bird's head, and catch it by the neck.'

'Have you any idea how many birds are caught here annually, young and old?'

'I cannot give a guess, probably thousands, but I cannot say.'

'How much does each head of a family catch?'

'One day I remember we were snaring the birds at Boreray, when we caught at least 1,000. There were twenty men of us.'

'That was an unusually large number?'

'I never saw or heard of so many being got.'

'Do you get any herring here?'

'We have no herring nets.'

'Would you catch any if you had nets?'

'Yes, I believe so; and we have spoken of it several times, but we have never got herring nets.'

'Do you catch any solan geese [gannets]?'

'We catch some solan geese.'

'Is it for the oil or feathers, or both?'

'We catch the young ones for their oil and feathers. We eat them a little. We salt some.'

'Is there any diminution in the number of birds,' asked Lord Napier, 'or are there just as many as there used to be long ago?'

'The number of birds varies, apparently, like other crops,' said Donald MacDonald, 'more some years, and less other years.'

'Is any shooting with fire-arms allowed?'

'It is forbidden to shoot birds when they are hatching.'

'Who forbids it?' asked Cameron of Lochiel.

'It has been a rule in the island as long as I remember.'

'But do you allow shooting on the island the rest of the year?' asked Lord Napier.

'There is no prohibition during the rest of the year.'

'If you had herring nets, would you be able to use them?'

'We would try, at any rate.'

'Do you know that the herring comes here, close to the island?'

'Yes, it does sometimes come into this loch. There were Lewis men fishing here and getting herring three years ago.'

'If you got a pier convenient for yourselves,' asked Charles

Fraser-Mackintosh, 'and bigger boats and nets, would you be enabled thereby to do with less meal than you are paying for?'

'If we had to buy the same meal, we would be more able to pay for it.'

'When the new roofs were put upon your houses many years ago by Sir John Macpherson McLeod, was the rent readjusted at the time you got those new roofs?'

'He made no difference on the rent on account of the improvement of the houses.'

'Did he put any rise on the land?'

'We had some complaints here about twenty years ago, for being made to pay for the rocks on which we caught the birds. We paid at that time £1 for the land and £1 for the rocks. When the complaint was made, the laird took £1 off the rocks and laid it upon us for the island of Boreray, for which we had been formerly paying 5s. a head.'

'Are you acquainted with the history and traditions of the island?'

'I am not very skilled in these things, but I have heard some of them.'

'In the oldest history that is written about St Kilda, there is mention made of a cross upon which the people were accustomed to take an oath. Have you ever heard of that?'

'I never heard of that.'

'Does the man sitting behind you know?'

'We cannot say anything about the oath, but there is a cross cut upon the rock at Boreray, the steep island over there.'

'But my inquiry was about a movable cross which would be held up by a party taking the oath, and it was either of gold or silver?'

'We never heard of it.'

'Was any object of curiosity or art ever found in the island – any old coin or old articles?' asked Lord Napier.

'We never heard of anything of the kind being found here.'

'Or any stones shaped like knives or spears?'

'There have been such things found.'

'Like arrow heads?'

'Yes; I have heard of such arrow heads being found, and I have also heard of little crocks made of clay. I have seen them myself. I have seen such found where we were digging, of the size of little bowls.'

Donald MacDonald then stood down and Angus Gillies, the third and final St Kildan to testify, took his place. Lord Napier asked Gillies: 'Have you heard what the previous witness has said?'

'Yes.'

'Have you anything else to say?'

'I have some little addition to make to it,' said Angus Gillies. 'We are complaining a little that our rent has not been fixed according to our present possession, but according to what it was when the present laird came into possession of the island. And as you have come to this island to see us, I hope that one change will be effected by it, and that henceforward we shall be provided with a doctor, the want of one being very much felt. We trust that this great boon will be provided for us by Government. In the next place, with regard to the school, we trust that the justice that is being done to the rest of the Highland Isles will be done to this island of St Kilda, so that the children may be taught to speak the English language as well as their mother tongue. We have suffered very much too, by the loss of a large boat which we had for the purpose of conveying us to the mainland, or to the islands, and which was lost in a storm, and we have now only our small skiffs.'

'Was it a decked boat?'

'She was not a very large boat, but bigger than those we have, and undecked. Mr [John] Sands collected the money with which that boat was provided for us. We felt the loss of the boat very much after that, when we wrote to Edinburgh, understanding there were funds there of which we were entitled to get the benefit. We did get a boat, but it appears there was not sufficient money to provide us with a boat of the kind we required, and the one we have got is so small as to be of no use, beyond those we have already. That boat was sent us by Mr Menzies of the Highland Society.'

'Would you like to have a decked boat?'

'A boat with a deck would be of no use here. A boat would be of no use to us of a greater weight than we could haul up on the shore, at present.'

'What is the length of keel of the boat you would like?'

'Twenty-five feet keel, with nine feet seven inches of breadth in the beam.'

'There was some destitution last year in the island?' asked Alexander Nicolson.

'We were much worse off last winter and spring than in former years.'

'What was the cause of that?'

'The crop was bad, and we ran out of food. The land did not produce of its abundance.'

'Where did you get help from?'

'We went in that little boat I have mentioned to the factor at Dunvegan, and he sent over a vessel with meal for us. We could not bring it in the little boat ourselves. I believe there were very few people in any of the Western Islands that would have undertaken the risk we did.'

'As regards the larger boat you want,' interrupted Lord Napier, 'is it of any use to have half a deck, or a place to keep things dry in the boat?'

'Oh yes, that would be useful. We would not be the worse of that.'

'You state that the factor pays 3s. per Scotch yard for the cloth,' continued Alexander Nicolson. 'Do you ask a higher price from Lowland customers?'

'We would need to have a little more from them than from the factor. There is a difference between the landlord and anybody else, because he will take things from us when nobody else would.'

'Is there any of the old breed of [Soay] sheep on the island?' asked Napier.

'There are some, but they are mostly in possession of the laird.'

'What is the breed, the wool of which you use for the cloth?'

'We mix together the white wool and the wool of the black sheep.'

'Is the wool of the old original sheep much finer?'

'Some of them; it is at least as fine.'

'Where has the proprietor the sheep in the island?' asked Donald MacKinnon.

'On the island of Soay.'

'How many has he got there?'

'I cannot say positively. No shepherd goes there at present; but I believe there are at least 200.'

'Where does the man who is in charge of them live?'

'They are under the charge of the ground officer here, but they are on that island like deer.'

'Has the proprietor always had that island in his own possession?'

'It has been in the hands of the laird since time immemorial.'

'Does he send over to shear the sheep?'

'Not always. I believe it is about three years since there has been any shearing there. Unless you go there at Whitsunday it is no use to go afterwards, for they cast off the wool.'

'What does he do with the young ones? Does he take them away or sell them?'

'They are left there, all mixed together.'

'Does he never sell any?'

'He does sometimes. We ourselves are the chief purchasers.'

'What do you pay for them?'

'They are very small, and we don't pay a great price for them.'

'We have had complaints laid before us in Skye, and the other islands we have been in,' said Alexander Nicolson, 'as to the smallness of the quantity of land that is in the hands of the crofters. Have you any such complaint?'

'We have none, because the proprietor can give us no more than we have except the little island [Soay] which he has for his sheep.'

'Do you complain that the rent is too high?'

'We have no complaint as to the rent except what we have made already.'

Lord Napier and his commissioners did not discover in St Kilda any of the militant land hunger that they encountered elsewhere in the Highlands and Islands. There were too few people and, as Angus Gillies pointed out, excepting the small island of Soay the St Kildans already had the run of the archipelago.

Following the hearing Lord Napier received a vaguely irritated letter from the factor of St Kilda, John MacKenzie in Dunvegan:

I am fifty-four years of age. I am well acquainted with Skye, having lived there the greater part of my life. I hold various public offices of trust.

I am also factor for St Kilda. I observe that the Commissioners visited that island on the 1st of June. I read the evidence given before them on that occasion. I have no comments to offer thereon; suffice it to say that Mr McKay omitted to mention that a medicine chest is kept on the island under his own charge, and that he himself is possessed of some skill in the proper dispensing of those medicines.

Angus Gillies, in his evidence, when he said the factor sent a vessel with meal on 3rd May, omitted to mention that in addition to meal, there was also sent flour, seed oats, and potatoes. The potatoes were, by Miss McLeod's special orders, given at half price, viz., 5s. a barrel, she undertaking to pay the other half out of her own private means.

The natural products of the island, such as feathers and oil, are falling out of view, other industries taking precedence.

Prosperity lies before the St Kildeans in the fishing occupation, which made a start a few years ago. Unfortunately certain circumstances have hitherto retarded its progress. I am glad, however, to say, that a fresh start has again been made with every appearance of success, if encouraged in the right direction and in the proper way.

Napier took note of what he heard. His commission's report noted that:

On the islands of St Kilda, Foula, and Fair Isle, a landing can be effected only when the ocean is at rest. The most productive fishing-grounds, both for herring and white fish, are generally off the most inaccessible shores. It is evident, therefore, that these banks cannot be fished to full advantage unless suitable places of shelter are made, where large boats can run for safety in stormy weather. Further, in several localities where the lochs and arms of the sea form a natural harbour, piers or landing-places are required in order to render them suitable fishing-stations. The circumstances of the country are such, that little or no part of the expense beyond local labour could be contributed in the districts where the works are chiefly needed. If harbours or piers are to be constructed, it must be mainly at the public expense ...

There are three islands of exceptional interest for their isolated position and the peculiar industries of their inhabitants – Foula, Fair Isle, and St Kilda. The access to all three offers great but perhaps not insurmountable difficulties. Without suggesting the creation of extensive harbour works, which would not be justified by the importance of the localities in question, we think that Government might institute a special inquiry with the view of ascertaining whether boat shelters of the simplest character might not be excavated or constructed at these places, in which a landing in rough weather could be effected.

With regard to the mail and other communications, it was proposed that 'improved postal service be provided for the whole of the Long Island [the Western Isles] ... and that one or other of the local steamers should be engaged to call off St Kilda once in every two months in summer, and at least once during winter.'

In time most of those things would come to pass. But the major short-term benefit to the St Kildans of the surprise visit of Lord Napier and his commissioners came just three years later, when the Crofters' Holdings (Scotland) Act of 1886 entered the statute books.

With the exception of Charles Fraser-Mackintosh and possibly Donald MacKinnon, it is fair to say that none of the members of the Napier Commission either wanted or welcomed what became known as the Crofters' Act. It was certainly not the intention of the titled, landowning commissioners. But their painstaking assembly of oral and written evidence from all across the Highlands and Islands, whose transcription ran to five thick printed volumes, presented such a powerful justification of the crofters' grievances that Prime Minister William Gladstone was persuaded to grant them legal security of tenure at fair rents which were adjudicated by an impartial land court known as the Crofters Commission.

After 1886 MacLeod of MacLeod or any other Highland landlord had substantially less power over his tenantry, in St Kilda or elsewhere, than ever before. The hegemony of the landowning classes was not broken, but it was seriously fractured. The freedom of crofters from whimsical or malicious eviction was secured. The saying '*Is treasa tuath na tighearna*' – 'The people are mightier than a lord' – had been justified. John MacKay, Angus Gillies and Donald MacDonald of Village Bay had played their own small part in the victory.

A year after the Napier Commission's visit, on 5 August 1884, the twenty-one year-old Finlay MacQueen married the twenty-four year-old Mary Jemima Otter Gillies, the daughter of Norman and the late Ann Gilliés.

A year later, in July 1885, Norman and Ann Gillies's oldest son, twenty-seven year-old Finlay married Catherine, the thirty-four year-old orphaned daughter of John and Flora Gillies who had been raised by her Uncle Roderick and Aunt Catherine. We know something about those marital ceremonies because Hugh MacCallum, who was the annual schoolteacher in Village Bay at the time of both Finlay and Mary MacQueen's and Finlay and Catherine Gillies's weddings, described the ceremony, their *reitach*, or pre-wedding rituals, and the aftermath to the English *Glasgow Herald* journalist Robert Connell.

One fabled St Kildan courting ritual was mentioned by MacCallum and Connell only as having fallen into disuse. At the south-west side of Hirta a cliff-top slab of rock reaches like a diving board up and out over the void.. This had become known – significantly in English rather than Gaelic – as the Lovers' Stone or Mistress Stone. The legend had it that in days gone by,

> … a young St Kildian who wished to make one of the fair maids of the island his own was required to accomplish a most dangerous feat in order to prove possibly the sincerity of his love, but, more probably, his ability to support a wife …
>
> The aspirant to the hand of a fair St Kildian had to climb this giddy, dangerous height, and, planting his left heel on the outer edge, with the sole of his foot entirely unsupported, he extended his right leg forward beyond the other and grasped the foot with both hands, holding it long enough to satisfy his own and the lady's friends gathered below …

It is likely that on some occasions in the long history of the islands a St Kildan bachelor did attempt to impress his friends of both genders in such a manner. But it was never mentioned as a rite of passage until Victorian times and, as a method of wooing girls, it has the ring of invented tradition.

Instead, by the 1880s the formalities were recognisably Hebridean. Connell reported,

> Three Sabbaths before the interesting ceremony, the banns are proclaimed in church by one of Mr Mackay's elders.
>
> A week before the marriage day a repast consisting of the chief luxuries of the island is provided for the whole of the islanders in the bridegroom's house. The 'luxuries' include tea – which is drunk out of bowls – cheese, butter, Scotch bannocks, and last, but not least, 'a wee drappie o't.' But, added my informant [Hugh MacCallum], the islanders are 'moderates' of the best kind, and they never disgrace such feasts with drunkenness. Their Gaelic word for this little affair is reitach, meaning contract, and it corresponds with a custom

once common in other parts of Scotland known as the 'bottling'.

A curious feature of the gathering is that the sexes are kept by themselves in different parts of the house. For the comfort of the people, tables and chairs are provided, and in the event of the supply running short the women have to remain standing …

When the wedding-day comes everybody gathers into the church, including the bride and bridegroom, attended by the best-man and bridesmaid. They are rigged out in their Sunday finery, and are privileged with a front seat to the left of the pulpit.

Everybody is agog with excitement, for the occasion is a great one. Soon there enters the Rev. Mr Mackay, Bible in hand. Mounting the precentor's box the minister engages in a Gaelic prayer. Then follows a sermon on the duties of husband and wife. The sermon over, Mr Mackay goes through the marriage ceremony in the orthodox fashion. There is another prayer, and then the curtain falls.

After the marriage a right jolly feast is provided in one of the houses in the village, but to this, with a peculiar exclusiveness, only natives are invited. The 'strangers', who include the schoolmaster [Hugh MacCallum from Inverness], the old nurse [Ann Mackinlay from Skye], and the minister himself [John MacKay from Wester Ross and Inverness], hie themselves to the manse, where they attempt to make merry in a humble kind of way, and the newly married couple are gracious enough to look in for a minute or two and smile upon the proceedings. The husband and wife bring provisions with them, generally mutton, it being considered unlucky that they should come empty-handed. Tea is supplied in great abundance by the housekeeper [Ann MacDonald], who has opinions of her own on the subject of tea-drinking. A bumper is drunk to the health and prosperity of the newly-wedded pair, and this formality over the company breaks up. The couple are seen to rest for the night, and the event is at an end.

There is a difficulty usually about the honeymoon. It is the correct thing to spend it from home, but there is only the choice of going to a friend's house ten yards off, or one twice the distance … Few of them have the native simplicity of a couple who were married shortly before my visit, and of whom it is not possible to speak but with approbation. They spent the honeymoon in their own house, going about their usual callings. The very first day both were on the top of the house thatching the roof.

The couple which honeymooned by thatching one of the old black-houses was almost certainly Finlay and Catherine Gillies.

Not one member of the two couples could write his or her own name: they all marked their marriage certificate with a cross.

Each couple, however, benefited from the hygienic reforms introduced by Nurse MacKinlay. Unlike their parents, they quickly had children who lived for longer than a fortnight. Finlay and Catherine Gillies, who moved to live with Catherine's elderly widowed Uncle Roderick, would raise five healthy children.

Finlay and Mary MacQueen, who continued at first to live in the house of Finlay's grandparents, had four sons and two daughters, the eldest of whom was christened Annie in memory of Finlay's natural mother, Ann MacDonald, who had recently left St Kilda for Skye. Such a survival rate would have been unthinkable twenty years earlier.

Those children grew up in a place which had changed only slightly from the days when their grandparents were young. In the middle of the 1880s 'The men were dressed, after their fashion, in heavy garments made of blanketing, and muffled to the ears with big coarse cravats twisted round their necks roll upon roll ... The women made a much more picturesque group. They were all barefoot, wore short petticoats and dresses reaching only to about their knees, and for head-dress disported bright Turkey-red napkins.'

Their diet was similarly traditional. Shortly after the weddings of the two Finlays, Mary and Catherine a visitor asked about and then noted down their diet. It was:

Breakfast – Porridge and milk, with the flesh of the fulmar afterwards occasionally, the bird being boiled in the porridge.

Dinner – Mutton, or the flesh of the fulmar or solan goose, with potatoes when there are any.

Tea – Tea and bread and cheese, the flesh of the fulmar occasionally, and sometimes porridge.

The islanders take breakfast between nine and ten; dinner generally not till about four, and sometimes an hour or two later, on their return from the rocks or the fields; and tea about nine in summer, and as late as eleven in winter, when they sit up at their looms till about two in the morning. There is a complete absence of variety in their food ...

Milk and sea-birds' eggs are consumed in considerable quantities during the summer; tea, sugar, and flour are now used in nearly every house; potatoes are the only vegetables procurable – the quantity grown on the island is small and the quality bad, and the supply is only available usually for six months. It therefore follows that the diet of the people is practically devoid of vegetables for the half of each year. Such condiments as vinegar, pepper, mustard, and pickles are not used. Whisky is relished very much, and every man keeps his bottle, but nobody drinks to excess.

Following the departure of the Napier Commission a series of temporary but qualified teachers such as Hugh MacCallum was sent to the island, as had been stipulated by the 1872 Education Act in Scotland but not immediately applied to the exceptional community in Village Bay.

MacCallum was succeeded by the third of those peripatetic teachers, a man from Sutherland called George Murray. Murray, who taught in Village Bay between June 1886 and June 1887, kept a diary. It indicates that he did not have the happiest of times in St Kilda.

It started well enough. Murray, who had previously worked in North Uist, was a confident if not entirely fluent Gaelic speaker and he determined to use his time in St Kilda to improve both his verbal and literary mastery of the language. He found himself writing letters for the St Kildans – presumably in English – to their Australian relatives. When the tourist steamers came in he welcomed the extra life and busyness of the place, and the fact that they often carried doctors who attended to such minor ailments as sprains.

Three months after his arrival the ss *Hebridean* turned up 'with a number of passengers' and stayed from noon to midnight.

> They bought a deal of cloth and stockings from the natives. Before they parted from us they & all the inhabitants of St Kilda assembled outside the minister's garden just as [it] was getting dark. The whole together constituted a small congregation. Three Gaelic tunes were sung at the request of one of the strangers. Then, in English, we sang the Hundredth Psalm & the Hymn 'How my comrades see the signal!', after which the minister prayed in Gaelic. It was an evening I will long remember, with not so much as a breath of wind to drive the sound one way more than another, there we stood under the cloudless

canopy of heaven singing 'All people that on Earth &c'. Few as we are on this remote island, it is comforting to think that we can, in unison with the rest of the world, 'Sing to the Lord with cheerful voice'.

The schooling offered by George Murray and his colleagues was more effective than the earlier Gaelic-medium scriptural efforts of Reverend John MacKay. Within fifteen years a third of the population of St Kilda, including almost everybody under the age of twenty and past infancy, could speak English as well as Gaelic, and many more of them could read and write in either language. 'There are fifteen children attending school at present,' wrote a visitor in 1886 of George Murray's little institution, 'and they are divided into three classes.'

The senior class (ages from 13 to 14) read the Fifth English Reader and the History of Scotland, and they also are put through their pacings in geography, grammar, and arithmetic as far as bills of parcels. They are made to translate their English lessons into Gaelic, and this is a very useful exercise. In this class there are at present two boys and three girls. The boys speak English very well, but the girls, more bashful and reticent, are further behind.

In the next class (ages about 9 and 10) there are three boys and two girls, and the class book is the Fourth English Reader. The third class (ages from 6 to 8) read the Second English Reader, They also do a little writing on slates and in arithmetic are exercised in addition and subtraction. There are one girl and four boys in this class.

I had the pleasure of attending a kind of non-official examination during my stay on the island, and I am able to speak the more confidently from what I saw and heard of the good work that is being accomplished in the education of the young St Kildians. Their teacher has, of course, many obstacles to contend with, but all the same the children are becoming good English scholars. The school is held in the building known as the church. It is noticeable that the schoolmaster, although he is allowed to make use of the sacred edifice itself for the purposes of his school, is not at liberty to use the church bell.

George Murray found the tight, insular socio-politics of the place difficult to embrace. In the second half of the nineteenth century St Kilda was at heart a tiny, extremely isolated and insecure community of people living in the constant presence of want and premature death. Any group of fifty or sixty adults clustered hugger-mugger on top of each other was bound to manifest strain, especially in the long, dark winter months. The 200 square yards of Village Bay could be a harsh, closed and claustrophobic place, blanketed by low cloud, battered by gales and drenched by constant rain. In such weather there were no excursions to Boreray, Soay or the stacks to relieve the mundane routines of daily existence. The St Kildans had known each other's quirks since infancy. Their habits and mannerisms and tempers and idiosyncrasies were exaggerated in such circumstances. An organised, talkative woman such as Finlay MacQueen's mother Ann MacDonald would be no more than another opinionated tea-shop habituee in Edinburgh. In St Kilda she was disparaged as unusually domineering. A bad-tempered elderly man or woman would find at least some friends in Glasgow. In St Kilda he or she could with a single outburst offend a whole community.

At first George Murray would, at the end of the day, wander down Main Street to pick up from his new neighbours what he called the 'Evening News'. By October he was noting 'A great deal of gossip floating at present, also rows in parts of the place. I take no side in the gossip. I listen and keep my opinions, as I have learned that, in St Kilda as in many other places, "Silence is better than gold".'

A couple of weeks later he was told one morning that 'few on the island saw such a night as there was last night. An old woman of eighty fighting with her daughter, a married woman. It came to blows. Others got entangled in the row, & a son of the old woman with his family left the house where he stayed with his mother. This was about midnight … After breakfast I went up the hill for a walk. I had not gone far when I saw the people removing furniture from one house to another. A family removed in consequence of the row.'

He would also shortly learn that keeping quiet was not enough to insure himself against such village feuds. Some of the St Kildans considered the twenty-six year-old bachelor to have designs on 'their' young women. An old man who was also a Church elder took strongly against George Murray, accused him of all the sins typical of people from Sutherland, and the two men maintained an uncordial silence for the rest of the winter.

Although he was not yet married and had no children of his own,

George Murray had a bitter taste of the enduring tragedy of Hirta. The tetanus bacterium was so rife that it not only attacked the severed umbilical cords of newborn babies and their mothers. It also infected the grazes, cuts and other small wounds of children and adults. Adults were usually strong enough and, even in St Kilda, had immune systems which were robust enough to survive the infection. But not always.

Late in February 1887 ten year-old Annie Ferguson, the illegitimate daughter of Christina Gillies and the deceased John Ferguson, was 'seized with that terrible disease the "Lock-jaw", which works such havock amongst the St Kildians.' Annie was 'one of the most promising' of George Murray's scholars. 'On Thursday last she was unable to read as usual in school in the forenoon. I thought it was merely her throat that was sore, for so I was told.'

It was worse, much worse than that. Annie Ferguson lingered in agony for two weeks. 'The muscles of [her] body appear to be in a state of lasting rigidity,' recorded George Murray while the girl was still alive, 'while at the end of every three or four minutes paroxysms of spasms occur ... She cannot rest in the same position five minutes; but must be turned from side to side, or kept sitting or standing.'

Throughout it all, while her body fought its losing battle, Annie Ferguson's mind was clear and even alert. She welcomed Murray's visits and spoke to him as best she could. Towards the end her throat was so constricted that she was unable to swallow the nurse's medicine, let alone take gruel. She died on 10 March 1887 and was buried during a snowstorm in the graveyard above Main Street two days later. 'On the part of the women,' wrote Murray, 'there was loud weeping and wailing and no wonder for from amongst them there was suddenly snatched away a quiet, inoffensive and very obedient girl.'

In the following few weeks a boy and three girls took ill with pains to the neck and jaw. They all recovered. George Murray took to recording the ailments of his neighbours. His notes confirm that the recently married twenty-five year-old Finlay MacQueen and the sixty-three year-old Norman Gillies both suffered from headaches.

During the 1880s two of the surviving emigrants to Australia in 1852 drifted back to St Kilda, at least for a short period of time. Their reappearance proved unsettling. It indicated that the spectre of emigration, even of wholesale desertion of the island, had never been entirely banished and was in some quarters welcome.

In the late summer of 1885 the island suffered its worst harvest failure in memory. Early in September a tremendous storm swept in from the North Atlantic and devastated their crofts. 'It began about three o'clock on the afternoon of Saturday, September 12, and raged till the Monday morning following. Great showers of salt spray from the sea were blown over Ruaval Point, on the west side of the Bay of St Kilda, and carried over the whole of the eastern slope of the island on which the islanders grow their scanty crops.'

Such ferocious gales were neither unprecedented nor unusual, even in summer and autumn. Reverend John MacDonald of Ferintosh on the Black Isle north of Inverness, one of several respected evangelists to earn the description 'the Apostle of the North', was the intermittently resident pastor of St Kilda between 1822 and 1830. On 8 July 1830 Reverend MacDonald noted in his diary: 'A view of a St Kilda storm was certainly presented to us this day. The sea all in a commotion – its billows rising mountains high, and dashing with fury against the lofty rocks all around, which oblige them in their turn to retire and sink into their mother ocean – the columns of spray which issue out of this conflict and overlap the highest mountains – all these present a sight awfully grand and sublime.' Reverend MacDonald subsequently preached to his flock from Isaiah 32:2 – 'And a man shall be as an hiding place from the wind, and a covert from the tempest; as rivers of water in a dry place, as the shadow of a great rock in a weary land.'

In 1830 the St Kildans had little option other than to suffer wearily in the shadow of their great rock, and make the most of their reserves. By 1885 they had fewer crops and higher expectations of assistance from the outside world.

September 1885 was the end of the tourist season and the beginning of the long, isolated winter. In normal circumstances the St Kildans could expect no further visits from any kind of ship, naval or otherwise, until the following spring, by which time the destruction of their seed crops would have left them destitute. Reverend John MacKay instantly wrote to Dr Robert Rainy, the Moderator of the Free Church in Edinburgh, begging 'leave to intimate to you that I am directed by the people under my charge on this island to tell you that their corn, barley, and potatoes are destroyed by a great storm which passed over this island on Saturday and Sabbath last. You will be kind enough to apply to Government in order to send us a supply of corn seed, barley, and potatoes. This year's crop is quite useless. They never before saw such a storm at this time of the year. They have lost one of their boats; but happily there was no loss of life.' MacKay's appeal was carried out on the last tourist steamer of the year.

Relief was organised; the *Hebridean* was despatched and a few days afterwards an inspecting officer of the Board of Supervision for the Relief of the Poor in Scotland named Malcolm MacNeill was sent to Hirta on a naval vessel. In the following year, 1886, MacNeill submitted his report.

> During the year 1884 a former emigrant from St Kilda to Australia returned, and resided for some months on the island ... his teaching has produced an effect which probably he did not anticipate, for within the past eighteen months a strong desire to emigrate has sprung up, and, with the exception of one or two old men, I found none who were not anxious to be transferred either to the mainland or to Australia. It may well be worth consideration by her Majesty's Government whether, in view of this disposition of the people, it may not be wise, and, in the end, economical, to assist them in attaining their object, and thus to avoid a recurrence of the anxieties which their isolated position must periodically produce.

The *Glasgow Herald* journalist Robert Connell, who had also been alerted to the news of catastrophe in the most far-flung outpost of the British Isles, arrived in St Kilda a few days before MacNeill with the relief ship ss *Hebridean*. Connell told Reverend John MacKay that a number of letters had appeared in the *Herald* which suggested 'that the island of St Kilda ought to be abandoned finally, with all convenient speed, and the people transplanted in a body to some other island of the Outer Hebrides, or to the mainland'.

MacKay, reported Connell, thought the proposal to be 'fair and reasonable ... but it was for the people themselves, and not for him to pronounce upon it'. John MacKay's housekeeper and Finlay MacQueen's mother Ann MacDonald, however 'declared that St Kilda was the biggest prison in all the world. Would she be willing to leave it? Well, she would go if the minister went; no matter whether her brothers went or not. In reply to a further observation she expressed her feelings for the good men who had made the proposal. She wished that they might never die, but that if they must die that they should go to the "good place".'

In common with a lot of other people Robert Connell thought that evacuating St Kilda was a very good idea. He returned in 1886 – coincidentally on the same ship which delivered that year's schoolteacher George Murray – and this time stayed for a fortnight. He was able then 'to learn with much fulness the views of the great bulk of the community on the question [of emigration]':

The first day of my sojourn on the island the minister informed me that the subject of emigration had been much discussed immediately after my first visit, but that it was now forgotten, and was never even referred to by man, woman, or child … Emigration, like many other subjects, took hold of their imaginations for a day. So long as the fit lasted it engrossed their minds, to the exclusion of everything else. The amount of zeal they showed was extraordinary, and could most easily be explained by supposing that the simple idea of wholesale emigration had never before occurred to their childlike minds as a practical suggestion. But it was dead now, the minister said. It was fated, however, to a very speedy resurrection.

Our smack … carried Her Majesty's mails. They embraced eight months' correspondence to the islanders … The letters which we fetched to the native islanders amounted to the handsome total of nine, and that, it appears, is a fair average for eight months. It represents one letter to every two families. Still the islanders are not without friends who advocate an improved mail service. The point that I want to bring out, however, is that six of the nine letters forwarded by the mail were from St Kildians in Australia.

The St Kildians settled in that colony appear all to have done well, and, in writing home to their relatives, they strongly advised them to betake themselves to the new country. In one instance the writer enclosed a sum of money to pay the passage out of a recently-married couple, under-taking also to find them a comfortable living on their arrival in Australia. All the letters spoke in the most tempting way of the good living to be obtained in Australia. Only one drawback was pointed out, and that by a female. She said in her letter that the preaching of the Word in Australia gave her cause for much uneasiness. It was not so pure or so pointed as in St Kilda. She was, moreover, wounded in spirit at the playing of godless organs and the singing of 'profane songs' in church. To the St Kildian this matter is more important even than meal and potatoes. It was, therefore, satisfactory that another of the colonists reported hopefully on this crucial question. In this case the writer was a man, and he reported that the preaching of the Gospel in Australia suited his taste exactly.

The receipt of this budget of news revived the topic of emigration, but no definite opinion was expressed in the absence of some of the men at Boreray. On their return to St Kilda on the night of Saturday, June 19, the matter provoked the liveliest discussion. In the end three able-bodied men, two of them married, made up their minds to emigrate to Victoria, where a number of the islanders are already settled, and the vessel which brought me back to Dunvegan carried in the mail-bag a letter addressed to the agent of the Victoria Government in London, making application for assisted passages on behalf of the three men.

The opinion in favour of emigration was almost unanimous, the only dissentients being one or two old men, whom it would be folly to ask to go to a new settlement at their time of life. In some instances, too, the families of the old men would prefer not to leave St Kilda at present. Without exception the islanders, if they are to leave their home at all, would prefer Victoria to any other part of the world, for the simple reason that a number of their friends are settled there already. I have no doubt that many of the people could readily be induced to go to any other of the Australian Colonies which offer the advantage of assisted passages. Go when and where they may the people will have to be assisted, most of them being very poor.

Still, they will make capital colonists, being strong and hardy and well fitted to turn their hand to any kind of out-door work. A general emigration of the community being for the present out of the question, the proper thing to do would be to take out those families who are willing to go, leaving the others to follow, as they almost certainly will, as soon as circumstances permit them. Surely some of the Australian Colonies will be found ready to establish a new St Kilda.

This much is certain, that if nothing is done and things remain as they are the condition of the islanders will go from bad to worse, and destitution periods will recur oftener. The produce of the island is steadily decreasing – feathers, oil, cloth, fish, cheese, and cattle, all show a remarkable falling-off. No doubt this has been compensated for to some extent in recent years by the visits of tourists, but for whom indeed the islanders would have been by this time near starvation point. But this source of wealth is a fickle one, and not to be always relied upon.

Both MacNeill and Connell first arrived and reported from St Kilda when the morale of the islanders was unusually low. Following the great storm of September 1885 it was unsurprising that many islanders were susceptible to the notion of evacuation to some happier place. It was equally unsurprising that a year later their disquiet should have eased. The temptation of mass emigration was clearly still alive, but it ebbed and flowed with the fortunes of the island.

Ten years later, during a period of relative health and stability in 1896, an English visitor who came to know and like Finlay MacQueen discovered that,

The St Kildans have a deep love for their rocky home. I playfully invited several of them to accompany me on leaving the island, but they shook their heads, and told me they couldn't live without 'going to the rocks' ...

My view is that they lead a very happy life, that they are better housed and better fed than any other people in their rank of life, and that it would be a great misfortune to them to be removed from their present home, and, of course, I find that none of them wish to leave. I do not mean that I would discourage emigration. If any of them wish to push their fortunes in other parts of Scotland or in the colonies, by all means let them do so, and let them have every encouragement and assistance. Probably, as they become more educated, many of them will become discontented with their primitive life and wish to take a more active part in the progress of the world.

All I say is that I do not believe it will add to their happiness. Theirs is indeed a happy life. They have plenty to do, but can do everything at their own time and in their own way. They have good houses, ample food, and no worries ... If they were removed en masse and given a start in one of the colonies, or even in Skye, some would succeed, but many would fail, and it would not be a step towards the greatest happiness of the greatest number.

One woman at least took her opportunity to leave the island. Having seen her son Finlay marry and give her grandchildren, Ann MacDonald left St Kilda at the same time as the man for whom she had kept house, Reverend John MacKay, who departed in 1889 at the age of seventy-two with the words, 'I think it is time I was leaving them now.' Nurse MacKinlay had left a year earlier, supposedly still frustrated by the unhygienic traditions of some St Kildans.

Ann MacKinlay was replaced as nurse by a Mrs Urquhart and then by Jessie Chisnall. Nurse Chisnall was brought in by John MacKay's replacement, the missionary Angus Fiddes. Fiddes, a 'kindly and strong' man whose hair turned 'iron grey' in the next twelve years, would also serve as schoolteacher on the island, which brought to an end the unsatisfactory regime of short-term teachers being sent annually to St Kilda. On one occasion towards the end of his pastorship Angus Fiddes required a holiday and another peripatetic replacement was shipped to the school. It was a disaster. The new schoolmistress knew Arabic and Greek but not Gaelic. She had been told that there was a store in Village Bay, but not that it was a featherstore for export produce, so she had carried no provisions. Once the minister left on his vacation 'she had great difficulty in getting anything to eat'.

When he arrived in 1889 Angus Fiddes was forty-seven years old and not long out of divinity college in Glasgow. He was a native of the parish of Tarbat on the south side of the Dornoch Firth in the far north-east of Scotland. He was also a native Gaelic speaker, which testifies yet again to the widespread use of the language in the middle of the nineteenth century. Jessie Chisnall from Stratherrick in central Inverness-shire was also a Gaelic speaker.

The new missionary would immediately be presented with an extreme test of his authority, the nadir of the local tourist industry and a trial of the St Kildan character.

NINE

The Royal Wedding

✳

IN 1890 ANN FERGUSON was a twenty-four year-old single woman and John Gillies, who was known as Iain Ban, was a twenty-eight year-old widower.

Nine years earlier John Gillies had married Catherine MacKinnon, who was three years his senior. After just fourteen months of marriage Catherine died in February 1884, aged twenty-four years and three months, of a short but unspecified illness. The couple had no surviving children.

Ann was a descendant of the famous Ferguson boatman from Berneray who had stayed in St Kilda for love after the early eighteenth-century smallpox epidemic. For some reason, possibly connected to her good looks, Ann Ferguson had, like Betsy Scott before her, been dubbed 'the queen'. John Ross, who was the schoolteacher in Village Bay in the summer of 1889, wrote: 'Ian Ban is engaged to Ann Ferguson – the Queen of St Kilda. The only marriageable man is to marry the Queen of St Kilda, and who can blame him. They would have been married before we left but unfortunately the minister did not get a sufficiently comprehensive licence to meet the requirements of such a place as St Kilda and so we had to forego the honour of "getting the Queen's wedding". They are going to Glasgow next summer for that very purpose. It must be a sight worth seeing as neither party has ever left St Kilda before and the younger man is rather a bashful and excitable fellow, although he has had the experience of passing through the marriage ceremony once already.'

By the failure to get 'a sufficiently comprehensive [marriage]

243

licence' for John Gillies and Ann Ferguson, John Ross meant simply that Reverend MacKay had left Village Bay and his replacement Angus Fiddes was as yet merely a missionary and unqualified to hold a wedding ceremony. Ross communicated this information, and more, to a man named James Gall Campbell, who owned a printing business in the north-eastern English port of Sunderland. Despite his surname, Campbell had no immediate Highland ancestry. His father John Campbell was also from Sunderland and his mother, Mary Gall, had been born in Leith outside Edinburgh.

By the late nineteenth century people on the United Kingdom mainland did not need Highland connections to avow an intimate relationship with St Kilda. James Gall Campbell professed such a devotion. When he learned that the 'queen' of the island was to marry, the temptation to express his fondness and fascination became too great. The result was a highly expensive farce which echoed around the world.

The farce was partly grounded in St Kilda's role as a blank slate for foreigners – the same blank slate which led others at the same time to visualise the islanders as an uncorrupted anarchist or communist society. It was highly unlikely that Ann Ferguson had ever seriously been described as a princess or a queen by her family, friends and neighbours. Hebridean islanders would occasionally ironically impose such monarchical labels upon their bossier and more prosperous fellows. But there was no hereditary line of royalty in that or any other little crofting community.

The irony was lost on the likes of James Gall Campbell because they perceived St Kilda as a miniature kingdom, as a tiny simulacrum of the rest of Europe. It was well known that even primitive Polynesian islanders had their chieftains. St Kilda, therefore, must have developed in parallel evolution its own royal family. The wedding of Hirta's 'queen' was no small matter. It represented an occasion to be observed and celebrated with all the munificence available in the larger parent kingdom.

Thrilled beyond reason by the prospect, down in Sunderland James Gall Campbell began to organise a ceremony of his own. He wrote to John Ross to ask for Ann Ferguson's measurements so that he could order a suitable wedding gown. Having failed to discover the size of her ring finger, Campbell bought three rings of different circumferences. He persuaded a minister of the United Presbyterian Church in Sunderland, Reverend J S Rae, to travel to St Kilda and perform the honours.

Encouraged by John Ross, who was leaving St Kilda but still found time to say: 'You have done for them, sir, what they cannot sufficiently appreciate, you have led the way, and that well, in bringing St Kilda into true civilisation and making it part of Great Britain', Campbell then began to organise a fully fledged expedition. By word of mouth and by placing advertisements in the local press he attracted thirty fellow members of the County Durham bourgeoisie to sail with him and Reverend Rae to St Kilda, laden with wedding presents. In the last week of May 1890 this formidable party travelled by train to Oban in Argyllshire and chartered the steamer *Clydesdale* to carry them across the North Atlantic to Village Bay. They stopped at Lochboisdale in South Uist to pick up the schoolteacher John Ross.

The gifts were extraordinary. As well as their own contributions, the thirty uninvited wedding guests carried a number of items donated by friends and well-wishers who had sadly to remain behind in Sunderland. They included an American pump organ, or harmonium, a musical instrument which was popular in small English churches and chapels but which was excoriated by the Free Church of Scotland, three dozen pairs of spectacles, various cough and digestive syrups, fly-catchers, hair restorers, powder for the relief of corns, silver spoons, a silver teapot, two dozen microscopes, fireworks, feeding bottles, jars of Bovril, a large pork pie and a wedding cake. As his own special contribution James Gall Campbell took with him, carefully boxed up, 640 books to form the basis of a Free Library in St Kilda. He also took along 'several professional and amateur photographers, an artist and several newspaper reporters'. The latter quickly found themselves with an unexpectedly good story.

Most of the gifts never left the ss *Clydesdale*. The ship anchored in Village Bay on Wednesday, 28 May. Ann Ferguson's father Donald and her brother Alexander rowed out to the steamer. Unlike his father, his older sister and her husband-to-be, the seventeen year-old Alexander Ferguson spoke English. He informed the party on the *Clydesdale* that there would be no wedding. He translated his father as saying: 'What business have you with a wedding? When we want a wedding, we can arrange it for ourselves.'

James Gall Campbell, John Ross, Reverend Rae and the reporters then took one of the ship's boats ashore. The St Kildans promptly set out their wares for sale and John Gall Campbell found Annie Ferguson retailing eggs and home-woven stockings on Main Street. Unable to converse with her or with her fiancé John Gillies – who was standing by 'unconcernedly' – Campbell tried the rings on her finger until he found one to fit. He went off to discuss matters with Angus Fiddes at the manse.

Fiddes had known for several weeks of the Sunderland group's imminent arrival. He was offended for several reasons. Reverend J S Rae might be – as Rae persistently pointed out – a Presbyterian minister, but he was not a minister of the Free Church of Scotland, which was perfectly capable of conducting its own weddings in its own congregations.

Moreover, Angus Fiddes had reason to believe that the entire circus had a commercial motivation. He suspected James Gall Campbell of profiteering from the excursion. He thought that the corn cures, syrups and hair restorers had been donated by their manufacturers in order to exploit the unsuspecting 'Queen of St Kilda' in advertising campaigns. He also, along with most if not all of the islanders, disliked the condescending shoddiness of the occasion. Angus Fiddes politely told John Gall Campbell and Reverend J S Rae that a Free Church minister would arrive from Harris in June, and then the wedding could properly be conducted.

By then the rest of the tourists had found their way ashore from the *Clydesdale* and 'there was no small disappointment when it was learned that there was no prospect of a wedding'.

'Those who could approach the natives in their vernacular,' reported *The Scotsman*, 'had no great difficulty in finding out why they objected to the wedding. They did not want a Sassenach minister to come down and marry them, one fellow said, and the general opinion was that the whole affair had been got up to enable these visitors to have a little amusement at their expense, and they objected, they said, to make sport for the Philistines.'

By way of compensation a cliff-scaling exhibition was provided. When they returned from Conachair, Campbell and Ross renewed their efforts. James Campbell was in favour of ignoring Angus Fiddes and coaxing Ann Ferguson and John Gillies into an eleventh-hour wedding independently of their own Church and minister. He was dissuaded by Reverend Rae, who 'thought the affair had been carried far enough, and that it would give rise to a scandal if they persisted in going any further with it'. Rae might by then have been informed that the prospective groom, Iain Ban Gillies, 'was a very religious man from his youth up' and was unlikely to offend against his own Church.

A number of the *Clydesdale*'s disgruntled and probably tipsy passengers nevertheless attempted to gain entry to the manse. They were halted by one of the vessel's stewards, who told them that he had been instructed to tell visitors that the missionary was not at home. Posting one of his crew as a guard at the manse indicates the sympathies of the captain of the *Clydesdale*. The travellers returned to their ship, passing on the rocks by the shore 'a number of strongly-bound boxes'. They were James Gall Campbell's books for a St Kilda library. Nothing was heard of them again.

At 9.00 p.m. the *Clydesdale* lifted anchor and took her disappointed human cargo on the twenty-two-hour passage back to Oban. They were greeted there by a large crowd which had already been informed of the previous day's events 'and many of them were not a little amused'. According to *The Scotsman*'s man on the spot, the future of the redundant pork pie had not yet been decided.

If there was, then or later, any lesson to be drawn from the occasion it was that the St Kildans were not so much in thrall to the tourist industry as had been suggested. They had rejected on a point of principle a shipful of gifts. Some of them were curious if not worthless gifts, but others had material value which the people of Village Bay chose to spurn. They would not at any cost 'make sport for the Philistines'. They had for many years been treated by tourists 'as if they were wild animals at the Zoo', wrote the sympathetic Norman Heathcote later in the 1890s. 'They throw sweets to them, openly mock at them, and I have seen them standing at the church door during service, laughing and talking, and staring in as if at an entertainment got up for their amusement.' In the summer of 1890 the St Kildans drew a line in the sand.

Fully four years later news of the incident reached the south end of the South Island of New Zealand. Otago had been settled fifty years earlier by emigrant members of the Free Church of Scotland, and the *Otago Witness* reported in 1894 that 'if the tourist is stupid and tactless he may spend a very unpleasant hour on St Kilda indeed. An experience of this kind is what came to a shipload of excursionists who went to the island expecting to carry on some very high jinks with the islanders … the wedding might have gone off all right if the persons concerned had been left to themselves. With a strange mixture of perverted generosity and vulgar stupidity, a large number of people put their heads together and, for a time at least, spoilt this matrimonial intention.'

The matrimonial intention was luckily not spoilt for long. Annie Ferguson and John Gillies were married in St Kilda Free Church of Scotland four weeks after the arrival and departure of the tourists from Wearside. The service was conducted by the visiting Free Church minister Angus Stewart of Whiting Bay in the most southerly Hebridean island of Arran. It was witnessed by Angus Fiddes and by Ann's brother Alexander. Over the next three decades, in what became a short but welcome Indian summer for the community of St Kilda, John and Annie raised five healthy boys in their cottage and on their croft at the southern end of Main Street. John died at the age of sixty-four from a severe bout of influenza in May 1926.

By the time Angus Fiddes came to take the 1891 census in Village Bay he had been ordained a minister. His enumeration of the population in that year revealed seventy-one residents. That was slightly fewer than ten years earlier and showed that the island had not recovered from the mass emigration to Australia and from the pandemic of neonatal fatalities. But a careful look at the statistics indicates some small positive signs.

The average age had fallen slightly, from thirty-eight in 1881 back down to thirty-six in 1891. The presence of nurses helped the old as well as the very young and the island now had its share of octogenarians. There was Lachlan MacKinnon at eighty-three, Finlay MacQueen's grandparents John and Jessie MacDonald at eighty-three and eighty respectively, Neil Ferguson at eighty-four, and living next to the newlyweds John and Annie Gillies was the grannie of them all, the eighty-eight year-old Ann Gillies. But there were also twenty-two children of school age or younger. If there was still a severe shortage of young men and women, at least they could look behind them and see boys and girls approaching maturity with the ability to share their seasonal tasks.

Among those younger children were the offspring of Finlay and Mary MacQueen and Finlay and Catherine Gillies. The Gillieses had three youngsters in 1891, the oldest of whom was a six year-old boy named Donald. The MacQueens had two children, including a two year-old girl called Annie.

A recovery was underway in Village Bay. The nurses of the 1880s had identified tetanus as the cause of the island's gross level of infant mortality and had introduced hygienic prophylactic measures and the application of antiseptics. In the 1890s a tetanus anti-toxin was developed which could cure almost all mild, early forms of the condition. Infant mortality in St Kilda plummeted. Parents began to hope that their newborn would live. An insufferable burden was lifted from the community. Young Donald Gillies and Annie MacQueen not only reached maturity themselves; they could also expect their own children to survive.

Over the next twenty years the population of St Kilda increased. It was a small increase, from seventy-one in 1891 to seventy-seven in 1901, to eighty in 1911. It was nonetheless significant. It reversed a decline which had appeared irreversible since the 1852 emigrations. It was almost unique in the north-west Highlands and Islands, where in the same period the populations of other islands and parishes were falling dramatically.

By 1911 the average age of the eighty people in St Kilda was just twenty-nine years. Thirty-eight of those eighty people were under the age of twenty. It was a remarkable transformation. In human terms it meant that those who were lucky enough to be alive after 1890 watched their community not only grow, but grow younger. It had gone in three decades from an island where the sound of children's laughter was scarce and was constantly muffled by the wails of the deceased, to a place where young people outnumbered their elders, where large families were commonplace and for a short but precious period a future seemed possible.

Life in that period was both traditional and modern. Although Gaelic remained the everyday language of the community, almost everybody who attended school from the 1880s onwards also spoke English. The adults continued to identify themselves as crofters, but cragsmanship, egg-collecting and bird-catching continued and their production and export of tweed rapidly increased.

Increasing numbers of boats carrying curious visitors from over-seas anchored in the bay. Towards the end of the nineteenth century their parties were swollen by amateur and professional naturalists who were, by and large, more interested in the flora and fauna of those remote islands than in their human inhabitants. St Kildans, especially those young men who could now speak some English, quickly learned to add the role of bird-guide to their skills. The English ornithologist Charles Dixon was unapologetic about the fact that 'The chief object of my visit to Doon [Dun] was to obtain the eggs of the Fork-tailed Petrel, and I was successful beyond my highest expectations.'

… We crossed the bay in a small boat belonging to the smack, danger-ously overcrowded, as many St Kildans as could scramble into her going with us to search for eggs and catch birds. Landing on this rock-bound islet was difficult work, owing to the strong swell. As we approached the shore one of the St Kilda men leapt out of the boat with a rope and assisted the rest to land. After taking off our boots we climbed up the cliffs, and over the grassy slopes to the summit, where Donald told me we should find the birds we wanted.

The place where the Petrels breed is on that portion of the island nearest to St Kilda and at the summit. We had not been there long before Donald, who had been searching the numerous holes, drew forth a struggling Petrel from its nest, and I was delighted to find that it was the Fork-tailed species. Handing me the bird, he quickly drew forth the single white egg, and I then waited until he found another nest within a yard or so of the first. Inserting my arm to the full extremity I felt the little bird fluttering over its egg and drew it out.

This nest also contained a single egg; and as I was catching the bird it uttered a few squeaking notes; excepting this, no other sound was heard during our stay. When held in the hand, it emits a small quantity of oil, precisely similar to that vomited by the Fulmar. Most of this oil comes from the mouth, but occasionally a little is squirted from the nostrils.

Whilst I was packing the eggs Donald found another nest, which I took; and in less than half-an-hour I had taken eleven nests of this rare little bird …

One of the birds which we caught, I let go again to watch its flight. It flew about for a few moments in a very erratic manner, as if dazed by the light, and then darted up and down, and flew round and round with rapid beats of its long wings, very much like a Swallow or a Swift. We finally lost sight of it as it flew behind a large stack of rock and went out to sea.

In 1896 the Yorkshire brothers Richard and Cherry Kearton reached Village Bay. Richard was a naturalist and Cherry was a wildlife photographer who would later become a celebrated maker of documentary films and a broadcaster. In that sense at least, the young Kearton brothers took the first whispers of the twentieth century to Village Bay.

They travelled from Glasgow on the *Dunara Castle*, and were joined on their way by the factor John MacKenzie. Their reception differed from that which was offered to visitors a few years earlier. They were received almost with complacency – at least by the people. Richard Kearton wrote,

> The St Kildans had no knowledge of the date of our coming, and the dogs, numbering between thirty and forty, were the first to discover our presence in the bay and tear pell-mell down to the water's edge. The dogs of Hirta – which is the Gaelic name of St Kilda – are a distinct feature of the place, and whenever a boat is being launched or hauled in there they all are congregated at the water's edge, engaged in furious barking, which generally ends in a fight, and a bundle of three or four, closely locked together, rolling into the sea.
>
> As nobody was to be seen, our captain blew the ship's whistle, but although he succeeded in making a prodigious din which echoed and re-echoed amongst the crags, causing the sheep to scamper away up the steep hill-sides, he produced not a sign of human life on the place. After waiting a few minutes, he sent forth another loud blast, which frightened the Kittiwakes off their nests and sent them wheeling like a little snow-cloud across the bay. In a while, a small boy, who was evidently more curious or energetic than the rest of the population, came running down to the shore to gaze at us ...
>
> I think that the clean, shining faces, and smooth, glistening hair of the women, and general Sunday appearance of the men, afford an explanation. They are caught in what they consider an unpresentable state, and the time taken up between the arrival of a boat in the bay

and the putting off of the natives is occupied in washing and tidying themselves up a bit.

By-and-by a boat put off and came alongside. I was particularly anxious to hear the first words of salutation from men who, though actually living within the confines of the British Isles, are in reality more out of touch with their country than the natives of Vancouver Island or Timbuctoo. As I could not get on deck in time, I popped my head out of a port-hole, and was startled to hear the minister [Angus Fiddes] wish everybody 'A happy new year'. [Kearton was understandably ignorant of the Gaelic tradition of exchanging that greeting at the first meeting of acquaintances after New Year's Day, even if the meeting did not take place until June.]

When we got ashore, we found most of the women and children had come down to the place of landing with great checked handkerchiefs full of birds' eggs, chiefly those of Guillemots and Razorbills, for which they found a ready sale at a penny a piece amongst the passengers and crew.

The Keartons stayed in St Kilda for almost two weeks, sleeping on hammocks in the Factor's house. There,

... after sweeping out the plaster that had fallen off the walls during the preceding twelve months and lighting a fire on a grateless hearth, we began to set things to rights. The place being half buried in the base of a steep hill called Oisaval was fearfully damp, and when my brother, with the instinct of the photographer, commenced to prowl around in search of a 'dark' room, the boards were in such a rotten condition on the ground floor that he fell through.

After tea we walked down to the beach to watch the natives bring their provisions ashore. The men conveyed the bags of meal and flour from the steamer to the rocks in their boat, whilst the women performed the far more arduous task of carrying them on their backs up the steep path to the cottages ...

We arose early the following morning, and, it being the Sabbath Day, were prepared for service. Eleven o'clock came round, but there was not a sign of anybody astir on devotions bent. We waited with patient curiosity until half-past twelve, when an old ship's bell, erected on the top of a wall near the church, began to summon worshippers to the House of Prayer by a weird out-of-place kind of tinkle, tinkle, tinkle.

In our ignorance we supposed that time was a little out of joint on the island, but afterwards learnt that the indulgent minister, Mr Fiddes, had considerately given his little flock an hour and a half's grace out of compassion for them, on account of their extra toil and exertion in landing their provisions the previous day.

The church, which is also used as a day-school, slopes considerably from the door at which the people enter to the end at which the pulpit or rostrum stands. The floor, except just beneath the feet of the worshippers, where there is a loose scaffold board, consists entirely of Mother Earth. The aisle is roughly laid with cement, put down by the minister's own hands …

The service was conducted in Gaelic, and consisted of reading the Scriptures, singing the psalms, prayer, and a very long sermon, all of which I flatter myself I sat under for the space of an hour and a half without lowering an eyelid, although I understood not a single word uttered. The collection was taken in two boxes, affixed to long handles. With these the platemen easily gathered the harvest of coppers as they walked up the aisle, without pushing in front of the congregation or bothering anybody for assistance in getting the boxes up and down the pews. They were primitive, but exceedingly sensible kind of boxes.

As soon as the minister had left, the women all filed silently out of church before a man stirred from his place. I was greatly pleased with this custom, thinking it to be a courteous deference shown to the fair sex of St Kilda, whose industry and modesty render them entirely worthy of it … In evidence of the religious fervour of the St Kildans – which can, I suppose, to some extent be reckoned up by census methods – I noticed that over 75 per cent of the entire population were in church.

Despite their language barrier the Kearton brothers befriended both Finlay Gillies, who was forty-one years old in 1896, and the thirty-four year-old, gregarious, 'big' Finlay MacQueen. One evening out on Boreray,

As we sat chatting in semi-darkness it suddenly occurred to Finlay McQuien [sic] to ask me, through a younger man who could speak

English, to tell them something about London. As they are all so good in St Kilda I knew it was of no use entering the great metropolis in a competition of that kind, so went at once to the opposite extreme and told the most dreadful stories I could remember or invent of pickpockets and other bad characters, and showed McQuien what they would probably do to him if he ever happened to wander so far south.

This fetched him, with a vengeance. He seized a lump of timber lying close by, put himself in a slaying attitude, rolled his eyes to heaven, and showed his fine set of pearly-white teeth in imitative rage. I was greatly pleased with the effect I produced, but fear I have sown the seeds of a bitter harvest for any member of the Fagin brotherhood who may happen to cross the path of the champion cragsman of St Kilda.

They were soon made aware that,

One of the civilities demanded by the etiquette of the place is that you shall shake hands with everybody you come in contact with night and morning.

The first thing they ask you in the morning is whether you have had a good sleep. If an answer in the affirmative be given they are satisfied, but if, on the contrary, you have not enjoyed a good night's rest, they follow up their solicitation after your welfare by inquiring whether you have eaten a good breakfast. Should this be the fact, they think you have no serious reason for complaint; but should the contrary be the case, they are alarmed, and show a great deal of natural sympathy.

Although extremely pious and well-behaved, they are deeply interested in the great life and death struggles of the outer world; and one of the first questions they ask, upon being visited by strangers, is whether the Queen is at war with any other country, and, if so, who is getting the best of the conflict. Nothing delights them more (men and women alike) than to hear that the enemy is being smitten hip and thigh.

They watched the two Finlays go fowling together – 'Finlay Gillies tied a rope round the body of McQuien, who stealthily crept down, rod in hand, until he came within reach of the unsuspecting birds, when he quietly pushed the instrument forward till the open noose at the end was just in front of the head of the one he had selected for his victim. By a dexterous twist of the wrist the fatal circle of horse-hair and Gannet quills fell round the neck of the Fulmar, which instantly spread out its wings and sprang forward, only to tighten the noose, and by its fluttering frighten all its companions away.'

They persuaded Finlay Gillies,

… to lay a Puffin snare on a rock which jutted out seawards, and was considered the favourite spot on all the St Kilda group of islands for the sport. Before he laid the engine of destruction down, the crag had been covered with birds; but the sight of the bit of rope, weighted at either end with a stone and crowded with horse-hair nooses in the middle, made them fight shy of it for a while as they flew past in perfect clouds.

By-and-by one individual, bolder than the rest, alighted on the rock, and with an air of foolish curiosity commenced to step along sideways towards where the snare was set. He pulled several of the nooses about with his beak, and after examining them for awhile grew bolder. Poor bird! his inquisitiveness cost him something; for in the course of his investigations one of his feet slipped through a noose, and when he came to lift his leg he discovered that he was a prisoner …

Finlay Gillies stepped along the crag, and sitting down upon one of the stones securing the snare – with as much, and probably far more, composure than he would have shown in a studio – had his portrait taken, along with that of the birds he had secured, in a position from which the slightest slip would have meant a headlong plunge of 500 feet into the ocean below.

One day Richard and Cherry Kearton walked to the end of Ruaival. Finlay MacQueen and some other men rowed out to take them from there by boat to Dun. Richard wrote afterwards:

We took off our boots and descended the slippery rock to embark. Seeing a chance of some fun with big Finlay McQuien, who turned out to be one of the rowers, I tied my boots together by the laces, and having no fear of their sinking on account of one of them being composed largely of cork – a necessity caused by an early climbing accident – I purposely threw them short of where he stood in the bows of the boat ready to make a catch, and they fell with a splash into the sea.

Poor McQuien! I shall never forget his look of alarm at what he supposed to be a very awkward accident, nor his astonishment when he saw the cork boot float and support its companion in the water. When he recovered them he squeezed the former, rolled up the whites of his eyes, and exclaimed, 'Vary khood, vary khood!'

In common with earlier visitors the Keartons observed the curiosity that 'in a community where crime is unknown' the St Kildans had secured their old blackhouses with crude wooden locks. The locks had been present in Village Bay since the eighteenth century and possibly earlier. They were occasionally affixed to the doors of cleits as well as houses and were clearly intended to discourage petty theft. The habit of lifting a neighbour's eggs was well-established in St Kilda. Occasionally more serious offences were committed, in which case the men preferred to deal with the crime and punishment themselves. Early in the 1890s 'one of them was accused of sheep-stealing [prob- ably from MacLeod's flock on Soay], and an inspector of police came up to take the offender into custody, but he wandered up and down the village street without finding any one to point out the delinquent's house, and when at last he spotted his man on the shore, he found him surrounded by all the other inhabitants, and eventually had to retire southwards alone, having ignominiously failed to vindicate the majesty of the law.'

When the people moved into the row of cottages on Main Street they made new locks for their new houses. 'The locks and keys are made entirely of wood,' wrote Richard Kearton, 'save for the two or three nails holding together the parts of the former ... A small piece of hard wood working up and down a perpendicular kind of box inside the lock drops into a mortise in the bolt, and effectually prevents it from being withdrawn until the hidden perpendicular bolt, for such it may be described, has been raised by the key, which is fashioned so as to fit into a part of it.'

They watched the women at work and at rest. They noted that 'The married women are distinguished from the unmarried ones by a white frill which is worn in front of the head-shawl or handkerchief and serves the part of a wedding ring, which is unknown in St Kilda.'

They thought it peculiar that Finlay Gillies's wife Catherine, and Finlay MacQueen's wife Mary Jemima Otter, had their clothes made by their husbands on the loom,

… whilst their future wearers dig the potato-beds or pull dock-leaves for the cows.

As a result of this, the dresses are neither fashionably made nor very close-fitting. I saw one young woman in church with her frock skirt hung upon her hips by the aid of a large French nail, the head and an inch or so of which protruded awkwardly from the material it was pinning together …

The younger women wear hats and bonnets whilst in church, but the elder ones still adhere to the picturesque, many-coloured handkerchief and shawl over their shoulders. I was considerably struck by the brooches with which they fasten their shawls. These are of two sorts – one, a large copper ring, said to be made from an old penny beaten out, and the other consisting simply of a ship's brass washer, with a wire pin attached to it. In both cases the sides of the shawl to be fastened are pulled through the ring and then transfixed by the pin.

I was much puzzled by seeing the women tramping about amongst the grass in the enclosure round the Village bare-foot and bare-leg with their skirts tucked up to their knees, pulling dock leaves. It turned out upon inquiry that the cows refuse to be milked unless they are being fed the while with this weed. Poor women of St Kilda! Theirs is a hard lot. They shoulder an immense load of dock leaves which they carry up the tremendously steep hill separating the Village from the Glen [Mor], where the cows are milked, and often fetch back an equally great load of turf in addition to their buckets of milk.

They also milk a number of ewes on the island, but although we tried every device to get them to allow my brother to photograph them in the act we failed. They would not permit this to be done for love or money, under the impression that people who saw the picture would laugh at them.

John MacKenzie the factor had of course business to do in Village Bay. He had to collect rent in kind, buy for export other surplus goods and sell or exchange what hardware and mainland clothing was required by the islanders.

The factor and the people were soon hard at work buying and selling oil, feathers, and cloth, on the one hand, and pails, spades, and similarly useful articles, on the other, down at the storehouse [the featherstore] by the sea ... The chattering and excitement were incredible.

In the afternoon of the same day all the women and children assembled in our cottage to munch sweets and go through the packages of many-coloured kerchiefs, shawls, and petticoats the factor had brought with him for their inspection and purchase. And for six mortal hours did Mackenzie, poor man! withstand with the utmost equanimity a continuous fusilade of questions and badinage.

But this was not all. At eleven o'clock at night a soft tap-tapping was heard upon the door, and in they all trooped to re-open their bargaining. I wonder what the average Bond Street shopkeeper would say to being invaded at this hour by a crowd of lady customers who had been unable to make up their minds in the afternoon.

Richard Kearton offered a sympathetic perspective on the St Kildans' supposed corruption by tourism and the materialism of the mainland.

I had heard and read a good deal about the unblushing greed and covetousness of the St Kildans, and must admit that I was staggered when one of them asked me in laboured English 'ten shilling' as an inducement for him to put back a Wren's nest where he had found it – inside one of his cleits – in order that my brother might photograph it ... [But otherwise] The men never objected to our photographing them, nor, so far as I could gather, expected anything for allowing us to do so, though had they done we could not have had serious reason for complaint.

I was anxious to obtain two pictures in order to show the difference in the head-gear worn by married and single women, and offered half-a-crown each to anybody who would sit; but to my surprise no one would consent, and it was only by strategy, and a positive assurance that their portraits were not being taken to make fun of them, that we succeeded in obtaining what we wanted.

Before passing judgment on these poor creatures, it is only fair to them to take evidence on both sides of the question of their selfishness, and then throw in a little consideration for the influence of their utter isolation and the folly of tourists and other visitors ...

Whilst we were about on the different islands with the men, those who took anything to drink in the shape of milk or whey with them in the boat gave us freely of their beverage if our own supply ran short; and after they came to know what manner of man I was, some of them would not accept anything for specimen birds which they caught for me.

Again, on the morning of my departure from the island, I was rowed to the steamer in the local boat along with a number of excursionists who had been paying a hurried visit ashore. When we got midway betwixt the land and the vessel, one of the St Kildan rowers took off his bonnet and began to make a collection, as payment for the boat and men. I was putting a shilling into the hat when the man stopped me and said that he wouldn't accept anything from me – I was one of themselves.

Two years after the Kearton brothers departed from Village Bay, in 1898 another couple went to stay in the Factor's House. The thirty-five year-old John Norman Heathcote and his beloved thirty-four year-old sister Evelyn May Heathcote were cousins of MacLeod of MacLeod – their maternal grandfather had been the 25th chief who had regained St Kilda and had died in Paris in 1895. They had been born and brought up at their affluent father's properties in London and Huntingdonshire, but they were naturally familiar with their mother's home island of Skye. They also travelled west on the *Dunara Castle* with the factor John MacKenzie. Heathcote would return in 1899 and later write up his impressions of the islands. On his first visit Norman Heathcote had expected the *Dunara Castle* to be full of day-trippers. He had not anticipated that others would also travel with the intention of spending a week or two on St Kilda. Most of those were masons and carpenters who had been commissioned to build a new schoolroom inside the church. Until they found lodgings they slept by the shore. There were also 'two young Englishmen who had rashly neglected to inquire about accommodation, and talked about sleeping in a tent. John MacKenzie, jun., who goes to St Kilda every year in his capacity of factor or agent for the owner, MacLeod of MacLeod, assured us that no tent could stand against the squalls that come down off the hills, and from what we experienced afterwards I can quite believe it. However, they did not have occasion to put it to the test, as they got lodgings in a native cottage.'

Norman Heathcote also found himself holidaying on St Kilda with the young novelist Charles John Cutcliffe Wright Hyne, who wrote as Weatherby Chesney and had recently published his bestseller *Adventures of Captain Kettle*. The St Kildans apparently deduced that as Hyne did not go to church and had been seen out of doors in a white mackintosh which they took for sacrificial robes, he was a Roman Catholic priest.

Despite such first-hand evidence of the advent of modernity as a gang of builders, two English campers and a travelling author in the Hebrides, Heathcote clung to late-Victorian fragments of noble savagery, writing:

> To people living in the midst of the turmoil and bustle of a London life, it seems almost incredible that there should be a place within the confines of the British isles where not only is there no telegraph or railroad or a horse; where the inhabitants have no conception what a town is like, and have never seen anything in the shape of a tree or shrub; an island fifty miles from the nearest land, having no communication with the outer world except during the three months of summer; an island of towering precipices surrounded by the relentless waves of the Atlantic, where no sound is heard except the cry of a seagull and the roar of the breakers on the rocks; where drunkenness and crime are unknown, where no policeman has ever been seen, and a doctor rarely comes.
>
> Yet such a place is St Kilda.

Once on the ground Heathcote was confronted by the realities of St Kildan life. Like the Keartons and others before him he could not help but notice the extraordinary labours of the women and girls.

> They do most of the carrying of goods up from the shore and peats down from the hills; they walk over to the glen, a distance of about two miles, over a pass 800 feet high, twice every day during the summer, to milk the cows and ewes; they work on the crofts, and when not otherwise employed, occupy themselves with spinning and knitting.
>
> The girls begin carrying weights at a very early age. [I saw] a child of about eleven bringing two pails full of water up from the well; and I have seen a girl of about the same age with a smaller child on one arm and a bucket of water in the other, coming over the hill with a sheep on her back.

For all the efforts of the women and girls, Norman Heathcote noticed that the arable land on the crofts was in poor repair. This had been the case for a number of years, and Heathcote was certainly alerted to the fact by the factor he knew familiarly as Johnnie MacKenzie. It had been the reason why severe summer storms made such a devastating impact on the islanders' remaining crops. It was certainly a hangover from the mid-nineteenth century shortage of active, able-bodied men who had too many other duties to perform on the sea and on the cliffs. It would have even more serious effects in the near future.

'The amount of cultivated land is now very limited,' wrote Heathcote in an ominous paragraph, 'and the people say that when they can get meal, &c., from the South it pays better to let the grass grow than to try cultivating corn or potatoes. There is probably some truth in this … At the present time their agricultural efforts are not at all worthy of praise. Their crops looked poor and uncared for, and showed an utter want of system … I came across a barley field that was certainly not more than two square yards in extent.'

With the help of Finlay MacQueen, Norman Heathcote despatched some letters to himself in a small mailboat. They arrived at his English home via Norway four months later. More crucially, he noticed the beginning of a more convenient means of communication.

As well as a new schoolroom and a renovated church – the first was 'very comfortable, and there is a good supply of apparatus' reported a schools inspector in 1900, and the second 'has been neatly matchboarded throughout, the floor has been levelled and boarded' – a large stone jetty was built below the manse in Village Bay in 1899 and 1901. 'The engineer who was looking after the construction of the pier … wished to be able to report progress from time to time, and made arrangements with the trawlers to act as postmen.' It was the start of the thirty-year relationship between the people of St Kilda and the steam trawlers of Fleetwood and elsewhere.

Norman and Evelyn Heathcote were given a taste of the adventure tourism which male St Kildans had discovered to be more interesting and profitable than cultivating grain. Finlay MacQueen arranged for them and some other visitors to take a day trip to Boreray. Heathcote wrote:

It seemed a most promising morning. Finlay MacQuien did say, 'Ah! we shall spend the night in Boreray,' but I thought he was only joking, especially as the others all agreed that it was a good day to go, and that the landing would be easy. Our party consisted of my sister and myself, three young Englishmen, who generally went by the name 'the boys', because they were a good deal younger than we were, and three natives. The 'Sassenachs' being new to St Kilda, did not venture up Stac Lii, but Finlay, my sister, and I got ashore with some difficulty and had a most satisfactory climb [both Norman and Evelyn Heathcote, whose father was a celebrated sportsman, were formidably accomplished climbers] ... it was close upon 5 p.m. before we had climbed down the cliffs and all got on board again. As soon as we had rowed round the corner, it became evident that we should have a job to get home.

They stayed overnight in their boat by a cave in the lee of Boreray.

We had had visions of landing and spending the night in a hut with a bright fire and roast puffins for dinner, but no such luxuries were in store for us. The men said that, if the wind were to shift to the south, the cave would be unsafe, and they would have to leave at a moment's notice ... all that remained from luncheon was a piece of cake, a few biscuits, and some chocolate, while the men had some cheese and cold tea. It was an occasion on which a non-smoker is at a great disadvantage. I have seldom enjoyed a smoke more than my after-dinner pipe that night.

Presently Norman MacKinnon, the only English-speaking member of our crew, told us that they were going to 'make worship', and then followed one of the most impressive services I have ever attended. I could not understand a word, but the earnestness of the men, the intoning of their prayers, the weirdness of the Gaelic tune to which they sang a psalm, and the solemn grandeur of the place, combined to make it a most interesting and impressive ceremony.

They reached Village Bay again on the following morning. 'There was great excitement on the shore. The hand-shaking was more than usually energetic and prolonged, and one of the natives could only give utterance to his feelings by the somewhat unexpected exclamation "By Jove!".'

The Heathcotes found the local tweed industry to be thriving. Norman wrote that,

> The wool of the St Kilda sheep is most beautifully soft, and the cloth made from it is first-rate stuff. Personally I habitually wear it in the country, but many people object to it because, being made of undyed wool, it is rather light in colour.
>
> The St Kildans use indigo for their own clothes, in fact you hardly ever see a native wearing a suit made from the natural wool, but for export they never use any dye. When they take the trouble to collect the wool from the Soay sheep, which is even finer and softer than the rest, they mix the brown wool with the white and produce a rather darker cloth, but they are always rather slack about getting it, and some years do not bother about it at all.

Heathcote's observations were confirmed in the 1901 census, where virtually every adult male identified his occupation as 'handloom weaver of wool', virtually every woman as 'hand spinner of wool', and very few as 'crofter'.

When the *Spectator* magazine reviewed Norman Heathcote's short book on St Kilda in November 1900, it commented: 'A change of minister is, perhaps, the most important event in the island chronicles, and this does not happen often.'

The *Spectator* spoke too soon. The St Kildans were not only about to change their minister; they would change their church. In 1900 Angus Fiddes had been in Village Bay for eleven years. He was not especially happy there. Referring to himself ironically as the 'Bishop of St Kilda', he periodically complained of his 'lonely life ... Nine weary months out of every year without a chance of exchanging a word with an educated person.'

More importantly, the St Kildans were increasingly unhappy with Reverend Fiddes. It was noted by the supervisor of the squad building the new pier, which would be completed in 1901, that Fiddes 'was not appreciated by the natives. He built a stone wall round his garden. They pulled it down, saying he was getting too worldly'.

Reverend Fiddes's worldliness had brought benefits to St Kilda. He had consulted Lowland experts about the neonatal tetanus deaths, had taken sound advice and put it to good use on the island. The widespread use of antiseptic and then anti-tetanus inoculations, building upon the hygienic improvements urged by the nurses, was largely due to the minister. He had campaigned successfully for the new pier, and for a post office which was opened in Village Bay in 1900 and was used not only by the locals but also by tourists sending letters and postcards bearing the precious St Kilda frank.

In 1900 Reverend Angus Fiddes decided to change his church. The Free Church of Scotland had suffered several schisms since its establishment in 1843. None of them had affected St Kilda for the dual reasons that the islanders had hardly heard of the divisions and were almost entirely dependent on their minister to inform and lead his flock.

The creation in 1900 of the United Free Church of Scotland was an attempt to bridge one of those confessional divides. It represented the union of an earlier offshoot, the United Presbyterian Church, and most members of Angus Fiddes's Free Church of Scotland. (A minority of Free Church adherents, mostly in the Highlands and Islands, remained outside the union and contested in the courts its right to Free Church assets and properties. They lost their case but felt themselves to be vindicated in 1929, when the United Free Church was voluntarily subsumed back into the established Church of Scotland.)

On St Kilda, Angus Fiddes went with the majority and took his congregation into the United Free Church. According to their minister the St Kildans accepted it 'with satisfaction ... Ecclesiastically, they are very pleased with the union of the Churches'.

If they were satisfied by the United Free Church, which is by no means certain, they were less pleased with Angus Fiddes himself. It is possible that no minister could spend more than a decade in the hothouse of Village Bay without making enemies. Whatever bad feeling had grown up between the St Kildans and Reverend Fiddes was irritated further by their 'bishop's many periods of absence at the turn of the century, and may have reached its nadir when the people realised that, almost uniquely in the Protestant Hebrides, they had been bounced out of their familiar Free Church.

The relationship had run its course. 'When I saw the last steamer leave [St Kilda] for the year,' Fiddes reflected shortly afterwards, 'a lump came in my throat. I was shut off from the world, and from all those who were near and dear to me.'

For their part, the St Kildans may or may not have been broadly content with their new Church, but they certainly considered it was time for a new minister. When Angus Fiddes returned to Hirta after a month on the mainland in August 1901, the locals let him ashore but – having already dismantled his garden wall – refused to land his coal and other supplies. Two months later in October a Fleetwood trawler carrying essentials for the minister was despatched by the United Free Church. The St Kildans refused to help but the trawler's crew managed to get the supplies to the manse.

It was clearly an unsustainable situation. In June 1902 a deputation from the United Free Church arrived on the SS *Hebrides*. Reverend Angus Fiddes left for the south. He returned just once more in the following month to collect his belongings and say his farewells. For the time being the St Kildans were left in the spiritual care of a missionary from the island of Tiree named Lachlan MacLean. No future minister or missionary would spend more than seven years on St Kilda, and most of them would stay there for less than half that period of time.

In September 1903 the missionary Lachlan MacLean buried Norman Gillies. The father of Mary Jemima Otter MacQueen and Finlay Gillies, husband first of their deceased mother Ann and of their surviving step-mother Mary, Norman passed away at the age of seventy-nine, of a supposed heart attack at 7.30 in the morning, in the presence of his twenty-three year-old youngest son Ewen. As a boy in the 1830s Norman had been thrown sweets by the first tourists on the SS *Glenalbyn*. As a man he had scaled the rocks for food and feathers and for display. He had rowed the boats, raised his family and given his best clothes to a shivering shipwrecked Austrian sailor. Until the very end he spoke only the soft, sibilant, lisping Hirtan Gaelic language. As a young man in 1852 he had rejected the opportunity to emigrate to Australia. There is no evidence that he ever left Hirta, unless it was to go to Soay, Boreray and the stacks, and no evidence that he desired to do so. The St Kilda archipelago had been Norman Gillies's world, entire unto itself.

Later in 1903 Lachlan MacLean was replaced by another United Free Church missionary from the Ross of Mull named John Fraser. To John Fraser fell the unfortunate task of burying Norman Gillies's precious daughter and Finlay MacQueen's dear wife, Mary Jemima Otter MacQueen. Mary died three years after her father, on 16 May 1906, after suffering from a uterine haemorrhage for three weeks. She was just forty-six years old. She died in the presence of her big, amiable husband Finlay MacQueen, who was left a widower with six of their children to raise. Finlay never remarried.

On 27 September of the following year, 1907, Alice MacLachlan, the English wife of the current United Free Church missionary Peter MacLachlan, noted in her diary: 'Went into William [MacDonald]'s house where there was an assembly of women. There I heard the astonishing intelligence that Annie MacQuien – daughter of Finlay – is to have a baby in a month or two & that the father is our friend Donald Gillies, son of poor Finlay Gillies. We are awfully sorry about it ...'

Alice MacLachlan's sorrow was groundless. Finlay MacQueen's oldest daughter, the eighteen year-old Annie MacQueen, duly gave birth to little Mary Gillies on 30 October. Mary's twenty-two year-old father Donald Gillies – the oldest son of Finlay and Catherine Gillies – accepted full responsibility and gave the baby his surname. Ten months later, in August 1908, the young couple were formally married by the missionary and registrar Peter MacLachlan at the St Kilda United Free Church.

The occasion afforded the MacQueen and Gillies families some overdue cause for celebration. Donald and Annie were both grand-children of the late Ann and Norman Gillies, which was as close to a necessary consanguinity as was accepted among the few families of Village Bay. The wedding was witnessed by Donald Gillies's mother Catherine. Donald and Annie were married on the same day as their aunt Annie Gillies, the thirty-five year-old daughter of Norman Gillies, who wed an older widower called Calum MacDonald.

At the respective ages of twenty-three, nineteen and one, Donald, Annie and Mary Gillies moved into Number 14 Main Street. They took over the house and croft at that site which had recently been vacated by the death of Donald's great-aunt Betsy MacDonald.

Two years later, at 5.00 p.m. on 3 September 1910, Annie Gillies was delivered of another baby girl. She was christened Rachel Annie Ferguson Gillies. The 'Ferguson' was a homage to Donald's mother's relatives. It would soon be lost from Rachel's life. As she grew up, as she went to the village school, as she travelled away by steam trawler to look for work and a new life in Lancashire, as she returned to St Kilda and then sailed away for one last time to spend the rest of her life in Argyllshire and elsewhere on the Scottish mainland, she would be known as Rachel Ann Gillies.

TEN

An Indian Summer

✷

RACHEL ANN GILLIES and her contemporaries, and indeed their parents' generation, would know a vastly different life from that of their grandfather and great-grandfather Norman Gillies. They were substantially different people.

They were born into a St Kilda from which the spectre of infant mortality had largely been removed, and whose population was as a consequence growing for the first time in half a century. But it was not growing as much as it should have grown.

By the turn of the nineteenth century into the twentieth, St Kilda's contacts with the outside world were hugely increased. It may have been the most visited destination of all the Outer Hebridean islands. Journalists and other writers from across Europe and even the United States came to call. To climbers – a hobby which grew apace in the late nineteenth century – St Kilda was a distant but desirable location. Post-Darwinian naturalists sought its examples of unique species and parallel evolution. Fishing boats and their crews also congregated all year round in its home waters and sought shelter in Village Bay – not only the long-distance steam trawlers of Fleetwood, but also drift-netters and trawlers from the north and north-east of Scotland and long-line fishing skiffs from the other western islands. On one winter's day in 1913 a St Kildan boy 'counted twenty ships of all sizes sheltering in Village Bay; practically all of them were from countries such as Norway, Sweden and France'. St Kilda's nine-month isolation from the rest of the world became almost a thing of the past. It may have taken them almost a year to hear about the Battle of Waterloo in 1815, but when Queen Victoria died on 22 January 1901 the news arrived in Village Bay on a sailing ship in February. The *Titanic* sank on 15 April 1912. The St Kildans heard of the tragedy 'from a passing boat' in May.

Those people found in Village Bay a young community with whom, thanks to the schoolteachers of the 1880s and later, they could converse in English. The relationship between St Kildans and their visitors changed from one of largely uncomprehending barter and exchange to one of real, direct, face-to-face human interaction. Peterhead trawlermen could tell young St Kildan men and women about the fishing. Fleetwood trawlermen could tell them about the wonders of the modern world. Naturalists, climbers and other tourists could describe the sights of Edinburgh and New York.

That generation's grasp of English also gave them the confidence to seek work, housing, new lives and new friends in Glasgow and London and even the colonies. The result was not mass emigration as in 1852, when the thirty-six islanders had departed for Australia in a defensible Gaelic-speaking corral, but a trickle of individual departures which steadily became a flood. As the early twentieth-century St Kildans would have known, they were not alone in their abandonment of their birthplace. Between 1881 and 1921 the combined populations of Eriskay and the larger Outer Hebridean islands of South Uist and Benbecula fell from 5,842 to 4,479 people. That was not the effect of the compulsory clearances which had reduced those islands earlier in the nineteenth century. It was the result of 'voluntary' economic migration by younger people to find salaried work in the industrial south.

In 1900 Norman Heathcote made tantalising mention of 'One or two of the young men who have recently obtained situations in Glasgow have tried selling some of the produce of the island on their own account.' Those young men were Alexander and Donald Ferguson, who had both been taught English, had left St Kilda in 1892 and 1896 respectively and had subsequently established themselves at a premises on Hope Street in the city as A G Ferguson & Co, St Kilda and Harris Tweed Factors. Alexander Ferguson was the younger brother of Annie, the 'Queen of St Kilda' whose show marriage he had helped to prevent. In future years Alexander – who returned regularly to Village Bay – would offer his home to St Kildan émigrés until they found their feet in the Lowlands.

Statistics compiled by Mary Harman suggest that between 1901 and 1920 at least a further ten men and women of marrying, child-bearing ages emigrated by themselves or in pairs. The figure may well be higher than ten, but even that number is equal to the total of individual departures – that is, excluding the emigration to Australia – between the 1820s and 1890. And they were just the first blood to be lost in the final haemorrhage.

As the twentieth century dawned, once again observers began to question the future viability of St Kilda not on its own terms, as a place in which humans could eat, drink, reproduce and stay alive, but in the more demanding remit of the modern world. 'What will happen to St Kilda in the future?' wondered Norman Heathcote at the start of the new century in 1900.

'Will it remain the lonely island home of a primitive people and continue to afford a charming refuge for those who wish for a while to escape from the rush of life? Will it be deserted by the present inhabitants and become the breeding-place of yet greater numbers of birds than are to be found there now? Or, lastly, will it be invaded by the purveyor of health or amusement, and shall we see a hydropathic establishment erected on the slopes of Connacher and an esplanade round the shores of Village Bay?'

In the same year the *Spectator* magazine was more brutal. 'The future suggests not a few problems which are by no means easy of solution,' it pointed out. 'The primitive ways of the island, the conducting of business by barter, for instance, it will hardly be possible to keep to, as it becomes more and more part of the great world.'

Donald John Gillies was born in Village Bay in May 1901. He was the youngest son of John and Annie Gillies, whose imminent marriage had been the cause of the invasion from Sunderland in 1890. When he was seven years old Donald and Annie Gillies moved in next door and Donald John and his brothers had their girls Mary and Rachel Ann with whom to play hide-and-seek and football, which had replaced shinty as the team sport of preference in almost all of the Outer Hebrides.

As was then required throughout the whole of Scotland, Donald John Gillies attended school between the ages of five and fifteen years. His first teachers in 1906 were the missionary Peter MacLachlan and his wife Alice. Peter would take school in the morning and the 'charming

... tall, kind-hearted and well educated' Alice in the afternoon. She also taught the girls sewing, knitting and singing.

There were twenty children in the school in Village Bay when Donald John first appeared, carrying his daily peat for the schoolroom fire, at the start of the educational year in 1906. They were almost immediately visited by a school inspector who arrived on the ss *Hebrides*. He reported that reading and arithmetic had improved over the previous year, 'but English composition shows no advance, and the new teacher is accordingly urged to make a special effort to effect the requisite improvement in this very important subject. Lessons in conversational English in all classes and written composition in the Senior classes should be a much more prominent feature of the instruction than hitherto, and greater neatness and accuracy in the handwriting and general style of the written work should be insisted on. The older pupils should be encouraged to make use of the well-equipped school library.'

Thus was English taught as a foreign language, to children whose parents, grandparents, uncles and aunts could barely utter a word of it, in the farthest corner of the Scottish *Gàidhealtachd* early in the twentieth century.

Attendance was flexible. The younger barefoot children often did not walk the short distance to school in the worst winter weather. All of the pupils were customarily given the day off if the *Dunara Castle* or any other tourist steamer arrived in the bay, and the afternoon off when a trawler came in with the mail and other goods. The school was closed during the weeks of church communion, and again when the children were needed to help carry peat from the bogs to the cleits. In May 1907 Peter MacLachlan wrote in the school log: 'School kept open but attendance unsatisfactory as the children are wanted to help their parents with the turf cutting. There is so much of outdoor work of all kinds at this season at which the children have to assist that as we are going for our holidays we have decided to give the children theirs at the same time so no interim teacher will be required.'

When Donald John Gillies was five years old Miss Zillah Hannah Goudie arrived in the island. Goudie, a redoubtable English ornithologist and water-colourist, embodied the new, modern version of St Kildan tourism. She was a thirty-four year-old woman, and she was there to climb, hunt birds and then write about her adventure in the public prints.

At the end of the nineteenth century gannets from Boreray and the stacks fell out of favour as a foodstuff in St Kilda and were replaced by the slightly more accessible fulmars. One early-twentieth-century boy in Hirta recalled being told, to his slight surprise, that his father's generation had dined on gannets rather than fulmar. Zillah Goudie's account of going on a fulmar hunt on a bright and clear August day in 1906 indicated that however their prey might have changed, crags-manship was still in the blood of the twentieth-century St Kildans. Even as they spun and wove increasing quantities of tweed, caught fish and sold their goods to tourists, even as they ate more mutton and imported other foodstuffs from the mainland, and were therefore less dependent on bird flesh to stay alive, even as they offered climbing demonstrations to tourists for cash, 'going to the rocks' would remain a fundamental focus of life on St Kilda. Zillah Goudie's experience showed that their extraordinary skills on rock faces, of whose every ledge and cleft they had encyclopaedic knowledge, continued even in modern times to be passed down from father to son. There was good reason for that. Without the cliffs they would have been just another subsistence community scratching a living on the edge of nowhere. With them, they could be heroes in a heroic landscape.

That August morning in 1906 Finlay MacQueen, Finlay Gillies and the other men left early to walk over into Gleann Mor and across to the cliffs between Cambir and Soay – 'by eight o'clock not a man remained in the tiny village on the bay'.

An hour later, at 9.00 a.m., the women and children followed, carrying sacks and accompanied by Zillah Goudie. They joined up with the men, preparing their long ropes and 'making ready for the descent', at the top of Cambir. As usual the men worked in pairs and bare-foot, 'for it would be impossible to get the toe of a boot into some of the cracks along which these expert cragsmen make their way'. They noosed or grabbed the birds and then the women drew the catch up to the summit.

As Zillah Goudie admired the 'magnificent and awe-inspiring' scenery,

> … one of the older men came behind me and, laughing, slipped a rope round my waist and knotted it, inviting me by signs to join in the hunt. The women expostulated shrilly in Gaelic, fearing, I suppose,

that 'Mees' might take an involuntary 'header' into the waves below. But the opportunity was not to be lost ... so with my heart in my mouth and an uneasy feeling at the pit of my stomach, I gaily followed my guide along a twelve-inch ledge with a distinct list to seaward.

After about five minutes of this we came to the first corner. The ledge narrowed to four or five inches, and it became necessary to face the cliff, hugging it with both arms, with the cheerful assurance that one's heels were over about 800 feet of nothingness.

I was the last of three on the rope, and we were divided by about thirty feet of slack. Bird after bird was seized, killed, and slung on to a rope round the shoulders of the men. Every now and again we stopped on a ledge a little wider than the rest, and one man let down the other to work the ledges below us. Any easy catch they left to me ... I caught them and passed them to the men to be killed, and was laughed at for my pains.

Up and down we went, now along a wide ledge, now working our way with toes and fingers along a mere crack. There was no time to feel dizzy. All one's energies were taken up in seeking toe and finger hold and scanning the cliff for birds. Now and again on some good wide ledge we stopped, and tied all our birds together by the neck, and one of the men gave a wailing call which brought the women to the edge above. They let down a rope and hauled up the birds.

At last we came to what looked like the end of things. A fault in the cliff raised the continuation of our ledge some twenty feet above our heads, and the rock rose perpendicular and smooth at right angles to our path. It seemed to me that only a fly could crawl up there. The first man stopped, looked up and down, and then began climbing the edge of the rock. I watched, expecting every moment to see him fall headlong. I suppose it was not two minutes, but it seemed an hour before he reached the ledge above. Then up went the second man with some assistance from the rope. Now it was my turn, but to go up that saw-like edge was more than I could manage, and I shook my head.

The man grinned and began to haul in the slack, and the next minute I was ignominiously dangling at the end of the rope. Nothing astonished me more during my stay on the island than the amazing strength of arm the men have. I am a heavy woman, but that man hauled me up, hand over hand, with no more trouble than if I had been a child.

The doughty Zillah Goudie made it back to the summit with cut and bleeding bare feet. A storm blew up and she worried that she might be stranded on St Kilda, but a tramp trawler out of Hull named the *Water Rat* put into Village Bay for shelter and Miss Goudie made her escape. Shortly afterwards she left the United Kingdom for Chile. For the moment, the St Kildans remained.

The MacLachlans left St Kilda in 1909. Peter MacLachlan's missionary work was taken on by Dugald MacLean from the Argyllshire island of Tiree. Dugald MacLean's oldest daughter Annie became the schoolteacher. They were replaced in 1912 by Calum MacArthur and his sister, and in 1914 the Skyeman Alexander MacKinnon and his wife moved into the manse.

On Dugald MacLean's and Calum MacArthur's short watches two shock waves rippled through St Kilda. In May 1912 the trawler *Strathmore* landed its catch at Aberdeen. Its captain reported that he had been fishing around St Kilda and had found the inhabitants to be 'practically starving … The supplies of tea, sugar, and meat had become entirely exhausted, and only a small quantity of flour remained. For the past week or two the people had been living mostly on birds' eggs, but they have been suffering from want of bread. Temporary relief was afforded by the arrival during the week of a Hull trawler, the captain of which gave as large a supply of provisions as he could spare.'

The captain of the *Strathmore*, Donald Craig, was a familiar and well-liked face in St Kilda. There is reason to doubt certain aspects of his account of a famine there in the spring of 1912. The St Kildans had run out of tea and sugar and run short of grain, but it is inconceivable that an island containing so many sheep would then or ever find its meat supplies 'entirely exhausted'. They had certainly received no mail and very few visitors since before Christmas, but they were not starving. They were not even incapacitated. On 2 May 1912 Annie MacLean wrote in the school log that 'As all the islanders are busy at work on the crofts, the [school] attendance was very bad as children are required to help.'

The conscience of the nation, which had become sensitively attuned to St Kilda, was nonetheless pricked. The First Lord of the Admiralty, Winston Churchill MP, ordered the Commander-in-Chief of the Home Fleet to send a cruiser stocked with provisions to Village

Bay. Miss MacLean dourly reported in her log: 'School closed on 20th and 21st May as HMS *Achilles* had arrived with food, the report having gone out that the inhabitants of St Kilda were starving.'

A year later the scare turned into reality. On 9 June 1913 Calum MacArthur wrote feebly in the school log, 'School closed today. Teacher has been unwell.' There were no further entries until 26 June, when a District Medical Officer scrawled in the neglected log, 'Visited school and found it closed in consequence of an epidemic of influenza.'

The whole island was prostrated. Donald John Gillies, who was twelve years old at the time, recalled that the epidemic was so severe that 'the food was practically all gone and I remember our family had to use the potatoes we had set aside for seed.'

The Admiralty responded yet again. HMS *Active* was despatched to the island, where she found 'practically the entire population of the island ill with influenza. Most of them were confined to bed, and were without medical aid and could do no work. Although food was plentiful there was no-one to cook it.'

The *Active*'s officers landed a doctor, two nurses and food, turned the church into a field hospital and the schoolroom into a supply stores. The Inverness-shire county medical officer ordered one of his staff to St Kilda with a supply of medical stores, which is why the medical officer's brief inscription appeared in the school log on 26 June. By that time HMS *Active* had returned to Devonport and reported that the condition of the people of St Kilda 'had greatly improved'.

On 23 June 1913 the concern of the nation in general for St Kilda was expressed when the Secretary of State for Scotland was asked to explain the incident to the House of Commons. Thomas McKinnon Wood said:

> I received information through the Admiralty, and also from The MacLeod of MacLeod, the owner of the island, to the effect that a trawler reported in Harris that there had been a serious outbreak of influenza or pneumonia in St Kilda, and that assistance was urgently needed.
>
> I at once communicated with the Admiralty, who, at my request, were good enough to arrange for the dispatch of His Majesty's ship *Active*, from Lamlash, to visit the island, and report. The *Active* reached St Kilda on Saturday afternoon and reported that the islanders were

suffering from an epidemic of influenza, which had attacked seventy-three out of the seventy-nine inhabitants, out of whom twenty-eight were convalescent. The commander of the *Active* took all steps in his power to render immediate medical assistance.

Meanwhile, I had instructed the Local Government Board for Scotland to be prepared, in case of need, to send to St Kilda a doctor, nurses and medical stores, and on receipt of the report from the *Active*, the Admiralty, at my request, sent instructions for the cruiser to leave her doctor at St Kilda, to proceed to Oban, and there to pick up the relief party. Dr Dittmar, medical inspector under the Local Government Board and two nurses, with the necessary medical stores, accordingly left Edinburgh early yesterday morning, joined the *Active* at Oban yesterday afternoon, and arrived at St Kilda late last night.

The relief expedition had been prompt and effective, but it could only cushion the impact of yet another psychological blow. The St Kildans may not in 1913 have suffered from the Stranger Sickness, but their herd immunity was clearly still low, and they were a very long way from help.

There had been talk for a number of years of erecting a radio mast on St Kilda. Such a means of communication could, it was argued, ease the locals' sense of isolation and enable them more quickly and easily to keep the authorities informed of their condition. The Postmaster General had dismissed the idea as too expensive an undertaking for so few people.

In 1912 the *Daily Mirror* newspaper, which had developed a sentimental anxiety about the island, opened a private subscription to erect a mast. They raised the money comfortably but the equipment was not installed until the panics of 1912 and 1913 lent a fresh urgency to the project. In July 1913 two masts were delivered by the ss *Hebrides* to Village Bay, hauled by the St Kildans off the beach, carried up the shore and through the crofts and erected directly in front of the factor's house. Although food and other supplies could never be delivered by radio wave, it did appear that the days of the functional St Kilda mailboat were over.

A technician taught the missionary Calum MacArthur how to operate the station. The first wireless message from St Kilda was sent on 29 July 1913 via the station at Lochboisdale in South Uist to King George

V in London. It read: 'Your Majesty's loyal subjects in the lonely island of St Kilda respectfully beg to offer to your Majesty on the occasion of the opening of the wireless station installed here by the Daily Mirror newspaper their most heartfelt thanks for the valuable assistance rendered by the officers and men of the cruiser Active to St Kildans when they were all stricken with illness. The inhabitants deeply appreciate the kindness extended to them in their hours of peril. They hope that peace and prosperity will continue to bless your Majesty's reign.'

His Majesty's peace would last for only another thirteen months.

By 1914, in the confusion of Calum MacArthur leaving St Kilda and the arrival of Alexander MacKinnon, who knew nothing about radio transmission; with the *Daily Mirror* and the General Post Office bickering about who had responsibility for the maintenance of the masts and station, St Kilda's wireless connection had fallen into disuse. It was saved by the First World War, which Great Britain entered on 4 August 1914. Two St Kildans fought in that conflict. Finlay MacQueen's son John joined the Royal Naval Reserve. John MacDonald, who was eighteen years old in 1914 and had moved to the mainland a year earlier, joined the British Army, survived the Dardanelles campaign and made it back alive. He was allowed one home visit during the war. In August 1916 a naval vessel from Stornoway in Lewis dropped him off for forty-eight hours' leave in Village Bay. The other men happened to be over in Soay catching sheep. They were informed of the lad's return and rushed back to greet him and say farewell again.

In his short time at home John MacDonald would have noticed that St Kilda was busy on the home front. With the advent of a war fought partly in the North Atlantic Ocean, the islands suddenly had a valuable function as a sentinel in the Western Approaches. A twentieth-century role which did not involve tourism or the manufacture of tweed had been discovered for Hirta. It would become a military base.

In November 1914 the Admiralty set about reviving the wireless station and sent two dozen men to St Kilda. Three sleeping huts, a cookhouse and a dining hut were erected near the church. The northwestern islands of Scotland and their surrounding ocean would be patrolled by about seventy armed trawlers and drifters and motor boats, which after 1915 were commanded from Stornoway.

A naval reservist from the west side of Lewis later told his son:

His assignation was rather unusual in that he did not serve on any conventional naval ship. Instead, he became a crew member of a small fishing boat with instructions to discard naval uniform in favour of fisherman's garb. On the deck of the tiny craft was a small gun hidden away by draped fishing nets. All very mysterious.

Orders were given to proceed to the sea area between Lewis and St Kilda, where an explanation of the proposed operation was revealed. Rendezvous was made with a submarine and a communicating cable was attached to both vessels. The plan was to keep a lookout for any enemy activity. If the innocent 'fisherman' spotted a hostile ship, contact could be made by cable with the submarine, which would then take appropriate action. A somewhat similar arrangement took place in World War Two. Such vessels were known as 'Q' Ships.

On one occasion, it so happened that the fishing boat was running short of fresh water used for cooking and drinking. The skipper decided to head for St Kilda to replenish supplies. Duncan MacDonald, with one or two others, was detailed to go ashore at Village Bay in the hope of finding a well or fresh water loch. It was never an easy task to land on St Kilda because of heavy swell. Gaelic was spoken.

Having scrambled ashore, the Navy men approached a small hamlet where they met an elderly female resident whom my father engaged in conversation – Gaelic of course. During the conversation, Duncan expressed the view that living in such a remote part posed many problems and asked if the inhabitants considered life on the mainland where they would enjoy easier living conditions. The response was instant and emphatic. '*Gu dearbh, cha tàinig a' smuain a-steach orm. Chan fhaca mise a-riamh àite a chuirinn air thoiseach air an eilean bheag bhòidheach agam fhin.*' ('Indeed never did such a thought enter my head. I have never seen a place that I would prefer to our own beautiful little island.').

Suddenly there was well-paid work on St Kilda. Local men built the huts and defences and formed a local volunteer force in case of German invasion. Several of them, including Finlay MacQueen's sons Donald and John, were given 15 shillings a week to keep watch for enemy shipping from the tops of their hills. At first the look-outs signalled to the radio station in the village by semaphore. When the hilltops were covered in mist they sent runners. Finally telephone cables were installed between cleits on the summits and the wireless station in Village Bay. The St Kildans were able to purchase food and other modern goods from the Navy stores. They were able to travel off the island on naval vessels and consequently had regular contact with the other islands and the mainland in all seasons of the year. The islands had never been busier or fiscally wealthier, and had never felt more important.

Their importance to the war effort was brutally emphasised on the calm and sunny morning of 15 May 1918. Neil Gillies, who had been keeping overnight watch with three companions from a cleit on top of Mullach Mor, recalled: 'We were up there and we made hot tea, we would sleep and take it in turns to watch. We spotted the sub coming in very slowly. We watched and he stopped over by the Dun. We had a phone down to the wireless and we phoned down that the submarine was making for the bay. He came close, to the point where you could have flung a stone right down his conning tower.'

Down in Village Bay, Finlay MacQueen was convinced that the submarine was a friendly craft and he was making plans to row out into the bay with fraternal greetings. She was not friendly. She was the German *U-90* under the command of Captain Walter Remy. The naval personnel onshore quickly realised her hostile intent and a pre-rehearsed plan was quickly activated. The men seized rifles and the women and children ran for the hills. Young Donald John Gillies 'found myself in Ruaival, so I took shelter in a cave'.

It was as well that they ran. Remy had spotted the military huts and the two radio masts. He also considered that the featherstore might have a military function. He sighted his stern gun on the wireless masts in front of the factor's house and fired a warning shot. Then Remy, who did not know that the operational wireless hut sat out of sight behind the factor's house, aimed for the masts.

He missed the masts in spectacular fashion. He fired seventy-four shells. He hit the factor's house behind the masts. He hit the church, the featherstore, the manse, the nurse's cottage, the barrack huts and three houses on Main Street. He smashed up two rowing boats and left shell craters on the machair. He did not hit the schoolroom. The St Kilda school was nonetheless suspended for the next six weeks as military personnel squatted in the premises while their own accommodation was repaired.

Accidentally, Walter Remy's *U-90* also damaged without destroying the radio hut. But aiming for the masts must have been like trying to hit a pair of needles with a pistol from a moving deck, and they were untouched. Signals were resumed within days of the departure of U-90. The only casualty was a lamb. After almost an hour of constant shelling Commander Remy's U-boat sailed out of Village Bay to the sight of old Donald Ferguson shaking a stick at them from the top of Oiseval. The islanders' property damage was made good by the government's Air-raid Compensation Committee.

Three months later, in August 1918, a 25-pound gun was shipped to St Kilda, laboriously carried ashore and mounted above the featherstore below Oiseval. Local men were paid to build its position and dig a deep protective trenchway between the cannon and a munitions store and shelter burrowed into the foothills of Oiseval. The artillery piece fired some practice shots into the bay, sending dead fish floating to the surface. On 11 November 1918 the Armistice was signed. On 12 November Alexander MacKinnon wrote in the school log: 'A boat came today with news that the terrible war was over. Children given a holiday in honour of the great event.' The big gun was never fired in anger.

In 1919 the servicemen left as suddenly as they had arrived, two of them taking away St Kildan girls as their wives. The wartime wages stopped. The food store was removed. The naval boats no longer came and went. St Kilda spiralled into a swift and irreversible decline. In the words of Donald John Gillies, who was then in his late teens, until the war 'the Islanders never experienced such a change from poverty line to a surplus' and in 1919 'most of the Islanders now were not prepared to go back to the life and custom they were used to before the 1914 War'.

In other parts of the west Highlands and Islands the years following the return of surviving soldiers and sailors from the Great War were marked by a renewal of the land wars of the late nineteenth century, as those demobilised men attempted to make good the prime minister David Lloyd George's promise in 1918 of 'a land fit for heroes to live in'. To Hebrideans, a land fit for heroes translated as a land with enough secure crofts and common grazings to support them all. When on the islands of Skye, Lewis, Harris, Uist and Raasay landowners were reluctant to apportion that land, people seized it. News of those land raids inevitably reached St Kilda, and the Hirtans made a half-hearted claim for the landowner's traditional grazing island of Soay. MacLeod of MacLeod paid it no attention and the claim fizzled out. The St Kildans soon had more pressing problems on their hands.

Their rediscovered vulnerability was stressed in April 1920 when the faithful trawlerman Donald Craig once more arrived back in Aberdeen carrying bad news from Hirta. 'Out of the sparse population of some eighty islanders,' he told the press, 'sixty were prostrated with illness, in most cases influenza. All work in the island, the tending of sheep flocks, the spinning of wool, and fishing, is at a complete standstill …'

This time Captain Craig was not exaggerating. A new missionary and his wife, Donald and Mary Cameron, had arrived in Village Bay the previous year, relieving Alexander and Mary MacKinnon after their long wartime service. On 15 April 1920 Mary Cameron wrote in the school log: 'School had to be closed today for an indefinite period on account of a severe outbreak of influenza from which one of the schoolchildren – Christina MacDonald – succumbed this morning.'

By the middle of May the epidemic had passed and its single young victim had been buried. But a sea-change had occurred in Village Bay. Instead of stoically accepting their lonely fate and returning to the loom, the lambing and the peats, one after another the young adults went away. Donald John Gillies, who himself emigrated in 1924 at the age of twenty-two, estimated that thirty-two St Kildans left for the mainland between 1923 and 1930. At least another five had gone between 1919 and 1922.

Neil Gillies, Angus MacDonald, Donald MacDonald and Finlay MacQueen's son Donald, all of whom were in their twenties and thirties, went to work in Clydeside shipyards. In 1926 Angus and Donald's younger brother Lachlan went to visit them in Glasgow. Lachlan returned to St Kilda but his widow remembered many years later that the trip had 'unsettled him. He thought it a leisured life because it was very hard work on St Kilda'.

Another of Finlay MacQueen's sons, the twenty-three year-old John, took up employment with the Clyde Trust. In the next few years all but one of Finlay's three sons and three daughters would leave St Kilda. The exception, his oldest daughter Mary Ann MacQueen, would make history by becoming a partner in the last wedding to be conducted in Village Bay when she married Neil Ferguson in 1925.

In August 1924 an entire large young family, William and Mary Ann MacDonald and their seven children aged between thirteen and twenty-eight, left together for the islands of Harris and then Lewis. In June 1922 a school inspector had reported that there was 'a total island population of seventy-three'. In May 1925 the skipper of the ss *Hebrides* reported to the mainland that, 'There are now only forty-six natives on the island, a decrease on last year due to one death and emigrations.'

In the course of this exodus, those who were left behind had no option other than to try to live normal lives, even if they were the lives 'they were used to before the 1914 War'. In one way or another they were thwarted.

In 1913 and 1919 Donald and Annie Gillies had produced two more baby girls at Number 14 Main Street. They christened them Christina and Flora respectively. Christina and Flora Gillies arrived in a happy and popular household – 'one of kindness, loyalty and friend-ship,' remembered their neighbour Donald John Gillies, 'where father and mother had a great respect for one another ... where even the tea kettle sings for happiness.'

In June 1922, when little Flora Gillies was three years old, and her older sisters Christina, Rachel Ann and Mary were nine, eleven and fourteen years respectively, her father Donald went on an expedition to Boreray. By that time Boreray was used almost exclusively for herding and shearing sheep. The islanders who sailed there took basic provisions and straw for their bedding. On arrival they cut peat and stored it in cleits to dry, and burned the peat that had been left by previous expeditionaries.

Such a trip was almost without danger and so for the first time Donald took along his nine year-old daughter Christina, for no reason other than that he 'loved her dearly', said a neighbour. While on Boreray in that June of 1922 Donald Gillies took ill with 'acute internal trouble'. A strip of turf was cut from the Boreray hillside as a signal and a rescue boat was launched from Village Bay. It arrived too late. Donald Gillies had already died on Boreray after fifteen hours of pain, in the presence of young Christina. 'The islanders maintain,' said one of them, 'that he died of appendicitis.' He was thirty-seven years old. When his body was returned to Village Bay, Donald's father Finlay, who was sixty-six years old, witnessed his son's death certificate with a shakily sketched 'X'.

Two and a half years later, in January 1925, Christina Gillies died at home of unexplained causes. She was eleven years old and had been ill for three weeks. Christina was attended by the resident nurse but at that time of year no medical help was available from the mainland, even if it had been considered necessary. Her grandfather Finlay, who had watched her die as Christina had watched his son and her father die on Boreray, once again marked 'X' on a death certificate.

At the age of thirty-six Ann Gillies had known enough sorrow to fill a lifetime. She was a widow with three surviving daughters to raise. She and her children represented the terrible conundrum of 1920s St Kilda. Their prospects on the island were impossibly bleak. Their contemporaries were either leaving or had left. Their older relatives and friends were dying. But other than those who had recently emigrated, they had no immediate relatives or other close connections outside St Kilda. Even had Ann Gillies wanted to leave Hirta, where was she to go? In 1928 she sent her middle daughter Rachel Ann away to seek a new life in Lancashire, but Rachel lasted only four months before homesickness overcame her and she returned to the place she knew and was happiest, to be with her dear mother and sisters and the few people on earth who spoke her language.

By the middle of the 1920s it was clear to most people outside St Kilda and to many within it that the community was doomed. In September 1926 it was reported nationally that they were once again running out of flour and sugar and 'there is a fear that the St Kildans have not much in reserve'. In 1927 the Ordnance Survey, making its first official expedition to the archipelago, discovered that 'the cultivated soil is poor, and yields a poor return ... At one time about eighty acres were under cultivation, barley being the chief crop. Now the acreage tilled has fallen to half that extent, and the crop is mainly potatoes.' In February 1928 the steam trawler *Alberia* anchored in Village Bay. Some St Kildan men rowed out to her in their only boat, 'a small disused lifeboat', asked for tobacco and delivered orders 'for urgently needed provisions ... especially flour'.

'The young folk had left the island,' wrote Donald John Gillies, 'and the elderly that was left was unable to do all the chores that were necessary to keep the fire burning. Islanders depended on the birds for a livelihood. These birds would have to be gathered from the other Islands adjacent to St Kilda, such as the Dun and Soay. Peat cutting and securing it for winter fuel: manpower was not available to do the work as it should be done ... Those who remained on the Island found it very difficult to make a living as they used to, on account of the lack of manpower.'

In February 1930 Dr Alexander Shearer of the Scottish Department of Health, who had paid particular personal attention to St Kilda during the 1920s, was summoned urgently to St Kilda to attend upon a thirty-five year-old married woman named Mary Gillies. Mary was pregnant and was suffering from such severe stomach pains that the resident nurse, Williamina Barclay, felt obliged to call for expert help even in the dead of winter.

Dr Shearer arrived and departed with his patient aboard the fisheries cruiser *Norna*. Mary Gillies was admitted to Stobhill Hospital in Glasgow. Alexander Shearer said: 'A serious situation is arising in St Kilda owing to the dwindling male population. There are at present thirty-eight natives on the island, of whom fifteen are males, including some children. It seems likely that in the near future they will not be able to man boats to go to the neighbouring islands of Boreray and Soa, where they have sheep, on the wool of which they depend for the making of cloth. The economic position of the islanders will in that event be precarious.'

Mary Gillies died in Stobhill Hospital on 26 May 1930 of a pulmonary embolism and lung abscess. A caesarean section had delivered her of a baby daughter thirteen days earlier. The little girl had been christened Annie. Despite the efforts of medical staff, in a vile echo of the nineteenth-century eight-day sickness, Annie Gillies died of 'congenital debility' just three and a half hours after her mother. Mary Gillies left behind on St Kilda her bereft husband John and their five year-old son Norman John. Seventy-five years later Norman John Gillies spoke of the last time he saw his mother: 'My most precious memory is of her being rowed out to the ... ship, with her shawl over her head, and waving to me on the shore. That is a real treasure that I will remember all my life.'

Shortly before the death in Glasgow of Mary and little Annie Gillies, the St Kildans had decided to give up their unequal struggle. On 10 May 1930 they sent a petition to the Secretary of State for Scotland William Adamson, a coalminer and union official who became the Labour MP for West Fife.

It read: 'We, the undersigned natives of St Kilda, hereby respectfully pray and petition His Majesty's Government to assist us all to leave the island this year and to find homes and occupations for us on the mainland.'

A journalist from the *Glasgow Herald* who arrived shortly after the petition had been posted reported that,

> ... there is scarcely enough men to do the ordinary work of the island. Some of the younger men have decided to go this summer, and the position of the others will be impossible ... The young men and women are all anxious and determined to go. All the older people now accept the inevitable. Even old Finlay MacQueen, who a few weeks ago said that when the last of the others went he would retire to his cottage, and his bed would be his coffin and his cottage his grave, now wants to go with the others ... What has happened apparently is that the standards of living have risen beyond the natural resources of the place, emigration denudes the man power, and in the end there is a final decision to seek richer pastures.

'We have had enough of islands,' said one St Kildan to the journalist.

William Adamson's under-secretary was a radical Labour MP called Tom Johnston. Johnston, who would later do considerable service to the Highlands as 'the greatest Scottish Secretary of the century', was in 1930 delegated to deal with the St Kilda issue. On 12 June Tom Johnston arrived in St Kilda and held a general meeting in the school to discuss the evacuation.

Five days later, on 17 June 1930 Tom Johnston told the House of Commons:.

> My right hon. Friend [William Adamson] received a petition dated 10 May last from the inhabitants of St Kilda praying that they might be removed from the island before winter. The petition which is signed by all householders now on the island, is attested by the missionary and the nurse, and reached him in ordinary course of post.
>
> I recently visited St Kilda in order to make full inquiries on the spot, and on my report my right hon. Friend has decided to accede to the prayer of the petition. The arrangements for carrying out the evacuation and for placing the inhabitants are now receiving attention.

There is not in view any scheme for the re-settlement of the island by my right hon. Friend …

I would be greatly obliged if hon. Members would not press me for details at the moment. It is obvious that every endeavour will be made to sell the sheep and apply the proceeds to the cost of the evacuation, and any balance to the future subsistence of the islanders … Every care will be taken to meet the needs of the individual families, but it is obviously impossible to make a settlement en masse.

While Tom Johnston finalised arrangements to relocate as many of the thirty-seven islanders who so desired to Forestry Commission homes and jobs on different parts of the mainland – 'We have had enough of islands' – the St Kildans prepared to leave. They did so under the gaze of the rest of the Western world. The news of their evacuation was reported in Missouri, Milwaukee and New South Wales. 'The desire of the inhabitants to leave the island is evidently genuine,' reported the national Sunday newspaper *The Observer* on 1 June 1930, 'and is proved by the fact that they have planted neither potatoes for their own use nor sown oats as provender for their cattle'.

On 27 June 1930 Dugald Munro, the last missionary and school-teacher in St Kilda, shut the schoolroom doors at the end of the spring term and entered in the log: 'Attendance perfect for last week. School closed today, with a small treat which the children seemed to enjoy. Today very probably ends the School in St Kilda, as all the inhabitants intend leaving the island this summer. I hope to be away soon.'

'It is expected,' said a national daily on 6 July, 'that by the end of August or beginning of September, the lone island in the Atlantic will be left to the seabirds.

'The chief difficulty was to find suitable employment for the ten able-bodied men … This had been removed by the proposal of the Forestry Commission to settle the majority of the men as foresters on the estate of Ardtornish in the Morvern district of Argyllshire … In the case of two other able-bodied men suitable crofts may be provided by the Department of Agriculture … It may not be possible to keep the whole community of St Kildans together, but, at any rate, the problem is being dealt with in a sympathetic spirit.'

Later in July their numbers were reduced from thirty-seven to thirty-six. The twenty-two year-old Mary Gillies, the eldest daughter of the widow Annie Gillies and sister of Rachel Ann and Flora, had been ill since April. She had been attended by Nurse Williamina Barclay and even visited from a Fleetwood trawler by the faithful Dr Alexander Shearer. Transference to a mainland hospital – which had been the fate of her older namesake earlier in the year – had been deemed inappropriate as Mary was 'too ill to be moved'. Annie Gillies was waiting for the wholesale evacuation to take her and all three of her daughters to Morvern, where they could restart their lives within reach of regular medical attention.

Mary died at Number 14 Main Street early in the morning of 21 July 1930. Some men went down to the old featherstore, collected the planks which were stored there for the purpose, made young Mary Gillies's casket and painted it black. They then carried the coffin to Number 14 Main Street. The entire population gathered to mourn in the house and the missionary Dugald Munro conducted worship. Mary Gillies then became the last native St Kildan who had died in the islands to be buried in the small graveyard above Main Street.

The St Kildans began to sell some of their spinning wheels for 30 shillings each to their last summer tourists. Rusted fulmar oil lamps went for as much as £1 sterling. One man put a notice in the window of an abandoned house on Main Street the sign: 'St Kildan Relics For Sale. Apply within. THE SIMPLE RACE.' Most of the island's sheep, which the Department of Agriculture would sell on their behalf, were taken to Oban on the *Dunara Castle* early in August. On 6 August 1930 the under-secretary of state Tom Johnston told the *Glasgow Herald* that the evacuation of people would take place 'during the last few days of August … All the men had been offered jobs, and [Johnston] did not anticipate any trouble'.

Johnston was keenly aware of the possibility of the evacuation being turned into another undignified circus. He refused to offer any government facilities to sightseers, journalists and photographers, and he ordered the Royal Navy to ensure that all such people were removed from Village Bay a day before the St Kildans departed. 'It would be very unfortunate indeed,' he said, 'in the interests of these poor people if their misfortunes were to be turned into a public show.'

An evacuation schedule was provisionally arranged for whichever day in the last week of August 1930 was favoured by the weather. Inevitably, a handful of journalists reached St Kilda in the preceding week. They were permitted to sleep on the schoolroom floor but were told to leave with the remaining sheep on the ss *Dunara Castle* before the islanders themselves boarded the Admiralty fisheries cruiser HMS *Harebell*.

On Sunday, 24 August, the three dozen St Kildans put on their best clothes, the men in suits and the women in shawls and coffered mutches, and they all went to church together for the last time. On Monday the 25th the women washed clothes in the burns and clean white sheets fluttered from the cottage doors. They began to pack. The men and boys gathered in the remaining sheep from the hills and quartered them in the huge enclosures on An Lag. The *Dunara Castle* arrived in Village Bay on Wednesday, 27 August. The man from the *Glasgow Herald* reported,

All [Thursday] morning, between quay and steamer they plied with sheep, cows, dressers, tables, and canvas bags to be lodged on the *Dunara Castle*.

The embarkation of the shaggy Highland cattle was extraordinary. The great tan beasts followed in the wake of the boats which towed them from shore to ship until, alongside, they were hoisted aboard by a noose around the horns, their big eyes bulging and their necks taut with the bellying weight below.

Before the morning sun had melted the mists on Conachair, the pens between decks on the *Dunara Castle* were packed with the hill sheep, Blackfaced and crossbred soays, that look like Nubian goats, while the holds were stowed with the frugal household goods of a unique race.

'The final outgoing dispatch,' reported *The Times* 'was by far the heaviest that ever left St Kilda. A number of passengers went ashore from the *Dunara Castle* and crowded round the little village post-office in their anxiety to procure any remaining relics of the island. They bought large supplies of stamps, picture postcards showing local scenes, and many pieces of woollen goods manufactured by St Kilda women from the fleeces of the famous St Kilda sheep.'

On Thursday the *Harebell* arrived and 'the evacuation was suddenly dramatised by the advent of the Navy. Bugles sounded on the deck. Presently a boat was lowered from the davits. Three braided officers were pulled away to the shore by navymen in white ducks.' The naval officers discovered that a foolish young author and civil servant named Alasdair Alpin MacGregor, who was also covering the occasion for *The Times*, intended to hide on the island until after the evacuation. They summarily ordered him aboard the *Dunara Castle*.

The St Kildans ate their last meals of salted mutton, porridge, scones and syrup, dried fish, salted puffin and roasted fulmar. They continued to load up the *Dunara Castle*. Dugald Munro carried away the communion service. The dogs 'dance madly, barking along the shore' before all but two of them were poisoned or drowned in the bay.

> Finlay MacQueen, white-bearded and sixty-nine [he was sixty-eight years old], had a heavy box strapped to his shoulders. The aquiline head suggested power and strength and this appearance was not deceptive ...
>
> Behind Finlay MacQueen came Finlay Gillies, equally loaded, the only septuagenarian on St Kilda and the only old-age pensioner [Finlay Gillies was seventy-four years old]. A girl of fifteen carried a table on her back, but most of the porters were barefooted women, adorned with red scarfs, striped shawls and petticoats. They were stooping under the weight of enormous tea and provisions boxes filled with domestic necessities ...
>
> Stone querns for grinding corn and oatmeal and wooden kirns for cheese-making are being despatched to order on the *Dunara Castle* ... The churns are curios and the handmills are with the collectors. St Kilda is of the historied past. The play is ended.

They were going 'without a tear and almost in an atmosphere of jocularity. The suggestion that some of the St Kildans would refuse to leave at the last moment proved a complete myth'. The *Glasgow Herald*'s journalist wondered.

> Why should St Kilda lose its people and one more tract of Scotland be left to nature?
>
> I talked with the St Kildans in their homes and heard the answer. The evacuation is the end of a movement that began with the war, that great instrument of social change.

Before the war the St Kildan was a recluse in his island … they were content, for they knew no other life; but after the peace the young men went over the water and came back with news of other places, their romance and opportunities. The germ of knowledge of isolation was introduced, and the sickness followed. St Kilda is cut off from communication from the mainland from September to February – the conditions last year – except by the grace of a Fleetwood trawler.

The number of young people dwindles. The life of St Kilda makes it imperative that there should be a fixed minimum of adult labour. Below that minimum life is imperilled. This was reached some years ago …

At noon on Thursday, 28 August the *Dunara Castle* weighed anchor, swung around and headed for the exit to Village Bay. Her siren shrieked farewell blasts which echoed off the sides of Oiseval, Ruaival and Conachair. She sailed to Oban with the livestock, furniture and journalists.

At daybreak on Friday, 29 August the thirty-six St Kildans – by sinister coincidence, exactly the same number as had left for Australia in the penultimate mass emigration seventy-eight years earlier – packed the last of their things. They visited the graveyard to bid farewell to their dead. Indoors they banked up their fires with unlit peat and left their Bibles open. Boats from the *Harebell* put ashore. Sailors carried packages and bundles down through the crofts from Main Street and helped the older women to the fly-boats at the battered and crumbling jetty. Finlay MacQueen, Finlay Gillies, the widowed former 'Queen of St Kilda' Ann Gillies, her namesake the forty-one year-old widowed Annie Gillies and her two remaining fatherless daughters Rachel Ann and Flora joined their relatives, friends and neighbours on their last voyage from St Kilda.

At 8.30 a.m. HMS *Harebell* sailed out of Village Bay in perfect weather. The officers and crew served tea and biscuits to the women and children. Up on deck, looking back at the morning sun on Dun and Conachair, in a sudden surge of anguish Finlay MacQueen said: 'May God forgive those that have taken us away from St Kilda.' Lachlan MacDonald, who was twenty-four at the time, said later: 'I wasn't sorry to leave. I wanted to go. It was a hard life and there was nothing left for the young, no one to look after the widows.'

Along with twenty-four of their fellow evacuees, Annie, Rachel Ann and Flora Gillies were taken off the *Harebell* that evening and transferred to their new homes in Lochaline overlooking the Sound of Mull. The other nine continued south to Oban, where they were met at dusk by crowds of sightseers before being put into motor cars and driven to hotels. 'I was on the boat right to Oban,' remembered one St Kildan many years later, 'and we were all ashore round about nine o'clock at night. There were no reporters on the boat but there were plenty reporters when we arrived in Oban. I landed at the pier in Oban, alongside the pier, the crowds – you would think you were going to a football match with the crowd waiting. And I says, "What are you looking at? There's nae hairs on us."'

There were also people waiting for Annie, Rachel Ann and Flora at Lochaline. Forestry Commission joiners were still working on the St Kildans' houses that morning. A motor launch full of journalists and photographers had arrived at the small settlement in the afternoon. When the smoke from the *Harebell*'s funnel appeared in the west, 'news of the ship's approach spread rapidly over Lochaline, and within a few minutes motor cars and motor cycles with pillion riders were bringing the curious villagers to the pier.'

A boat went out from Lochaline to the *Harebell* and carried twenty-seven St Kildans to shore. 'As the vessel drew nearer, features became discernible, and it was something of a surprise to note that the expressions showed neither joy nor sorrow. Rather did they signify sullen apprehension.

'The villagers cheered and waved a friendly welcome, but the St Kildans made no response. Some smiled, but others simply stared.'

As the launch approached Lochaline pier, the St Kildans first tossed onto dry land a feather broom tied to a home-made ladder. That symbolic gesture completed, they went ashore. The grown women carried spinning wheels. Their young daughters and sons held baskets containing hens and cats.

On Lochaline pier the party of islanders was broken into family units and escorted to the motor cars which would take them to their separate dwelling places. That final, irrevocable division in an unfamiliar place of an obstinate, inter-dependent bloodline of ancient lineage provoked, said one observer, 'the only flood of tears in the whole story so far'.

Afterword

✵

THIRTY-SIX PEOPLE left that day. Thirty-six was not only coincidentally the same number of St Kildans as had left for Australia in 1852, it was also approximately the same number of islanders who were alive at the previous nadir in 1728, following the catastrophic smallpox epidemic.

But this time there would be no civilian repopulation of St Kilda, from Skye or anywhere else. MacLeod of MacLeod did not want it. The government of the United Kingdom had just committed a lot of thought and a good many resources to executing a well-planned and sensitive evacuation and was unlikely to reverse the process.

Most importantly, nor did the St Kildans themselves wish to repopulate their islands. The thirty-six evacuees of August 1930 had taken the only realistic course. They included only two married couples with young families, and six widows between the ages of thirty-six and sixty-seven years, three of whom had school-aged children to raise, and three widowers, one of whom had a six-year-old son. Without the social security of other able-bodied neighbours and relatives their futures on St Kilda were hopeless. Even those who, like Finlay MacQueen, would remain regretful about leaving their homes no longer had any human cause to remain, far less to go back.

Reginald, the 27th MacLeod of MacLeod, his hereditary duties done, promptly sold the islands to the young Earl of Dumfries, John Crichton-Stuart, who was a keen ornithologist. Crichton-Stuart insisted that no commercial activities should be permitted in his new properties. He based a keeper there for much of the time and used

St Kilda as an extravagant personal resort. The St Kildans having removed their own flocks from Hirta, the landlord's traditional Soay sheep were shipped over from that island and left to run on Hirta, wild and unmolested except by passing ships in need of mutton.

When the Second World War was declared in September 1939 St Kilda did not resume its earlier duties as a guardian of the Western Approaches. Airstrips built on the islands of Lewis and Benbecula filled that function. So when in three separate incidents British aeroplanes flying back in bad weather from duties in the North Atlantic Ocean crashed into Soay and Hirta, although it seems certain that their crews died instantly, nobody was present to reclaim and respect their bodies.

John Crichton-Stuart, who by then was the 5th Marquess of Bute, died in 1956 and bequeathed St Kilda to the National Trust for Scotland. A year later the archipelago was officially designated as a National Nature Reserve – just in time for the return of the military. In 1957 a rocket testing range was established on the west side of South Uist. Its function was to fire missiles out into the Atlantic Ocean and its location was chosen in part because, 50 miles west of the Uist rangehead, stood an uninhabited island from which the rockets' trajectory could be tracked.

Accommodation huts, a radar station at the summit of Conachair and a small reservoir below An Lag were built. They would be followed by the replacement of diesel generators with an electricity generating station, a complex of military buildings surrounded by cleits, adjacent to the empty and crumbling houses on Main Street and a helipad below Ruaival. The soldiers of the Royal Artillery left in 2001 to be replaced by the defence contractors QinetiQ, but the islands' role remained the same. Less than thirty years after the evacuation of Finlay MacQueen and Rachel Ann Gillies and their families and neighbours St Kilda was indeed repopulated, but by a shifting roster of soldiers, engineers and computer operators, augmented seasonally by National Trust staff and volunteers.

The first impressions of new arrivals changed hardly at all. One Royal Engineer in 1993 echoed the words of many a nineteenth-century visitor:

My first image of the Island was its craggy cliff bound outline silhouetted against the night sky and later as the LCL [light landing craft] made its way into the village bay, the dimly lit slipway and short string of street lights against the total dark background of Hirta is an image that will stay with me forever. It wasn't until the following day that I realised just how desolate a place St Kilda actually is. I think it's fair to say that the small military site looks like the dreariest soul destroying place ever built by the men in green!

That said I can't think of a posting, tour or visit to any part of the world that has fascinated me so much, only the total philistine would fail to realise that they had arrived somewhere special. The sheer isolation of St Kilda was made up for entirely by the friendly, laid back atmosphere of its inhabitants (Sappers!).

The presence of this Cold War military base had no deleterious effect on St Kilda's growing international reputation. The islands became a UNESCO World Heritage Site in 1986 and shortly afterwards became the only location in the United Kingdom – and one of just twenty-nine in the world – to be designated a 'mixed site' because of both its natural and archaeological assets. St Kilda has become the subject of documentary films, an opera, innumerable poems, a couple of novels and countless works of history and memoir.

During his twenty-five year sovereignty John Crichton-Stuart had no objection to native St Kildans returning to their old homes for short visits. So year after year throughout the 1930s, until the Second World War broke out in 1939 and most of the west Highlands and Islands became for security reasons a restricted zone, parties of exiled St Kildans reoccupied Main Street during the summer and even wove tweed on looms which they had left behind.

When they were both well into their seventies, Finlay Gillies and Finlay MacQueen took the steamer from Glasgow back to Village Bay, mounting to the bridge of the vessel when the summits of Conachair, Boreray and the stacks appeared on the horizon, 'anxious for a first glimpse of his beloved home'. Once he had settled back in his old house on Main Street, observed a fellow visitor in 1932, Finlay Gillies's 'face brightens as he tramps over the ground hallowed to him by seventy years of memories'.

For decades after the war the pattern continued. Elderly St Kildans returned with their children and their grandchildren, for day-trips, for a week, or to be buried and lie forever more in the old cemetery.

The very last such visit took place in June 2005. Accompanied by the journalist Torcuil Crichton, a Gaelic speaker from the island of Lewis, Norman John Gillies, the five year-old who in 1930 had waved to his mother Mary as she sailed out of Village Bay to her death in a Glasgow hospital, returned to Hirta for the final time. Crichton reported,

> From the deck, eighty year-old Norman John Gillies gazes into the far horizon. He has been straining like a pointer on a leash since the boat left Harris. One of the last St Kildans, he is heading home. Gillies left St Kilda as a five year-old. He's been back twice but today is special because he is accompanied by his son, John, and that midwife of modern history, a television crew. It's early morning and he's the most smartly dressed and energetic of the dozen passengers aboard the *Orca*, a purpose-built boat that can race from Harris to St Kilda and back in a day.
>
> Being St Kildan, Gillies ought to have a Gaelic burr, but the language has died on his lips. He pronounces the word 'Gaylic' in the anglicised accent of his adopted home, Ipswich, an object lesson in how displacement shattered the St Kildan culture. He is, though, 100 per cent, genuine islander, one of only three remaining evacuees ... History flows through him to his son, who shares his father's passion. Even the Gillies house in Ipswich, where Norman John has lived with his wife for fifty-seven years, is called St Kilda.
>
> You cannot expect a five year-old to shoulder an entire heritage and Gillies has only fragmented memories of what life was like on St Kilda before he left, with the others, for Lochaline on the Morvern peninsula. Most of all, he remembers his mother, and they are beautiful memories that provide an umbilical link to the past. To step ashore on St Kilda with him is to walk across the bridge. If you touch the hand of this old man, and he touches the wall of the house he was born in, you are back there.
>
> 'I've got memories,' he says, standing outside the doorway of his old home. 'We lived at number 10; there was a dyke in front of it. This dyke. If I was playing at one end of the mainland or the other end of the village street, my mother would stand on the wall and call out: "Tormod Iain, time to come home for dinner".'

Notes

ONE

p. 3 'never leave St Kilda again', *Manchester Guardian*, 17 July, 1924

p. 3 'They thought I was someone . . . but I assured them I was quite tame.' *Manchester Guardian*, 28 April 1928

p. 3 'and the ride amazed Miss Gillies . . . too excited to express herself', *Manchester Guardian,* 28 April 1928

p. 4 'sat transfixed. Her facial expression . . . I never knew there were such things.' *Manchester Guardian*, 1 May 1928

p. 4 'She soon learned to dislike . . . never again to forsake the quiet of her home.' *Manchester Guardian*, 31 July 1928

p. 5 'It was really quite sad … back again.' *Glasgow Herald*, 24 Augut 1955

p. 5 'The deep-sea fishermen of Fleetwood . . . in the eyes of every deep-sea fisherman.' *Manchester Guardian*, 22 August 1930

p. 7 'May God forgive those . . . away from St Kilda.' *Glasgow Herald*, 30 August 1930

pp. 8–9 'Please see the bearer . . . and go elsewhere.' *Manchester Guardian*, 14 October 1930

TWO

p. 12 'a diverse range of animals . . . even sabre-toothed cats' Chris Stringer FRS, 'The First Britons', The Royal Society, 2010

p. 17 'Hebridean vessels are characteristically deep jars … in feasting and ritual activities . . .' Ian Armit, *The Archaeology of Skye and the Western Isles*, 1996

p. 19   'Formerly they were used . . . his crops in the open air.' Robert
         Connell, *St Kilda and the St Kildians*, 1887

p. 21   'This is an incredibly significant . . . living there in the first place.'
         'Evidence of Ancient Settlement Found on Boreray', RCAHMS,
         2011

p. 27   'The stones of which this . . . above ground.' Kenneth Macaulay,
         The History of St Kilda, 1764

pp. 30–31   'During the reign of Popery . . . to perform miraculous cures',
             Kenneth Macaulay, *The History of St Kilda*, 1764

p. 32   'A son of the king of Lochlin . . . until this day.' Miss Anne
         Kennedy, letter quoting Euphemia MacCrimmon, 1862

THREE

p. 36   'to the islands that are called Hirtir' Saga Guðmundar Arasonar,
         circa 14th century

p. 41   'The fountain water of St Kilda . . . parts of the Long-Island.'
         Kenneth Macaulay, *The History of St Kilda*, 1764

p. 46   'the progenitors of the St Kildans . . . you to St Kilda.' *With Nature
         and a Camera*, Richard Kearton, 1898

pp. 47–48   '[T]here was one Coll M'Donald . . . reasonless reasons they
             were satisfied.' Martin Martin, *A Late Voyage to St Kilda*, 1698

p. 62   'It usually begins with a cold sensation . . . extends itself over the
         whole community.' George Seton, *St Kilda Past and Present*, 1878

FOUR

p. 75   'men and women and children were sporting . . . gooding or
         manure for their Land.' Michael Robson, *St Kilda: Church, Visitors
         and Natives*, 2005

p. 76   'The people of . . . children to school.' Michael Robson, *St Kilda:
         Church, Visitors and Natives*, 2005

p. 77   'in the filthiest gutter . . . doun black gutter' Michael Robson, *St
         Kilda: Church, Visitors and Natives*, 2005

p. 80   'On one occasion, the rope having given . . . the yawning gulf
         below.' George Seton, *St Kilda Past and Present*, 1878

p. 84   'The cattle of St Kilda feed . . . people sickened upon drinking it.'
         Kenneth Macaulay, *The History of St Kilda*, 1764

p. 85   'One day shortly after my arrival . . . was wanted immediately.' John Sands, *Out of the World, or, Life on St Kilda*, 1876

p. 86   '. . . noticed three or four strips . . . they may make for assistance.' *With Nature and a Camera*, Richard Kearton, 1898

p. 87   'Donald Macdonald lived in St Kilda . . . who continue in the island yet.' Miss Anne Kennedy, letter quoting Euphemia MacCrimmon, 1862

p. 94   'whole time was devoted to weeping . . . carrying tidings to her friends in Edinburgh', John Lane Buchanan, *Travels in the Western Hebrides: from 1782 to 1790*, 1793

pp. 95–96   'She was kind to the peasantry . . . not such as to gain their esteem.' Robert Chambers, *Traditions of Edinburgh*, 1868

FIVE

pp. 111–17   'had finished his education . . . burdened with the care of them', William Otter, *The Life and Remains of Edward Daniel Clarke*, 1824

p. 117   'Before being used they are thoroughly fumigated . . . until they have been again roasted.' *With Nature and a Camera*, Richard Kearton, 1898

pp. 120–121   'armed to the teeth . . . swarthy complexion and foreign aspect'. James Wilson, *A Voyage Round the Coast of Scotland and the Isles*, 1842

p. 121   'their remote . . . from the ships of that enemy', John MacCulloch, *A Description of the Western Islands of Scotland*, 1819

SIX

p. 126   'Sir Thomas and his lady . . . help them build new houses . . .' Michael Robson, *St Kilda: Church, Visitors and Natives*, 2005

pp. 127–28   'very respectable-looking slated house . . . as well as priest . . .' James Wilson, *A Voyage Round the Coast of Scotland and the Isles*, 1842

pp. 134–35   'the vital statistics of St Kilda . . . ultimately approximate to that of Faroe.' John E. Morgan, 'Diseases of St Kilda', *British and Foreign Medico-Chirurgical Review*, 1862

p. 135   'At the time of birth, there . . . indisposition to take the breast.' John E. Morgan, 'Diseases of St Kilda', *British and Foreign Medico-Chirurgical Review*, 1862

p. 138 'The little creature is wrapped . . . before a single stitch is sewed.' Robert Connell, *St Kilda and the St Kildians*, 1887

p. 138 'If it's God's will that babies . . . can do will save them.' Robert Connell, *St Kilda and the St Kildians*, 1887

p. 138 'it was discovered that . . . with accidents in fowling expeditions.' George Seton, *St Kilda Past and Present*, 1878

pp. 139–40 'was not a native of . . . very little work for two years', Calum MacQueen, *St Kilda Heritage: Autobiography of Callum MacCuithinn (Malcolm MacQueen)*, 1995

SEVEN

p. 145 'He was vexed . . . to the established Church of Scotland.' Calum MacQueen, *St Kilda Heritage: Autobiography of Callum MacCuithinn (Malcolm MacQueen)*, 1995

p. 148 '. . . with the narrow sound of the Dune . . . it runs at the rate of three miles an hour.' Captain Charles Otter, 'Sailing Directions for the West of Scotland', Hydrographic Department, 1886

p. 148 'imprisoned to all appearance . . . all hands are piped to prayer', Michael Robson, *St Kilda: Church, Visitors and Natives*, 2005

pp. 149–50 'As to the mortality of the children . . . strength of the mother's milk while nursing . . .' Captain Charles Otter, letter to *The Times*, 1871

p. 154 'nine panes of glass in each . . . the entrance-door.' George Seton, *St Kilda Past and Present*, 1878

pp. 154–55 'All the houses in St Kilda . . . birds' eggs that adorn nearly every window.' *With Nature and a Camera*, Richard Kearton, 1898

p. 155 'cloth, salt-fish, and other . . . the owners wished to exchange for gold', George Seton, *St Kilda Past and Present*, 1878

p. 156 'Towards night the wind changed . . . the announcement was of no ordinary kind.' George Seton, *St Kilda Past and Present*, 1878

p. 156 'unfaithful, and deserted her husband . . . other dependent relatives.' John MacDiarmid, 'St Kilda and its Inhabitants', *Transactions of the Highland and Agricultural Society*, 1878

p. 158 'an old man sitting on the low wall . . . and other exciting incidents'. George Seton, *St Kilda Past and Present*, 1878

p. 158 'was much affected by . . . who met his death on the cliffs of Soa.' George Seton, *St Kilda Past and Present*, 1878

Notes

p. 162   'It is the product of far-away thinking . . . the Highlands and Islands.' Alexander Carmichael, *Carmina Gadelica*, vol. I, 1899

p. 165   'some perfectly unobjectionable . . . they could not be accepted', George Seton, *St Kilda Past and Present*, 1878

p. 165   'The minister has several volumes . . . Sir John Herschell's Astronomy.' John MacDiarmid, 'St Kilda and Its Inhabitants', *Transactions of the Highland and Agricultural Society*, 1878

p. 165   'I found the reverend gentleman . . . simmering in a small broken grate.' Robert Connell, *St Kilda and the St Kildians*, 1887

p. 167   'The minister is one who commands . . . his wife's side immediately.' John Sands, *Out of the World, or, Life on St Kilda*, 1876

p. 167   '. . . not only an earnest and honest . . . more reason to feel proud of.' George Seton, *St Kilda Past and Present*, 1878

pp. 168–69   'I think they are better ... perhaps they may have, but I don't hear.' Evidence to Napier Commission, 1884

p. 169   'So unusual was the sight . . . and told them to go away.' *With Nature and a Camera*, Richard Kearton, 1898

pp. 169–70   'None of the men . . . we severed ourselves from MacLeod's interest.' John MacDiarmid, 'St Kilda and Its Inhabitants', *Transactions of the Highland and Agricultural Society*, 1878

p. 175   'They are a mongrel breed ... the dogs will quickly "do" for him.' Robert Connell, *St Kilda and the St Kildians*, 1887

pp. 175–76   'They have a wonderful intuition . . . and soon begin barking again.' Norman Heathcote, *St Kilda*, 1900

pp. 182–83   'At present they are in the habit . . . importation of a few ponies or donkeys.' Norman Heathcote, *St Kilda*, 1900

pp. 184–85   'In October, when the nights . . . Their industry astonished me.' John Sands, *Out of the World, or, Life on St Kilda*, 1876

p. 185   'His loom is in operation . . . It is the same every winter.' Robert Connell, *St Kilda and the St Kildians*, 1887

pp. 186–87   'Among recent visitors to St Kilda . . . on the fifteenth of June 1877 . . .' George Seton, *St Kilda Past and Present*, 1878

p. 187   'The children looked very healthy . . . no brudder, no sister', Michael Robson, *St Kilda: Church, Visitors and Natives*, 2005

p. 187   'One cannot be long . . . the St Kildian is to teach him to help himself.' Robert Connell, *St Kilda and the St Kildians*, 1887

pp. 189–90   'Before you have long . . . divided among the lucky sixteen.'
Robert Connell, *St Kilda and the St Kildians*, 1887

p. 191   'The dwelling is something . . . of sheep and birds of various
kinds.' *With Nature and a Camera*, Richard Kearton, 1898

p. 192   'As I had expressed a desire . . . forcibly of my stay on the island.'
With Nature and a Camera, Richard Kearton, 1898

p. 195   'As certain conditions . . . fished for ling and also cod, no parliament.' Donald John Gillies, *The Truth About St Kilda: An Islander's
Memoir*, 2014

p. 197   'the manner in which . . . pot or basket containing hot stones',
George Seton, *St Kilda Past and Present*, 1878

p. 197   'two circular stones of granite . . turned the handle with great
rapidity.' George Seton, *St Kilda Past and Present*, 1878

p. 200   '. . . we soon emerged from the Hebridean . . . when the steamer
entered the bay.' George Seton, *St Kilda Past and Present*, 1878

pp. 201–02   'The minister having made suitable . . . possessed of a
nervous system.' George Seton, *St Kilda Past and Present,* 1878

EIGHT

p. 207   'no hesitation in attributing the disease to improper food and
treatment', Robert Connell, *St Kilda and the St Kildians*, 1887

pp. 207–08   'but so small was the faith . . . operated upon a single child',
With Nature and a Camera, Richard Kearton, 1898

p. 208   'they were remarkably clean . . . St Kildan mode of greeting.'
Norman Heathcote, *St Kilda*, 1900

p. 208   'every man follows five . . . fisherman, weaver, tailor, and cobbler.'
Robert Connell, *St Kilda and the St Kildians*, 1887

p. 210   'How is the Crofter Question . . . in a boat to record their votes',
Robert Connell, *St Kilda and the St Kildians*, 1887

pp. 211–29   'There is no stated visit on the part . . . least once during
winter.' 'Report of Her Majesty's Commissioners of Inquiry Into
the Condition of the Crofters and Cottars in the Highlands and
Islands of Scotland', 1884

p. 230   '. . . a young St Kildian who wished . . . the lady's friends gathered
below . . .' Robert Connell, *St Kilda and the St Kildians*, 1887

pp. 230–31 'Three Sabbaths before the ... the house thatching the roof.' Robert Connell, *St Kilda and the St Kildians*, 1887

p. 232 'The men were dressed ... head-dress disported bright Turkey-red napkins.' Robert Connell, *St Kilda and the St Kildians*, 1887

pp. 232–33 'Breakfast – Porridge and milk ... but nobody drinks to excess.' Robert Connell, *St Kilda and the St Kildians*, 1887

pp. 233–34 'They bought a deal of cloth ... Lord with cheerful voice', George Murray, *St Kilda Diary*, 1886

p. 234 'The senior class (ages from 13 to 14) ... liberty to use the church bell.' Robert Connell, *St Kilda and the St Kildians*, 1887

p. 236 'seized with that terrible disease ... sore, for so I was told.' George Murray, *St Kilda Diary*, 1886

pp. 239–41 'The first day of my sojourn ... and not to be always relied upon.' Robert Connell, *St Kilda and the St Kildians*, 1887

p. 241 'The St Kildans have a deep love for their rocky home ... the greatest number.' *With Nature and a Camera*, Richard Kearton, 1898

NINE

pp. 250–51 '... We crossed the bay ... and went out to sea.' Charles Dixon, *Seebohm's History of British Birds*, 1883

pp. 251–59 'The St Kildans had no knowledge ... I was one of themselves.' *With Nature and a Camera*, Richard Kearton, 1898

p. 259 'two young Englishmen ... as they got lodgings in a native cottage.' Norman Heathcote, *St Kilda*, 1900

p. 260 'To people living in the midst ... with a sheep on her back.' Norman Heathcote, *St Kilda*, 1900

p. 262 'It seemed a most promising ... interesting and impressive ceremony.' Norman Heathcote, *St Kilda*, 1900

p. 266 'Went into William ... are awfully sorry about it ...' Alice MacLachlan, *St Kilda Diary*, 1907

TEN

pp. 269–70 'charming ... tall, kind-hearted and well educated', Donald John Gillies, *The Truth About St Kilda: An Islander's Memoir*, 2014

p. 270 'but English composition ... the well-equipped school library.' St Kilda School Log, 1906 pp. 271–72   '. . . one of the older men . . . than if I had been a child.' Zillah Goudie, 'Fulmar Hunting in St Kilda', *Manchester Guardian*, 21 March 1907

p. 277   'His assignation was rather unusual . . . our own beautiful little island.' Donald MacDonald, West Side Historical Society

p. 278   'We were up there and we made hot tea . . . flung a stone right down his conning tower.' R. Morris, *Defending St Kilda*, 2013

p. 279   'the Islanders never experienced . . . were used to before the 1914 War'. Donald John Gillies, *The Truth About St Kilda: An Islander's Memoir*, 2014

p. 284   '. . . there is scarcely enough men . . . to seek richer pastures.' *Glasgow Herald*, 12 May, 1930

pp. 284–85   'My right hon. Friend . . . to make a settlement en masse.' Hansard, 17 June, 1930

p. 285   'It is expected . . . dealt with in a sympathetic spirit.' *Manchester Guardian*, 6 July, 1930

p. 287   'All [Thursday] morning . . . household goods of a unique race.' *Glasgow Herald*, 29 August, 1930

p. 288   'Finlay MacQueen, white-bearded . . . The play is ended.' *Glasgow Herald*, 29 August, 1930

p. 290   'news of the ship's approach . . . in the whole story so far', *Glasgow Herald*, 30 August, 1930

AFTERWORD

p. 292   'My first image of the Island was its craggy cliff bound . . . atmosphere of its inhabitants (Sappers!).' John 'Foz' Foster, www.sappers.co.uk

p. 293   'anxious for a first . . . by seventy years of memories', *Manchester Guardian*, 15 July, 1932

p. 294   'From the deck, eighty year-old . . . come home for dinner",' *Sunday Herald*, 26 June, 2005

Selected Bibliography

❊

Acland, A. 1981 *A Devon Family: The Story of the Aclands*, Phillimore & Co., Chichester

Admiralty 1865 Chart 2474 Hebrides or Western Isles from Barra Head to Scarpa Island, and subsequent editions

Allen, J. 1880 'Notes on wooden tumbler locks', *Proceedings of the Society of Antiquaries of Scotland* 14, (1879–80), 149–162

Ancrum, M. 1985 Nomination of St Kilda for inclusion in the World Heritage List, Edinburgh

Anon. c.1594 'A short Description of the Western Isles of Scotland, lying in the Deucalidon Sea, being above 300. Also the Isles of Orknay and Shetland or Hethland' printed as part of Certain Matters concerning the Realme of Scotland composed together, London

Anon. 1595 'The Description of the Isles of Scotland' (probably 1577–95) printed as appendix to Skene, W.F., *Celtic Scotland*, 1880–3, 428–440

Anon. 1732 Description at St Kilda The most western Isle of Scotland, giving an account of its situation, extent, soil, product, bay, and adjacent island of rocks, Register of the Great Seal of Scotland Ms. 914.117, Edinburgh

Anon. 1751 *A Voyage to Scotland, the Orkneys and the Western Isles of Scotland*, C. Corbet, London

Basham, S. 1991 'Subterranean structures on Hirta, St Kilda, Scotland', *Bulletin Subterranea Britannica* 27, 5–6

Baxter, C. and Crumley, J. 1988 *St Kilda. A portrait of Britain's remotest island landscape*, Colin Baxter Photography, Lanark

Boece, Hector 1527 *Scotorum Regni*, Description f xiiii: part of: *Scotorum Historiae Prima Gentis Origine cum aliarum et rerum et gentium illustratione non vulgari*, Paris (another edition 1574, (f 8))

Boswell, J. 1785 *The Journal of a Tour to the Hebrides*

Buchan, A. 1727 *A Description of St Kilda*, Lumisden and Robertson, Edinburgh (reprinted with substantial alterations by Miss Buchan, 1752)

Buchanan, G. 1762 *The History of Scotland*, Edinburgh

Buchanan, J.L. 1793 *Travels in the Western Hebrides: from 1782 to 1790*, London

Buchanan, M. 1983 *St Kilda: A Photographic Album*, William Blackwood, Edinburgh

Buchanan, M. (ed.) 1995 *St Kilda: The Continuing Story*, HMSO, Edinburgh

Burrill, J.E.O. 1958 'Gunners on St Kilda', *Journal of the Royal Artillery*, 85, 97–101

Cameron, M. 1969 'Our childhood on St Kilda', *Scots Magazine*, March, 567–71

Cameron, M. 1973 *Childhood days on St Kilda*, S. Barker Johnson, Gairloch

Campbell, J.L 1953 'Smallpox on St Kilda', *Scots Magazine*, May, 168–72

Campbell, R. 1799 An Account of the Island of St Kilda and Neighbouring Islands, Visited August 1799. National Library of Scotland, Ms. 3051

Carmichael, A. 1928 *Carmina Gadelica* vol. I (1928a) Oliver and Boyd, Edinburgh and London

Carmichael, A. 1928 *Carmina Gadelica* vol. 2 (1928b) Oliver and Boyd, Edinburgh and London

Carmichael, A. 1941 Carmina Gadelica vol. 4 (1941) Oliver and Boyd, Edinburgh and London

Carmichael, A. 1954 *Carmina Gadelica* vol. 5 (1954) Oliver and Boyd, Edinburgh and London

Carmichael, A. 1971 *Carmina Gadelica* vol. 6 (1971) Oliver and Boyd, Edinburgh and London

Carruthers, R. 1843 *The Highland Notebook; or sketches and anecdotes*, A and C Black, Edinburgh

Chambers, William 1874 'The Story of Lady Grange', *Chambers Journal* 551, July 14, 1874, 449–52

Charnley, B. 1989 *Last Greetings from St Kilda*, Stenlake and McCourt, Glasgow

Charnley, B. 1993 A Voyage to St Kilda, Maclean Press, Portree

Cheyne, I.A., Foster, W.M. and Spence, J.B. 1974 'The incidence of disease and parasites in the Soay sheep population of Hirta', chapter 13 in Jewell, P.A, Milner, C. and Boyd, J.M. (eds) *Island Survivors: the Ecology of the Soay Sheep of St Kilda*, Athlone Press, London

Chudleigh, R.A. 1886 'The strangers' cold' *British Medical Journal* 4, 484

Clegg, E.J. 1984 'Some factors associated with island depopulation and the example of St Kilda', *Northern Scotland* 6, 3–11

Cockburn, A.M. 1935 'The Geology of St Kilda', *Transactions of the Royal Society of Edinburgh* 58, 511–48

Collacott, R.A. 1981 'Neonatal Tetanus in St Kilda', *Scottish Medical Journal* 26, 224–27

Collacott, R.A. 1985 'Medical and nursing services to St Kilda', *Scottish Medical Journal* 30, 181–83

Connell, R. 1887 *St Kilda and the St Kildians*, Hamilton, Adams & Co., London

Cooper, J.B. 1931 The history of St Kilda from its first settlement to a city and after 1840 to 1930 compiled by the order of the St Kilda city council by JBC, Melbourne

Dixon, H.G. 1886 'The strangers' cold', *British Medical Journal*, 286

Dryden, J. 1930 'St Kilda's Floating Mail', *Gibbons Stamp Monthly*, December 1930

Duckworth, C.L.D. and Langmuir, G.E. 1950 *West Highland Steamers*, Richard Tilling, London

Dunn, D. 1981 *St Kilda's Parliament*, Faber and Faber, London

Dwelly, E. 1920 *The Illustrated Gaelic–English Dictionary*, E. MacDonald and Co., Herne Bay

Elliot, J.S. 1895 'St Kilda and the St Kildans', *Journal of the Birmingham Natural History and Philosophical Society* 1, 113–35

Ershine, W. 1799 Epistle from Lady Grange to Edward D, esq.: written during her confinement in the Island of St. Kilda. Printed for Mundell & Son, Edinburgh

Ewing, W. 1914 *Annals of the Free Church of Scotland* 2 vols, T.&T. Clark, Edinburgh

Fenton, A. and Hendry, C. 1984 'Wooden tumbler locks in Scotland and beyond', *Review of Scottish Culture* 1, 11–28

Ferguson, M. 1885 *Ramblers in Skye, with sketch of a trip to St Kilda*, Irvine

Ferguson, T. 1958 'Infantile Tetanus in some Western Isles in the second half of the nineteenth century', *Scottish Medical Journal* 3, 140–46

Fleming, A. 1995 'St Kilda: stone tools, dolerite quarries and long-term survival', *Antiquity* 69, 25–35

Fleming, A. 2000 'St Kilda: Family, Community, and the Wider World', *Journal of Anthropological Archaeology* 19, 348–68

Fleming, A. and Edmonds, M. 2000 'St Kilda: quarries, fields and prehistoric agriculture', *Proceedings of the Society of Antiquaries of Scotland* 129, 119–60

Fleming, J. 1828 *A History of British Animals (Great Auk)*, Edinburgh 129–30

Forbes, R. 1895 *The Lyon in Mourning* (ed.) Henry Paton, Scottish History Society, Edinburgh

Fordun, John of 1871 *Chronica Gentis Scotorum, 1* (ed.) W.F. Skene, Edmonston and Douglas, Edinburgh 1871

Fordun, John of 1872 *Chronica Gentis Scotorum 2* (ed.) W.F. Skene, Edmonston and Douglas, Edinburgh 1872

Gibson, G. 1928 'The tragedy of St Kilda', *Caledonian Medical Journal* April 1928, 50–62

Gillies, D., 2014, *The Truth About St Kilda: An Islander's Memoir*, Birlinn, Edinburgh

Gillies, D. 1930 School Exercise Book, Scottish Record Office GD 1/817/1

Gillies, D.J. 1988 Autobiographical notes, in: Quine, D.A. *St Kilda Portraits*, Ambleside, 39–51

Gillies, J. (ed.) 1786 *A Collection of Ancient and Modern Gaelic Poems and Songs transmitted from gentlemen in the Highland of Scotland, etc.,* Perth

Gillies, N. 1988 Autobiographical notes, in: Quine, D.A. *St Kilda Portraits*, Ambleside, 37–39

Gilmour, H. 1958 'Mail boat from St Kilda', *Post Office Magazine*, December 1958

Gladstone, J. 1928 'Notes on the flora in St Kilda' (ed. J. Mathieson), *Scottish Geographical Magazine* 44 (2), 77–79

Gordon, S. 1933 *Islands of the West*, Cassell and Co., London

Gordon, S. 1937 *Afoot in the Hebrides*, Cassell and Co., London

Grant, I.F. 1959 *The Macleods: The History of a Clan*, Faber and Faber, London

Great Britain, The Nature Conservancy 1969 *National Nature Reserve: St Kilda*, Edinburgh

Green, E.E. 'Notes on the Coccidae of Scotland', *Scottish Naturalist*, 25–30, 55–59

Grenfell, B.T., Price, O.F., Albon, S.D. and Clutton-Brock, T.H. 1992 'Overcompensation and population cycles in an ungulate', *Nature* 355, 823–26

Grieg, S. 1940 'Viking antiquities in Scotland' in Shetelig, H. (ed.) *Viking Antiquities in Great Britain and Ireland*, Oslo

Grieve, S. 1885 *The Great Auk or Garefowl*, London

General Register Office for Scotland. St Kilda. Censuses. Registers of Baptisms, Marriages and Deaths

Hamp, Eric P. 1991 'A few St Kilda toponyms and forms', *Nomina* 14, 73–76

Harman, M. 1979 'An incised cross on Hirt, Harris', Proceedings of the Society of Antiquaries of Scotland 108, 254–58

Harman, M. 1997 *An Isle Called Hirte. A History and Culture of St Kilda to 1930*, Maclean Press, Skye

Hay, G.D. 1972 'Scottish wooden tumbler locks', *Post-Medieval Archaeology* 12, 125–127

Heathcote, E. 1900 'A night in an ocean cave', *Wide World Magazine*, August, 91–96

Heathcote, E. 1901 'A Summer Sojourn in St Kilda', *Good Words* 42, 460–67

Heathcote, J.N. 1900 'On the Map of St Kilda', *Geographical Journal* 15, London, 142–44 and map

Heathcote, J.N. 1901 'Climbing on St Kilda', *Scottish Mountaineering Club Climbing Journal* 6, 146–51

Heathcote, N. 1900 *St Kilda*, Longmans Green & Co., London

Heron, R. 1794 *General View of the Natural Circumstances of the Hebrides*, John Paterson, Edinburgh

Inglis, H. et al. 1934 *The Early Maps of Scotland*, Edinburgh

Kearton, R. 1897 *With Nature and a Camera*, London (reprint Melven Press, Inverness 1978)

Kearton, R. 1899 'Strange life of Lone St Kilda',*Wide World Magazine* 2, 69–77

Kennedy, A. 1875 'Letter from St Kilda by Miss A. Kennedy communicated with notes by Capt. F.W.L. Thomas', *Proceedings of the Society of Antiquaries of Scotland* 10, 702–11

Kennedy, J. 1932 *The Apostle of the North; the Life and Labours of the Rev. Dr. J MacDonald*, Northern Counties Newspaper and Printing and Publishing Co., Inverness

Kennedy, W.S. 1924 *Ultissima Thule*, Edinburgh

Kissling, W. 1943 'Character and purpose of the Hebridean Blackhouse', *Journal of the Royal Anthropological Institute* 73, 75–100

Knox, J. 1787 *A Tour through the Highlands of Scotland and the Hebride Isles in 1786*, London

Laing, D. 1876 'Mrs Erskine, Lady Grange, in the island of St Kilda', *Proceedings of the Society of Antiquaries of Scotland* X, 722–30

Laing, D. 1877 'An episode in the life of Mrs. Rachel Erskine, Lady Grange, detailed by herself in a letter from St Kilda, January 20, 1738, and other original papers', *Proceedings of the Society of Antiquaries of Scotland* XI, 593–608

Lawson, R. 1903 A Flight to St Kilda in July 1902, Paisley

Lawson, W.M. 1976 'Na Hiortaich', *Gairm* 94, 168–73

Lawson, W.M. 1981 'Families of St Kilda', *St Kilda Mail* 5, 38–43

Lawson, W.M. 1993 *Croft History: Isle of St Kilda*, Bill Lawson Publications, Northton

Lawson, W.M. 1993 *St Kilda and its Church*, Bill Lawson Publications, Northton

Logie, D.W. 1889 *An Account of a trip from Stirling to St Kilda in S.S. Hebridean of Glasgow 12–17 August 1889*, Stirling

Love, John A., 2006 *A Natural History of St Kilda*, Birlinn, Edinburgh

Lungatoo, F.M. 1906 'St Kilda mail via Shetland' *St Martins Le Grand* 16, 211–12

Macaulay, K. 1764 *The History of St Kilda*, T. Beckett and P.A. de Hondt, London

Macaulay, K. 1765 *A Voyage to, and History of St Kilda*, Dublin

MacCallum, H. 1907 'St Kilda', *Caledonian Medical Journal* 8, 18–24

MacCulloch, J. 1824 *The Highlands and Western Isles of Scotland* 4, London

MacCulloch, J. 1819 *A Description of the Western Isles of Scotland* 2 and map 3, 75, Hurst, Robinson and Co., London

MacDiarmid, J. 1877 *St Kilda and its Inhabitants*, Edinburgh

MacDiarmid, J. 1878 'St Kilda and its inhabitants', *Transactions of the Highland and Agricultural Society* 10 (4th ser.), 232–54

MacDonald, C.R. 1886 'St Kilda: Its inhabitants and the diseases peculiar to them', *British Medical Journal* 2, 160–63

MacDonald, F. 2001 'St Kilda and the Sublime' *Ecumene* 8(2), 151–74

MacDonald, J. 1811 *General View of the Agriculture of the Hebrides*, Edinburgh

MacDonald, J. 1823 Journal and Report of a visit to the Island of St Kilda (appendix to SSPCK sermon preached by Rev. W A Thomson, June 6 1822)

Macgillivray, J. 1842 'An account of the island of St. Kilda, chiefly with reference to its natural history; from notes made during a visit in July 1840', *Edinburgh New Philosophical Journal*, 32, 47–178

MacGregor, A.A. 1931 *A Last Voyage to St Kilda*, London

MacGregor, A.A. 1931 'The folklore of St Kilda' *Scottish Field*, October 128–29; November, 168–69

MacGregor, A.A. 1969 'St Kilda's mailboats', *Country Life*, October, 2

MacGregor, D.R. 1960 'The island of St Kilda – a survey of its character and occupance', *Scottish Studies* 4, 1–48

MacIain 1886 Note in *Celtic Magazine* 11, 124–26

MacInnes, J. 1899 *The Brave Sons of Skye*, Norman MacLeod, Edinburgh

MacInnes, J. and MacQueen, D. 1982 'St Kilda mail', *Tocher* 36–7, 446–50

MacInnes, J. and MacQueen, N. 1961 'A folktale from St Kilda', *Scottish Studies* 5, 215–19

MacIntosh, C.F. 1897 *Antiquarian Notes*, Inverness

MacKay, J.A. 1963 St Kilda, *Its Posts and Communications*, Scottish Postmark Group, Edinburgh

MacKay, J. 2002 *Soldiering on St Kilda*, Token Publishing Ltd, Honiton

MacKay, J.A. 1978 *Islands Postal History: Harris and St Kilda*, James A Mackay, Dumfries

MacKay, J.A. 1959 'Hiort an Diugh' *Gairm* 30, 145–47

MacKay, J.A. 1964 'Scotland's remotest wireless station', *Scots Magazine*, October 37–43

MacKay, W.R. 1985 'Early St Kilda – a reconsideration' *West Highland Notes and Queries* 26, 13–19, and 27, 17–21

MacKenzie, A. 1881 *History of the MacDonalds,* A. and W. MacKenzie, Inverness

MacKenzie, A.D. and MacKinnon, A.D. 1883 *The Family of MacKinnon Edward Stanford*, London

MacKenzie, H.R. 1885–86 'St Kilda', *Celtic Magazine* 11, 9–16, 62–69, 121–26

Mackenzie, J.B. 1905 'Antiquities and old customs in St Kilda, compiled from notes made by Rev. Neil Mackenzie, minister of St Kilda, 1829–43', *Proceedings of the Society of Antiquaries of Scotland* 39, 397–402

Mackenzie, J.B. 1911 *Episode in the Life of the Rev. Neil Mackenzie at St Kilda from 1829 to 1843* (privately published)

MacKenzie, M. 1921 Account of visit in MacKenzie, O.H. (1853) in *A Hundred Years in the Highlands*, Edward Arnold, London

MacKenzie, Sir George of Tarbat 1681–84 An Account of Hirta and Rona, published in MacFarlane, W. *Geographical Collections* 1908, 3, 28

Mackenzie, Sir George Steuart of Coul 1817 'An account of the misfortunes of Mrs Erskine of Grange, commonly known as Lady Grange', *Edinburgh Magazine* 1, 333–39 (published under 'Gael')

Mackenzie, W.C. 1905 *The Lady of Hirta: a tale of the Isles, being the narrative of the Rev. Ferchard Ross*, A.M. Paisley

MacKenzie, W.C. *The Lady of Hirta* (novel)

MacKenzie Papers 1872–1897 Letters sent to J. T. MacKenzie, factor, in National Trust for Scotland Archive

MacLachlan, Alice 1906–9 Typescript copy of diaries in National Trust for Scotland Archive

MacLean, C. 1972 *Island on the Edge of the World: The Story of St Kilda*, Tom Stacey Ltd (revised edition Canongate, Edinburgh 1996)

MacLean, L. 1838 Sketches on the island of St Kilda McPhun, Glasgow:

MacLennan, M. 1925 *Gaelic Dictionary* John Grant, Edinburgh

MacLeod, D. 1814 'Notices on the present state of St Kilda', *Scots Magazine*, December, 912–13

MacLeod, D.J. 1952 'Eilean Hiort', *Gairm* 1, 15–17

MacLeod, J. 1792 *Parish of Harris: Old Statistical Account 1791–9* (ed.) John Sinclair 13, 342–92

MacLeod, J.M. 1871 'St Kilda: letter to the Editor', *The Times* 26 August, 10

MacLeod, J. 1910 *Reminiscences Moray and Nairn Newspaper Co. Ltd.*, Elgin

MacLeod, W. (Theophilus Insulanus) 1763 *A Treatise on the Second Sight, Dreams and Apparitions*, Ruddimans, Auld and Co., Edinburgh

Mactaggart, F. 1999. St Kilda (Hiort) *Site of Special Scientific Interest (Part II: Geomorphology)*, Earth Science Site Documentation Series, Scottish Natural Heritage, Edinburgh

Major, J. 1740 *Historia Majoris Britanniae tam Angliae quam Scotiae*, Edinburgh (first edition 1521)

MacQueen, Calum, Kelman and Ewan McQueen (eds) 1995, *St Kilda Heritage: Autobiography of Callum MacCuithinn (Malcolm MacQueen)*, St Kilda Heritage Scottish Genealogy Society, Edinburgh

Martin, M. 1698 *A Late Voyage to St Kilda*, London (reprint 1986 James Thin, The Mercat Press Edinburgh)

Martin, M. 1698 'Several observation on the North Islands of Scotland', *Philosophical Transactions of the Royal Society* 19, 727–29

Martin, M. 1716 *Description of the Western Isles of Scotland*, London

Martin, M. 1753 *A Voyage to St Kilda* (4th edn), London

Martyn, K.P. 1988 *Provisional Atlas of the Ticks (Ixodoidea) of the British Isles*, Institute of Terrestrial Ecology, Huntingdon

Matheson, W. 1952 'Mary MacLeod: her family connections; her forgotten songs', *Transactions of the Gaelic Society of Inverness* 41, 11–25

Mathieson, J. 1928 'St Kilda', *Scottish Geographical Magazine* 44, 65–90

Mathieson, J. 1928 'The antiquities of the St Kilda group of islands', *Proceedings of the Society of Antiquaries of Scotland* 62, 123–32

Mathieson, J. 1928 Map of St Kilda or Hirta and Adjacent Islands and Stacs, Ordnance Survey

Mathieson, J. 1930 'Lone St Kilda', *Scottish Motor Traction Magazine* August

Mathieson, J. 1930 'The evacuation of St Kilda', *Scottish Geographical Magazine* 46

Mathieson, J. and Cockburn, A.M. 1929 'St Kilda', *Transactions of the Edinburgh Geological Society* 12, 287–88

Matthews, A.E.H. 1969 'Sappers at St Kilda – 1900', *Sapper Magazine* 78–79

McIver, E. 1905 *Memoirs of a Highland Gentleman*, Constable, Edinburgh

Milner, W.M.E 1848 'Some account of the people of St Kilda, and of the birds in the Outer Hebrides', *The Zoologist*, 2054–62

Mitchell, A. 1865 'Consanguineous marriages on St Kilda', *Edinburgh Medical Journal* 10 April, 899–904

Mitchell, A. 1901 'List of some accounts of visits to St Kilda 1549–1900', *Proceedings of the Society of Antiquaries of Scotland* 35, 440–42

Moore, P. 1987 'Gannet hunter's bothy on Stac Lee, St Kilda', *Vernacular Buildings* 11, 12–14

Moray, R. 1678 'A Description of the island of Hirta', *Philosophical Transaction of the Royal Society of London* 12, 927–29

Morgan, J.E. 1861 'The Falcon among the Fulmars; or six hours in St Kilda' *MacMillan's Magazine* June, 104–11

Morgan, J.E. 1862 'The diseases of St Kilda', *British and Foreign Medico-Chirurgical Review* 29, 176–191

Morris, R., 2013, *Defending St Kilda*, Islands Book Trust, Isle of Lewis

Morrison, A. 1966 'The Contullich Papers', *Transactions of the Gaelic Society of Inverness* 44, 33–97

Morrison, A. 1968 'The Harris Estate Papers', *Transactions of the Gaelic Society of Inverness* 45, 33–97

Morrison, A. 1969 'The Island of Pabbay', *Clan MacLeod Magazine* 6, 17–23

Morrison, A. 1974 *The MacLeods: The Genealogy of a Clan* 4, 1974

Muir, T.S. 1858 *St Kilda, A Fragment of Travel*, Edinburgh

Muir, T.S. and Thomas, F.W.L. 1860 'Notice of a beehive house in the island of St Kilda', *Proceedings of the Society of Antiquaries of Scotland* 3, 225–32

Muir, T.S. 1861 *Characteristics of Old Church Architecture etc in the Mainland and Western Isles of Scotland*, Edinburgh 213–23

Muir, T.S. 1885 *Ecclesiological Notes on Some of the Islands of Scotland*, Edinburgh 61–66

Munro, D. 1774 Description of the Western Isles of Scotland, called Hybridies; with genealogies of the chief clans of the Isles Edinburgh (Also contains Account of Hirta and Rona, by Sir George McKenzie of Tarbart. Description of Saint Kilda by Alexander Buchan Voyage to Saint Kilda in 1697, by Martin Martin.)

Munro, D. 1818 Description of the Western Isles of Scotland called Hybrides, by Mr Donald Munro, High Dean of the Isles, who travelled through most of them in the year 1594, *Miscellanea Scotica* 2

Munro, J. and Munro R.W. 1986 *Acts of the Lords of the Isles 1336–1493*, Scottish History Society, Edinburgh

Munro, R.W. 1982 'Hirta of Harris?' *West Highland Notes and Queries* 18, October, 16–19

Murray, A. 1735 A Politicall Whim concerning St Kilda one of the Western Isles of Scotland written in the year 1735 National Library of Scotland Adv.Ms. 29.1.1vii ff 169–72

Murray, G. 1886–7 *St Kilda Diary of George Murray*, National Trust for Scotland Archive

Napier Commission 1884 'Highland Crofters: Report of her Majesty's Commissioners of Enquiry into the Conditions of the Crofters and Cottars in the Highlands and Islands of Scotland'

Newstead, R. 1903 *Monograph of the Coccidae of the British Isles* 2, London

Nicolson, J. 1937 'John Sands', *Shetland Times* 3 July

Oswald, D.A. 1925 'St Kilda' *Scots Magazine* September, 419–21

Oxford University Press 1931 *St Kilda Papers*

Peacock, J.D., Austin, W.E.N., Selby, I., D.K., Harland, R. and Wilkinson, I.P. 1992 'Late Devensian and Flandrian palaeoenvironmental changes on the Scottish continental shelf west of the Outer Hebrides', *Journal of Quaternary Science* 7, 145–61

Pennie, I.D. 1958 'Early medicine in the Highlands and Islands', *Scottish Medical Journal* 3, 398–408

Pomfret, A.A. 1931 'The evacuation of St Kilda', *Journal of the Royal Naval Medical Service*, 17

Powell, L.F. 1940 'The history of St Kilda', *Review of English Studies* 16, 44–53

Powell, M. 1990 *Edge of the World*, Faber and Faber, London

Power, W.A. 1983 *The Log of the Olivia Richmond*

Quine, D.A. 1982 *St Kilda Revisited*, Dowland Press, Frome (revised edition 1989)

Quine, D.A. 1988 *St Kilda Portraits*, Dowland Press, Frome

Quine, D.A. 1991 'Australian MacQueens – Links with St Kilda', *St Kilda Mail* 15, 4–9

Quine, D.A. 2000 *St Kilda*, Colin Baxter Island Guides, Colin Baxter (revised edition)

Quine, D.A. (ed.) 2001 *Expeditions to the Hebrides by George Clayton Atkinson in 1831 and 1833*, Maclean Press, Isle of Skye

Quine, T.A. 1983 Excavations in Village Street, Hirta, St Kilda 1983, Ms. report to National Trust for Scotland, Edinburgh

Rae, B.R. 1954 'Heron on St Kilda', *Scottish Naturalist* 66, 39

Richards, E. 1982 'Highland emigrants to South Australia in the 1850s' *Northern Scotland* 5 (no. 1), 1–29

Richards, E. 1992 'The decline of St Kilda: demography, economy and emigration', *Scottish Economic and Social History* 12, 55–73

Robertson, A.W. 1960 'The St Kilda "Mailboats"', *Strand Stamp Journal* 4 no. 2, 109–11

Robertson, A., Hiraiwa-Hasegawa, M., Albon, S.D. and Clutton-Brock, T.H. 1992 'Early growth and sucking behaviour of Soay sheep in a fluctuating population', *Journal of Zoology* 227, 661–71

Robson, M. 2005, *St Kilda: Church, Visitors and Natives,*

Robson, R. 2001 *St Kilda (Hiort) Site of Special Scientific Interest (Part I: Geology)*, Earth Science Site Documentation Series, Scottish Natural Heritage, Edinburgh

Ross, A. 1884 'A visit to the island of St Kilda', Transactions of the Inverness Scientific Society and Field Club 3 (1883–8), 72–91

Ross, Alexander 1895 *Scottish Home Industries*

Ross, J.C. 1890 St Kilda Ms. Account. National Trust for Scotland, Edinburgh, Bute Box

Sands, J. 1876 *Out of the World; or, Life in St Kilda*, MacLachlan & Stewart, Edinburgh

Sands, J. 1877 'Life in St Kilda', *Chambers Journal* 1877, 284–87, 312–16, 331–34

Sands, J. 1878 'Notes on the antiquities of the island of St Kilda', *Proceedings of the Society of Antiquaries of Scotland* 12 (1876–8), 186–92

Seton, G. 1878 *St Kilda Past and Present Edinburgh* (1980 reprint, James Thin, The Mercat Press, Edinburgh)

Seton-Watson, R.W. 1931 'The strange story of Lady Grange', *History* 16, 12–24

Seymour, W.A. 1980 *A History of the Ordnance Survey*, Wm. Dawson and Sons, Folkestone

Shand, A.I. 1897 *The Lady Grange Smith*, Elder and Co., London (novel)

Spackman, R.A. 1982 *Soldiers on St Kilda*, Uist Community Press, Uist

Steel, T. 1994 *The Life and Death of St Kilda*, HarperCollins, London

Stell, G.P. and Harman M. 1988 *Buildings of St Kilda*, Royal Commission on the Ancient and Historical Monuments of Scotland/HMSO, Edinburgh

Stewart, A. 1877 'The St Kilda Maids' Song', *Gael* 6, April 1877, 125

Stone, J. 1989 *The Pont Manuscript Maps of Scotland: Sixteenth Century origin of a Blaeu Atlas,* Tring

Taylor, A.B. 1969 'Norsemen in St Kilda', *Saga Book* 17 (1966–9), 116–44

Taylor, A.B. 1969 'The name "St Kilda"', *Scottish Studies* 13, 145–58

Thomson, R. 1891 *A Cruise on the Western Isles,* Glasgow

Thornber, I. 1990 'St Kildans no more', *Scots Magazine*, December, 278–88

'Viator' 1818 'St Kilda poetry', *Scots Magazine*, March, 241–42

Walker, J.R 1883 "Holy Wells' in Scotland', *Proceedings of the Society of Antiquaries of Scotland* 17, 152–210

Watson, W.J. 1926 *The History of the Celtic Place Names of Scotland*, Edinburgh

Wilson, J. 1842 *A Voyage round the Coasts of Scotland and the Isles* 2, Adam & Charles Black, Edinburgh

Wilson, J. 1842? St Kilda: letter addressed to John Tawse, esq., secretary Society for Propagating Christian Knowledge

Wilson, J. 1842 'Additional Notice Regarding St Kilda', *Edinburgh New Philosophical Journal* 32, 178–80

Withers, C.W.J. 1999 'Reporting, Mapping, Trusting: Making Geographical Knowledge in the Late Seventeenth Century', *Isis* 90, 497–521

Index

Index

Heathcote, Norman 247, 259, 260, 261, 262, 263
  community at Village Bay and 247, 259–63,
    268–9
ss *Hebridean* 211, 233, 238
Hebridean Blackface sheep 25
Hebridean Gaels 5
Hebridean Terrane 11, 15
Hebridean Ware 17
ss *Hebrides* 9. 265, 270, 275, 281
Hebrides, settlement of 6
Heisker (Monach Islands) 6, 7, 92, 94, 96
Henri II of France 39
Herbert, Lady Catherine, Countess of Dunmore
  184
Herschell, Sir John 165
Highland Agricultural Society of Scotland
  (HASS) 149, 175, 216, 225
Hirta
  naming of 40–41
  see also St Kilda; Village Bay
historical references 36–70, 71–108, 111–12,
  114, 117–19, 121, 138, 161, 172, 291
History of Scotland (Buchanan, G.) 42
The History of St Kilda (Macaulay, K.) 98–106
History of the Scottish People (Boece, H.) 43
Hoare, Lydia 125
Holy Well (Tobar a' Chleirich) in Village Bay 39
Hope, Thomas of Rankeillour 94, 95
Humboldt, Karl Wilhelm von 63
Hume, David 96
Hyne, Charles John Cutcliffe 260

Ice Age in Scotland (and post-Ice Age) 12, 13, 16
Iceland 2, 26, 36–7, 69
  Christian heritage of 37
infant mortality see neonatal and infant mortality
influenza
  epidemic (1913), and relief of 274–5
  susceptibility of people to 62, 69, 113, 196,
    248, 280
Inverness (and Inverness-shire) 7, 25, 35, 69, 88,
  105, 165, 209, 210, 211, 231, 237, 242, 274
Inverness Courier 133
Ipswich 294
Ireland 2, 11, 12, 17, 22, 23, 24, 26, 39, 42, 45,
  46–7, 142, 206
Irish and Scottish Gaeldom, transnationalism
  of 46–7
Iron Age 17, 23–4
Islay 12, 13, 34, 35, 46, 70
Isle of Man 24, 33, 34, 35, 43
isolation
  from news of world events 267–8
  position of St Kilda, isolated nature of 2, 18,
    25, 63–4, 69, 72, 96, 136, 148, 181, 193–5,
    211, 228, 234–5, 237–8, 257, 258, 275, 289,
    293

HMS *Jackal* 199
Jacobite Risings 97
James IV 46
Jenner, Edward 207
jetty at Village Bay, absence of 148–9
John the Baptist 73, 74
Johnson, Dr Samuel 62, 105, 106
Johnston, Tom 284, 285, 286

Kearton, Cherry 251, 252
Kearton, Richard and Cherry 253, 255, 256,
  259, 260
  community at Village Bay and 251–9
Keats, John 185
Kemble, John 129
Kennedy, Anne 159, 160, 161, 165
Kennedy, Duncan 145, 147, 150, 157, 158, 159,
  165, 172, 184
Kintyre, Mull of 23, 34, 78
Kyle of Lochalsh, Wester Ross 8, 9
Kyle-to-Dingwall railway line 9

Ladies Association (Free Church), Edinburgh
  212
The Lady of St Kilda (ocean-going schooner)
  125–6
Lady of the Isles (yacht, arrival at St Kilda June
  1877) 187
An Lag bho'n Tuath (The Hollow from the
  North) 29
Laimhrig na Gall (Foreigner's Anchorage) 29
Lancashire 3–4, 266, 282
land, overuse of 179–81
land at Village Bay 14, 40–41
Landnámabók (*Book of Settlements*) 37
last St Kildans sail out of Village Bay 4–5, 6–7,
  286–90, 291–2
Latin land divisions 37–8
Lauder, Sir Thomas Dick 127, 128, 130, 132,
  133, 201
Laurentia, prehistoric continent of 11, 15
legends of St Kilda, survival of 158–63, 191–5
Leith 244
Leod, Torcuil 35
Leod, Tormod 35
Leotard, Jules 202
Lewis 2, 7, 13, 22, 35, 39, 40, 43, 44, 45, 54, 65,
  70, 75, 88, 97, 156, 184, 192, 209, 279, 281,
  292, 294
  Butt of 34
Lewisian Complex in Hebridean Terrane 11
Liberal Government 209
linguistic difficulties 3
Lloyd George, David 279
Loch a' Glinne (Glen Bay) 31
Lochaber 6
Lochaline Estate 8, 9, 290, 294

Index